THE LAW OF REFUGEE STATUS

James C. Hathaway

LL.B., LL.M., J.S.D.
Osgoode Hall Law School
York University

Research funding
was generously
provided by

Canadian
Legal
Information
Centre

Centre
canadien
d'information
juridique

LexisNexis™
Butterworths

The Law of Refugee Status

© LexisNexis Canada Inc. 1991

Members of the LexisNexis Group worldwide

Canada	LexisNexis Canada Inc, 75 Clegg Road, MARKHAM, Ontario
Argentina	Abeledo Perrot, Jurisprudencia Argentina and Depalma, BUENOS AIRES
Australia	Butterworths, a Division of Reed International Books Australia Pty Ltd, CHATSWOOD, New South Wales
Austria	ARD Betriebsdienst and Verlag Orac, VIENNA
Chile	Publitecsa and Conosur Ltda, SANTIAGO DE CHILE
Czech Republic	Orac sro, PRAGUE
France	Éditions du Juris-Classeur SA, PARIS
Hong Kong	Butterworths Asia (Hong Kong), HONG KONG
Hungary	Hvg Orac, BUDAPEST
India	Butterworths India, NEW DELHI
Ireland	Butterworths (Ireland) Ltd, DUBLIN
Italy	Giuffré, MILAN
Malaysia	Malayan Law Journal Sdn Bhd, KUALA LUMPUR
New Zealand	Butterworths of New Zealand, WELLINGTON
Poland	Wydawnictwa Prawnicze PWN, WARSAW
Singapore	Butterworths Asia, SINGAPORE
South Africa	Butterworth Publishers (Pty) Ltd, DURBAN
Switzerland	Stämpfli Verlag AG, BERNE
United Kingdom	Butterworths Tolley, a Division of Reed Elsevier (UK), LONDON, WC2A
USA	LexisNexis, DAYTON, Ohio

Canadian Cataloguing in Publication Data

Hathaway, James C.
    The law of refugee status

Includes bibliographical references and index.
ISBN 0-409-91479-7

1. Refugees – Legal status, laws, etc. – Canada.
I. Title.

KE4454.H3 1991   342.71'083   C91-093330-8

Reprint #1, 1996
Reprint #2, 1996
Reprint #3, 1998
Reprint #4, 2001
Reprint #5, 2003

Printed and bound in Canada.

Preface

A Convention refugee is a person who is outside her[1] country because she reasonably believes that her civil or political status puts her at risk of serious harm in that country, and that her own government cannot or will not protect her.

The Convention refugee definition is of singular importance because it has been subscribed to by more than one hundred nations in the only refugee accords of global scope. Many nations have also chosen to import this standard into their domestic immigration legislation as the basis upon which asylum and other protection decisions are made.

Yet this legal definition of a refugee is at odds with the ordinary, social perception of refugee status. We commonly refer to persons who have been forced to flee to another region of their country as refugees. We normally assume that a person who is prepared to abandon her home, her family, her security is a refugee, without inquiring into the accuracy of the concerns which cause her to flee. We recognize the logic of escape from natural disasters, or from generally oppressive political regimes as much as from the possibility of persecution. Too, our sense of compassion drives us to relieve the suffering of involuntary migrants without first conducting a detailed inquiry into the circumstances which gave rise to their distress, or the reasons that a return home or a prolonged stay in a country of first asylum are untenable.

This book is an attempt to explain the scope of the Convention refugee definition as drafted, and as it has evolved in practice. While this definition was not intended to, and does not in fact, address the whole range of concerns which prompt involuntary migration, a generous interpretation of the Convention can go some distance to meeting the needs of at least the most acutely at risk populations outside the borders of their own nation. It remains tragically true that international human rights law — the intended means of permitting the world community to respond to wrongs committed by a country within its own territory — has not been permitted to evolve to a state of genuine efficacy.

---

[1] Pronouns herein are phrased in the feminine voice in recognition of the fact that "refugee women and girls constitute the majority of the world refugee population, and that many of them are exposed to special problems in the international protection field": Executive Committee of the UNHCR Programme, Conclusion No. 39 (1985).

v

The Convention refugee definition may be viewed as comprising five essential elements, each of which must be established before status is appropriately recognized. Following an introduction to the development of the international refugee definition in Chapter 1, this book addresses each of these five criteria in a distinct chapter.

The first essential definitional element, comprehending a range of contextual concerns, is referred to here as *alienage*. The Convention definition includes only persons who have left their country of nationality, or in the case of stateless persons, their country of former habitual residence. This criterion raises several related questions of claims grounded in post-departure events; the relevance of official authorization to emigrate; so-called direct flight requirements which suggest a duty to seek protection in the first potential state of refuge; the implication of entry into an asylum state in contravention of applicable immigration laws; and the means by which the country of reference for a particular refugee claim is defined. Each of these concerns is examined in detail in Chapter 2.

Second, the refugee claimant must be *genuinely at risk*. It is not enough that she truly believe herself to be in jeopardy. Rather, there must be objective facts to provide a concrete foundation for the concern which induces her to seek protection in another state. Chapter 3 addresses the historical and practical reasons which underpin the Convention's focus on the prospective assessment of objective risk, and its exclusion of claims based on purely subjective apprehensions. The nature of the threshold test, as well as the means of establishing this objective risk — including consideration of human rights data, the claimant's own testimony, and evidence of harm to persons similarly situated — are canvassed in detail.

Third, the claimant's flight must be motivated by the prospect of "persecution", that is, *risk of serious harm* against which the state of origin is *unwilling or unable to offer protection*. Chapter 4 defines this serious harm as the sustained or systemic violation of core, internationally recognized human rights. The nature of both civil and political rights and socio-economic human rights is addressed, and the distinction is drawn between the violation of human rights and generalized hardship or lack of opportunity. Most important, this chapter attempts to explain the nature of a state's duty to protect its population, failure of which is at the heart of refugee protection. This leads to a consideration of state accountability for the actions of non-official persecutors, and responsibility for localized failure to protect.

Fourth, the risk faced by the refugee claimant must have some nexus to her race, religion, nationality, membership in a particular social group, or political opinion. The critical question is whether but for her *civil or political status* she could reasonably be said to be at risk of serious harm. The meaning of each of the recognized forms of civil and political status is examined in Chapter 5. In particular, this chapter looks to issues of unexpressed political opinions, and of political opinion implicit in conduct. The malleability of the social group criterion is canvassed in relation to issues of gender, sexual orientation, family, class or caste, and membership in voluntary associations. Finally, the compatability of the civil or political status requirement with claims grounded in criminal status, refusal to perform military service, and flight from war or violence is explored.

Fifth and finally, there must be a genuine need for and legitimate claim to protection. The *cessation* clauses of the Convention provide that refugee status is not warranted if the refugee can either reclaim the protection of her own state, or has secured an alternative form of enduring protection. The *exclusion* clauses ensure that serious criminals and persons whose actions have exhibited disregard for basic norms of human dignity cannot invoke international protection. Chapter 6 looks at each of the cessation and exclusion clauses in detail, in an effort clearly to delineate the recognized exceptions to the duty of protection.

The examination of each of the five essential elements of the Convention definition draws on three sources. First, the drafting history of the Convention is canvassed as a means of understanding the intentions which underlie the protection regime. Second, the views of legal and other scholars who have informed the development of refugee law are presented. Third, the rich refugee jurisprudence developed in Canada since the incorporation of the Convention definition into domestic law in 1973 is employed to illustrate the Convention's actual and potential scope. The approximately 3000 judgments of the Supreme Court of Canada, Federal Court of Appeal, and Immigration Appeal Board considered in preparing this book have proved invaluable to the development of a contextual understanding of the definition. The caselaw was surveyed to January 1, 1989, with the exception of superior court judgments and decisions of the new Immigration and Refugee Board relating to exclusion and cessation (which clauses were incorporated in Canadian law only as of January 1, 1989), which have been considered to July 1, 1990. Judgments of determination authorities in other countries are drawn upon only very selectively, particularly in relation to aspects of the definition not yet adequately elaborated in Canadian law. All of these sources are extensively footnoted in response to the concerns expressed to me by many scholars, practitioners, and decision-makers, that there was a need for a consolidation in one volume of the best of the relevant international legal materials, scholarship, and caselaw.

I have benefitted from an extraordinary support structure over the several years during which this book was in preparation. The Canadian Law Information Council generously provided core research funding, supplemented by assistance from the United Nations High Commissioner for Refugees. Deans John McCamus and Jim MacPherson and Executive Officer Norma Doran of the Osgoode Hall Law School were instrumental in providing me the opportunity and facilities to realize this project. The staff of the York University Law Library — in particular, Maureen Boyce, Norma Eakin, and Marianne Rogers — never failed to track down whatever obscure document or reference I needed to consider. George Gonsalves, Terri Offen, Wendy

Rambo, Kassandra Sharpe and Margaret Stockton provided me with ever-patient secretarial assistance, and helped me cope with unending computer crises. Charmian Harvey of Butterworths was the model of the supportive and good-humoured editor.

A special thanks is due to Guy Goodwin-Gill, who cajoled me to get my ideas onto paper, and who introduced me to the research facilities at UNHCR, Geneva; and to the late Atle Grahl-Madsen, who generously shared his ideas and writing strategy with me. Gervase Coles, Susan Davis, and Diane Pask helped to shape my views on refugee protection. I also owe a great debt to several of my colleagues at Osgoode's Refugee Law Research Unit. Steven Tress designed the computer system which allowed me to organize an extraordinary volume of material, and continued to give generously of his research skills long after embarking on his own legal career. Suzanne Egan, Gary Evans, David Petrasek, Lori Pope, and Maureen Smith provided invaluable help in revising and updating research materials, and in forcing me to defend, and frequently to rework, my conceptual framework. Two outside experts also did their best to keep me on track: Deborah Anker of the Harvard Law School coached me on American case law; and Toronto lawyer Colin Campbell provided helpful critiques from an advocate's vantage point.

While preparing this book, I have been privileged to work with the members, legal staff, and hearing officers of Canada's new Immigration and Refugee Board. The somewhat intimidating, but always rewarding, experience of training those who will make the law has convinced me that the fair-minded and conscientious application of the Convention definition can go a substantial distance toward reinvigorating the highly imperfect international protection regime.

My final and particular appreciation is to Lisa Gilad, social anthropologist and author, now refugee decision-maker, who provided frequent commiserations during the writing phase, and who generously and carefully reviewed my final draft; and to John Moreau, whose patient support and caring sustained my resolve to complete this project.

Toronto
August, 1990

Acknowledgments

The authors and publishers of these articles and textbooks have been most generous in giving permission for the reproduction in this text of work already in print. References, of course, appear where necessary and possible in the text. It is convenient for us to list below, for the assistance of the reader, the publishers and the authors for whose courtesy we are most grateful.

Allen, Unwin	Vernant, Jacques. *The Refugees in the Post-War World* (1953).
The American Society of International Law	Martin, David A., in C. Sumpter. "Mass Migration of Refugees — Law and Policy" (1982), 76 A.S.I.L. Proc. 13. Reprinted with the permission of The American Society of International Law and the author.
Archiv des Völkerrechts	Grahl-Madsen, Atle. "International Refugee Law Today and Tomorrow" (1982), 20 Archiv des Völkerrechts 411.
Australian Law Journal	Hyndman, Patricia. "Refugees Under International Law with a Reference to the Concept of Asylum" (1986), 60 Australian L.J. 148. Reprinted with the permission of The Law Book Company Limited, Australia.
A.W. Sijthoff, Leyden	Grahl-Madsen, Atle. *The Status of Refugees in International Law*, Vol. 1 (1966).
British Yearbook of International Law	Weis, Paul. "The Draft United Nations Convention on Territorial Asylum" (1979), 50 British Y.B. Intl. L. 151. By permission of Oxford University Press and the author.

California Western
International Law Journal

Saari, V. and R. Higgins Cass. "The United Nations and the International Protection of Human Rights: A Legal Analysis and Interpretation" (1977), California W. Intl. L.J. 591.

Canada Law Book Inc.

LaForest, G. *Extradition to and from Canada* (1977). Reproduced with the permission of Canada Law Book Inc., 240 Edward Street, Aurora, Ontario L4G 3S9.
Wydrzynski, Christopher J. *Canadian Immigration Law and Procedure* (1983). Reproduced with the permission of Canada Law Book Inc., 240 Edward Street, Aurora, Ontario L4G 3S9.

Case Western Reserve
Journal of International
Law

Fragomen, A.T., Jr. "The Refugee: A Problem of Definition" (1970), 3 Case Western Reserve, J. Intl. L. 45.

Center for Migration Studies

Coles, G.J.L. "Some Reflections on the Protection of Refugees from Armed Conflict Situations" (1984), 7 In Defense of the Alien 78.

Cleveland State Law Review

Brill, Kenneth D. "The Endless Debate: Refugee Law and Policy and the 1980 Refugee Act" (1983), 32 Cleveland State L. Rev. 117.

Columbia Human Rights
Law Review

Helton, Arthur C. "Persecution on Account of Membership in a Social Group as a Basis for Refugee Status" (1983), 15 Columbia Human Rights L. Rev. 39.

Columbia Law Review

Gross, Douglas. "The Right of Asylum Under United States Law" (1980), 80 Columbia L. Rev. 1125. Copyright © 1980 by the Directors of the Columbia Law Review Association, Inc. All Rights Reserved. This article originally appeared at 80 Colum. L. Rev. 1125 (1980). Reprinted by permission.

Department of Employment and Immigration — Minister of Employment and Immigration. *New Refugee Status Advisory Committee Guidelines on Refugee Definition and Assessment of Credibility.* Ottawa: Department of Employment and Immigration (1982). Published with the permission of Employment and Immigration Canada and Supply and Services Canada, 1990.

Harvard Law Review — (Student) Note. "Political Legitimacy in the Law of Political Asylum" (1985), 99 Harvard L. Rev. 450. Copyright © 1985 by the Harvard Law Review Association.

Human Rights Quarterly (The Johns Hopkins University Press) — Gibney, Mark. "A 'Well-Founded' Fear of Persecution" (1988), 10(1) Human Rts. Q. 109.
Hyndman, Patricia. "The 1951 Convention Definition of Refugee: An Appraisal with Particular Reference to the Sri Lankan Tamil Applicants" (1987), 9 Human Rts. Q. 49.
Tsamenyi, B.M. "The 'Boat People': Are They Refugees?" (1983), 5 Human Rts. Q. 348.

International Commission of Jurists — Alston, Phillip. "The Universal Declaration at 35: Western and Passé or Alive and Universal?" (1983), 31 I.C.J. Rev. 60.

International and Comparative Law Quarterly — Gilbert, Geoffrey S. "Right of Asylum: A Change of Direction" (1983), 32 I.C.L.Q. 633. Extracts are reproduced from (1983), 32 I.C.L.Q. 633 with permission from the publishers The British Institute of International and Comparative Law.
Krenz, Frank E. "The Refugee as a Subject of International Law" (1966), 15 I.C.L.Q. 90. Extracts are reproduced from (1966), 15 I.C.L.Q. 90 with permission from the publishers The British

	Institute of International and Comparative Law.
Japanese Annual of International Law	Shimada, Yukio. "The Concept of the Political Refugee in International Law" (1975), 19 Japanese Ann. Intl. L. 24.
Journal du droit international	Weis, Paul. "The concept of the refugee in international law" (1960), 87 J. du droit international 928.
McGill Law Journal	Wydrynski, Christopher J. "Refugees and the *Immigration Act*" (1979), 25 McGill L.J. 154. Reprinted with the permission of The McGill Law Journal and the author.
Nordisk Tidsskrift for International Ret	Foighel, I. "Legal Status of the Boat People" (1979), 48 Nordisk Tidsskrift for Intl. Ret 217.
Notre Dame Law Review	Petrini, Kenneth R. "Basing Asylum Claims on a Fear of Persecution Arising from a Prior Asylum Claim" (1981), Volume 56, Issue 4, Notre Dame Lawyer 719. Reprinted with permission. © by Notre Dame Law Review, University of Notre Dame. Any errors which have occurred in reprinting or editing are the responsibility of Butterworths.
Office of the United Nations High Commissioner for Refugees, Geneva	UNHCR. *Handbook on Procedures and Criteria for Determining Refugee Status* (1979), and extracts from drafting histories of the Refugee Convention, Protocol, UNHCR Statute, Conference on Territorial Asylum.
Oxford University Press	Goodwin-Gill, Guy. *The Refugee in International Law*. Oxford: Clarendon Press (1983). By permission of Oxford University Press. *The Oxford English Dictionary* (1961). By permission of Oxford University Press.

Sieghart, Paul. *The International Law of Human Rights.* Oxford: Clarendon Press (1983). By permission of Oxford University Press.

Trubek, D. "Economic, Social, and Cultural Rights in the Third World: Human Rights Law and Human Needs Programs", in Theodor Meron, ed., *Human Rights in International Law*, p. 205. Oxford: Clarendon Press (1984). By permission of Oxford University Press.

San Diego Law Review

Heyman, M. "Redefining Refugee: A Proposal for Relief for the Victims of Civil Strife" (1987), 24 San Diego L. Rev. 449. Copyright 1987 San Diego Law Review Association. Reprinted with permission of the San Diego Law Review.

Plender, Richard. "Admission of Refugees: Draft Convention on Territorial Asylum" (1977), 15 San Diego L. Rev. 45. Copyright 1977 San Diego Law Review Association. Reprinted with permission of the San Diego Law Review.

Scandinavian Studies in Law

Melander, Goran. "The Protection of Refugees" (1974), 18 Scandinavian Studies in Law 153.

Stanford Journal of International Law

Gagliardi, Donald P. "The Inadequacy of Cognizable Grounds of Persecution as a Criterion for According Refugee Status" (1987-88), 24 Stanford J. Intl. L. 259. Reprinted with the permission of the Stanford Journal of International Law. Copyright © 1988 by the Board of Trustees of the Leland Stanford Junior University.

University of Chicago Press

Shacknove, Andrew R. "Who is a Refugee?" (1985), 95 Ethics 274. © 1985 by the University of Chicago. All rights reserved. 0014-1704/85/9502-0002$01.00

Vanderbilt Journal of
Transnational Law

Sexton, Robert C. "Political Refugees, Nonrefoulement and State Practice: A Comparative Study" (1985), 18 Vanderbilt J. Transntl. L. 731.

Virginia Journal of
International Law

Goodwin-Gill, Guy. "Non-Refoulement and the New Asylum Seekers" (1986), 26(4) Va. J. Intl. L. 897.
Hailbronner, Kay. "Non-Refoulement and 'Humanitarian' Refugees: Customary International Law or Wishful Legal Thinking?" (1986), 26(4) Va. J. Intl. L. 857.

World Refugee Survey

Jaeger, Gilbert. "The Definition of 'Refugee': Restrictive versus Expanding Trends", [1983] World Refugee Survey 5.

Zed Books

Independent Commission on International Humanitarian Issues. *Refugees: The Dynamics of Displacement* (1986).

Table of Contents

H

P

Q

R

S

1

The Development of the Refugee Definition in International Law

Legal formulations of refugee status are a product of recent Western history. Prior to this century there was little concern about the precise definition of a refugee, since most of those who chose not to move to the "New World" were readily received by rulers in Europe and elsewhere. The practice of sheltering those compelled to flight was not perceived as a burden, but rather as a necessary incident of power, and indeed as a source of communal enrichment:

> Central governments pursued their own interests by facilitating immigration and discouraging or even forbidding emigration. Whether to be taxed, to contribute to the growth of manufactures and commerce, to offer specialized knowledge, or to join the military, talented or affluent foreigners were frequently deemed useful to society and welcomed with open arms by European monarchs or municipalities.[1]

This freedom of international movement accorded to persons broadly defined as refugees was adversely impacted by the adoption of instrumentalist immigration policies in Western states during the early twentieth century.[2] Immigration came to be seen less as a means of allowing individuals to exercise their right to self-determination, and more as a vehicle to facilitate the selection by states of new inhabitants who could contribute in some tangible way, such as skill or wealth, to the national well-being. International migration was no longer to be a function of the particularized needs or ambitions of the would-be immigrants, but was instead to be closely controlled to maximize advantage for sovereign nation states.[3]

---

[1] M. Marrus, *The Unwanted: European Refugees in the Twentieth Century*, pp. 6-7 (1985).

[2] "The twentieth century has been witness to substantial developments in immigration law and control. States have pressed on, assuming the right of exclusion to be 'inherent in their sovereign powers' . . . ": G. Goodwin-Gill, *International Law and the Movement of Persons Between States*, p. 96 (1978).

[3] "It was only with the rise of nationalism, and the resulting growth of State power, that international law became explained in terms of the sovereignty of States. This was only a natural development, grown out of the necessity of regulating the relationships between the all-powerful States": F. Krenz, "The Refugee as a Subject of International Law" (1966), 15 I.C.L.Q. 90, at 95.

1

The desire of European states to establish normative standards and control mechanisms to stem the arrival of immigrants perceived as non-contributing clashed head-on with the enormity of a series of major population displacements within Europe during the early part of the twentieth century.[4] The most prominent migrations were the flight of more than one million Russians between 1917 and 1922, and the exodus during the early 1920s of hundreds of thousands of Armenians from Turkey in order to avoid persecution and massacre by the government of that country.[5] The social crisis brought on by the *de facto* immigration of so many refugees convinced governments that their laws would have to recognize the reality of forced international movements of people. Because political and other disruptions would inevitably induce involuntary migration, policies of selecting immigrants on the basis of national advantage alone were obliged to yield in such circumstances: indeed, in some instances, the nation concerned had no practical power to control the flow of humanity.[6]

Refugee law was designed to effect a compromise between the reality of this largely unstoppable flow of involuntary migrants across European borders and the broader policy commitment to restrictionism in immigration.[7] At least in its initial form, refugee law constituted a humanitarian exception to the protectionist norm,[8] in that immigration screening was dispensed with for large groups of unprotected migrants.

1.1 International Refugee Definitions Before 1951

Analysis of the international refugee accords entered into between 1920 and 1950 reveals three distinct approaches to refugee definition. Each of these perspectives — juridical, social, and individualist — was dominant during a part of the initial decades of refugee law.

1.1.1 The Juridical Perspective

From 1920 until 1935, refugees were defined in largely *juridical* terms, which meant that they were treated as refugees because of their membership

---

[4] "[O]ne of the really pressing problems which arose in the wake of the First World War and the ensuing great revolutions, was the exodus of the great masses of human beings seeking refuge in foreign countries": A. Grahl-Madsen, "The League of Nations and the Refugees" (1982), 20 A.W.R. Bull. 86, at 86.

[5] Conférence des organisations russes, *Memorandum sur la question des réfugiés russes*, p. 4 (1921); J. Simpson, *Refugees: Preliminary Report of a Survey*, pp. 21-22 (1938).

[6] "In situations of mass migration, the fact is that those states wishing to control their own borders are often those most completely unable to do so . . . . Even though asylum is recognized in customary law as at the discretion of nation states, discretion can seldom be used when one is faced with thousands of people encamped on one's borders": M. Chamberlain, "The Mass Migration of Refugees and International Law" (1983), 7 Fletcher Forum 93, at 102.

[7] *See* M. Marrus, *supra*, note 1, pp. 51-81.

[8] The exclusive jurisdiction of states to control the entry of persons into their territory is now constrained by an increased recognition of protection as a humanitarian duty: G. Goodwin-Gill, *supra*, note 2, p. 138.

in a group of persons effectively deprived of the formal protection of the government[9] of its state of origin.[10] The purpose of refugee status conceived in juridical terms is to facilitate the international movement of persons who find themselves abroad and unable to resettle because no nation is prepared to assume responsibility for them.[11]

These first refugee definitions were formulated in response to the international legal dilemma caused by the denial of state protection. The withdrawal of *de jure* protection by a state, whether by way of denaturalisation or the withholding of diplomatic facilities such as travel documents and consular representation, results in a malfunction in the international legal system. Because the then existing international law did not recognise individuals as subjects of international rights and obligations, the determination of responsibilities on the international plane fell to the sovereign state whose protection one enjoyed.[12] When the bond of protection between citizen and state was severed, no international entity could be held accountable for the individual's actions. The result was that states were reluctant to admit to their territory individuals who were not the legal responsibility of another country.[13] The refugee definitions adopted between 1920 and 1935 were designed to correct this breakdown in the international order, and accordingly embraced persons who wished to have freedom of international movement but found themselves in the anomalous situation of not enjoying the legal protection of any state.

The most fundamental form of *de jure* withdrawal of state protection is, of course, denaturalisation.[14] It was the general policy of the League of Nations to extend protection to groups of persons whose nationality had been involuntarily withdrawn.[15] As well, the League recognised that persons who could not obtain valid passports were entitled to international protection.[16] Both of these groups received League of Nations identity certificates which

---

[9] L. Holborn, *The International Refugee Organization: A Specialized Agency of the United Nations*, p. 311 (1956); R. Nathan-Chapotot, *La qualification internationale des réfugiés et personnes déplacées dans le cadre des Nations Unies*, p. 47 (1949); J. Simpson, *The Refugee Problem*, p. 227 (1939); R. Jennings, "Some International Law Aspects of the Refugee Question" (1939), 20 British Y.B. Intl. L. 98, at 99; P. Weis, "Legal Aspects of the Convention of 25 July 1951 relating to the Status of Refugees" (1953), 30 British Y.B. Intl. L. 478, at 480.

[10] *Report by the High Commissioner*, League of Nations Doc. 1927. XII. 3 (1927) at 13.

[11] R. Nathan-Chapotot, *supra*, note 9, p. 20.

[12] 1 A. Grahl-Madsen, *The Status of Refugees in International Law*, p. 57 (1966).

[13] J. Vernant, *The Refugee in the Post-War World*, p. 14 (1953).

[14] (1930) 11(11) League of Nations O.J. 1463.

[15] "In 1929, the Advisory Commission for Refugees clearly indicated that the characteristic and essential feature of the problem was that persons classed as 'refugees' have no regular nationality and are therefore deprived of the normal protection accorded to the regular citizens of a State": *Report by the Secretary-General on the Future Organisation of Refugee Work*, League of Nations Doc. 1930.XIII.2 (1930) at 3.

[16] *Minutes of the Inter-Governmental Conference on Refugee Questions*, League of Nations Doc. R/I.G.C.-10-1926 (1926) at 4; *Report by the High Commissioner*, League of Nations Doc. 1926.XIII.2 (1926) at 5.

contracting states agreed to recognise as the functional equivalent of passports.

The definitions of this era contained a criterion of ethnic or territorial origin, coupled with a stipulation that the applicant not enjoy *de jure* national protection. Only persons applying from outside their country of origin were eligible for refugee recognition.[17] This is consistent with the notion of the refugee as an international anomaly: while the unprotected individual remained within the boundaries of her home state, there was no question of another country being confronted with a person outside the bounds of international accountability and, accordingly, no need to include her within the scope of League of Nations protection.

1.1.2 The Social Perspective

In contrast to the initial juridical focus, the refugee agreements adopted between 1935 and 1939 embodied a *social* approach to refugee definition. Refugees defined from the social perspective are the helpless casualties[18] of broadly based social or political occurrences which separate them from their home society. Assistance in migration is afforded refugees not, as from the juridical perspective, with a view to correcting an anomaly in the international legal system, but rather in order to ensure the refugees' safety or well-being. The categories of persons eligible for international assistance encompassed groups adversely affected by a particular social or political event, not just those united by a common status *vis-à-vis* the international legal system.[19]

The essence of this second definitional approach was to continue to assist persons without formal national legal protection, but to assist as well the victims of social and political events which resulted in a *de facto*, if not a *de jure*, loss of state protection. For the most part, these agreements sought to protect persons caught up in the upheaval and dislocation caused by the National Socialist regime in Germany.[20] The substantive scope of this era's definitions was defined by an *en bloc* reference to general, situation-specific categories of persons affected by adverse social or political phenomena.

---

[17] *Report by the High Commissioner, supra,* note 10, at 13.

[18] J. Vernant, *supra,* note 13, p. 3.

[19] The response of the League of Nations to the Saar crisis in 1935 was the first recognition in international law that protection was required for persons on the basis of *de facto,* rather than merely formal, loss of state protection: (1935) 16(6) League of Nations O.J. 633.

[20] *Provisional Arrangement concerning the Status of Refugees coming from Germany,* July 4, 1936, 3952 L.N.T.S. 77; *Convention concerning the Status of Refugees coming from Germany,* February 10, 1938, 4461 L.N.T.S. 61; *Council Resolution on Refugees from Sudetenland,* January 17, 1939, (1939) 20(2) League of Nations O.J. 73; *Additional Protocol to the Provisional Arrangement and to the Convention concerning the Status of Refugees coming from Germany,* September 14, 1939, 4634 L.N.T.S. 142.

1.1.3 The Individualist Perspective

The third phase of international refugee protection, comprising the accords of the 1938-1950 era, was revolutionary in its rejection of group determination of refugee status. A refugee by individualist standards is a person in search of an escape from perceived injustice or fundamental incompatibility with her home state. She distrusts the authorities[21] who have rendered continued residence in her country of origin either impossible or intolerable,[22] and desires the opportunity to build a new life abroad. Refugee status viewed from this perspective is a means of facilitating international movement for those in search of personal freedom.

This individualist approach first affected the determination procedure: the decision as to whether or not a person was a refugee was no longer made strictly on the basis of political and social categories. Rather, the accords of the immediate post-war era prescribed an examination of the merits of each applicant's case.[23] Moreover, the move to a more personal conception of refugeehood altered substantive notions. The essence of refugee status came to be discord between the individual refugee applicant's personal characteristics and convictions and the tenets of the political system in her country of origin.

The subjective concept of a refugee was not universally embraced by the international community. During debate in the United Nations in 1946, for example, the socialist states asserted the impropriety of including political dissidents among the ranks of refugees protected by international law.[24] It was argued unsuccessfully that political émigrés who had suffered no personal prejudice ought not be protected as refugees under the auspices of the international community as a whole, but should instead seek the assistance of those states sympathetic to their political views.[25] The voting strength and influence of the Western alliance, however, led to a movement away from a focus on group *de jure* or *de facto* disfranchisement, and toward a personalized evaluation of incompatibility between state of origin and refugee

---

[21] A. Grahl-Madsen, "Further Development of International Refugee Law" (1964), 34 Nordisk Tidsskrift for International Ret 159, at 160.

[22] A. Grahl-Madsen, *supra*, note 12, p. 74.

[23] For example, the heart of the definition employed by the International Refugee Organisation (1946-1951) classified as refugees all persons who "in complete freedom and after receiving full knowledge of the facts . . . expressed valid objections to returning to [their country of origin]": 1(2) UNGAOR (67th plen. mtg.) at 1454.

[24] "[H]e had wanted to distinguish between refugees and displaced persons, on the one hand, and political émigrés on the other, as he did not think that countries of origin could be expected to support the latter. He had therefore suggested that the new organisation should be responsible for the people in the former categories and the receiving countries, and they only, should be responsible for those in the latter, under such international agreements as they could conclude": 1(2) UNESCOR Spec. Supp. 1 (1946) at 20, U.N. Doc. E/REF/75 (1946).

[25] *Id.*

claimant in search of personal freedom and liberty.[26] This initiative to define the refugee concept in a manner consistent with the ideology of the more powerful states set the stage for the development of contemporary international refugee law.

1.2 The 1951 Convention Definition of Refugee Status

The primary standard of refugee status today is that derived from the 1951 *Convention relating to the Status of Refugees*.[27] In addition to continuing protection for all persons deemed to be refugees under any of the earlier international accords,[28] the mandate of the Convention includes any person who

> . . . as a result of events occurring before 1 January 1951 and owing to well-founded fear of being persecuted for reasons of race, religion, nationality, membership of a particular social group or political opinion, is outside the country of his nationality and is unable or, owing to such fear, is unwilling to avail himself of the protection of that country; or who, not having a nationality and being outside the country of his former habitual residence as a result of such events, is unable or, owing to such fear, is unwilling to return to it.[29]

Provisions dealing with dual or multiple nationality[30] and the circumstances in which one may either cease to be a refugee[31] or be excluded from the benefits of refugee status[32] are also set out.

The Convention was drafted between 1948 and 1951 by a combination of United Nations organs, *ad hoc* committees, and a conference of plenipotentiaries. The two main characteristics of the Convention refugee definition are its strategic conceptualization and its Eurocentric focus.

The strategic dimension of the definition comes from successful efforts of Western states to give priority in protection matters to persons whose flight was motivated by pro-Western political values. As anxious as the Soviets had been to exclude political émigrés from the scope of the Convention for fear of exposing their weak flank,[33] so the more numerous and more powerful

---

[26] 1(1) UNGAOR (8th mtg.) at 23.

[27] 189 U.N.T.S. 2545, entered into force on April 22, 1954 (*"Convention"*).

[28] "For the purposes of the present Convention, the term 'refugee' shall apply to any person who: (1) Has been considered a refugee under the Arrangements of 12 May 1926 and 30 June 1928 or under the Convention of 28 October 1933 and 10 February 1938, the Protocol of 14 September 1939 or the Constitution of the International Refugee Organization. . .": *Convention, supra*, note 27, at Art. 1(A)(1).

[29] Convention, *supra*, note 27, at Art. 1(A)(2).

[30] "In the case of a person who has more than one nationality, the term 'country of his nationality' shall mean each of the countries of which he is a national, and a person shall not be deemed to be lacking the protection of the country of his nationality if, without any valid reason based on well-founded fear, he has not availed himself of the protection of one of the countries of which he is a national": *Convention, supra*, note 27, at Art. 1(A)(2), para. 2.

[31] *Convention, supra*, note 27, at Art. 1(C). *See* Chapter 6, *infra*.

[32] *Convention, supra,* note 27, at Art. 1(D), (E), (F). *See* Chapter 6, *infra*.

[33] "The U.S.S.R. delegation considers that persons who collaborated in any way with the

Western states were preoccupied to maximize the international visibility of that migration.[34] In the result, it was agreed to restrict the scope of protection in much the same way as had been done in the post-World War II refugee instruments:[35] only persons who feared "persecution" because of their civil or political status would fall within the international protection mandate. This apparently neutral formulation facilitated the condemnation of Soviet bloc politics through international law in two ways.

First, the persecution standard was a known quantity, having already been employed to embrace Soviet bloc dissidents in the immediate post-war years.[36] It was understood that the concept of "fear of persecution" was sufficiently open-ended to allow the West to continue to admit ideological dissidents to international protection.[37]

---

enemies of the democratic countries should not be regarded as refugees or enjoy the protection of the United Nations. It considers it essential to exclude from the category of persons who receive United Nations assistance not only those who, during the war, fought actively on the side of the enemy against the people and government of their country, but all those other traitors who are refusing to return home to serve their country together with their fellow citizens": Statement of Mr. Soldatov of the U.S.S.R., 5 UNGAOR (325th Mtg.) at 671, December 14, 1950.

[34] "[T]he definition of the term 'refugee'. . . was based on the assumption of a divided world. If, however, it was considered that a single text should cover both refugees from Western Europe seeking asylum beyond the 'Iron Curtain' and refugees from the latter countries seeking asylum in Western Europe, he wondered what the moral implications of such a text would be. The problem of refugees could not be considered in the abstract, but, on the contrary, must be considered in the light of historical facts. In laying down the definition of the term 'refugee', account had hitherto always been taken of the fact that the refugees principally involved had always been from a certain part of the world; thus, such a definition was based on historical facts. Any attempt to impart a universal character to the text would be tantamount to making it an 'Open Sesame' ": Statement of Mr. Rochefort of France, U.N. Doc. A/CONF.2/SR.22, at 15, July 16, 1951.

[35] The United Nations Relief and Rehabilitation Administration (UNRRA) insisted on "concrete evidence" of persecution, and the successor International Refugee Organization (IRO) required the demonstration of "valid objections" to return to the country of origin: UNRRA European Region Order 40(I), July 3, 1946; Constitution of the International Refugee Organization, Part I(C)(1), 18 U.N.T.S. 3.

[36] "The representative of France had observed that the definition of neo-refugees could be interpreted very broadly. The fact was that it already appeared in the IRO constitution where its meaning was quite clear: it would have to have the identical meaning in the convention. It did not apply to all types of refugees wherever they might be, but only to those who had become refugees as a result of events which had followed the outbreak of the Second World War": Statement of Mr. Henkin of the U.S.A., U.N. Doc. E/AC.32/SR.5, at 5, January 30, 1950.

[37] "As to refugees, both present and future, arriving in central and western Europe from eastern European lands, he considered that, having regard to the terms of the draft convention and the observations of the High Commissioner for Refugees, [there need be] no fear that such refugees would not be covered by the present text": Statement of Mr. Warren of the U.S.A., U.N. Doc. A/CONF.2/SR.21, at 15, July 14, 1951. *Accord* Mr. Robinson of Israel: ". . . [T]he word 'events' had originally been included. . . in an attempt to designate, in a somewhat camouflaged manner, the new categories of post-war refugees that had emerged as a result of the political changes which had supervened in parts of central and eastern Europe": U.N. Doc. A/CONF.2/SR.22, at 6, July 16, 1951.

Second, the precise formulation of the persecution standard meant that refugee law could not readily be turned to the political advantage of the Soviet bloc. The refugee definition was carefully phrased to include only persons who have been disfranchised by their state on the basis of race, religion, nationality, membership of a particular social group, or political opinion,[38] matters in regard to which East bloc practice has historically been problematic.[39] Western vulnerability in the area of respect for human rights, in contrast, centres more on the guarantee of socio-economic human rights[40] than on respect for civil and political rights. Unlike the victims of civil and political oppression, however, persons denied even such basic rights as food, health care, or education are excluded from the international refugee regime (unless that deprivation stems from civil or political status). By mandating protection for those whose (Western inspired) civil and political rights are jeopardized, without at the same time protecting persons whose (socialist inspired) socio-economic rights are at risk, the Convention adopted an incomplete and politically partisan human rights rationale.

In addition to their desire for the refugee definition to serve strategic political objectives, the majority of the states that drafted the Convention sought to create a rights regime conducive to the redistribution of the post-war refugee burden from European shoulders.[41] The Europeans complained that they had been forced to cope with the bulk of the human displacement caused by the Second World War,[42] and that the time had come for all members

---

[38] *Convention, supra*, note 27, at Art. 1(A)(2), para. 1.

[39] *See* generally Amnesty International, *Report 1987*, pp. 279-332 (1987). For example, in regard to the U.S.S.R., the Report (at p. 320) notes ". . . no improvement in the harsh and arbitrary treatment of prisoners of conscience in 1986. Although it has learned of fewer political arrests, Amnesty International was disturbed that the Soviet authorities continued to imprison many citizens whose conscience led them to dissent peacefully from official policies, and to apply compulsory psychiatric measures to others."

[40] "We vote for officials every two or four or six years. We never vote on those who occupy the land. We do not live in an economic democracy. Many of those who are now in wealth did not become so because of brilliance and hard work and character, but because of royal blood and inheritance and growth at the expense and exploitation of other people . . . . This generation cannot speak of political democracy apart from human rights, cannot speak of human rights apart from development. The great issues of our day transcend party, race, region, religion, and sex": J. Jackson, "Measuring Human Rights and Development by One Yardstick" (1985), 15 Ca. W. Intl. L.J. 453, at 456-60.

[41] "One region in the world was ripe for treatment of the refugee problem on an international scale. That region was Europe. One problem was ready to form the subject of an international convention, namely, the problem of European refugees": Statement of Mr. Rochefort of France, U.N. Doc. A/CONF.2/SR.19, at 12, November 26, 1951. Mr. Desai of India summarized the redistributive purpose succinctly: "In effect, an appeal was made to all governments to accord the same treatment to all refugees, in order to reduce the burden on contracting governments whose geographical situation meant that the greater part of the responsibility fell on them": U.N. Doc. E/AC.7/SR.166, at 18, August 22, 1950.

[42] "All previous international instruments concluded on behalf of refugees had been couched and conceived in respect of those European countries, of which Italy was one, that had first been affected by the problem and made sacrifices to relieve it. The proposed geographical restric-

of the United Nations to contribute to the resettlement of both the remaining war refugees and the influx of refugees from the Soviet bloc.[43] Refugees would be more inclined to move beyond Europe if there were guarantees that their traditional expectations in terms of rights and benefits would be respected abroad. The Convention, then, was designed to create secure conditions such as would facilitate the sharing of the European refugee burden.[44]

Notwithstanding the vigorous objections of several delegates from developing countries faced with responsibility for their own refugee populations,[45] the Eurocentric goal of the Western states was achieved by limiting the scope of mandatory international protection under the Convention to refugees whose flight was prompted by a pre-1951 event within Europe.[46] While states might opt to extend protection to refugees from other parts of the world, the definition adopted was intended to distribute the European refugee burden without any binding obligation to reciprocate by way of the establishment of rights for, or the provision of assistance to, non-European refugees. It was not until more than fifteen years later that the *Protocol relating to*

---

tion was essential . . . ": Statement of Mr. Del Drago of Italy, U.N. Doc. A/CONF.2/SR.21, at 4, July 14, 1951.

[43] "[T]he Secretariat had sent out 80 invitations to the present conference. Yet the conference gave the appearance of being nothing more than a meeting of the Council of Europe slightly enlarged . . . . it meant that it was really European refugees who were still involved; it meant, too, that the non-European countries in whose territories European refugees were living did not wish to enter into commitments in respect of them": Statement of Mr. Rochefort of France, U.N. Doc. A/CONF.2/SR.3, at 12, November 19, 1951.

[44] "It was . . . one thing to frame a definition in the desire to assist all refugees irrespective of their country of origin, and quite another to adjust that definition to the remaining provisions of the Convention . . . . If, when considering the articles other than article 1, the Conference had been aware that the Convention was to apply to all refugees without distinction, it would undoubtedly have proceeded differently. As it was, the provisions so far agreed upon had been adapted specifically for application to refugees from European countries": Statement of Mr. Warren of the U.S.A., U.N. Doc. A/CONF.2/SR.22, at 16, July 16, 1951. *Accord* Mr. Del Drago of Italy: "If the Convention covered Europeans who wanted to settle in overseas countries with a western civilization, the rights and duties of the refugee and the receiving country could be defined": U.N. Doc. A/CONF.2/SR.19, at 15, November 26, 1951.

[45] "[T]he French text seemed to approach the question from a purely European point of view, and might not therefore be entirely suitable for an international convention. He believed that due consideration should be given to refugee problems existing outside the continent of Europe": Statement of Mr. Caledron Puig of Mexico, U.N. Doc. E/AC.7/SR.160, at 4, August 18, 1950. *Accord* Mr. Brohi of Pakistan: "The Pakistan delegation was of the opinion that the problem of refugees was not a European problem only and thought, therefore, that the definition of the term 'refugee' should cover all those who might reasonably fall within the scope of that term": 11 UNESCOR (399th mtg.) at 215, August 2, 1950.

[46] "For the purposes of this Convention, the words 'events occurring before 1 January 1951' in Article 1, Section A, shall be understood to mean either: (a) 'events occurring in Europe before 1 January 1951' or (b) 'events occurring in Europe or elsewhere before 1 January 1951' and each Contracting State shall make a declaration at the time of signature, ratification or accession, specifying which of these meanings it applies for the purpose of its obligations under this Convention . . . ": *Convention, supra,* note 27, at Art. 1(B)(1).

the Status of Refugees[47] expanded the scope of the Convention definition to include refugees from all regions of the world.[48]

1.3 The Impact of the 1967 Protocol on the Convention Definition

The 1967 Protocol achieved the formal, but not the substantive, universalization of the Convention definition of refugee status. The obvious restriction in the Convention definition — the requirement that the claim relate to a pre-1951 event in Europe — was prospectively eliminated by the Protocol.[49] However, there was no review conducted of the substantive content of the definition.

Even after the elimination of temporal and geographic limitations, only persons whose migration is prompted by a fear of persecution on the ground of civil or political status[50] come within the scope of the Convention-based protection system. This means that most Third World refugees remain *de facto* excluded, as their flight is more often prompted by natural disaster, war, or broadly based political and economic turmoil than by "persecution",[51] at least as that term is understood in the Western context.[52] While

---

[47] 606 U.N.T.S. 8791, entered into force on October 4, 1967 (*"Protocol"*).

[48] Those states which had already made the declaration under Article 1(B)(1)(a) of the Convention to restrict its application in their jurisdiction to European refugees could, however, maintain that restriction: *Protocol, supra*, note 47, at Art. I(3).

[49] "For the purpose of the present Protocol, the term 'refugee' shall . . . mean any person within the definition of article 1 of the Convention as if the words 'As a result of events occurring before 1 January 1951 and . . . ' and the words ' . . . as a result of such events', in article 1(A)(2) were omitted. The present Protocol shall be applied by the States Parties hereto without any geographic limitation, save that existing declarations made by States already Parties to the Convention in accordance with article 1(B)(1)(a) of the Convention, shall, unless extended under article 1(B)(2) thereof, apply also under the present Protocol": *Protocol, supra*, note 47, at Article I(2)-(3).

[50] "[S]i la persécution est toujours une réalité trop fréquente, elle est loin de constituer la seule raison que amène les individus à fuir leur pays ou à refuser sa protection": F. Julien-Laferrière, "Réflexions sur la notion de réfugié en 1978" (1978), A.W.R. Bull. 30, at 30.

[51] "[I]n addition to political persecution and the ravages of war, the modern refugee flees the whole range of problems which acompany underdevelopment in the post-colonial period, including civil strife, political instability, and harsh economic conditions. Though the post-World War II refugee and the modern refugee are . . . treated differently under international law, the actual position of both groups is the same. Hence, the argument continues, both groups should be accorded the same rights under international law": E. Lentini, "The Definition of Refugee in International Law: Proposals for the Future" (1985), 5 Boston Coll. Third World L.J. 183, at 184.

[52] "[F]or the great masses there will be a presumption, hard for them to disprove, that they have fled more in order to escape economic misery than because they fear political persecution . . . . It may seem as if there is a tendency to draw the line differently, depending on the differences of economic levels between the countries in question. If the flow is from one of the poorest countries in the world into one of the richest, as is the case of the Haitians trying to get into the United States, the scales may be heavily weighted against the newcomers . . . ":

these phenomena undoubtedly may give rise to genuine fear and hence to the need to seek safe haven away from one's home,[53] refugees whose flight is not motivated by persecution rooted in civil or political status are excluded from the rights regime established by the Convention.

1.4 International Expansion of the Refugee Concept

The Convention refugee concept has been expanded in practice through the evolution of the institutional competence of the United Nations High Commissioner for Refugees, the effort to prepare a United Nations convention on territorial asylum, the establishment of regional refugee protection arrangements, and the practice of states. While these developments do not constitute formal amendments to the Convention definition, they are nonetheless indicative of a widening of the circumstances in which persons may be said genuinely to be in need of international protection. In keeping with Recommendation E[54] of the Conference that adopted the Convention, states which are parties to the Convention may be expected to consider these developments in determining the extent to which persons outside the strict contractual scope of the Convention will be protected as refugees.

1.4.1 Enhanced Competence of the United Nations High Commissioner for Refugees

Developments in the refugee definition employed by the United Nations High Commissioner for Refugees[55] are salient particularly because this institu-

---

A. Grahl-Madsen, "International Refugee Law Today and Tomorrow" (1982), 20 Archiv des Völkerrechts 411, at 422.

[53] "[T]he Convention and Protocol, and thus several domestic laws, designate as refugees only those who have fled from persecution and exclude fugitives from natural disasters and from civil and international war. This limitation on the designation of refugee owes its origins to the fact that the refugee was designated as a person who stands in need of international protection because he or she is deprived of that in his or her own country. Such reasoning and definition may well be appropriate for the purpose of determining whether an individual should receive an international travel document and should be eligible for the diplomatic protection afforded by the High Commissioner's representatives; however, it appears inappropriate for the purpose of determining whether an applicant qualifies for admission to a country of asylum and to freedom from 'refoulement.' The compassionate claim of a fugitive from persecution may, after all, be no greater than that of a person displaced by an earthquake or a civil war": R. Plender, "Admission of Refugees: Draft Convention on Territorial Asylum" (1977), 15 San Diego L.Rev. 45, at 54-55.

[54] "The Conference, [e]xpresses the hope that the Convention relating to the Status of Refugees will have value as an example exceeding its contractual scope and that all nations will be guided by it in granting so far as possible to persons in their territory as refugees and who would not be covered by the terms of the Convention, the treatment for which it provides": *Final Act of the United Nations Conference of Plenipotentiaries on the Status of Refugees and Stateless Persons*, 189 U.N.T.S. 37.

[55] "The competence of the High Commissioner shall extend to . . . [a]ny other person who is outside the country of his nationality, or if he has no nationality, the country of his former

tional definition and the Convention definition were drafted simultaneously by the same organs of the United Nations. Since the adoption of the 1967 Protocol, moreover, the two definitions are quite similar.[56]

The individualistic character of the refugee definition contained in the 1950 UNHCR Statute[57] made it difficult initially for the organization to respond in a meaningful way to the needs of refugees outside Europe.[58] Becauses refugees in Africa and Asia tend to move in large groups, the type of individuated, case by case application of a refugee definition contemplated by the Statute (like the Convention) was simply not a practical possibility.[59] The UNHCR was thus technically unable to exercise its universal mandate, and sought the authority to deal with refugee situations outside Europe in a more collective fashion that would not involve a process of individualized assessment.[60]

Since 1957, the General Assembly, the Economic and Social Council, and the Executive Committee of the UNHCR have moved by a variety of means

---

habitual residence, because he has or had well-founded fear of persecution by reason of his race, religion, nationality or political opinion and is unable or, because of such fear, is unwilling to avail himself of the protection of the government of the country of his nationality, or, if he has no nationality, to return to the country of his former habitual residence": *Statute of the Office of the United Nations High Commissioner for Refugees*, U.N.G.A. Res. 428(V), December 14, 1950 ("*Statute*").

[56] The differences of importance include (a) the omission of any reference to claims grounded in membership of a particular social group in the UNHCR Statute; (b) the UNHCR Statute's inclusion of persons who have either a present or a past fear of persecution; (c) the explicit exclusion under the UNHCR Statute of persons whose refusal to return is for reasons of personal convenience or of an economic character; (d) the clarification in the UNHCR Statute that it is the actual receipt of assistance from another U.N. agency, rather than eligibility for the same, that results in exclusion from the refugee definition; and (e) the more narrow criminal exclusion in the UNHCR Statute. *See UNHCR Statute, supra*, note 55, and *Convention, supra*, note 27.

[57] *Supra*, note 55.

[58] "The UNHCR Statute . . . contains an apparent contradiction. On the one hand, it affirms that the work of the Office shall relate, as a rule, to groups and categories of refugees. On the other hand, it proposes a definition of the refugee which is essentially individualistic, requiring a case by case examination of subjective and objective elements. The escalation in refugee crises over the last 30 years has made it necessary to be flexible in the administration of UNHCR's mandate. In consequence, there has been a significant broadening of what may be termed the concept of 'refugees of concern to the international community' ": G. Goodwin-Gill, *The Refugee in International Law*, p. 6 (1983).

[59] "An eligibility procedure — however devised — is inevitably very time-consuming. When the Statute of the Office of the UNHCR and the Convention were adopted it was quite possible to recognize refugees on an individual basis. Since 1951, however, there have been occasions when new refugee problems have arisen and the number of refugees involved has been so large as to make it impossible to recognize persons on an individual basis": G. Melander, "The Protection of Refugees" (1974), 18 Scandinavian Studies in Law 153, at 161.

[60] "[T]he High Commissioner has been authorized to assist refugees without having to decide on an individual basis whether the persons in question were mandate refugees. The High Commissioner has — to use the official terminology — been authorized to lend his good offices to persons in need of assistance": G. Melander, *supra*, note 59, at 161.

to respond to non-European refugee-producing situations.[61] Styled variously as requests for the UNHCR to "extend its good offices", or to act on behalf of groups "of concern" to the international community, the *de facto* sphere of responsibility has expanded radically from its relatively constrained statutory base. UNHCR has been authorized to aid the full range of involuntary migrants, including the victims of all forms of both man-made[62] and natural[63] disasters. Moreover, the organization has been requested to assist refugees who remain within their country of origin,[64] and to contribute to the resettlement of refugees who are returning home.[65] The essential criterion of refugee status under UNHCR auspices has come to be simply the existence of human suffering consequent to forced migration. While this enhanced definition is linked primarily to eligibility for material assistance, UNHCR has also been authorized with increasing frequency to extend international legal protection to persons within its broader mandate.[66] In functional terms, few distinctions are now made between the role of UNHCR in regard to refugees within its statutory mandate and those within its extended competence.

1.4.2 The Attempt to Draft a Convention on Territorial Asylum

A second indication of the expanded scope of refugee status derives from the abortive effort to draft a convention to define the circumstances in which

---

[61] "The U.N. High Commissioner for Refugees (UNHCR) has enjoyed an expansion of his mandate and responsibility and authority under successive resolutions of the General Assembly, until now that responsibility extends far beyond the classic U.N. definition of 'refugee' to include a great many other 'displaced persons' ": D. Martin in C. Sumpter, "Mass Migration of Refugees — Law and Policy" (1982), 76 A.S.I.L.P. 13, at 17. *See generally* P. Maynard, "The Legal Competence of the United Nations High Commissioner for Refugees" (1982), 31 I.C.L.Q. 415.

[62] "It has been said that the High Commissioner's competence in relation to protection as well as to assistance has been extended gradually to all victims of man-made disasters": G. Coles, *Problems Arising From Large Numbers of Asylum-Seekers: A Study of Protection Aspects*, p. 15 (1981).

[63] Independent Commission on International Humanitarian Issues, *Refugees: The Dynamics of Displacement*, pp. 48-49 (1986).

[64] "Since the early 1970s, UNHCR has been requested on numerous occasions to assist refugees once they have returned to their home country. From time to time, it has been called on to help people who have been uprooted and displaced within their own country": Independent Commission on International Humanitarian Issues, *supra*, note 63, p. 48.

[65] "[I]nternational action, whether at the universal or regional level, to promote voluntary repatriation requires at the outset of a refugee movement consideration of the situation within the country of origin . . . . It was not to be excluded that conditions within the country of origin could be improved significantly and beneficially as a result of timely and helpful international intercessions whether of a political or economic nature . . . . Material assistance for the reintegration of returnees provided by the international community in the country of origin was recognized as an important factor in promoting voluntary repatriation": Executive Committee of the High Commissioner's Programme, "Refugee Aid and Development", U.N. Doc. A/AC.96/662 (1985) paras. 32 and 39.

[66] "The type of assistance which might be given [to non-mandate refugees] was initially limited, often to the transmission of financial contributions, but that restriction was soon dropped": G. Goodwin-Gill, *supra*, note 58, p. 7.

territorial asylum should be guaranteed to refugees. The need for such a convention stems from the failure to include in the Convention any obligation beyond "non-refoulement",[67] that is, the duty to avoid the return of a refugee to a country where she faces a genuine risk of serious harm. While willing to provide emergency protection against return to persecution the states that participated in the drafting of the Convention insisted that they be allowed to decide who should be admitted to their territory, who should be allowed to remain there, and ultimately who should be permanently resettled.[68]

In view of this deficiency in the Convention, and in an effort to effectuate the right to seek and enjoy asylum contained in the Universal Declaration of Human Rights[69] and the Declaration on Territorial Asylum,[70] a draft convention on territorial asylum was prepared and submitted to a conference of plenipotentiaries in 1977.[71] While the purpose of the proposed accord was essentially to enhance the scope of protection available to Convention refugees,[72] its most noteworthy achievement may in fact have been the degree of consensus attained on changes to the definition of refugee status for purposes of entitlement to international legal protection.

The expert draft of Article 2 of the proposed asylum convention recommended important changes to the definitional standard derived from the Convention, as amended by the Protocol. Clarifications of the notions of "political opinion" to include opposition to apartheid and colonialism, and of "persecution" to embrace prosecution grounded in persecutory intent were

---

[67] "The Convention does not address the granting of asylum. The reasons for this appear to be two-fold. First, because states are the proper subjects of international law, individuals have neither rights under nor access to it. More importantly, the right to grant asylum remains within the unfettered discretion of a state as an incident of sovereignty; in the absence of contrary treaty obligation, a state is not bound to grant or deny political asylum to any person": R. Sexton, "Political Refugees, Nonrefoulement and State Practice: A Comparative Study" (1985), 18 Vand. J. Transntl. L. 731, at 737-738.

[68] "States the world over consistently have exhibited great reluctance to give up their sovereign right to decide which persons will, and which will not, be admitted to their territory, and given a right to settle there. They have refused to agree to international instruments which would impose on them duties to make grants of asylum": P. Hyndman, "Refugees Under International Law with a Reference to the Concept of Asylum" (1986), 60 Australian L.J. 148, at 153.

[69] "Everyone has the right to seek and enjoy in other countries asylum from persecution. This right may not be invoked in the case of prosecutions genuinely arising from non-political crimes or from acts contrary to the purposes and principles of the United Nations": *Universal Declaration of Human Rights*, U.N.G.A. Res. 217 A (III), December 10, 1948, at Art. 14.

[70] U.N.G.A. Res. 2312 (XXII), December 14, 1967.

[71] *See generally* P. Weis, "The Draft United Nations Convention on Territorial Asylum" (1979), 50 British Y.B. Intl. L. 151.

[72] "The proposed new Convention, and the conference, were concerned more with increasing the degree of protection afforded to those falling within the existing definition of a *refugee* than with broadening the definition . . . ": R. Plender, *supra*, note 53, at 48.

proposed.[73] During the meeting of the 92 states, moreover, it was agreed *inter alia* that asylum should be accessible also to persons at serious risk of persecution due to kinship[74] or as a result of "foreign occupation, alien domination, and all forms of racism."[75] An important clarification of the definition agreed to by delegates was the replacement of the "owing to a well-founded fear of persecution" Convention-based standard with a requirement that a refugee be "faced with a definite possibility of persecution."[76] The expanded scope of protection as a whole, including both the expert group and conference amendments, which was approved by 47 votes to 14 with 21 abstentions, provided that:

> Each Contracting Stage may grant the benefits of this Convention to a person seeking asylum, if he, being faced with a definite possibility of:
> (a) Persecution for reasons of race, colour, national or ethnic origin, religion, nationality, kinship, membership of a particular social group or political opinion, including the struggle against colonialism and *apartheid*, foreign occupation, alien domination and all forms of racism; or
> (b) Prosecution or punishment for reasons directly related to the persecution set forth in (a);
> is unable or unwilling to return to the country of his nationality or, if he has no nationality, the country of his former domicile or habitual residence.[77]

While the drafting of the territorial asylum convention ended in a stalemate,[78] the affirmative vote in favour of an expanded definition of refugee

---

[73] The proposed Article 2, which set out the scope of the refugee concept read as follows: "A person shall be eligible for the benefits of this Convention if he, owing to a well-founded fear of:
(a) Persecution for reasons of race, religion, nationality, membership of a particular social group or political opinion, including the struggle against colonialism and *apartheid*, or
(b) Prosecution or punishment for acts directly related to the persecution as set forth in (a)
is unable to unwilling to return to the country of his nationality, or, if he has no nationality, the country of his former habitual residence."
P. Weis, *supra*, note 71, at 155.

[74] This Australian amendment was adopted by a vote of 40-24, with 15 abstentions: P. Weis, *supra*, note 7, at 162.

[75] This amendment, co-sponsored by Algeria, Egypt, Iraq, Jordan, Kuwait, Lebanon, Libya, Morocco, Saudi Arabia, Somalia, Sudan, Syria, Tunisia, United Arab Emirates and Yemen was adopted by a vote of 45-21, with 15 abstentions: P. Weis, *supra*, note 71, at 162.

[76] Paul Weis argues that "[t]he amendment adopted is more restrictive, providing for an objective test only, and would depart from the present practice of many States": P. Weis, *supra*, note 71, at 162. The position advanced herein is to the contrary: *see* Section 4.1, *infra*.

[77] P. Weis, *supra*, note 71, at 163-64.

[78] "[T]he Committee met for [more than] four weeks, and only three of the ten articles of the experts' draft were discussed and voted on . . . . As foreseen, the preoccupation of the majority of the states was that of safeguarding, to exasperation point, the sovereign right of a state to grant asylum": E. Lapenna, "Territorial Asylum — Developments from 1961 to 1977 — Comments on the Conference of Plenipotentiaries" (1978), 16 A.W.R. Bull, 1, at 4.

status is nonetheless indicative of a willingness on the part of the international community to conceive the refugee concept more broadly than as elaborated in the Convention and Protocol. In contrast to the concern in 1967 to avoid the reassessment of the substantive content of the refugee definition,[79] a majority of the 92 states that attended the Conference on Territorial Asylum agreed to update the definition in ways that were responsive to refugee movements in the developing world, and which recognized the collective nature of many refugee-producing phenomena. While no binding, conventional commitment was established toward refugees within this revised concept, the work of the 1977 conference remains the most recent expression of international consensus on the appropriate scope of refugee status in international law.

Three regional groups have enacted standards of refugee protection that extend the Convention definition in ways similar to the evolution of the UNHCR mandate and the scope of the proposed asylum convention. The work of each of the Organization of African Unity, the Organization of American States, and the Council of Europe is considered in turn.

1.4.3 The Organization of African Unity Definition of Refugee Status

The first regional arrangement was established by the Organization of African Unity (OAU) in 1969. In addition to respecting the Convention definition of a refugee, state parties to the OAU *Convention governing the specific aspects of refugee problems in Africa*[80] broke new ground by extending protection to all persons compelled to flee across national borders by reason of any man-made disaster,[81] whether or not they can be said to fear persecution:

> The term refugee shall also apply to every person who, owing to external aggression, occupation, foreign domination or events seriously disturbing public order in either part or the whole of his country of origin or nationality, is compelled to leave his place of habitual residence in order to seek refuge in another place outside his country of origin or nationality.[82]

---

[79] *See* text *supra* at note 49. The Colloquium that drafted the Protocol "considered that a revision of the Convention would be too lengthy and cumbersome to meet the need for urgency and therefore recommended the adoption of a Protocol. Although this does not appear from the Colloquium's Report, the members of the Colloquium freely admitted that a revision of the Convention would also be undesirable as it might lead to a political discussion in the General Assembly": UNHCR, "Draft Protocol to the 1951 Convention: Analysis of the present position", Internal memorandum, May 26, 1966.

[80] U.N.T.S. 14,691, entered into force June 20, 1974 ("*OAU Convention*").

[81] "The second part of the definition would virtually cover all man-made disasters and would embrace that class of persons sometimes called 'displaced persons' ": G. Coles, "Background Paper for the Asian Working Group on the International Protection of Refugees and Displaced Persons", p. 83 (unpublished, 1980).

[82] *OAU Convention, supra*, note 80, at Art I(2).

This standard represents an important conceptual adaptation of the Convention refugee definition, in that it successfully translates the core meaning of refugee status to the reality of the developing world.[83] From its inception, refugee status has evolved in response to changing social and political conditions[84] — the initial concern with *de jure* statelessness shifted to embrace *de facto* unprotected groups, and further to protect individuals at ideological odds with their state. The common thread is a recognition that it is reasonable for groups and individuals to disengage from fundamentally abusive national communities, at which point refugee law exists to interpose protection by the international community. Whether the particular form of abuse consists of a denial of formal protection, a campaign of generalized disfranchisement, refusal to allow individuals political self-determination, or calculated acts of deliberate harm, the definitional framework of international refugee law has evolved to respond to the imperative to protect involuntary migrants in flight from states which fail in their basic duty of protection.

The OAU definition accepts this rationale for refugee status. It does not, for example, suggest that victims of natural disasters or economic misfortune should become the responsibility of the international community, as a shift away from concern about the adequacy of state protection in favour of a more generalized humanitarian commitment might have dictated.[85] Rather, the OAU definition recognizes that four important modifications of the Convention definition are required in order to accommodate the specific context of abuse in states of the developing world.

First, the OAU definition acknowledges the reality that fundamental forms of abuse may occur not only as a result of the calculated acts of the government of the refugee's state of origin, but also as a result of that government's loss of authority due to external aggression, occupation, or foreign domination. The anticipated harm is no less wrong because it is inflicted by a foreign power in control of a state rather than by the government of that state *per se*. This modification simply recognizes the need to examine a refugee claim from the perspective of the *de facto*, rather than the formal, authority structure within the country of origin.

---

[83] "The 1951 Convention was primarily drawn up to deal with the situation of displaced persons in Europe immediately after the Second World War, and to provide protection for those persons. The States acceding to the Convention were anxious to make their obligations specific and to ensure that those obligations could not be extended indefinitely. Today, circumstances have changed and many people who need international protection of the kind provided by the Convention do not fall within its ambit": P. Hyndman, *supra*, note 68, at 150.

[84] *See generally* J. Hathaway, "The Evolution of Refugee Status in International Law: 1920-1950" (1984), 33 I.C.L.Q. 348, especially at 379-80.

[85] "Even this broader [OAU] definition would not cope with complex refugee situations with multiple causes, including ecological or economic disasters . . . . On humanitarian grounds, there is a strong case to be made for a broader approach . . . . Where a person's life, liberty or safety is threatened, it is immaterial whether that threat is the result of persecution or some other form of danger . . . ": Independent Commission on International Humanitarian Issues, *supra*, note 63, p. 46.

Second, the OAU definition reverts to the pattern of pre-World War II refugee accords in recognizing the concept of group disfranchisement.[86] By its reference to persons who leave their country in consequence of broadly based phenomena such as external aggression, occupation, foreign domination, or any other event that seriously disturbs public order, the OAU recognizes the legitimacy of flight in circumstances of generalized danger.

While the accommodation of abuse at the hands of a *de facto* government is little more than an extrapolation from the intent of the Convention definition, and while group-based refugee determination has its historical antecedents in European practice, there are two additional features of the OAU definition that are unprecedented in international refugee law.

The Convention definition and all of its predecessors link refugee status to the prospect of abuse *resulting from* some form of personal or group characteristic (in the case of the Convention, from one's civil or political status).[87] The OAU definition, on the other hand, leaves open the possibility that the basis or rationale for the harm may be indeterminate. So long as a person "is compelled" to seek refuge because of some anticipated serious disruption of public order, she need not be in a position to demonstrate any linkage between her personal status (or that of some collectivity of which she is a member) and the impending harm. Because the African standard emphasizes assessment of the gravity of the disruption of public order rather than motives for flight, individuals are largely able to decide for themselves when harm is sufficiently proximate to warrant flight.

The OAU Convention also extends international protection to persons who seek to escape serious disruption of public order "in either part or the whole"[88] of their country of origin. This, too, represents a departure from past practice in which it was generally assumed that a person compelled to flight should make reasonable efforts to seek protection within a safe part of her own country (if one exists) before looking for refuge abroad.[89] There are at least three reasons why this shift is contextually sensible. First, issues of distance or the unavailability of escape routes may foreclose travel to a safe region of the refugee's own state. Underdeveloped infrastructure and inadequate personal financial resources may reinforce the choice of a more easily reachable foreign destination. Second, the political instability of many

---

[86] *See* text *supra* at notes 10-20.

[87] A Convention refugee is a person outside her country " . . . owing to a well-founded fear of being persecuted *for reasons of* race, religion, nationality, membership of a particular social group or political opinion . . . ": *Convention, supra*, note 27, at Art. 1(A)(2).

[88] *OAU Convention, supra*, note 80, at Art. I(2).

[89] "The fear of being persecuted need not always extend to the *whole* of the refugee's country of nationality . . . . a person will not be excluded from refugee status merely because he could have sought refuge in another part of the same country, *if under all the circumstances it would not have been reasonable to expect him to do so*" [Emphasis added]: United Nations High Commissioner for Refugees, *Handbook on Procedures and Criteria for Determining Refugee Status*, pp. 21-22 (1979).

developing states may mean that what is a "safe" region today may be dangerous tomorrow. Rapid shifts of power and the consequent inability to predict accurately where safe haven is to be found may lead to a decision to leave the troubled state altogether. Finally, the artificiality of the colonially imposed boundaries in Africa has frequently meant that kinship and other natural ties stretch across national frontiers.[90] Hence, persons in danger may see the natural safe haven to be with family or members of their own ethnic group in an adjacent state.

The relevance of the OAU definition to conditions in the developing world has made it the most influential conceptual standard of refugee status apart from the Convention definition itself. It has provided the basis for enhanced UNHCR activity in Africa,[91] was at the root of the proposed conventional definition of persons entitled to territorial asylum,[92] and has inspired the liberalization of a variety of regional[93] and national[94] accords on refugee protection.

1.4.4 The Organization of American States Definition of Refugee Status

The most recent regional extension of the refugee definition is derived from the Cartagena Declaration, adopted by ten Latin American states in 1984.[95] In recognition of the inadequacy of the Convention definition to embrace the many involuntary migrants from generalized violence and oppression in Central America, the state representatives agreed to a refugee definition that

---

[90] "[Le] franchissement des limites territoriales, surtout en Afrique de l'Ouest, était fréquent avant que les pays accèdent à l'indépendance politique et que soient définies des frontières juridiques bien nettes . . . . Il importe, en outre, de souligner qu'à l'origine la définition des frontières à l'époque de l'administration coloniale n'avait qu'un effet minime puisque la plupart des migrants se déplaçaient très librement sans tenir compte de frontières artificielles": E.-R. Mbaya, *La communauté internationale et les mouvements des populations en Afrique*, p. 17 (1985).

[91] "UNHCR's competence in Africa has been recognized as extending also to refugees who have fled owing to external aggression, occupation, foreign domination or events seriously disturbing public order": G. Goodwin-Gill, "Refugees: The Functions and Limits of the Existing Protection System", in A. Nash, ed., *Human Rights and the Protection of Refugees under International Law*, p. 150 (1988).

[92] The successful amendment of the expert draft definition for purposes of the proposed asylum convention to embrace claims grounded in foreign occupation and alien domination (*supra*, note 75) parallels the major innovation of the OAU definition (*see* text *supra* at note 81).

[93] The Organization of American States refugee definition (discussed in text *infra* at note 95 ff.) embraces persons whose claims are grounded in generalized violence and foreign aggression, whether or not a well-founded fear of persecution can be demonstrated. The Council of Europe has also recommended a more expansive concept of *de facto* refugee status which extends to persons in flight from broad-based oppression (*see* text *infra* at note 104 ff.)

[94] *See* text *infra* at note 108 ff.

[95] *See Annual Report of Inter-American Commission on Human Rights 1984-85*, OEA/Ser.L/II.66, doc. 10, rev. 1, at 190-193.

is similar to that enacted by the Organization of African Unity. In addition to Convention refugees, protection as refugees was extended to

> . . . persons who have fled their country because their lives, safety, or free-dom have been threatened by generalized violence, foreign aggression, inter-nal conflicts, massive violations of human rights or other circumstances which have seriously disturbed public order.[96]

This definition was approved by the 1985 General Assembly of the Organi-zation of American States, which resolved "to urge Member States to extend support and, insofar as possible, to implement the conclusions and recom-mendations of the Cartagena Declaration on Refugees."[97]

The OAS definition shares some of the innovative characteristics of the OAU Convention. First, it acknowledges the legitimacy of claims grounded in the actions of external powers by virtue of its reference to flight stemming from foreign aggression. Second, it offers a qualified acceptance of the notions of group determination and claims in which the basis or rationale for harm is indeterminate. The qualification stems from the fact that while generalized phenomena are valid bases for flight, and while acceptance of a claim is not premised on any status or characteristic of the claimant or a group to which she belongs, all applicants for refugee status must nonethe-less show that "their lives, safety or freedom have been threatened."[98] This requirement that the putative refugee be demonstrably at risk due to the gener-alized disturbance in her country contrasts with the OAU Convention's defer-ence to individuated perceptions of peril.[99] Finally, the OAS definition, unlike its African counterpart,[100] does not explicitly extend protection to persons who flee serious disturbance of public order that affects only part of their country.

The references to claims grounded in "internal conflicts"[101] and "mas-sive violations of human rights"[102] provide helpful clarification of established principles, but in substantive terms do not break new ground. Any situation of internal conflict would surely "disturb public order"[103] and hence be included within the general language of both the OAU and OAS definitions. Moreover, while the granting of refugee status based simply on the existence of massive violations of human rights would have been a major innovation, this ground of claim as codified adds little to the Convention definition in

---

[96] Conclusion 3, *Declaracion de Cartagena, supra,* note 95.

[97] UNHCR, "OAS General Assembly: an inter-American initiative on refugees" (1986), 27 Refugees 5.

[98] *Supra,* note 96.

[99] *See* text *supra* at note ff.

[100] *See* text *supra* at note 88 ff.

[101] *Supra,* note 96.

[102] *Supra,* note 96.

[103] This criterion is contained in the OAU refugee definition. *See* text *supra* at note 80.

view of the obligation of refugee claimants to show that *their* lives, safety, or freedom have been threatened by such human rights abuses.

Overall, the OAS definition of refugee status marks something of a compromise between the Convention standard and the very broad OAU conceptualization. It expands the "persecution" standard of the Convention to take account of abuse that can result from socio-political turmoil in developing countries, yet constrains the protection obligation to cases where it is possible to show that there is some real risk of harm to persons similarly situated to the refugee claimant.

1.4.5 The Council of Europe Definition of Refugee Status

The Council of Europe has also introduced standards of refugee protection that go beyond the Convention definition, although the changes are significantly more modest than those of the OAU or OAS. In the Parliamentary Assembly's Recommendation 773 in 1976, the Council of Europe expressed its concern in regard to the situation of "*de facto* refugees", that is, persons who either have not been formally recognized as Convention refugees (although they meet the Convention's criteria), or who are "unable or unwilling for . . . other valid reasons to return to their countries of origin."[104] Member governments were invited to "apply liberally the definition of 'refugee' in the Convention"[105] and "not to expel *de facto* refugees unless they will be admitted by another country where they do not run the risk of persecution."[106]

To date, this Recommendation has been only partially implemented. While the Committee of Ministers has stipulated that Convention refugees not formally recognized as such should be protected from return,[107] no text has been adopted dealing with the rights of the broader class of refugees outside the scope of the Convention definition. Overall, it can be said that the Council of Europe has acknowledged the legitimacy of the claim to protection of an expanded class of refugees, but has not moved to formalize their status or rights.

1.4.6 The Refugee Definition in the Practice of States

There is also evidence of an expanding conceptualization of refugee status in the practice of those states which do not participate in a formalized regional refugee protection arrangement. Refugees in flight from situations of generalized danger or serious disturbances of public order are often protected through special programs or regulatory schemes, or by burden-sharing arrangements concluded between states of reception and resettlement coun-

---

[104] Council of Europe, Parliamentary Assembly Recommendation 773 (1976).
[105] *Id.*
[106] *Id.*
[107] Council of Europe, Committee of Ministers Recommendation R(84)1 (1984).

tries.[108] Because these voluntary initiatives are not subject to the formal constraints of the Convention-based protection scheme, states have a substantial margin of discretion in determining the scope of their efforts. It is nonetheless striking to note the virtual unanimity of state practice in affording some type of protection to refugees outside the formal scope of the Convention.

In Europe, the general moral commitment toward non-Convention refugees evinced in Council of Europe resolutions[109] is buttressed by an array of national protection arrangements. Perhaps the best known is the concept of "B" status in Swedish law, whereby persons outside the scope of the Convention who remain abroad for valid humanitarian reasons may be temporarily admitted and granted residence permits.[110] Similarly, Portugal grants asylum to persons in flight from armed conflict or broadly based human rights violations,[111] West German law tolerates the residence of persons who face civil war, foreign occupation, or adverse political conditions in their country of origin,[112] and Dutch law provides for the granting of asylum to persons at risk due to difficult political circumstances in their home state that fall short of "persecution".[113] Under Great Britain's discretionary refugee policy, persons perceived by authorities to have a valid reason for not returning to their country may be granted asylum, whether or not they meet the Convention refugee definition.[114] French policy, while more closely wedded to the Convention definition, has nonetheless authorized the admission of Cambodian, Laotian, and Vietnamese citizens, regardless of whether they meet the strict refugee definition.[115] In general, while European states have constructed policies that safeguard national sovereignty over the admission of refugees in flight from broadly based disturbances, there is a general practice of not returning persons to states in which there is a significant risk of danger due to internal upheaval or armed conflict.[116]

A similar range of special programs exists in the traditional countries of immigration. In Australia, no distinction exists in law between Convention

---

[108] "There is a widespread practice of states to respond by special programs or internal regulations to large refugee movements arising out of civil war, internal disturbances, foreign occupation, natural catastrophes, or a general situation of gross violations of human rights": K. Hailbronner, "Non-refoulement and 'Humanitarian' Refugees: Customary International Law or Wishful Legal Thinking?" (1986), 26(4) Virginia J. Intl. L. 857, at 887.

[109] *See* text *supra* at note 104 ff.

[110] K. Hailbronner, *supra*, note 108, at 881-82. *Accord* A. Grahl-Madsen, *supra*, note 52, at 424.

[111] Act 38/80, August 1, 1980, Art. 5, para. 2, amended by Act 415/83, November 24, 1983. Cited in K. Hailbronner, *supra*, note 108, at 881.

[112] Deutscher Bundestag, 10 Wahlperiode, Drucksache 10/3346 (1985). Cited in K. Hailbronner, *supra*, note 108, at 882.

[113] K. Hailbronner, *supra*, note 108, at 881.

[114] R. Sexton, "Political Refugees, Nonrefoulement and State Practice" (1985), 18 Vand. J. Transntl. L. at 791.

[115] K. Hailbronner, *supra*, note 108, at 882-83.

[116] Note on the Consultations on the Arrivals of Asylum-seekers and Refugees in Europe, U.N. Doc. A/AC.96/INF.174 (1985).

and other refugees, as a result of which persons displaced by serious disturbances of public order may benefit from asylum.[117] Moreover, Australia operates special humanitarian programs to facilitate the admission of persons in refugee-like situations, including Soviet Jews, East Timorese, Sri Lankans, Lebanese, Latin Americans, and the victims of apartheid in South Africa.[118] Canadian law authorizes the admission of persons "for reasons of public policy or due to the existence of compassionate or humanitarian considerations."[119] In reliance on this authority, special measures programs have in the past been established to permit persons in Canada who are nationals of certain countries that are experiencing adverse domestic events to benefit from temporary asylum. Like Australia, Canada also operates overseas refugee selection programs that result in the resettlement of members of non-Convention "designated class" refugees in accordance with regional target allocations.[120] The United States of America temporarily admits classes of persons outside the Convention refugee definition under the Attorney General's parole power, based on a combination of humanitarian and foreign policy considerations.[121] Too, the extended voluntary departure procedure, which delays departure or removal on a discretionary basis, has been invoked in the cases of such refugee-like groups as Afghans, Poles, Ugandans, and Lebanese.[122]

The practice of many developing countries is based on either the OAU[123] or OAS[124] expanded refugee concept. Even in those countries not subject to one of these regimes, however, there is evidence of a willingness to protect refugees who may not meet the Convention definition. Pakistan and Iran, for example, sheltered the largest concentration of humanitarian refugees in the world, made up of persons forced to flee from the Afghanistan conflict.[125] Similarly, Hong Kong[126], Thailand[127] and other Southeast Asian

---

[117] K. Hailbronner, *supra*, note 108, at 886.

[118] A. Nash, *International Refugees Pressures and the Canadian Public Policy Response*, p. 99 (1989).

[119] *Immigration Act*, R.S.C. 1985, c. I-2, s. 114(2).

[120] [A]ny person who is a member of a class designated by the Governor in Council as a class, the admission of members of which would be in accordance with Canada's humanitarian tradition with respect to the displaced and the persecuted, may be granted admission": *supra, Immigration Act,* note 119, at 6.s(2).

[121] 8 U.S.C. 1182(d)(5)(A) (1982). Cited in K. Hailbronner, *supra*, note 108, at 883-84.

[122] G. Goodwin-Gill, "Non-Refoulement and the New Asylum Seekers" (1986), 26(4) Virginia J. Intl. L. 897, at 901.

[123] *See* text *supra* at note 80 ff.

[124] *See* text *supra* at note 95 ff.

[125] "By the end of 1987, estimates of the total number of Afghan refugees stood at between five and six million, approximately one-third of Afghanistan's population . . . . The overwhelming majority of Afghans who left their country took refuge in Pakistan and in Iran — 3.1 million and 2.4 million respectively, according to the official statistics of these two governments": A. Billar, "An historic moment" (1988), 53 Refugees 8, at 9.

[126] R. Mushkat, "Hong Kong as a Country of Temporary Refuge: An Interim Analysis" (1982), 12 Hong Kong L.J. 157.

[127] A. Nash, *supra*, note 118, at 107.

states[128] have in most cases provided temporary refuge to Indochinese migrants in refugee-like situations pending their resettlement abroad. While refugee relief in developing countries has often been conditioned on the provision by the international community of either material assistance or resettlement opportunities,[129] there is nevertheless a clear pattern of granting non-Convention refugees basic protection from return once the security of the receiving state has been assured.

In sum, even in those states which have not formally committed themselves to the application of an expanded concept of refugee status through one of the regional accords, there is a consistent practice of recognizing as legitimate the protection needs of a class of refugees outside the scope of the Convention. A more difficult issue, given the predominance of discretionary and conditional programs for these humanitarian refugees, is the extent to which it can be said that they benefit from a *right* to international protection.

1.5 An Expanded Refugee Concept in Customary International Law?

Taking into account the consensus on the extension of the mandate of the UNHCR,[130] the agreement reached on broadening the refugee concept at the Conference on Territorial Asylum,[131] the conceptual advances of the three regional refugee accords,[132] and the consequent shifts in the practice of states,[133] can it be said that modern international law recognizes any duty toward a class of refugees more broad than as defined in the Convention and Protocol?

Guy Goodwin-Gill has argued[134] that a new class of refugees is recognized in customary international law. He believes that the obligation of states to observe the principle of "non-refoulement", implying at least temporary refuge in the face of imminent danger, now extends to persons outside the Convention refugee definition insofar as they may be said to lack governmental

---

[128] D. Greig, "The Protection of Refugees and Customary International Law" (1983), 8 Australian Y.B. Intl. L. 108, at 127.

[129] "In the developing world, recent state practice demonstrates that government are prepared to give at least temporary refuge to large numbers of distressed people, provided that the burden of caring for them and of seeking permanent solutions to their plight is shared by the international community. It was this principle of 'burden-sharing' that persuaded several South East Asian states which had initially been reluctant to admit Indo-Chinese boat refugees to change their policy": Independent Commission on International Humanitarian Issues. *Refugees: The Dynamics of Displacement*, pp. 44-45 (1986).

[130] *See* text *supra* at note 55 ff.

[131] *See* text *supra* at note 67 ff.

[132] *See* text *supra* at note 80 ff.

[133] *See* text *supra* at note 108 ff.

[134] G. Goodwin-Gill, *supra*, note 122.

protection against harmful events beyond their choosing or control.[135] Persons who flee situations of civil disorder, domestic conflict, or human rights violations should benefit from a presumption of humanitarian need, and may not be returned unless the state of refuge can rebut the presumed risk of danger.[136]

On the other hand, Kay Hailbronner[137] characterizes such views as "wishful legal thinking" on the basis that there is neither extensive and uniform state practice nor *opinio juris* sufficient to warrant an assertion of international rights for refugees outside the scope of the Convention. Hailbronner notes that most of the international practice in favour of the expanded class of refugees is in fact UNHCR institutional practice, which cannot be said to bind states in their own actions.[138] Moreover, regional standards have not been codified in binding terms, and national efforts on behalf of humanitarian refugees have been carefully defined as discretionary exercises of prerogative over immigration.[139]

Insofar as there is an international legal consensus on an expanded conceptualization of refugee status based upon custom, it surely is, as Goodwin-Gill concedes, "at a relatively low level of commitment."[140] In my view, Goodwin-Gill's assertion of a *right* to protection against "refoulement" overstates the extant scope of customary law in regard to non-Convention refugees. As noted by Hailbronner, developed states have felt free to reject members of the broader class of asylum seekers by the imposition of visa requirements, penalties on transportation companies, naval blockades, and

---

[135] "The central thesis of this paper is that the essentially moral obligation to assist refugees and to provide them with refuge or safe haven has, over time and in certain contexts, developed into a legal obligation (albeit at a relatively low level of commitment). The principle of non-refoulement must now be understood as applying beyond the narrow confines of articles 1 and 33 of the 1951 Refugee Convention": G. Goodwin-Gill, *supra*, note 122, at 898.

[136] "Whenever temporary refuge is sought, the existence of danger caused by civil disorder, domestic conflicts, or human rights violations generates a valid presumption of humanitarian need. This has important consequences for the process of determining the entitlement to protection of individuals or specific groups. In particular, the presumption should shift the burden of proof from the claimant to the state": G. Goodwin-Gill, *supra*, note 122, at 905.

[137] K. Hailbronner, *supra*, note 108.

[138] "Although the UNHCR fulfills its functions with the agreement of states, it remains a special body entrusted with humanitarian tasks . . . . the fact that the UNHCR continues to care for the interests of *de facto* refugees cannot be considered evidence of an *opinio juris* by states": K. Hailbronner, "Non-Refoulement and 'Humanitarian' Refugees" (1986), 26(4) Virginia J. Intl. L. 857 at 869.

[139] "There is no evidence at all for a generalized recognition of an individual right of humanitarian refugees not be returned or repatriated. On the contrary, states have generally taken care not to narrow the range of possible responses to mass influxes of aliens . . . . It is common knowledge that states no longer enjoy absolute sovereignty. The real question is to what extent states have subjected their sovereign power to admit aliens to public international law. Municipal law, in fact, shows that states are not prepared to surrender in advance the ultimate option of returning to their home countries large categories of persons not meeting the definition of the 1951 Refugee Convention": K. Hailbronner, *supra*, note 138, at 887.

[140] G. Goodwin-Gill, *supra*, note 122, at 898.

the establishment of strictly discretionary mechanisms to cope with those asylum seekers who do reach their territory.[141] Developing states have conditioned their willingness to protect humanitarian refugees on the agreement of the international community to underwrite the costs of temporary asylum and to relocate the refugees to states of permanent resettlement.[142] Even the UNHCR has been tentative in its assertion of an expanded scope for the refugee definition applicable in the context of legal protection decisions.[143]

On the other hand, Hailbronner overlooks the consensus at the global, regional, and national levels in favour of *addressing in some way* the claims of those persons in one's territory or at one's borders who fear harm in their country of origin as a result of serious disturbances of public order. No aspect of international practice has questioned the duty to examine their need for protection. The nature of the special consideration has varied, and the avoidance of "refoulement" has not been universal. Nonetheless, UNHCR practice, the international consensus at the Conference on Territorial Asylum, all three regional refugee accords, and relatively consistent state practice agree in their extension of *some opportunity for special consideration* to persons within a state's territory who have been victimized by serious disturbances of public order in their country of origin.

The level of commitment is lower than that suggested by Goodwin-Gill,[144] but an intermediate category of refugee protection does now exist. The customary norm rooted in international usage is a right to be considered for temporary admission, whether by formal procedure or administrative discretion, *on the basis of a need for protection.* That is, customary international law precludes the making of decisions to reject or expel persons who come from nations in which there are serious disturbances of public order without explicit attention being paid to their humanitarian needs. This duty may be met through the granting of formal status as is contemplated by the three regional refugee accords, through the discretionary programs of "B" status, special measures, or extended voluntary departure that exist in Western developed states, or by seeking the assistance of other states or the international community to share the burden of actual or impending refugee flows. The obligation is simply to do *something* which provides a meaningful response to the humanitarian needs of the victims of serious disruptions of public order. We have not yet reached the point, though, of assimilating such

---

[141] K. Hailbronner, *supra*, note 138, at 875.

[142] *Supra*, note 129.

[143] "The UNHCR Notes on International Protection of 1984 and 1985 do not assert that persons who have been forced to seek refuge outside their country of origin because of armed conflict or other political or social upheavals have an individual right of temporary refuge even if one interprets this term in the sense of non-repatriation. Instead, the High Commissioner referred to difficulties of a definition of the legal status of *de facto* refugees which *should* include at least protection against refoulement and permission to remain in the territory": K. Hailbronner, *supra*, note 138, at 870.

[144] *See* text *supra* at notes 135-136.

persons to Convention refugees for the purpose of stipulating a duty to avert return in all cases.

In sum, international law may be said to recognize four categories of refugees. First are refugees defined by the Convention and Protocol. Convention refugees are entitled to claim protection against return to a country in which they fear persecution from any of the more than one hundred state parties to these accords. They may also invoke the full range of rights set out in the Convention, and call upon the institutional support of the UNHCR. Second, there are refugees who are protected by a regional agreement.[145] Such persons may be at risk of return to a situation of serious disturbance of public order, rather than persecution. Nonetheless, at least within Africa and Latin America, they are generally protected against return, and may be entitled to other preferential rights akin to those afforded Convention refugees. Third, there are refugees who fear harm as a result of serious disturbances of public order, but who are not able to invoke the protection of a special regional arrangement. These refugees from man-made harm are entitled to special consideration prior to return to their state of origin, but they may not claim protection from return as of right except as stipulated in the national legislation of the asylum state. Finally, all persons who are involuntary migrants as a result of natural or man-made causes may claim the institutional support of UNHCR by way of material assistance, aid in voluntary repatriation or resettlement, and in some cases legal protection. This residual class of refugees, however, has no special claim to protection under international law.

This book is devoted to a study of refugee status as defined by the Convention and Protocol. While other legal and extralegal vehicles add important momentum to the protection system for refugees, it remains clear that state practice today is fundamentally anchored in the basic conceptual framework established by these accords. The chapters which follow strive to elaborate a clear, contextually sensitive understanding of the Convention refugee definition as it has evolved through confrontation with the needs of contemporary involuntary migrants.

---

[145] While OAS and Council of Europe resolutions endorse expanded definitions similar to that of the OAU, only the African standard is incorporated in a legally binding convention. *See* text *supra* at notes 97 (OAS recommendation) and 104 (Council of Europe recommendation).

2

Alienage

The first element of Convention refugee status is that the claimant must be outside her country of origin.[1] There is nothing intuitively obvious about this requirement: many if not most of the persons forced to flee their homes in search of safety remain within the boundaries of their state.[2] Their plight may be every bit as serious as that of individuals who cross borders, yet the Convention definition of refugee status excludes internal refugees from the scope of global protection.

The strict insistence on this territorial criterion[3] has prompted concern that there is a mismatch between the definition and the human suffering consequent to involuntary migration.[4] In one sense, the exclusion of internal refugees is clearly unfair: it does not recognize the existence of social, legal, and economic barriers which make it impossible for all to escape to international protection.[5] The Convention definition of refugee status therefore responds

---

[1] "The first requirement, that the refugee should be an alien, is undisputed": G. Jaeger, "The Definition of 'Refugee': Restrictive versus Expanding Trends" [1983], World Refugee Survey 5, at 5.

[2] "Many people may find themselves in refugee-like situations, and may have fled considerable distances, but if no border has been crossed they will not be considered to be refugees. An example of people in this situation would be the many displaced persons in Vietnam during the 1970s. Many people within Africa also fall within this category": P. Hyndman, "Refugees Under International Law with a Reference to the Concept of Asylum" (1986), 60 Australian L.J. 148, at 149.

[3] "It is a general requirement for refugee status that an applicant who has a nationality be outside the country of his nationality. There are no exceptions to this rule": United Nations High Commissioner for Refugees, *Handbook on Procedures and Criteria for Determining Refugee Status*, p. 21 (1979). *Accord* J. Patrnogic, "Refugees — A Continuing Challenge" (1982), 30 Ann. de droit international médical 73, at 74: "In the general concept, a refugee is a person who flees to find refuge and who feels compelled to leave his normal place of abode on account of any kind of circumstance . . . . In the international legal concept, a refugee is an alien who finds himself outside his country of origin or nationality for serious reasons . . . . Thus, while in municipal law the term refugee can also be applied to nationals, in international law the refugee is an alien."

[4] "The mismatch between a legal definition and actions of governments, and the inadequacies of a cold, legal definition in the face of human suffering, are all too apparent": C. Keely and P. Elwell, *Global Refugee Policy: The Case for a Development-Oriented Strategy*, p. 11 (1981).

[5] "Refugee flows occasioned by expulsion or flight are but one of the outcomes of political persecution; paradoxically, the refugees may be the more fortunate segment of the original tar-

in a less than even-handed way to the protection needs of persons similarly at risk of persecution.[6]

There is a threefold historical rationale for the requirement that only persons outside their state be eligible for Convention refugee status. First, the Convention was drafted with a specific purpose in the context of limited international resources. Its intent was not to relieve the suffering of all involuntary migrants, but rather to deal "only with the problem of legal protection and status."[7] Its goal was to assist a subset of involuntary migrants composed of persons who were "outside their own countries [and] who lacked the protection of a government",[8] and who consequently required short-term surrogate international rights until they acquired new or renewed national protection.[9] Internal refugee displacements, while of humanitarian note, "were separate problems of a different character",[10] the alleviation of which would demand a more sustained commitment of resources than was available to the international community.[11]

Second, there was a very practical concern that the inclusion of internal refugees in the international protection regime might prompt states to attempt to shift responsibility for the well-being of large parts of their own population to the world community.[12] The obligations of states under the Conven-

---

get, others of whom may be subjected to a worse fate, including not only immobilization but even murder": A. Zolberg, "The Formation of New States as a Refugee-Generating Process" (1983), 467 The Annals Am. Academy Pol. Soc. Science 24, at 27.

[6] The same advantages make it possible for some refugees to seek out more commodious states of asylum: "Refugees who are persistent and innovative (and who are overwhelmingly male) dominate the spontaneous arrivals into Canada; in camps, women and children predominate, and they and others in the camps rarely have the resources or the independence to make Canada a country of first asylum": H. Adelman, "Refuge or Asylum — A Philosophical Perspective" (1988), 1(1) J. Refugee Studies 7, at 9.

[7] Statement of Mr. Henkin of the U.S.A., U.N. Doc. E/AC.7/SR.161, at 7, August 18, 1950.

[8] Statement of Mrs. Roosevelt of the United States of America, 5 UNGAOR at 473, December 2, 1949.

[9] "The proposals of the Economic and Social Council were designed, however, to meet the needs of refugees who were outside their countries of origin for social, religious or political reasons, were unable to return thereto and required protection under international auspices until they acquired a new nationality or reassumed their former nationality": Statement of Mrs. Roosevelt of the United States of America, 5 UNGAOR at 363, November 29, 1950.

[10] Statement of Mrs. Roosevelt, *supra*, note 8.

[11] "[W]hile he would like to see the Convention drafted to cover as many refugees as possible, he nevertheless appreciated how difficult it would be for governments to provide what the Ad Hoc Committee had described as a blank cheque . . . ": Statement of Mr. van Heuven Goedhart, United Nations High Commissioner for Refugees, U.N. Doc. A/CONF.2/SR.21, at 12, July 14, 1951.

[12] "While, in principle, it favoured the elimination of all exceptions, the United States Government wanted to maintain that of refugees of German ethnic origin residing in Germany because it considered that group of nearly eight million persons as normally under the jurisdiction of the German Government and it did not want to encourage that government to renounce all responsibility toward them by placing them under international protection": Statement of Mr. Henkin of the U.S.A., U.N. Doc. E/AC.32/SR.5, at 5, January 30, 1950.

tion would thereby be increased, as a result of which fewer states would be likely to participate in the Convention regime.[13]

Third and most fundamental, there was anxiety that any attempt to respond to the needs of internal refugees would constitute an infringement of the national sovereignty of the state within which the refugee resided.[14] Refugee law, as a part of international human rights law, constitutes a recent and carefully constrained exception to the long-standing rule of exclusive jurisdiction of states over their inhabitants.[15] While it was increasingly accepted in the early 1950s that the world community had a legitimate right to set standards and scrutinize the human rights record of the various countries, it was unthinkable that refugee law would intervene in the territory of a state to protect citizens from their own government.[16] The best that could be achieved within the context of the accepted rules of international law was the sheltering of such persons as were able to liberate themselves from the territorial jurisdiction of a persecutory state.

None of the three factors which dictated the exclusion of internal refugees — limited resources, concern about state participation, or respect for sovereignty — was so much a matter of conceptual principle, as it was a reflection of the limited reach of international law. As Andrew Shacknove has observed, "alienage is an unnecessary condition for establishing refugee status. It . . . is a subset of a broader category: the physical access of the international community to the unprotected person."[17] In other words, the physical presence of the unprotected person outside her country of origin is not a constitutive element of her refugeehood, but is rather a practical

---

[13] "He felt that the extension of the Convention to internal refugees, which was implied in the [Belgian, Canadian, and Turkish] draft [U.N. Doc. A/C.3/L.130] could only encourage the diplomatic conference to adopt some other definition": Statement of Mr. Rochefort of France, 5 UNGAOR at 391, December 4, 1950.

[14] "Whatever [definitional] formula might ultimately be chosen, it would not and could not in any event apply to internal refugees who were citizens of a particular country and enjoyed the protection of the government of that country. There was no general definition covering such refugees, since any such definition would involve an infringement of national sovereignty": Statement of Mr. Rochefort of France, U.N. Doc. E/AC.7/SR.172, at 4, August 12, 1950.

[15] "Since the beginnings of the Law of Nations, one of its fundamental principles was that of national sovereignty, which reserves to each sovereign State the exclusive right to take any action it thinks fit, provided only that the action does not interfere with the rights of other States, and is not prohibited by international law on that or any other ground . . . . It follows from this principle that, in all matters falling within the 'domestic jurisdiction' of any State, international law does not permit any interference, let alone any intervention, by any other State": P. Sieghart, *The International Law of Human Rights*, p. 10 (1983).

[16] "[F]rom the legal standpoint refugee law was bound up with the existence of a multinational society and implies the existence of a variety of political and administrative systems in a number of comparatively watertight national territories. In a uninational society or in a federation of States there would doubtless be castaways, there might be political victims, but there would clearly be no refugees in the exact sense of them": J. Vernant, *The Refugee in the Post-War World*, p. 4 (1953).

[17] A. Shacknove, "Who Is a Refugee?" (1985), 95 Ethics 274, at 277.

condition precedent to placing her within the effective scope of international protection.

The territorial dimension of the Convention definition of refugee status, then, was dictated by the extant authority of international law. Its purpose was not to divide involuntary migrants into those who are worthy of assistance and those who are not deserving, but was instead to define the scope of refugee law in a realistic, workable way. As the authority of the international community over human rights has increased with the passage of time,[18] so too has the reach of refugee law expanded, at least tentatively, to protect some internal refugees.

First, since 1972 the United Nations High Commissioner for Refugees has been called on to provide material assistance to various groups of refugees within their national boundaries.[19] This assistance has been premised on the concurrence of the state concerned and the willingness of the international community to provide funding,[20] but is nonetheless indicative of an enhanced recognition of an international role in the protection of internal refugees. Second, and more dramatic, is the establishment of orderly departure programs in collaboration with refugee-producing states, whereby refugees may make application from within their country of origin for resettlement abroad under international auspices.[21] Both of these developments bear witness to Shacknove's position[22] that the territorial limitation in the Convention refugee definition is a function of "the art of the possible", which may decrease in importance as unprotected persons still within their states become more accessible to the international community.

The alienage requirement raises a number of specific issues. First, must an individual *leave* her country as a result of fear of persecution, or may

---

[18] "Whether or not national states will yield enough of their external sovereignty in our lifetime to make international government possible . . . one basic fact emerges from our study. It is that the individual, not the sovereign state, is the end purpose of the new legal order that has been erected in our generation under the title of Human Rights": J. Joyce, *The New Politics of Human Rights*, p. 225 (1978).

[19] P. Hartling, "Concept and Definition of 'Refugee' — Legal and Humanitarian Aspects", Inaugural lecture given on April 23, 1979, at the Second Nordic Seminar on Refugee Law, University of Copenhagen 14-15 (unpublished, 1979).

[20] It is noteworthy that the whole approach of UNHCR to the provision of assistance to non-mandate refugees is within the control of Western developed states. This is so because the only core funding that the United Nations provides the UNHCR is to cover routine administrative expenses. The operating budget of the organization is thus nearly completely derived from the voluntary contributions of a fairly small number of developed states: Executive Committee of the High Commissioner's Programme, "Voluntary Funds Administered by the United Nations High Commissioner for Refugees: Accounts for the Year 1987 and Report to the Board of Auditors Thereon", U.N. Doc. A/AC.96/707 (1988).

[21] "Calls for orderly departure agreements for the Vietnamese or the airlift agreement between Cuba and the United States in the 1960s indicate a willingness to extend the refugee label to people in their own country": C. Keely and P. Elwell, *supra*, note 4, at 9.

[22] *See* text *supra* at note 17.

she successfully claim Convention refugee status if her fear arises at a time when she is already abroad? Second, does it matter if the putative refugee left her country with or without the official authorization of her state? Third, must a refugee claim status in the country nearest her home, or in the first state to which she flees? Fourth, what is the implication of entry into an asylum state by fraudulent means or in contravention of applicable immigration laws? Finally, *what* country must an individual be outside of in order to qualify for Convention refugee status where she is, for example, possessed of dual or multiple nationality, or conversely is stateless?

2.1 Refugees *sur place*

The Convention refugee definition does not distinguish between persons who flee their country in order to avoid the prospect of persecution and those who, while already abroad, determine that they cannot or will not return by reason of the risk of persecution in their state of nationality or origin.[23] By virtue of its requirement that the claimant "*is* outside the country of his nationality . . . "[24] the Convention protects refugees *sur place* on an equal footing with those who cross a border after the risk of persecution is already apparent. This position is consonant with the general rule that the territorial requirement of the Convention definition is intended to identify those involuntary migrants within the effective reach of international law: whether already present or arriving in a foreign state, the refugee claimant is clearly able to benefit from protection against return.

2.1.1 Claims Grounded in Events in the Country of Origin

The classic *sur place* refugee claim[25] derives from a significant change of circumstances in the country of origin at a time when the claimant is abroad

---

[23] "A person who has left his country for whatever reason but subsequently owing to well-founded fear of being persecuted refuses or becomes unable to avail himself of being persecuted refuses or becomes unable to avail himself of the protection of that country or, in the case of a stateless person owing to well-founded fear of being persecuted refuses or becomes unable to return to the country of his former habitual residence, is equally a refugee. These persons have become known as *réfugiés sur place*": P. Weis, "The concept of the refugee in international law" (1960), J. du droit international 928, at 972. *Accord* UNHCR, *supra*, note 3, at 22.

[24] *Convention Relating to the Status of Refugees*, 189 U.N.T.S. 2545, entered into force April 22, 1954 ("*Convention*"), at Art. 1(A)(2).

[25] This type of claim was clearly contemplated by the drafters of the Convention. Mr. Rain of France, for example, stated that the definition extended to "not only those who had actually left their country owing to persecution, but also those who had already been outside their country before the persecution began and were unable to return for fear of persecution": U.N. Doc. E/AC.32/SR.17, at 3, February 6, 1950. Similarly, Mr. Robinson of Israel cited as an example of a refugee *sur place* persons who "went abroad on a diplomatic mission or to study and, while still abroad, were overtaken by a revolution which made it impossible for them to return": U.N. Doc. A/CONF.2/SR.23, at 9, July 16, 1951. *Accord* Mr. Petren of Sweden: U.N. Doc. A/CONF.2/SR.23, at 10, July 16, 1951.

for reasons wholly unrelated to a need for protection.[26] At the time of departure from her state, she may have intended only to vacation, study, or do business abroad, and then to return home.[27] If, however, events subsequent to her departure would put her at risk of serious harm upon return home, she may claim protection as a Convention refugee.

For example, the decision in *Chaudri v. Minister of Employment and Immigration*[28] involved a Pakistani citizen who had been an activist in the ruling People's Party of Pakistan prior to the military overthrow of 1979. Mr. Chaudri had been in Canada for some three years prior to the coup. In 1980, he learned that the new military government of Pakistan had issued a politically inspired warrant for his arrest that could lead to indefinite detention. The Federal Court of Appeal held that he was properly considered a Convention refugee *sur place* since his fear of persecution, while not extant at the time of his departure from Pakistan, was nonetheless well-founded in subsequent events. The same result was reached in the case of *Almaz Isebella Kebede Fernandes*,[29] involving an Ethiopian student abroad when the military ousted Emperor Haile Selassi. Her father, the Emperor's bodyguard, had been killed by the military, and all of her immediate family was either in detention or in receipt of asylum in other countries. In the circumstances, the Immigration Appeal Board found her to be a Convention refugee in that she "could not possibly return to her country at the present time and expect to be treated favourably by the military junta."[30]

A variant of the classical *sur place* situation involves the dramatic intensification of pre-existing factors since departure from one's home country. While distinguishable from the first category by the fact that the claimant may have been aware of, or even motivated to depart by, disturbing events in her home country, these cases are characterized by an escalation of events post-departure which is sufficient to give rise to a reasonable risk of persecution upon return.

In a series of decisions involving Eritrean seamen,[31] the Immigration Appeal

---

[26] "If he is outside his homeland when conditions change in such a manner that his return would lead to a well-founded fear of persecution, the person is classified as a refugee": A. Fragomen, "The Refugee: A Problem of Definition" (1970), 3 Case Western Reserve J. Intl. L. 45, at 55.

[27] "If he is outside his country he can make an application for asylum no matter why he left": G. Gilbert, "Right of Asylum: A Change of Direction" (1983), 32 I.C.L.Q. 633, at 646.

[28] (1986), 69 N.R. 114. *See also Mohammad Mushtaq*, Immigration Appeal Board Decision M81-1122, C.L.I.C. Notes 47.6, October 26, 1982, where the same result was reached in the case of a Pakistani abroad prior to the coup who arrived in Canada only after the Bhutto government was overthrown.

[29] Immigration Appeal Board Decision 77-1036, October 6, 1977.

[30] *Id.*, at 3, *per* J.-P. Houle.

[31] *Tekeste Kifletsion*, Immigration Appeal Board Decision 79-1136, C.L.I.C. Notes 20.3, February 29, 1980; *Kidane Ghebreiyesus*, Immigration Appeal Board Decision 79-1137, C.L.I.C. Notes 20.3, March 21, 1980; *Isaak Afework*, Immigration Appeal Board Decision 79-1139, C.L.I.C. Notes 20.3, May 21, 1980; and *Kidane Tegegne*, Immigration Appeal Board Decision M80-1034, February 25, 1981.

Board found that the long-standing mistreatment of this ethnic group by Ethiopian authorities had so intensified during the claimants' time abroad that it was reasonable for them to conclude that their lives or liberty would be at risk upon return to their country.[32] Similarly, in the case of *Thillainathan Srikanthan*[33] the Board determined that "*recent events* in the State of Sri Lanka lead the Board to believe that the applicant, although marginally involved in political events *at the time of his residence* in that country, may encounter some problems if he were to be returned . . . *at the present time* the applicant has good reason to fear persecution"[Emphasis added].[34] The Immigration Appeal Board also considered the intensification of harm doctrine in a number of cases involving allegations of increased governmental hostility toward Sikhs in the State of Punjab, but found that the changes in government policy there did not yet amount to a sufficiently serious risk of harm.[35]

2.1.2 Claims Grounded in the Asylum Seeker's Activities Abroad

In addition to claims grounded in either new circumstances or a dramatic intensification of pre-existing conditions in the country of origin, a *sur place* claim to refugee status may also be based on the activities of the refugee claimant since leaving her country.[36] International law recognizes that if while abroad an individual expresses views or engages in activities which jeopardize the possibility of safe return to her state, she may be considered a Convention refugee. The key issues are whether the activities abroad are likely to have come to the attention of the authorities in the claimant's country of origin and, if so, how they are likely to be viewed and responded to.

The leading Canadian authority on this point is the decision of the Federal Court of Appeal in *Mohamed Ahmed Urur v. Minister of Employment and Immigration*.[37] Responding to the Immigration Appeal Board's refusal to receive photographic evidence of the claimant's participation in a demonstration in Ottawa in front of the embassy of his country of origin, the Court

---

[32] "When the applicant left his country to work as a seaman, he did not have the intention of becoming a refugee, but as the situation deteriorated, he realized that his liberty and his life would be in jeopardy if he returned to Ethiopia. The United Nations Convention applies to someone who comes within the definition *sur place*": *Id.*, (common to all four decisions), *per* R. Tremblay.

[33] Immigration Appeal Board Decision T83-10351, May 23, 1985.

[34] *Id.*, at 5, *per* B. Suppa.

[35] *See*, e.g., *Lakhbir Gill Singh*, Immigration Appeal Board Decision V83-6279, February 13, 1986; *Mohinder Parmar Singh*, Immigration Appeal Board Decision V87-6247X, August 10, 1987; and *Santokh Bhopal Singh*, Immigration Appeal Board Decision V87-6245X, August 17, 1987.

[36] "[C]onduct in which the person has engaged while outside of his homeland may also give rise to a well-founded fear of persecution upon his return": A. Fragomen, *supra*, note 26, at 55. *Accord* UNHCR, *supra*, note 3, at 22.

[37] Federal Court of Appeal Decision A-228-87, January 15, 1988; affirming on other grounds Immigration Appeal Board Decision M86-1601X, April 8, 1987.

held that "[t]his refusal by the Board was manifestly wrong. An alien in Canada may be a refugee as a consequence of facts which have occurred since his arrival."[38] A *sur place* claim to refugee status was recognized, for example, in the case of *Irfam Ismailovski*,[39] who had helped to publish antigovernment propaganda directed to the Albanian exile community in Canada, thereby placing himself at risk of incarceration by his home authorities.

Other very similar claims have, however, been rejected. The Board in *Carlos Armando Guerra Morales*[40] denied refugee status to a Chilean émigré journalist who had been "since his arrival, engaged in many activities directed against the present regime in his native country."[41] Involvement with politically hostile emigrant groups has likewise been looked upon with scepticism,[42] even where such activity has been clearly publicized.[43] The Immigration Appeal Board has asserted that "it is not reasonable that a person may place himself in jeopardy with the laws of his country . . . and thereby claim special status if it is that act itself which creates the claim for refugee status."[44]

Canadian decision-makers are not alone in taking this position. Except where foreign policy goals are served, American authorities have also rejected most claims grounded in political activity in the United States.[45] Because per-

---

[38] *Id.*, at 2, *per* Pratte J. The Federal Court nonetheless dismissed this application for review because the Board had admitted oral evidence to the same end.

[39] Immigration Appeal Board Decision 75-10266, June 8, 1976.

[40] Immigration Appeal Board Decision 76-1057, March 10, 1977. While the claim to Convention refugee status was denied, the Board nonetheless chose to admit Mr. Guerra Morales under its then extant authority to direct landing in situations of unusual hardship.

[41] *Id.*, at 3, *per* F. Glogowski.

[42] *See*, e.g., the case of *Meril Meryse*, Immigration Appeal Board Decision M73-2608, April 30, 1975, in which active involvement with the Bureau de la communauté chrétienne des Haitiens à Montréal, an anti-Duvalier organization, was held to be an insufficient ground for refugee status; and *Charan Batth Singh*, Immigration Appeal Board Decision V86-6189, April 10, 1987, involving a Sikh claimant who had come to the attention of Indian authorities for preaching to the expatriate community in Canada. This approach is contrary to accepted doctrine: "Circumstances occurring outside a refugee's country of origin may also make his fear well-founded, e.g. a person may be considered as having well-founded fear of being persecuted in his country of origin if he can show that he is suspected of having associated with *émigré* circles considered hostile by the authorities in his country of origin": P. Weis, *supra*, note 23, at 972.

[43] In the case of *Leszek Adamczenko*, Immigration Appeal Board Decision 80-9339, November 20, 1980, the unsuccessful applicant had participated as a newsman, commentator and news announcer on a Canadian television program addressed to the Polish expatriate community. A *sur place* claim to refugee status was also denied in the case of *Manuel Antonio Rosario Estrella*, whose family home abroad had been searched following publication of his photograph in a Montreal newspaper: Immigration Appeal Board Decision M85-1097, C.L.I.C. Notes 83.13, August 19, 1985.

[44] *Lech Jankowski*, Immigration Appeal Board Decision V80-6410, C.L.I.C. Notes 26.11, January 5, 1981, at 4, *per* B. Howard.

[45] "In the cases of political refugees claiming to fear persecution resulting from activities within the United States in opposition to their native regimes, the courts have consistently denied refugee status to claimants from non-communist countries": J. Zimmer, "Political Refugees: A Study in Selective Compassion" (1978), 1 Loyola L.A. Intl. Comp. L. Ann. 121, at 134. *Accord* D. Roth, "The Right of Asylum Under United States Immigration Law" (1981), 33 U. Florida

sons might engage in oppositional activity strictly or primarily with the intention of placing themselves at risk, there is concern that such claims present a clear opportunity for abuse by persons who are not really in need of protection.[46]

Such an absolutist preoccupation with the possibility of fraud ignores the basic right of all persons to be free to express themselves, to associate with whomever they wish, to pursue the development of their own personalities.[47] Logically, visitors from abroad who exercise their right to speak out against their home government, who associate with opposition emigrant groups, or who otherwise engage in lawful activity perceived by their state of origin to be inappropriate should be protected from return where there is a serious risk of persecution as a result of those actions.[48] Since the voluntary issuance of the challenge to the home state is clearly lawful in and of itself, any reticence to acknowledge the validity of a claim to protection in such circumstances "chills an alien's constitutionally protected freedom of expression."[49]

Because the expression of oppositional opinion is lawful, there is no good reason to focus on the question of voluntariness *per se*.[50] The conceptual

---

L. Rev. 539, at 552-53. See also *Matter of Mogharrabi*, Board of Immigration Appeals Interim Decision 3028, June 12, 1987, in which the *sur place* claim of an Iranian citizen was recognized on the basis of the risk flowing from a dispute with Iranian consular officials in the United States.

[46] "Bootstrap refugees are people who had no problem in their home country before they left, but left anyway, came here and decided they wanted to stay. In most blatant form, bootstrap refugees are those who, having decided they want to stay here, then issue a statement denouncing the home government, which they promptly use as the basis of their asylum application. Surely, they argue, if the government hears about this, it will persecute us when we get home": D. Martin in C. Sumpter, "Mass Migration of Refugees — Law and Policy" (1982), 76 A.S.I.L.P. 13, at 15.

[47] "[R]efugee status is not restricted to martyrs. If an individual can demonstrate that flight was a manifestation of an opinion that would have resulted in persecution if expressed, should he be denied asylum if persecution would ensue upon deportation?": K. Brill, "The Endless Debate: Refugee Law and Policy and the 1980 Refugee Act" (1983), 32 Cleveland State L. Rev. 117, at 135.

[48] "Consider the situation of a student . . . who comes here from a repressive country, who may never have paid much attention to political developments there or may never have had an opportunity to think seriously or to speak out about the political situation in that country. The student comes here, indulges in the . . . freedoms of which we are justly proud, and awakens to the political repression, the problems that exist in the home country, and now begins to speak out. Whether the student did that consciously, knowing of the risk that she may be generating if she ever were to return, or not, we probably would agree that this country stands for encouraging that sort of awakening — at least so long as it reflects a real personal change and not a blatant attempt to affect immigration status. If that speaking out leads to a strong showing that she will be persecuted on return, I submit that most of us would not vote to send the student back to the home country": D. Martin in C. Sumpter, *supra*, note 46, at 16.

[49] D. Roth, *supra*, note 45, at 553.

[50] *But see* text at note 44, *supra*. Grahl-Madsen similarly emphasizes the issue of voluntariness: "[W]e may have to draw a distinction . . . between those who unwittingly or unwillingly have committed a politically pertinent act, and those who have done it for the sole purpose of getting a pretext for claiming refugeehood. The former may claim good faith, the latter may

awkwardness in recognizing these claims derives rather from the fact that not all instances of voluntary alienation give rise to a risk of harm which can readily be linked to one of the five forms of civil or political status set out in the Convention.[51] Specifically, it is legitimate to grant refugee status in this type of case only insofar as the claimant's post-departure activities may genuinely be seen to reflect her true political opinion, or alternatively where there is evidence that those activities may lead to the attribution to her of a political opinion by authorities in her home state. Otherwise, whatever consequences ensue from her actions abroad are the result only of her unfounded or untruthful assertions, a predicament outside the scope of the Convention definition.

In the case of persons who have chosen to be politically active in their state of origin, the authenticity of the political opinion underlying the activism is generally assumed. This is sensible, because an individual would be unlikely to make insincere attacks on her state at a time when she remains within its grasp. The ability of the state to exert control and to punish is an implied barometer of authenticity. In contrast, an individual *outside* the jurisdiction of her state of origin may be subject to no such automatic and effective control mechanism. It is thus more readily conceivable that an oppositional stance could be assumed simply for the purpose of fabricating a claim to refugee status,[52] and thus not reflect a political opinion as required by the definition. The challenge, then, is to respond to this real evidentiary difference without being dismissive of such protection needs as may arise from the expression of sincerely held convictions at a time when an individual is abroad.

This can be done by canvassing a number of issues. First, does the claimant retain close personal connections to family, friends, or institutions in her home state? Insofar as such a nexus exists, it affords a surrogate indicator of sincerity, as the claimant would be less likely to engage in unfounded opposition where persons who are important to her are at risk. Second, are the claimant's statements or actions abroad consistent with her behaviour prior to departure? If so, the consistency affords some evidence of veracity. If there is no consistency, are there valid reasons to explain the claimant's openness or change of views once abroad? Third, can the firmness of the claimant's newly expressed convictions be tested? To the extent that she has a clear understanding of relevant concerns and issues and has become significantly involved in their propagation, it is more likely that she genuinely embraces the belief underlying her statements or actions.

---

not"; 1 A. Grahl-Madsen, *The Status of Refugees in International Law*, p. 252 (1966). This dichotomy does not account for the possibility of fully *bona fide* expressions of opposition that may be voluntarily made while abroad.

[51] *See* Chapter 5, *infra*.

[52] "Asylum law protects those who *in good faith* need to be sheltered from persecution. This protection was not meant to encompass those who make political statements for the sole purpose of becoming refugees" [Emphasis added]: K. Petrini, "Basing Asylum Claims on a Fear of Persecution Arising from a Prior Asylum Claim" (1981), 56 Notre Dame Lawyer 719, at 729.

It does not follow, however, that all persons whose activities abroad are not genuinely demonstrative of oppositional political opinion are outside the refugee definition. Even when it is evident that the voluntary statement or action was fraudulent in that it was prompted primarily by an intention to secure asylum, the consequential imputation to the claimant of a negative political opinion by authorities in her home state may nonetheless bring her within the scope of the Convention definition. Since refugee law is fundamentally concerned with the provision of protection against unconscionable state action, an assessment should be made of any potential harm to be faced upon return because of the fact of the non-genuine political activity engaged in while abroad.[53]

This issue is most poignantly raised when it is alleged that the fact of having made an unfounded asylum claim[54] may *per se* give rise to a serious risk of persecution. While these cases provide perhaps the most obvious potential for "bootstrapping",[55] there must nonetheless be a clear acknowledgment and assessment of any risk to basic human rights upon return which may follow from the state's imputation of an unacceptable political opinion to the claimant. The mere fact that the claimant might suffer some form of penalty may not be sufficiently serious to constitute persecution,[56] but there are clearly situations where the consequence of return may be said to give rise to a well-founded fear of persecution. For example, in *Slawomir Krzystof Hubicki*[57] evidence was adduced that under then-prevailing Polish criminal law, the claimant would face imprisonment of up to eight years because he had made a refugee claim in Canada. In such situations, the basis of claim is not the fraudulent activity or assertion itself, but is rather the political opinion of disloyalty imputed to the claimant by her state. Where such an imputation exists, the gravity of consequential harm and other definitional criteria should be assessed to determine whether refugee status is warranted.

2.2 Departure from the State of Origin

The second aspect of alienage is concerned with the means by which the refugee claimant exited her country of origin. First, can the fact of illegal

---

[53] Such an approach would conform to the basic principle enunciated by Grahl-Madsen that "the behaviour of the persecutors is decisive with respect to which persons shall be considered refugees": A. Grahl-Madsen, *supra*, note 50, pp. 251-52.

[54] Not all cases based on the fact of a prior unsuccessful refugee claim are *per se* fraudulent. "[W]hen faced with an asylum claim based on a previous unsuccessful claim, the courts must determine (1) the applicant's background and conditions in his country of origin, (2) whether the first asylum claim had a good faith, substantive basis, and (3) whether the first asylum claim was simply a bootstrap for the second asylum claim": K. Petrini, *supra*, note 52, at 730.

[55] *Lech Jankowski, supra*, note 44.

[56] *See* Chapter 4, *infra*.

[57] Immigration Appeal Board Decision 81-6325, October 19, 1981. The claim to refugee status was denied by the Board without any explicit consideration of the potential criminal penalties upon return to Poland.

departure or stay abroad be said to give rise *per se* to a genuine risk of serious harm? Second, to what extent are issues of authorized or unauthorized departure probative of the genuineness of the claim to refugee status? Third, can a refugee claim arise where the state of origin not only authorizes, but in some sense facilitates the claimant's departure?

2.2.1 Illegal Departure or Stay Abroad

The mere fact that an individual either departs her country or stays abroad without authorization does not always entitle her to refugee status.[58] However, if two conditions are met, a genuine refugee claim may be established.

First, the country of origin must punish unauthorized exit or stay abroad in a harsh or oppressive manner.[59] The prospect of reasonable penalties for breach of a fairly administered passport law, for example, is not a harm of sufficient gravity to warrant protection as a refugee.[60] On the other hand, where the sanctions for illicit travel abroad are so severe that they effectively negate the fundamental human right to leave and return to one's country,[61] there is the basis for a claim to refugee status.[62]

---

[58] *See*, e.g., P. Nicolaus, "La notion de réfugié dans le droit de la R.F.A." (1985), 4 A.W.R. Bull. 158, at 159.

[59] UNHCR, *supra*, note 3, at 16. An excellent example of the need for protection is cited in G. Gilbert, *supra*, note 27, at 644-45: "Difficulties arise, however, where the offence for which he could be prosecuted is one which would be regarded as oppressive or contrary to human rights in the asylum State. This occurred recently in the United Kingdom in relation to Stancu Papusoiu, a Romanian. On his return Papusoiu would face prosecution for illegally leaving Romania . . . . In Papusoiu's case it is possible that the British Government has erred in deporting him. Of the past 11 years he has spent ten in gaol for attempting illegally to leave Romania."

[60] *See*, e.g., *Jacek Marian Olszak*, Immigration Appeal Board Decision T87-9085X, October 26, 1987, in which the Board found that the Polish claimant would face only minor disciplinary action for his violation of Polish emigration law, and was not therefore at risk of sufficient harm to be classed as a refugee. This is consistent with the appellate jurisprudence in the United States of America: *see Coriolan v. I.N.S.*, 559 F. 2d 993, at 1000 (5th Cir. 1977), cited in K. Brill, *supra*, note 47, at 132-33.

[61] "Everyone has the right to leave any country, including his own, and to return to his country": Universal Declaration of Human Rights, G.A. Res. 217A (III), December 10, 1948 ("*UDHR*"), at Art. 13(2). *Accord* International Covenant on Civil and Political Rights, G.A. Res. 2200 (XXI), December 19, 1966, entered into force March 23, 1976, at Art. 12(2-4): "Everyone shall be free to leave any country, including his own. The above-mentioned rights shall not be subject to any restrictions except those which are provided by law, are necessary to protect national security, public order ("ordre public"), public health or morals or the rights and freedoms of others, and are consistent with th other rights recognized in the present Covenant. No one shall be arbitrarily deprived of the right to enter his own country."

[62] R. DeVecchi, "Determining Refugee Status: Towards a Coherent Policy" (1983), World Refugee Survey 10, at 13. *Accord* D. Gross, "The Right of Asylum Under United States Law" (1980), 80 Columbia L. Rev. 1125, at 1142-143: "Leaving a country is not normally considered an act of political expression, and punishment based on departure or failure to return in violation of travel restrictions would not normally be considered persecution for political opinion. However, in its 1965 reforms, Congress evinced a general desire to protect aliens facing punishment for illegal departure. Some courts have shown a similar willingness to let such aliens remain

Second, the illegal departure or stay abroad must either be explicitly politically motivated, or the state of origin must view the unauthorized departure or stay abroad as an implied political statement of disloyalty or defiance.[63] Whether by law or administrative practice, it must be clear that the home country disapproves of illicit emigration, and views those who breach its rules on exit or travel abroad as non-conforming dissidents. This perspective is exemplified by those societies in which it is considered a crime to seek to withdraw from the national community by emigration, and which brand all those who leave as traitors.[64] Claims should not be denied simply because they are prompted by an intention to secure asylum abroad. As in the case of *sur place* claims based on post-departure voluntary acts,[65] refugee status should be recognized where there is a prospect of serious harm upon return[66] as the result of the imputation to the claimant of an unacceptable political opinion.[67]

Insofar as a refugee claimant can meet this two-part test, she falls within the scope of the Convention definition. She reasonably fears persecution because of her home government's established practice of harshly oppressive punishment. The reason she is at risk is moreover directly related to the political opinion that her government attributes to her unauthorized departure or stay, or to its view that her disloyal behavior has set her fundamentally apart from the national community.

Recent practice in North America has been less generous to persons who leave or remain outside their country illegally. In the United States, the individual's motives at the time of flight are viewed as determinative, whatever the position taken by the state of origin. Thus, unless the refugee leaves her country for specifically political reasons, she is not a refugee.[68] Cana-

---

in the United States, based on the idea that the crime of illegal departure imposes punishment for the exercise of a fundamental human right, the right to travel." This position has recently been codified in the United States: "The asylum officer or immigration judge shall give due consideration to evidence that the government of the applicant's country of nationality or last habitual residence persecutes its nationals or residents if they leave the country without authorization or seek asylum in another country": 8 C.F.R. 208.13(b)(2)(B)(ii), July 27, 1990.

[63] In reference to the Vietnamese "boat people", for example, it may be contended that although some may have departed for strictly economic reasons, " . . . by joining the exodus they may have put themselves in a situation where they are likely to suffer persecution if they ever return home . . . . The relevant reasons here must be their political opinion *because they have by implication expressed their disgust for Vietnamese political system* . . . . The attitude of the home government must be taken into consideration in such cases" [Emphasis added]: B. Tsamenyi, "The 'Boat People': Are They Refugees?" (1983), 5 Human Rts. Q. 348, at 369-70.

[64] "Some States have made it a crime to withdraw from society without permission ('Republikflucht'), and anyone who manages to escape may face stiff penalties if he ever returns": A. Grahl-Madsen, "International Refugee Law Today and Tomorrow" (1982), Archiv des Völkerrechts 411, at 421.

[65] *See* text *supra* at notes 49-52.

[66] *See* text *supra* at note 56 ff. at which relevant concerns are discussed.

[67] *See* text *supra* at note 53.

[68] K. Brill, *supra*, note 47, at 132.

dian courts have adopted a similar position: fear of reprisals for unauthorized departure or stay may be invoked as an auxiliary ground of claim, but is not sufficient to meet the refugee definition in and of itself.[69]

The Immigration Appeal Board consistently noted that "violating the laws of one's country and having to face the consequences does not make one a refugee."[70] Even where the penalties for the breach of controls on emigration are clearly inordinate, the Board refused to bend. For example, notwithstanding evidence that Polish law would impose a five-year prison term for illegal exit, it was held that " . . . if [the claimant] were to be imprisoned for leaving his country without proper authorization, this would not be considered persecution — but rather prosecution."[71] Similarly, even though it was shown that illegal departees from the Soviet Union " . . . under Russian law have committed treason and are subject to heavy penalties on their return",[72] it was decided that "[s]erious as this is for them, it is not persecution as defined in the Convention but the consequence of breaking Russian law."[73] This refusal to examine the substance of the state's response to unauthorized exit or sojourn (rather than just its form) is not in keeping with the Convention.[74] Extreme, clearly unreasonable penalties for the breach of travel restrictions convert what might otherwise have been routine prosecution into the type of serious harm encompassed by the notion of persecution.

The often callous disregard for the plight of persons who face severe penalties for illegal departure or stay abroad is further evinced by the Immigration Appeal Board's view that because the potential sanctions are the same for all nationals of the country of origin,[75] they are inherently non-

---

[69] The Immigration Appeal Board has adopted the view that "[a] person who flees his country by reason of a well-founded fear of persecution for reasons of race, religion, nationality, membership in a particular social group or political opinion, is justified in placing before the Board his additional fear of reprisal for leaving his country in an unlawful manner. *Such action, by itself, does not make a person a Convention refugee*" [Emphasis added]: *Stanislaw Julian Jodlowski*, Immigration Appeal Board Decision V81-6166, June 18, 1981, at 6-7, *per* D. Davey.

[70] *Henryk Stanley Komisarski*, Immigration Appeal Board Decision V81-6162, May 28, 1981, at 2, *per* C.M. Campbell. *Accord*, e.g., *Jean-Claude Delva*, Immigration Appeal Board Decision 74-1091, December 31, 1974;; *Gizella Litter*, Immigration Appeal Board Decision M77-1051, April 25, 1977; *Lech Jankowski*, Immigration Appeal Board Decision V80-6410, C.L.I.C. Notes 26.11, January 5, 1981.

[71] *Jerzy Malek*, Immigration Appeal Board Decision 76-9092, March 10, 1976, at 3, *per* A.B. Weselak.

[72] *Viatcheslav Drozd and Tatiana Drozd*, Immigration Appeal Board Decision T79-9395, C.L.I.C. Notes 18.12, March 6, 1980, at 3, *per* C.M. Campbell.

[73] *Id.*

[74] "Where there is reason to believe that a person, due to his illegal departure or unauthorized stay abroad is liable to such severe penalties, his recognition as a refugee will be justified" if causally related to a ground of protection enumerated in the Convention: UNHCR, *supra*, note 3, at 16.

[75] References to the inapplicability of refugee protection due to the general application of travel restrictions abound in the case law of the Immigration Appeal Board. *See*, e.g., *Vladimir Stojka*, Immigration Appeal Board Decision 74-10198, September 12, 1974, at 5, *per* A.B. Weselak ("This is the lot of all Czechoslovakians . . . "); *Edmund Kroszkini*, Immigration Appeal Board

persecutory.[76] It is simply incorrect to argue that the pervasive nature of the restriction makes refugee protection unviable or inappropriate. By way of comparison, many societies have rules of universal application against freedom of expression. Refugee law does not purport to assist all persons who live within these societies, but rather only those whose defiance of the generalized rule has placed them at risk of serious harm. Similarly, only the minority of persons at risk in consequence of broadly based migration restrictions — namely, those who have contravened the standards — merits protection as refugees. It is not, however, sensible to ignore the reality of the minority genuinely at peril simply because any member of the home society could, if similarly situated, also become at risk.

2.2.2 Inferences Based on the Legality of Departure

A related question is the extent to which issues of authorized or unauthorized departure are probative of the genuineness of a claim to refugee status. The general rule, of course, is that if a person faces the risk of serious harm, the means by which she left her country of origin is essentially irrelevant.[77] An individual may depart her country without impediment, even travel on a valid passport, and still be a genuine refugee[78] if the balance of the evidence in favour of recognition as a refugee is compelling. Moreover, the Federal Court of Appeal has held unequivocally that illegal departure, even involving forged documentation, is also no bar to a refugee claim. In *Benjamin Attakora v. Minister of Employment and Immigration*,[79] the Court noted:

> . . . [T]he Board found that the applicant's credibility was weakened by his statement that, while on the plane to Canada, he destroyed a passport, Canadian visitor's visa and airline ticket, all of which were in the name of a friend and had been used by him in order to get away. The Board, after noting that

---

Decision 75-10374, December 15, 1975, at 3, *per* A.B. Weselak ("This is the lot of all Poles . . . "); *Frantisek Horbal*, Immigration Appeal Board Decision T77-9138, April 27, 1977, at 4, *per* D. Petrie (" . . . [T]his is prosecution for breaking the law of his country, applicable to all, and not persecution").

[76] "If the appellant will be prosecuted and jailed on his return to Poland for deserting his ship, this is not tantamount to persecution, but only the implementation of the Polish law governing that state, which is applicable to all ship-deserters and not only to non-communist or Catholic ship-deserters. The fact that Mr. Mazur does not agree with the political situation in Poland does not permit the Board to recognize him as a political refugee as there must be several thousand who also do not agree with the present regime": *Jerzy Mazur*, Immigration Appeal Board Decision 76-9327, June 29, 1976, at 3, *per* U. Benedetti.

[77] G.J.L. Coles, "Background Paper for the Asian Working Group on the International Protection of Refugees and Displaced Persons" 102 (unpublished, 1980).

[78] "The fact that a person has left his country legally with a valid passport is no bar to refugee status": P. Weis "The concept of the refugee in international law" (1960), J. du droit international 928, at 972.

[79] Federal Court of Appeal Decision A-1091-87, May 19, 1989; setting aside Immigration Appeal Board Decision T86-10336X, October 14, 1987.

the applicant had said that he destroyed the documents because he was afraid that, if they were discovered, he might be arrested and sent back, concluded, without more, that this element of his testimony lacked credibility.

The Board's finding on this point is, to say the least, puzzling. There is certainly nothing inherently incredible in a refugee saying that he destroyed false documents in order to avoid detection and arrest once they had served their purpose. In the circumstances of this case, the destruction of such documents could not have had any conceivable relevance to any issue which the Board has to decide. I can only conclude that the Board's insistence upon its significance is founded upon some erroneous view of the law. Does the Board think that only persons who arrive with their travel documents in order can be refugees? Or that those who arrive with false documents have some obligation to preserve them?[80]

Nonetheless, there are two situations where it is appropriate to consider information on the mode of departure.

First, evidence of difficulty in securing official permission to leave may be probative of a negative relationship between the claimant and her state, and thus corroborate other evidence tending to show a genuine risk of harm. In *Joseph Khouri*,[81] for example, the Board looked to Syria's refusal of an exit visa to the claimant in order to substantiate the assertion that certain actions, which might otherwise have been politically ambiguous, were viewed by the government to have been traitorous. Too, evidence that bribery or influence was required in order to secure travel documents may infer the absence of a normal relationship between the claimant and her state,[82] and thereby support a claim to refugee status.[83] In *Shahram Nassirbake*,[84] for example, the Board acknowledged the probative value of the Iranian claimant's need to pay a substantial sum to be smuggled out of his country, in view of the government's policy of refusing passports to its opponents.

Second and conversely, where the evidence of serious risk is less than clear-cut, evidence of undue ease of departure tends to discredit a claim to fear serious harm at the hands of the state. At least in countries that have sophisti-

---

[80] *Id.*, at 3-4, *per* Hugessen J.

[81] Immigration Appeal Board Decision T82-9804, October 2, 1984.

[82] "Should the authorities assist a person in leaving the country of flight by means of illegal bribes, illegal issuance of travel documents, or illegal passivity, and if this is the only possible way in which the authorities could assist, such circumstances actually underline the situation of persecution. The fact that certain authorities — on financial or humanitarian grounds — are willing to break the law in order to assist persons in leaving the country is, incidentally, a familiar phenomenon under any regime and, so far, it has not led to any doubts regarding the international refugee status of the persons involved": I. Foighel, "Legal Status of the Boat People" (1979), 48 Nordisk Tidsskrift for International Ret. 217, at 224.

[83] "The Board also appears to have overlooked the fact that his passport may not have been obtained routinely since it was obtained through his brother's *contacts* who work in government offices": *Pedro Enrique Juarez Maldonado v. Minister of Employment and Immigration*, [1980] 2 F.C. 302 (C.A.), at 304, *per* Heald J. (setting aside a refusal to grant refugee status at the Immigration Appeal Board level).

[84] Immigration Appeal Board Decision V87-6134, April 23, 1987, at 15-16, *per* N. Mawani.

cated bureaucracies and information storage and retrieval systems, issuance of a passport or exit visa may indicate that the government has no particular concern to persecute the claimant. In the case of *Oscar Manuel Diaz Duran*,[85] for example, the Immigration Appeal Board legitimately questioned the credibility of the Chilean claimant's vague assertion of risk on the ground that he had been issued a valid passport and exit visa, in contrast to his government's established practice of refusing travel documents to its political opponents. In *Bakhshish Gill Singh*,[86] the Board observed that it had

> . . . heard many accounts of Indian police incompetence in refugee determination cases, but there is a limit to such claimed incompetence beyond which credibility disappears. In this connection, it is hard to believe that Mr. Gill would have succeeded in obtaining a "no objection certificate" and an extension of his passport, quite apart from succeeding in getting through controls at Delhi airport, were there any serious desire on the part of the authorities to arrest him.[87]

Evidence of this kind, whether positive or negative, is not however determinative, but should rather be weighed together with other facts to discern the true extent of the risk faced by the refugee claimant. There is an unfortunate tendency to be reflexively dismissive of claimants who have freely exited their country or who possess valid travel documents.[88] Suspicion is particularly high in the case of persons who have been actively assisted to leave their country.[89] Yet in even these situations where the refugee's departure is facilitated by the state of origin, a genuine claim to refugee status can be established. As Foighel has noted,[90] Convention refugee status is fundamentally a function of the risk faced by the claimant, not of her mode of departure; state practice has not resulted in the generalized denial of protection to refugees who were assisted to leave by their home state; geographical or political limitations may mean that for some refugees the collaboration of their government is the only means of escape; and the extensive exclusion clauses of the Convention make no reference to the issue of the facilitation of departure by home authorities. In the result, the role of evidence on mode of departure should be carefully confined to situations of evidentiary ambiguity, and should not be allowed to override the fundamental concern to identify persons who would be at genuine risk of serious harm upon return to their state of origin.

---

[85] Immigration Appeal Board Decision 80-9116, April 16, 1980; affirmed on other grounds, (1982) 42 N.R. 342 (F.C.A.).

[86] Immigration Appeal Board Decision V87-6246X, July 22, 1987.

[87] *Id.*, at 5, *per* D. Anderson.

[88] F.M. Marino-Menendez, "El concepto de refugiado en un contexto de derecho internacional general" (1983), 35(2) Revista española de derecho internacional 337, at 356.

[89] D. Roth, "The Right of Asylum Under United States Immigration Law" (1981), 33 U. Florida L. Rev. 539, at 554.

[90] *Supra*, note 82, at 224-25.

2.3 Choice of the Country of Asylum

There is no requirement in the Convention that a refugee seek protection in the country nearest her home, or even in the first state to which she flees. Nor is it requisite that a claimant travel directly from her country of first asylum to the state in which she intends to seek durable protection.[91] The universal scope of post-Protocol refugee law[92] effectively allows most refugees to choose for themselves the country in which they will claim refugee status.

This basic premise flows from the Universal Declaration of Human Rights,[93] and was confirmed, subject to minor qualification, by Conclusion 15 of the Executive Committee of the UNHCR:

> The intentions of the asylum-seeker as regards the country in which he wishes to request asylum should as far as possible be taken into account. Regard should be had to the concept that asylum should not be refused solely on the ground that it could be sought from another state. Where, however, it appears that a person, before requesting asylum, already has a connexion or close links with another State, he may if it appears fair and reasonable be called upon first to request asylum from that State.[94]

This basic standard unequivocally refutes the legitimacy of a so-called "direct flight" requirement, under which only persons coming directly to an asylum state from their country of origin would be eligible for protection.[95] It rather establishes the right of a state to *defer* its duty to protect where a claimant has a pre-existing connection or close links with another state. In such a case, if it is both "fair and reasonable," the country in which the asylum claim is made may suspend its procedures pending a decision by authorities in the state with which the claimant is affiliated. In *R. v. Immigration Appeal Tribunal, ex parte Steven Miller*,[96] for example, the English Divisional Court considered Conclusion 15 in deciding that a Jewish South African who had

---

[91] *See* e.g., the case of Mr. B. Conté, reported at [1981] Recueil des décisions du Conseil d'Etat 20-21, in which the French Conseil d'Etat considered the case of a Guinean who had resided for four years in Senegal before seeking asylum in France. Looking to the purposes and structure of the 1951 Convention, the Court properly held that Mr. Conté could be excluded only if determined to be a *de facto* national of Senegal, in accordance with Art. 1(E). Cited in E. Vierdag, "The Country of 'First Asylum': Some European Aspects", in D. Martin, ed., *The New Asylum Seekers: Refugee Law in the 1980s*, pp. 79-80 (1988).

[92] *See* Section 1.3, *supra*.

[93] "Everyone has the right to seek and to enjoy in other countries asylum from persecution": *UDHR, supra,* note 63, at Art. 14(1).

[94] Conclusion 15(XXX) of the Executive Committee of the High Commissioner's Programme, at para. (h)(iii)-(iv), U.N. Doc. HCR/IP/2/Eng./REV.1986 (1979).

[95] Goran Melander succinctly states the underlying rationale for this concept: "It is considered that any asylum seeker should ask for asylum in the state he first enters after his flight from a country in which he has a well-founded fear of persecution. He has no right to choose his country of asylum. The movement of refugees should be controlled . . . ": G. Melander, "Refugees in Orbit" (1978), 16 A.W.R. Bull. 59, at 60.

[96] [1988] Imm. A.R. 1.

resided in Israel for nearly four years before coming to the United Kingdom, and who appeared to be entitled to immigrant status in Israel pursuant to the Law of Return, ought reasonably to seek protection from Israel before claiming status elsewhere. Nonetheless, such a decision is suspensive only, since Conclusion 15 requires that status determination proceed in the event that the state with which the claimant has close links ultimately declines protection.

This principle, however, is increasingly questioned. At the international level, a conclusion of the Executive Committee[97] foreshadows the exclusion of "irregular" asylum seekers,[98] that is, refugees whose protection needs can be met in some other state. While not as yet fully defined, this notion could ultimately legitimate the refusal of claims from, for example, persons who have family connections or long-term work authorization in a safe intermediary country.[99]

Beyond this initiative at the universal level, European states are moving rapidly toward a system designed to limit the right of refugees to choose their place of asylum within that regional community.[100] Canada's new legislation, in this respect still not proclaimed, also authorizes the turning away of asylum seekers eligible to have the merits of their claim determined in another state.[101] Schemes of this sort are inconsistent with the spirit of the Convention, and reflect a weakening of the commitment to the refugee's right to decide for herself the most effective means of securing safety from persecution. Direct flight schemes also infringe the principle of burden-sharing, as those countries closest to the site of refugee movements will bear a disproportionate share of the collective duty of protection.[102]

At present, then, the only claims to refugee status which may be deflected under international law remain those from the narrow category of persons defined in Conclusion 15,[103] and then only insofar as the state with which they are affiliated agrees to extend protection. Otherwise, unless the refugee secures the actual or *de facto* nationality of another state,[104] she is entitled to have her claim to refugee status determined in the country of her choice.

---

[97] Conclusion 36(XXXVI) of the Executive Committee of the High Commissioner's Programme, at para. (j), U.N. Doc. HCR/IP/2/Eng./REV. 1986 (1985).

[98] *See* J. Hathaway, " 'Irregular' Asylum Seekers: What's All The Fuss?" (1988), 8(2) Refuge 1.

[99] *See*, e.g., comments of Dr. Marie-Odile Wiederkehr of the Council of Europe, quoted in E. Vierdag, *supra*, note 91, pp. 81-82.

[100] *See Convention Determining the State Responsible for Examining Applications for Asylum lodged in one of the Member States of the European Community* ("Dublin Convention"), June 1990.

[101] *Immigration Act, 1976*, now R.S.C. 1985, c. 1-2, s. 46.01(1)(b) [en. 1985, c. 28 (4th Supp.), s. 14].

[102] *See*, e.g., D. Hull, "Displaced Persons: 'The New Refugees' " (1983), 13 Georgia J. Intl. Comp. L. 755, at 772.

[103] *Supra*, note 94.

[104] *See* Sections 6.2.2 and 6.2.3, *infra*.

In Canada, there has been an attempt indirectly to incorporate a direct flight rule by impugning the credibility of claimants who do not claim refugee status in other countries of passage or residence. Persons who have spent substantial time in one[105] or more[106] countries, who have enjoyed short-term status in an intermediate state,[107] and even those who have merely transited through another country[108] have frequently been viewed with mistrust because of their failure to claim refugee status before arriving in Canada. As noted in the case of Ghanaian *Anthony Appiah Asamoah*,[109]

> . . . [T]he applicant's failure to seek asylum in any other country than Canada, although he passed through several intervening countries . . . is not consistent with an intention to flee from one's pursuers and therefore the concurrent imperative to seek haven wherever one can. Surely it is reasonable to expect one to seek help at the first convenient venue.[110]

---

[105] *See* e.g., *Jeno Pillmayer*, Immigration Appeal Board Decision V84-6254, November 20, 1986 (rejecting the claim of a Hungarian who failed to claim refugee status during nine years' residence in Sweden); and *Guadalupe Quintanilla Ruiz*, Immigration Appeal Board Decision V87-6662X, April 26, 1988 (in which the Salvadoran claimant's credibility was questioned because she failed to claim refugee status during two years' illegal residence in the United States).

[106] *See*, e.g., *Mahmoud Saddo*, Immigration Appeal Board Decision M80-1123, July 24, 1980; set aside on other grounds by Federal Court of Appeal Decision A-574-80, January 19, 1981; claim ultimately rejected by the Board on February 25, 1981, in which the Board commented negatively on the fact that the Ethiopian claimant had spent six years in Iraq, Sudan, Saudi Arabia, and Kuwait before coming to Canada; *Munir Mohamad Adem Suleiman*, Immigration Appeal Board Decision V81-6246, July 23, 1981; set aside on other grounds by the Federal Court of Appeal on October 6, 1982; claim ultimately rejected by the Board on November 16, 1983, in which the Board criticized the two years spent by the Ethiopian applicant in Sudan and Saudi Arabia as inconsistent with refugee status; and *Jasbir Singh*, Immigration Appeal Board Decision T83-9400, April 14, 1983, at 5, *per* D. Davey ("Whereas the Board has consistently held that it is not necessary to seek refugee status in the first country reached, it is not supportive of a genuine fear of persecution for a person to travel by ship to fifteen or sixteen countries without seeking refugee status."

[107] *See*, e.g., *Alfredo Nelson Salvatierra Villarroel*, Immigration Appeal Board Decision T78-9173, October 31, 1978; affirmed on other grounds by the Federal Court of Appeal at (1979), 31 N.R. 50 (in which the Board drew a negative inference from the failure of the Chilean claimant to remain in Spain, where he had resided for four months without permission to work); and *Harjinder Dhillon Singh*, Immigration Appeal Board Decision T84-9049, October 21, 1985, at 5, *per* B. Suppa (" . . . [H]e never claimed refugee status while he was in Sweden for three months . . . . Is this the behaviour of a man with a well-founded fear of persecution? In the opinion of the Board, it is not.")

[108] *See*, e.g., *Fernando Segundo Hidalgo*, Immigration Appeal Board Decision 74-10354, January 29, 1975; set aside on other grounds by Federal Court of Appeal Decision A-71-75, May 26, 1975; claim ultimately rejected by the Board on September 16, 1975, in which the Board criticized the Argentinian claimant's failure to seek protection during a one-day stop in the United States; and *Rajinder Prashad Sharma*, Immigration Appeal Board Decision V82-6401, January 27, 1984; set aside on other grounds by Federal Court of Appeal Decision A-1255-82, January 27, 1984, which took into account the failure of the Indian applicant to claim status during a stopover in the United Kingdom.

[109] Immigration Appeal Board Decision T87-9902, January 19, 1988.

[110] *Id.*, at 3, *per* J. Weisdorf.

By characterizing the issue as one of credibility, it is possible simultaneously to refuse the claims of persons arriving indirectly while maintaining a formal commitment to the impropriety of a direct flight rule:[111]

> . . . [I]f the applicant had experienced a well-founded fear, he had at least two opportunities of expressing and establishing it . . . . It is hard to believe that a person in the grip of an uncontrollable fear . . . does not make any effort to eradicate this fear when the opportunity arises. I use the expression "hard to believe" because I know that there is nothing in the Act that makes it compulsory for a person to apply for refugee status at the first port he reaches.[112]

Fortunately, the Federal Court of Appeal has intervened to constrain this implied direct flight rule. First, in its decision in *Marcel Simon Chang Tak Hue v. Minister of Employment and Immigration*,[113] the Court recognized that failure to make a claim to refugee status does not raise an issue of credibility if it can be explained, for example, by the absence of an immediate need for protection against *refoulement*:

> The Board rejected the Applicant's claim . . . on the sole ground that he had not made it in 1981 when he went to Greece and boarded his ship. This, for the Board, would show that the applicant's fear was not real and that his contention to that effect, his having waited so long before making it, was not credible. While we do not dispute that the delay in making a claim for refugee status may be an important factor to take into consideration in trying to assess the seriousness of the applicant's contentions, we disagree completely with the Board's reasoning in the present case. It seems to us obvious that the Applicant's fear is in relation to his having to return to the Seychelles and as long as he had his sailor's papers and a ship to sail on, he did not have to seek protection.[114]

The Federal Court expanded on this approach in *Charles Kofi Owusu Ansah v. Minister of Employment and Immigration*,[115] in which the Board had attacked the Ghanaian claimant's credibility because he had failed to claim protection in any of three countries visited before coming to Canada:

---

[111] "[T]here is nothing in the Convention that obliges a person fleeing his country owing to fear of being persecuted to seek refuge in the closest neighbouring country or in the first country he reaches. The Convention refers, simply, to a person who is outside the country of his nationality . . . ": *Juan Alejandro Araya Heredio*, Immigration Appeal Board Decision 76-1127, January 6, 1977, at 6, *per* J.-P. Houle.

[112] *Luis Omar Reyes Ferrada*, Immigration Appeal Board Decision T81-9476, September 18, 1981, at 4, *per* J.-P. Houle; affirmed by Federal Court of Appeal Decision A-572-81, May 3, 1982. *Accord Farah Shire Abdurahaman*, Immigration Appeal Board Decision T82-9419, C.L.I.C. Notes 50.8, November 3, 1982, at 8, *per* G. Tisshaw; affirmed on other grounds by the Federal Court of Appeal at (1983), 50 N.R. 315: "[W]as his fear well-founded if he never in any of the Western European democracies he visited approached the authorities for refugee status? It is not credible that he would prolong his ordeal under the circumstances."

[113] Federal Court of Appeal Decision A-196-87, March 8, 1988; setting aside Immigration Appeal Board Decision M87-1079X, March 25, 1987.

[114] *Id.*, at 2, *per* Marceau J.

[115] Federal Court of Appeal Decision A-1265-87, May 19, 1989; setting aside Immigration Appeal Board Decision T87-9386X, November 10, 1987.

It was, indeed, 53 days from the date the applicant left Ghana, May 30, until he arrived in Canada, July 23. He was at sea 16 of them but there were 37 days during which he might have claimed to be a Convention refugee in a country other than Canada, assuming, of course, that those countries are parties to the Convention and have implemented it by whatever domestic process prevails . . . . The significant point is that the Applicant did offer explanations as to why he had not sought to remain or claim to be a refugee in Togo, Nigeria and Brazil. Each explanation appears plausible.[116]

Specifically, Owusu Ansah did not seek status in Togo because he feared kidnapping by the nearby Ghanaian authorities; he avoided Nigerian authorities because he felt that country's military government could not be trusted to respect human rights; and he did not make a claim in Brazil because he preferred to come to an English-speaking country.

Reading these decisions together, the Federal Court's position is that a claimant's credibility cannot be discounted if there is a reasonable explanation for failure to claim refugee status during passage through or sojourn in other countries which adhere to the Convention. The Court has thus far accepted as plausible reasons the lack of impending threat of return, a desire to distance oneself from incursions by authorities of the home state, concern regarding the true adequacy of protection, and preference to make a claim in a country in which one's language is spoken. Similarly, one ought reasonably to take account of such factors as desire to be reunited with family, close friends, or an ethnic community; the compatibility of the asylum state with personal needs and goals; and a decision by the claimant to delay seeking status until in a country with a fully adequate determination procedure.

Even in those rare cases where no credible explanation for delay in claiming status is advanced, it does not follow that the refugee claim is necessarily unfounded. While the lack of a plausible account for delay may render the claimant's own testimony insufficiently credible for it alone to establish the need for protection, independent evidence of possible harm may nonetheless found the case for refugee status.

2.4 Illegal Entry or Stay in an Asylum State

A claim to Convention refugee status is not in any sense compromised by illicit arrival in the state in which protection is sought. Persons who sneak across frontiers or who disguise their true motive when they seek entrance may still be genuine refugees if they otherwise meet the requirements of the definition.

The eligibility of illegal entrants to qualify as refugees is clear from the absence of any reference in the Convention to legal admission as a criterion of refugee status. This possibility was explicitly raised and rejected at the

---

[116] *Id.*, at 3, *per* Mahoney J.A.

Conference of Plenipotentiaries by way of an unsuccessful Australian proposal to exclude fraudulent entrants from the scope of protection.[117]

To the contrary, the granting of refugee status to illegal entrants was specifically contemplated by incorporation in the Convention of Article 31, titled "Refugees unlawfully in the country of refuge."[118] In this provision, the Conference went so far as to require contracting states to exempt refugees from ordinary penalties that might attach to illegal entry or presence in their territory. While this article does not prohibit the eventual deportation of a refugee to a state in which she is not at risk,[119] it provides ample support for the position that illegal entry is not a sufficient concern to deprive an individual of the right to have her refugee claim determined in accordance with the Convention.

This approach is consistent with the predicament in which refugees find themselves. As Sadruddin Aga Khan has noted, most refugees do not enjoy the luxury of immigration through customary channels, and thus find themselves compelled to seek asylum by irregular entry to a safe country.[120] In contrast, the recent practice of states has often demonstrated a near obsession with the manner by which a refugee claimant has entered an asylum state. Historically, American case law has placed "an exaggerated — indeed, almost exclusive — emphasis on factors related to the applicant's manner

---

[117] "The present Convention shall not apply to a person who has been admitted to the territory of a Contracting State for a specific purpose and who did not at the time of entry apply for permission to reside permanently therein, unless such person can establish to the satisfaction of the Contracting State that since the date of his admission circumstances have arisen which justify his claiming the rights and privileges intended to be secured by this Convention for a *bona fide* refugee": Proposal for a new article submitted by Australia, U.N. Doc. A/CONF.2/42, July 6, 1951. This proposal was *not* incorporated in the final version of the Convention.

[118] "The Contracting States shall not impose penalties, on account of their illegal entry or presence, on refugees who, coming directly from a territory where their life or freedom was threatened in the sense of Article 1, enter or are present in their territory without authorization, provided they present themselves without delay to the authorities and show good cause for their illegal entry or presence": *Convention, supra*, note 24, at Art. 31(1).

[119] The Belgian and Canadian delegations in particular stressed that the prohibition in Article 31 on penalties on account of illegal entry or presence meant the imposition of a fine or imprisonment, and did not include deportation: Statements of Mr. Herment of Belgium and Mr. Winter of Canada, U.N. Doc. E/AC.32/SR.40 at 4-5, cited in 2 A. Grahl-Madsen, *The Status of Refugees in International Law*, p. 210 (1972). Nor does the prohibition in Article 32 on the expulsion of refugees apply to illegal entrants, as it is explicitly confined to the case of refugees "lawfully in [the state's] territory." Thus, the primary protection available to illegal entrant refugees is the prohibition on return to a country of persecution, found in Article 33.

[120] "The situation of a refugee differs . . . from that of an ordinary alien, who . . . holding a national passport, enjoys the protection of the authorities of his country, to which he may return if he so desires. This is not so in the case of a refugee. Having, in many cases, entered the country in an irregular manner, he is immediately at odds with the authorities of the country of reception . . . ": S. Aga Khan, "Legal Problems Relating to Refugees and Displaced Persons" (1976), Recueil des cours 287, at 313.

of entering the United States."[121] While the recent decision in *Matter of Pula*[122] has significantly restricted the importance to be attached to evidence of illegal entry, the circumvention of immigration rules nonetheless remains "a proper and relevant discretionary factor"[123] in determining an asylum claim.

Canadian practice conforms somewhat more closely to international standards, although it too demonstrates a frequently disproportionate concern with the refugee claimant's mode of entry to the asylum state.[124] The basic principle that illegal entrants are eligible to have their claims to Convention refugee status determined in accordance with law is nonetheless clear from the important dictum of Mr. Justice MacGuigan of the Federal Court of Appeal in the case of *Surujpal v. Minister of Employment and Immigration*:[125]

> It does not stand to the applicants' credit that, after entering Canada as visitors, they illegally obtained Canadian social insurance cards, worked illegally for approximately a year before they were found out and arrested, and then claimed refugee status. Nevertheless, since the law allows them to apply as refugees even in such circumstances, we must conclude that it does not intend that their refugee claims should be determined on the basis of these extraneous considerations. . . .[126]

This position respects the fundamentally protective purpose of refugee law, and reinforces the primacy in the determination process of the risk faced by the refugee claimant.[127]

The decision in *Khemraj Surujpal*,[128] however, impliedly approves of a

---

[121] D. Anker, "Discretionary Asylum: A Protection Remedy for Refugees Under the Refugee Act of 1980" (1987), 28(1) Virginia J. Intl. L. 1, at 4.

[122] Board of Immigration Appeals Interim Decision No. 3033, September 22, 1987, cited in D. Anker, *supra*, note 121, at 68.

[123] *Supra*, note 122, at 9.

[124] *See*, e.g., *St. Gardien Giraud*, Immigration Appeal Board Decision T81-9669, March 20, 1986, at 5, *per* B. Suppa: "His action in using a false passport in his attempt to enter Canada hardly supports his claim." *Accord Harjinder Dillon Singh*, Immigration Appeal Board Decision T84-9049, October 21, 1985 (no refugee claim until time of arrest); *Moustafa Salamat*, Immigration Appeal Board Decision M86-1142, April 13, 1987 (tearing up passport on plane); and *Santokh Bhopal Singh*, Immigration Appeal Board Decision V87-6245X, August 17, 1987 (two-year delay before presenting claim to refugee status).

[125] (1985), 60 N.R. 73 (F.C.A.). There is a foundation for these comments in two earlier judgments of the Federal Court of Appeal: *Lloyd Oswald Forbes v. Minister of Employment and Immigration*, Federal Court of Appeal Decision A-655-83, November 8, 1983, *per* Thurlow J.; and *Rajinder Prashad Sharma v. Minister of Employment and Immigration*, Federal Court of Appeal Decision A-1255-82, January 27, 1984, *per* Stone J.

[126] *Id.*, at 73-74, *per* MacGuigan J.

[127] "[P]rovisions on the punishment for unauthorised entry and sojourn . . . should be read in conjunction with art. 31 para. 1 of the Refugee Convention, which prescribes that a refugee who is coming directly from a territory where his life or freedom is threatened in the sense of art. 1, shall not be punished for his unauthorised entry, provided he present himself without delay": G. Melander, *supra*, note 95, at 61.

[128] *Supra*, note 125.

more limited role for evidence of illegal entry or presence in the assessment of the claimant's credibility.[129] While it is clearly inappropriate to disallow a refugee claim on the ground of illicit arrival or stay, the Convention establishes an obligation on refugees to "present themselves without delay to the authorities and show good cause for their illegal entry or presence."[130] It seems right, therefore, to inquire into the circumstances of any protracted postponement of a refugee claim as a means of evaluating the sincerity of the claimant's need for protection. As observed in *Jeno Pillmayer*:[131]

> The Board cannot assume that the niceties of Canadian immigration law were known by the applicant. However, it is reasonable to expect that given his stated intention to make a refugee claim, the applicant would have shown some due diligence in pursuing his claim after his arrival in Canada or at least provide the Board with an explanation for the delay.[132]

Where there is no reasonable excuse for the delay, an inference of evasion going to credibility is often warranted. Acceptable explanations would include, for example, lack of familiarity with or trust in the claims procedure[133] or reliance on events which have occurred only since arrival in Canada.[134]

The case of *Malik Abdul Majad*[135] offers a good example of the circumstances in which a negative assessment of credibility may reasonably be derived from the circumstances of illegal entry or stay. The claimant entered Canada as a visitor, and did not report to immigration authorities upon the expiration of his visa. He was arrested more than a year after his status in

---

[129] *Accord Bakhshish Gill Singh*, Immigration Appeal Board Decision V87-6246X, July 22, 1987, at 11-12 *per* D. Anderson: "Counsel for the Minister argued that the applicant's long delay in filing his claim to refugee status suggests that his claim is frivolous. At most, such delay might be a factor to be considered in assessing the credibility of the claimant . . . . "

[130] *Convention, supra*, note 24, at Art. 31(1). The text of this article is reproduced at note 118, *supra*.

[131] Immigration Appeal Board Decision V84-6254, C.L.I.C. Notes 100.17, November 20, 1986.

[132] *Id.*, at 10, *per* A. Wlodyka.

[133] "A claimant may be credible even though the claim was not made at the earliest possible opportunity. He may be in the country for some time before he becomes aware of the refugee claims procedure": *Rajinder Kumar*, Immigration Appeal Board Decision T83-9484, March 31, 1987, at 6, *per* E. Rotman.

[134] "Whether a person is a refugee or not is a matter that inevitably varies dramatically with political events in that person's country of nationality or country of former habitual residence. A person could meet the definition of Convention refugee one week, and the next, by reason of political events thousands of kilometres away, no longer meet that definition. Two weeks after that it is perfectly conceivable that the definition would be met once more. Under the circumstances . . . [i]t therefore appears appropriate that the concept of the continuing jurisdiction of the Board apply, in some degree at least, in refugee cases": *Palwinder Kaur Gill*, Immigration Appeal Board Decision V86-6012, July 11, 1986, at 8, *per* D. Anderson (dissenting). *Accord Bakhshish Gill Singh*, Immigration Appeal Board Decision V87-6246X, July 22, 1987, at 11-12, *per* D. Anderson: "[W]here he claims to be a refugee *sur place* delay can be of little relevance and on its own, hardly amounts to grounds for denying the claim."

[135] Immigration Appeal Board Decision T76-9507, December 17, 1976.

Canada had come to an end, and claimed refugee status at his special inquiry. There was evidence that Mr. Majad was well-acquainted with formal refugee determination procedures even before his arrival in Canada, and that he had attempted to bribe officials to grant him legal status. No explanation for delay in presenting his case was offered. In view of all of the evidence, the Immigration Appeal Board correctly concluded that the claimant had not "complied with the spirit of the Convention as set out in Article 31",[136] as a result of which the credibility of his claim to protection was weakened.

On the other hand, as Christopher Wydrzynski has noted, the Immigration Appeal Board has frequently "seemed to prefer form to substance in attempting to rank the honesty and openness of the applicant . . . . [Where] the applicant had lied on arrival and had only formulated his intent to apply for refugee status when deportation became inevitable, this was fatal to his claim."[137] This type of absolutism is unwarranted if there is a reasonable explanation for delay. For example, the case of *Ashfaq Ahmad Sheikh*[138] involved a citizen of Pakistan who had been advised by a lawyer upon arrival to keep a low profile in Canada in the hope that the situation in his home state would normalize in the short term, thus permitting his return. The Board nonetheless found it "incredible"[139] that he would not apply for refugee status in Canada if his claim were genuine, and dismissed the claim to refugee status. In *Oscar Manuel Diaz Duran*,[140] the Chilean claimant voluntarily presented himself to immigration authorities to make a refugee claim one day after the expiration of his visitor's visa. He delayed in approaching officials on the advice of an expatriate friend in Canada, presumably aware of the then prevailing rule against the issuance of interim work permits to persons who made refugee claims while lawfully in Canada. This explanation for delay, however, "[did] not make too much sense",[141] as a result of which the Immigration Appeal Board chose to discount the claimant's testimony and determined him not to be a refugee. The Immigration Appeal Board's perspective is typified by remarks made in the case of *Roberto Osvaldo Ramirez Rojas*:[142]

> . . . [I]t was not until after his arrest by immigration authorities, when he was liable to deportation or removal, that the applicant, for the first time, claimed

---

[136] *Id.*, at 3, *per* D. Petrie. *Accord Malkit Katnoria Singh*, Immigration Appeal Board Decision V84-6133, April 30, 1987, at 4, *per* B. Howard: "Furthermore the Board regards the explanation of his failure to apply for refugee status in Canada until after his arrest as far fetched and not credible in the light of his claimed attempts to earlier obtain refugee status in Jordan and West Germany."

[137] C. Wydrzynski, "Refugees and the *Immigration Act*" (1979), 25 McGill L.J. 154, at 177.

[138] Immigration Appeal Board Decision 77-3021, September 6, 1977; affirmed on other grounds by Federal Court of Appeal, [1981] 2 F.C. 161.

[139] *Id.*, at 6, *per* J. Campbell.

[140] *Supra*, note 85.

[141] *Supra*, note 85, at 1, *per* U. Benedetti.

[142] Immigration Appeal Board Decision M80-1010, January 29, 1980.

to be a Convention refugee. *A claim made in such a way is not that of an authentic visitor or true refugee.* [Emphasis added][143]

Both Christopher Wydrzynski[144] and Deborah Anker[145] criticize this approach on the ground that the duress under which asylum seekers live often leads them to be less than forthright in dealing with or even approaching officials of the asylum state. The fear of encounters with authority figures in their state of origin carries over to the state of reception, prompts many refugees to seek entry by any means, and induces them to go underground in order to avoid the risk of rejection or deportation at the hands of an unknown system.

The propriety of considering evidence of illegal entry or stay in the assessment of credibility is therefore dependent upon the willingness of the decision-maker to examine those facts *in context*. It does not follow that all refugee claims made at a time when deportation for an immigration offence is imminent should be discounted. The concern should be to identify those cases where the breach of immigration rules is fraudulent, and to discount the claimant's credibility accordingly. On the other hand, where the illicit arrival or overstay is a result of misunderstanding, bad advice, mistrust of officials, or fear of reprisal or penalty, the refugee claim should be examined on its merits without reference to the circumstances of entry or stay in the country of asylum.

2.5 Determining the State of Reference

Where a refugee claimant possesses a formal nationality, her claim to protection should be assessed with reference to conditions in the state of nationality. Issues of surrogate protection in another state may arise at the final stage of the determination process,[146] but the initial inquiry should be limited to an examination of the relationship between the claimant and the country of which she is formally a national.[147]

---

[143] *Id.*, at 10, *per* J.-P. Houle.

[144] "The desire not to return to a place where his life may be in danger is frequently the refugee's prime motivation. With little knowledge of the Canadian immigration process, the individual may not even know of the existence of the privilege to claim protection as a refugee under the Act. The timeliness of the application does not make an individual any more or less of a refugee until all the facts are examined": C. Wydrzynski, *supra*, note 137, at 177.

[145] "Misrepresentations or other irregularities in the entry process are excusable because of the special duress which compels the refugee, who lacks the protection of his country of origin, to take extreme measures in his search for protection and security elsewhere": D. Anker, *supra*, note 121, at 53.

[146] For example, a refugee claimant may have a right of residence in a country other than the country of her nationality, in which case her need for protection may already have been met. This issue is discussed *infra* at Section 6.2.3.

[147] "In order to be considered eligible, persons possessing a nationality must fear persecution in the country of their nationality . . . . Their nationality may, therefore, have to be determined as a preliminary question in eligibility proceedings": P. Weis, "The concept of the refugee in international law" (1960), J. du droit international 928, at 972.

This basic principle was incorporated in Canadian law by the Federal Court of Appeal in the decision of *Hurt v. Minister of Manpower and Immigration*.[148] The claimant was a Polish citizen who had resided in West Germany for five years before coming to Canada. The Immigration Appeal Board determined that he had no fear of persecution in West Germany, and declared him not to be a Convention refugee. The Federal Court of Appeal set this decision aside on the ground that the claim should have been assessed with reference to Poland, the claimant's country of nationality. The Court held that the issue of surrogate protection in West Germany, while relevant, was appropriately addressed as a matter of exclusion from refugee status, subsequent to the primary determination.[149]

This view is consistent with UNHCR recommendations,[150] and ensures that the central issue of risk upon return is addressed before alternatives to protection by the asylum state are canvassed. Because deportation or expulsion will normally be effected to the state of nationality,[151] an assessment of potential harm in that country is of the essence.

In most cases, the claimant's nationality can be discerned from her own testimony, buttressed by documentary evidence such as a passport, visa, or transportation ticket. In some cases, however, it will have been necessary for the refugee to secure false documentation in order to successfully exit her country, or in order to circumvent the visa controls imposed by some asylum states on the nationals of refugee-producing countries.[152] In these

---

[148] [1978] 2 F.C. 340 (C.A.). Prior to this decision, it had been held by the Immigration Appeal Board that "a claim must be determined in relation to the claimant's country of residence and not in relation to the country which originally prompted the emigration": C. Wydrzynski, *supra*, note 137, at 171.

[149] Adherence to this practice is demonstrated in the decisions of the Immigration Appeal Board, e.g., *Ashfaq Ahmad Sheikh*, Immigration Appeal Board Decision 77-3021, September 6, 1977; set aside on other grounds by the Federal Court of Appeal, [1981] 2 F.C. 161 (C.A.), in which the claim of a citizen of Pakistan resident in Bangladesh was determined by reference to Pakistan; and *Miwako Maejima*, Immigration Appeal Board Decision 80-1072, June 5, 1980, in which the risk faced by a Japanese citizen who resided in South Africa was assessed by reference to Japan.

[150] "Once a person's status as a refugee has been determined, it is maintained unless he comes within the terms of one of the cessation clauses. This strict approach towards the determination of refugee status results from the need to provide refugees with the assurance that their status will not be subject to constant review in the light of temporary changes — not of a fundamental character — in the situation prevailing in their country of origin": UNHCR, *supra*, note 3, at 26.

[151] Under international law, the state of nationality is generally obliged to admit its nationals who have been lawfully expelled or deported: G. Goodwin-Gill, *International Law and the Movement of Persons between States*, p. 136 (1978).

[152] "Since the current (Canadian) *Immigration Act* was passed, fifteen visa requirements have been levied, and eleven of them were imposed in response to growing volumes of refugee claims . . . ": R. Girard, "Speaking Notes for an Address at the Conference on 'Refuge or Asylum — A Choice for Canada' at York University" (1986), p. 4. In the result, "[v]isa requirements often block an important escape route to Canada which may be the most logical and accessible country of refuge for the claimant . . . ": M. Schelew, "A Lawyer's Perspective on Canadian Refugee Policy" (1984), 3(4) Refuge 11, at 14.

cases of conflict between the claimant's assertion and the corroborative evidence of nationality, primary regard should be had to the characterization of the claimant's status by the country whose travel document the individual holds, or which was her immediate point of departure for the asylum state. Because international law allows each state to determine for itself those persons who are its nationals,[153] a nationality cannot be attributed to a refugee claimant where the authorities of that state take a contrary position.

Thus, where the refugee claimant alleges that documentary or other indicia of nationality are inaccurate, the authorities of the asylum country have a duty to consult the apparent state of origin in an effort to verify the claimant's status.[154] If the country that issued the documentation cannot confirm the status of the claimant as its national, the need for protection should be determined with reference to the state which the claimant asserts to be her country of origin.[155]

2.5.1 Persons with Dual or Multiple Nationality

It is an underlying assumption of refugee law that wherever available, national protection takes precedence over international protection.[156] In the drafting of the Convention, delegates were clear in their view that no person should be recognized as a refugee unless she is either unwilling or unable to avail herself of the protection of *all* countries of which she is a national.[157] Even if an individual has a genuine fear of persecution in one state of nationality, she may not benefit from refugee status if she is a citizen of another country that is prepared to afford her protection.[158]

---

[153] P. Weis, *Nationality and Statelessness in International Law*, p. 92 (1956).

[154] In a trilogy of cases in which the claimants possessed Djiboutian passports, but alleged that they were not in fact nationals of that state, the Immigration Appeal Board held, on a full oral hearing ordered by the Federal Court of Appeal, that the Canadian government "could and should have checked the validity of the Djiboutian passports with the authorities of Djibouti . . . . This failure might be conclusive in an appropriate case . . . ": *Zahara Hassan Dembil*, Immigration Appeal Board Decision 80-1025, May 21, 1982; *Ismail Hassan Dembil*, Immigration Appeal Board Decision 80-1018, May 21, 1982; and *Hassan Ahmed Ali Dembil*, Immigration Appeal Board Decision 80-1026, May 21, 1982.

[155] "[W]hile the burden of proof in principle rests on the applicant, the duty to ascertain and evaluate all the relevant facts is shared between the applicant and the examiner. Indeed, in some cases, it may be for the examiner to use all the means at his disposal to produce the necessary evidence in support of the application. Even such independent research may not, however, always be successful and there may also be statements that are not susceptible of proof. In such cases, if the applicant's account appears credible, he should, unless there are good reasons to the contrary, be given the benefit of the doubt": UNHCR, *supra*, note 3, at 47.

[156] UNHCR, *supra*, note 3, at 24.

[157] "[P]ersons with dual or even plural nationality would be considered as refugees only after it had been ascertained that they were either unable or unwilling to avail themselves of the protection of the governments of any of their nationalities": Statement of Mr. Fearnley of the United Kingdom, U.N. Doc. E/AC.7/SR.160, at 6, August 18, 1950.

[158] "[S]o long as a person had one nationality and no reasons not to avail himself of the protection of the government concerned, he could not be considered as a refugee": Statement of Mr. Henkin of the U.S.A., U.N. Doc. E/AC.7/SR.160, at 7, August 18, 1950.

This principle of the Convention[159] is not explicitly incorporated in the *Immigration Act*.[160] However, the courts have seen fit to exclude, for example, the claim of an at-risk citizen and resident of Angola who retained Portuguese citizenship by virtue of his birth in that country.[161] The fear of return of a Turkish national was also examined from the perspective of the risk he would face in Australia, a country whose citizenship he had acquired through naturalization during childhood.[162] Even where the dual citizen has *never* set foot in her second country of nationality, refugee law requires an assessment of the degree of risk, if any, in that state as a prerequisite to international protection.[163] This principle was recently affirmed by the Federal Court of Appeal in *Attorney General of Canada v. Patrick Francis Ward*.[164] Explicitly citing the second paragraph of Article 1(A)(2) of the Convention, which, while "not binding upon us since it has not been incorporated into Canadian law, . . . is persuasive as forming a logical construction of the Convention refugee definition",[165] the Court held:

> . . . [I]f it is found that he has more than one country of nationality the claimant is obliged to establish his unwillingness to avail himself of the protection *of each* of his countries of nationality before he can be considered to be a Convention refugee.[166]

---

[159] "In the case of a person who has more than one nationality, the term 'the country of his nationality' shall mean each of the countries of which he is a national, and a person shall not be deemed to be lacking the protection of the country of his nationality if, without any valid reason based on well-founded fear, he has not availed himself of the protection of one of the countries of which he is a national": *Convention, supra,* note 24, at Art. 1(A)(2), para. 2.

[160] Notwithstanding the absence of reference to Art. 1(A)(2) of the Convention in the *Immigration Act,* reliance was placed on this provision in several decisions of the Immigration Appeal Board, including *Slobodan Popovich,* Immigration Appeal Board Decision M76-1081, March 4, 1977, and *Carlos Fernando Amara de Carvalho,* Immigration Appeal Board Decision 77-1071, May 19, 1977.

[161] *Agostinho de Oliveira Duarte,* Immigration Appeal Board Decision 76-9051, February 6, 1976.

[162] *Gelil Nuh,* Immigration Appeal Board Decision T81-9273, July 5, 1981.

[163] In three decisions involving Angolan citizens who retained Portuguese citizenship by virtue of their birth in Angola prior to independence, the Immigration Appeal Board correctly assessed their claims with reference to conditions in both Angola and Portugal, and denied refugee status on the ground that effective protection by Portugal was available to the claimants: *Americo Antonio da Costa,* Immigration Appeal Board Decision 76-9401, August 26, 1976; *Jose Manuel Costa de Carvalho,* Immigration Appeal Board Decision T77-9040, February 10, 1977; and *Carlos Fernando Amara de Carvalho,* Immigration Appeal Board Decision 77-1071, May 19, 1977. *Accord* R. Plender, "Admission of Refugees: Draft Convention on Territorial Asylum", (1977) 15 San Diego L. Rev. 45, at 55: "Persons displaced by the changes of government in Angola and Mozambique, eligible to claim or maintain Portuguese nationality, do not quality as refugees if willing to seek Portuguese protection. In the event of their emigration to Portugal, they are designated as *returnees,* though they may never have been in Portugal and may not be of Portuguese descent."

[164] Federal Court of Appeal Decision A-1190-88, March 5, 1990; leave to appeal granted by the Supreme Court of Canada on November 8, 1990: Supreme Court Bulletin 2347.

[165] *Id.,* at 19, *per* Urie J.

[166] *Id.,* at 18, *per* Urie J. *Accord* concurring judgment of MacGuigan J., *id.,* at 18.

The major caveat to the principle of deferring to protection by a state of citizenship is the need to ensure *effective*, rather than merely formal, nationality. It is not enough, for example, that the claimant carries a second passport from a non-persecutory state if that state is not *in fact* willing to afford protection against return to the country of persecution. While it is appropriate to presume a willingness on the part of a country of nationality to protect in the absence of evidence to the contrary, facts that call into question the existence of basic protection against return must be carefully assessed.

In the case of *Harbans Rai Singh*,[167] for example, the Immigration Appeal Board dismissed the applicant's alleged fear of persecution in his country of birth, India, on the ground that he possessed a British passport, and could accordingly expect to be protected by the United Kingdom. Evidence was adduced that the claimant's passport had been altered to delete his right of abode in the United Kingdom, thus raising the obvious possibility that the claimant's British nationality would provide him with less than fully effective protection. In these circumstances, the Board should have satisfied itself that its reliance on apparent second nationality was warranted before dismissing the claim.

Similarly, dual nationality is not to be equated with the right to claim a second nationality. In *James Patrick Gillen*[168] the Board treated the claimant's apparent right to qualify for a British passport as sufficient to constitute both his country of citizenship, the Republic of Ireland, and the United Kingdom as countries of reference. There was no evidence that the claimant had ever been admitted to British territory outside Northern Ireland; moreover, the claimant gave uncontradicted testimony that entry to the United Kingdom had in fact been refused to other persons similarly situated. The dilemma here is a logical extension of the concern to ensure *effective* nationality before assessing the adequacy of a refugee claim: only the degree of risk in those states that are known to be obliged to allow the re-entry of the claimant is relevant, as it is to one of those states that the putative refugee would in most cases be sent back if not admitted to the country of refuge.

2.5.2 Stateless Persons

Refugee law exists to interpose the protection of the international system where a domestic government fails to protect an individual or collectivity under its national jurisdiction. The position of stateless persons is thus anomalous: Are all stateless persons refugees because by definition they do not benefit from national protection? Or conversely are stateless persons excluded from refugee status because their dilemma stems not from the failure of a national government to protect them, but rather from the absence of a state that can be said to have a duty of protection toward them?

---

[167] Immigration Appeal Board Decision T82-9359, C.L.I.C. Notes 44.7, July 8, 1982.

[168] Immigration Appeal Board Decision T83-9750, August 15, 1984. *See also Attorney General of Canada v. Patrick Francis Ward*, *supra*, note 164.

This conceptual confusion is historically explicable. In the first phase of international refugee law, formal statelessness was a condition precedent to recognition as a refugee.[169] The expanded focus of refugee law in the years leading up to the Second World War recognized *de facto* lack of protection as an equally compelling basis for international protection, but continued to protect stateless persons adrift in the international system as refugees.[170] The divorce of *de jure* statelessness and refugee status came only during the drafting of the 1951 Convention.

The background study prepared by the Secretary General in 1949[171] proposed a revised and consolidated convention relating to the status of all persons without national protection. The Economic and Social Council approved the drafting of a convention which would extend comprehensive humanitarian protection to both persons who lacked formal or *de jure* protection ("stateless persons") and persons who lacked *de facto* protection, notwithstanding their retention of a particular nationality ("refugees").[172] The Conference of Plenipotentiaries, however, was of the view that refugees presented a more serious problem of humanitarian need:[173] the problems of stateless persons were characterized as distinct,[174] less urgent than the needs of refugees,[175] and fundamentally giving rise to less of a social problem[176] than the international protection of refugees. As such, it was agreed to restrict the scope of the Convention to those persons who required protection from a state to which they were formally returnable, and to leave the problems of the stateless population to be dealt with by a later and less comprehensive conventional regime.[177]

---

169 *See* Section 1.1.1, *supra*.

170 *See* Section 1.1.2, *supra*.

171 U.N. Doc. E/1112, February 1, 1949.

172 *Id.*, at 1.

173 "The applicability of the draft convention should . . . be limited to refugees. It should not be based upon a confusion between the humanitarian problems of refugees and the primarily legal problems of stateless persons, which should be dealt with by a body of legal experts, but should not be included in the proposed convention": Statement of Mr. Henkin of the U.S.A., U.N. Doc. E/AC.32/SR.2, at 6, January 26, 1950.

174 "Like the French Government, the Government of the United States considered that the problem of refugees differed from that of stateless persons and ought to be considered separately": Statement of Mr. Henkin of the U.S.A., U.N. Doc. E/AC.32/SR.2, at 5, January 26, 1950.

175 "It was . . . indisputable that refugees and *de facto* stateless persons were more unfortunately placed than *de jure* stateless persons, and it was therefore more urgent to remedy their situation": Statement of Mr. Gurreiro of Brazil, U.N. Doc. E/AC.32/SR.3, at 4, January 26, 1950. Several other delegates, including the representatives of both Denmark and Turkey, agreed: U.N. Doc. E/AC.32/SR.3, at 6, January 26, 1950.

176 "[I]ncluding in the convention provisions to cover stateless persons who were not refugees . . . was secondary in the sense that the situation of stateless persons who were not refugees did not raise any urgent social or humanitarian problem": Statement of Mr. Rain of France, U.N. Doc. E/AC.32/SR.3, at 4, January 26, 1950.

177 The *Convention relating to the Status of Stateless Persons*, 360 U.N.T.S. 5158, did not come into force until June 6, 1960. While the structure of the two conventions is quite similar, "[t]he draft Convention on the Status of Refugees, however, gave somewhat greater benefits,

It is thus clear that statelessness *per se* does not give rise to a claim to refugee status.[178] On the other hand, the drafters of the Convention were equally unequivocal in their view that stateless persons could, in some situations, qualify as refugees.[179] Where a stateless person has been admitted to a given country with a view to continuing residence of some duration,[180] and subsequently finds herself in a position of being deprived of the protection of that state, she may find herself in a predicament comparable to that of a refugee with a nationality. This is only so, however, when the stateless person can be said to have a country of "former habitual residence" in the sense of a state that has evinced some degree of willingness to allow her to remain in its territory and to which she would be returnable if refugee protection were not granted.[181]

To qualify as a refugee, then, the stateless person must stand in a relationship to a state which is broadly comparable to the relationship between a citizen and her country of nationality. Because the notion of a "former habitual residence" is intended to establish a point of reference for stateless refugee claimants that is the functional equivalent of a country of nationality,[182] it implies some degree of formal responsibility for protection of the putative refugee.[183] A purposive interpretation of "former habitual residence"

---

it being assumed that States would be willing to go further in respect of refugees than in respect of stateless persons generally, in view of the greater humanitarian factors involved": Statement of Mr. Henkin of the U.S.A., U.N. Doc. E/AC.7/SR.158, at 13, August 15, 1950.

[178] "The problem of stateless persons who were not refugees should, however, be kept separate from the question of refugees, especially since there were doubtless stateless persons who were in no need of protection by the United Nations": Statement of Mr. Henkin of the U.S.A., U.N. Doc. E/AC.32/SR.2, at 8, January 26, 1950.

[179] [T]here were two categories of stateless persons: those who were also refugees, who would, of course, benefit from the draft convention, and those who were not refugees. Almost all refugees were in need, a fact which gave the problem its special urgency. The same could not be said of stateless persons who were not also refugees": Statement of Mr. Rain of France, U.N. Doc. E/AC.32/SR.2, at 7, January 26, 1950.

[180] Statement of Sir Leslie Brass of the United Kingdom, U.N. Doc. E/AC.32/SR.3, at 3, January 26, 1950.

[181] "[T]he real difference between a refugee and a stateless person was that whereas the former might have some sort of travel document, and a particular country might claim his allegiance, the stateless person [who is not also a refugee] would have neither a travel document nor a country of allegiance": Statement of Mr. Robinson of Israel, U.N. Doc. A/CONF.2/SR.31, at 19, July 20, 1951.

[182] The notion of a "country of his former habitual residence" as an appropriate state of reference is applicable only to stateless persons: *see Convention, supra*, note 24, at Art. 1(A)(2), para. 1. This structure was intended to meet the concern expressed by the Director of the International Refugee Organization during the drafting process: "The term 'former habitual residence' has been interpreted by the IRO to apply only to stateless persons . . . . It is, therefore, suggested to reconsider the wording of para. A(2)(i). In case the words 'former habitual residence' should be retained, they might at least be qualified by the terms 'in the case of stateless persons' ": U.N. Doc. E/AC.32/L.16, at 3, January 30, 1950.

[183] "[T]he sub-paragraph had been intended to include persons who had been given the status of refugee by the receiving countries although they had not come under the conventions in force when they entered those countries": Statement of Mr. Henkin of the U.S.A., U.N. Doc. E/AC.32/SR.17, at 7, February 6, 1950.

focuses on the nature of the ties between the claimant and countries in which she has resided, with a particular view to the identification of one or more countries to which she is readmissible. Since refugee law is essentially a means of preventing the sending back of an individual to a state in which a risk of persecution exists, the proper point of reference is the country to which the claimant would normally be expected to return if not admitted to the asylum state.

Under this rubric, Atle Grahl-Madsen's argument that country of former habitual residence should usually be equated with the state in which the stateless claimant first experienced persecution[184] is not fully sustainable. The country from which flight first occurred *is* often the state to which the refugee claimant retains the greatest formal legal ties, simply because subsequent states of residence which admitted her on the basis of her fear of persecution may not have granted her an unconditional right to return.[185] On the other hand, the refugee claimant may have as strong or stronger formal ties to some other country or countries, in which case the claim to need protection should be assessed in relation to any and all countries to which she is formally returnable. This position respects the need for symmetrical treatment of persons with and without nationality, since in the case of the former group the Convention requires proof of lack of protection in all states of nationality.[186]

Conversely, where the stateless refugee claimant has no right to return to her country of first persecution or to any other state, she cannot qualify as a refugee because she is not at risk of return to persecution. Assessment of the claimant's fear of returning to the country of first persecution is a nonsensical exercise, as she could not be sent back there in any event. Thus, when it is determined that the claimant does not have a right to return to any state, and does not therefore have a country of "former habitual residence", her needs should be addressed within the context of the conventional regime for stateless persons[187] rather than under refugee law.

Canadian practice has not clearly interpreted "former habitual residence" in the context of applications by stateless persons, but has defined the notion

---

[184] "[T]he country from which a stateless person had to flee in the first instance remains the 'country of his former habitual residence' throughout his life as a refugee, irrespective of any subsequent changes of factual residence": 1 A. Grahl-Madsen, *The Status of Refugees in International Law*, p. 162 (1966).

[185] In contradistinction to nationals, refugees who choose to leave a country which has provided them with asylum are not necessarily readmissible to that country. While under Article 28 of the *Convention, supra*, note 24, states are obliged in most circumstances to issue a Convention travel document to refugees lawfully staying in their territory, they are entitled to impose a temporal limitation on return: *see Convention, supra*, note 24, at Annex, para. 3. Refugees who fail to return to the issuing state by the specified date may find themselves without the protection of that country. Moreover, refugees who do not travel on either a Convention travel document or a document issued by the state of asylum may have no right of re-entry at all.

[186] *See* Section 2.4.1, *supra*.

[187] *See* note 177, *supra*.

in relation to prior protection. First, the case law has required a significant period of *de facto* residence in the putative state of reference: one year appears to be accepted as a reasonable threshold standard,[188] although most relevant decisions have in fact involved persons who resided in a foreign state for several years.[189] Second, former habitual residence implies *de facto* abode, and not merely ongoing transient presence.[190] Third, and most important, a state is a country of former habitual residence only if the claimant is legally able to return there.[191] These indicia conform to the basic tenets of the concept of former habitual residence in international law, and provide the basis for a jurisprudence interpreting the criteria for determining when a stateless person may properly invoke the protection of refugee law.

---

[188] "It is apparent from the appellant's declaration under oath that she found refuge in France; whether she actually chose France as a country of refuge or whether she went there with her family is immaterial; the fact remains that she did indeed find refuge in France *where she had her last habitual residence for at least one year* before coming to Canada"[Emphasis added]: *Thi Chien Le*, Immigration Appeal Board Decision 77-1099, June 20, 1977, at 3, *per* J.-P. Houle.

[189] For example, six years' residence in the United States as a refugee by a Czech national: *Jiri Kovar* (1973), 8 I.A.C. 226; more than sixteen years' residence in the United Kingdom by a citizen of Hungary: *Gregor Steven Harmaty* (1976), 11 I.A.C. 202; a Hungarian who had accumulated eleven years' combined residence in Switzerland and Austria: *Magdolna Haidekker* (1977), 11 I.A.C. 442; and two years in the Netherlands in the case of a Chilean refugee: *Mireya del Carmen Arriagada Lopez*, Immigration Appeal Board Decision 77-9216, May 31, 1977.

[190] "The (Ethiopian) appellant left home to make a life at sea in 1968 . . . . He established a base and a way of life in the Greek economy . . . . He never applied for refugee status in Greece where he had established a base or in any other country he visited": *Teum Mehamed Abubeker*, Immigration Appeal Board Decision V76-6125, August 26, 1977, at 6, *per* C. Campbell. The claim to refugee status in Canada was granted in the circumstances, as his connection to Greece was insufficient to constitute that country a state of reference.

[191] *Guillermo Sergio Francisco Valenzuela Ponce*, Immigration Appeal Board Decision 81-1231, C.L.I.C. Notes 38.12, November 12, 1981. In this case, the Immigration Appeal Board declined to consider the appellant's claim to be a refugee from his country of refuge, Argentina, on the ground that he did not possess status in that country sufficient to permit his return there.

3

Well-Founded Fear

The hallmark of a Convention refugee is the inability or unwillingness to return home due to a "well-founded fear of being persecuted". Not all involuntary migrants qualify as refugees in law: only those who face a genuine risk of persecution in their state of origin are entitled to the protections established by the Convention. The scope and meaning of persecution will be discussed in Chapter 4, while this chapter addresses the notion of well-founded fear.

It is generally asserted that "well-founded fear" entails two requirements. The first[1] criterion is that the refugee claimant perceive herself to stand in "terror of persecution";[2] her very personal response[3] to the prospect of return to her home country must be an extreme form of anxiety that is neither feigned nor overstated, but is rather sincere and reasonable.[4] Second, the subjective perception[5] of risk must be consistent with available information on conditions in the state of origin, as only those persons whose fear is reasonable can be said to stand in need of international protection. This chapter argues that this two-pronged approach to the definition of "well-founded fear" is neither historically defensible nor practically meaningful. Well-founded fear has nothing to do with the state of mind of the applicant for refugee status, except insofar as the claimant's testimony may provide some evidence of the state of affairs in her home country.[6] The concept of well-founded fear is rather inherently objective, and was intended to restrict the scope of protection to persons who can demonstrate a present or prospective risk of persecution, irrespective of the extent or nature of mistreatment, if any, that they have suffered in the past.

---

[1] It has been argued that " . . . the significance of the Convention's definition of refugee in the realm of international refugee law consists of its substantial, if not predominant, reliance on *subjective* elements": R. Sexton, "Political Refugees, Nonrefoulement and State Practice: A Comparative Study" (1985), 18 Vanderbilt J. Transntl. L. 731, at 733.

[2] Y. Shimada, "The Concept of the Political Refugee in International Law" (1975), 19 Japanese Ann. Intl. L. 24, at 33.

[3] A. Fragomen, "The Refugee: A Problem of Definition" (1970), 3 Case Western Reserve J. Intl. L. 45, at 53.

[4] G. Melander, "The Protection of Refugees" (1974), 18 Scandinavian Studies in Law 153, at 158.

[5] M. Posner, "Who Should We Let In?" (1981), 9 Human Rts. 16, at 18.

[6] *Accord* K. Petrini, "Basing Asylum Claims on a Fear of Persecution Arising from a Prior Asylum Claim" (1981), 56 Notre Dame Lawyer 719, at 724.

3.1 Fear: The Requirement for Prospective Assessment of Risk

In a linguistic context, it is understandable that the reference to "fear" in the Convention definition has led many commentators to assume the relevance of a psychological assessment of the claimant's reaction to conditions in her state of origin.[7] While the word "fear" may imply a form of emotional response,[8] it may also be used to signal an anticipatory appraisal of risk.[9] That is, a person may fear a particular event in the sense that she apprehends that it may occur, yet she may or may not (depending on her personality and emotional makeup) stand in trepidation of it actually taking place. It is clear from an examination of the drafting history of the Convention that the term "fear" was employed to mandate a forward-looking assessment of risk, not to require an examination of the emotional reaction of the claimant.[10]

3.1.1 Historical Foundation of the Prospective Risk Requirement

The immediate legal predecessor of the modern refugee convention was the Constitution of the International Refugee Organization.[11] The IRO definition of a refugee included persons who expressed "valid reasons" for not returning to their country of nationality, including "[p]ersecution, or fear, based on reasonable grounds of persecution . . . . "[12] That is, the Organization had competence over persons who had *already* suffered persecution in their home state, as well as over persons judged by the administering authorities to face a *prospective risk* of persecution were they to be returned to their own country.

---

[7] "An evaluation of the *subjective element* is inseparable from an assessment of the personality of the applicant, since psychological reactions of different individuals may not be the same in identical conditions": United Nations High Commissioner for Refugees, *Handbook on Procedures and Criteria for Determining Refugee Status*, p. 12 (1979). *Accord* P. Weis, "The concept of the refugee in international law" (1960), 87 J. du droit intl. 928, at 970; S. Aga Khan, "Legal Problems Relating to Refugees and Displaced Persons" (1976), Recueil des cours 287, at 297; M. Chemille-Gendreau, "Le concept de réfugié en droit international et ses limites" (1981), 28 Pluriel 3, at 9; P. Hyndman, "The 1951 Convention Definition of Refugee: An Appraisal with Particular Reference to the Sri Lankan Tamil Applicants" (1987), 9 Human Rts. Q. 49, at 68.

[8] "Fear" may defined as "[t]he emotion of pain or uneasiness caused by the sense of impending danger": IV *The Oxford English Dictionary* 117 (1961).

[9] "Fear" may also mean "a particular apprehension of some future evil . . . (an) [a]pprehensive feeling towards anything regarded as a source of danger, or towards a person regarded as able to inflict injury or punishment": *The Oxford English Dictionary, supra,* note 8.

[10] Such an interpretation is consistent with the French-language text of the Convention definition ("*craignant* avec raison d'être persécutée") [Emphasis added]: *Convention relating to the Status of Refugees*, 189 U.N.T.S. 2545, entered into force April 22, 1954 ("*Convention*"), at Art. 1(A)(2).

[11] 18 U.N.T.S. 3, 15 December 1946 ("IRO Constitution"). The IRO was established as a temporary specialized agency of the United Nations, and functioned between 1946 and the establishment of the United Nations High Commissioner for Refugees in 1950.

[12] *Id.,* at s. C(1)(a)(i).

The second part of this definition was particularized in that it took cognizance of "factors in the attitude of the individual himself".[13] From the state perspective, it was also functionally subjective: for political and strategic reasons, the Western states which dominated the IRO were prepared to assume the existence of the risks alleged by the refugee claimants to exist in their East Bloc states of origin.[14] The definitional framework itself nonetheless authorized an *objective* assessment of risk: Was the refugee claimant an individual who, even though she had not already been persecuted, might be in jeopardy in her state of origin because of who she was or what she believed? The establishment of the alternative formulation of refugee status was thus intended to recognize the importance not only of sheltering those who had already been persecuted, but equally of extending protection to those who could be spared from prospective harm. Both groups were viewed as having "valid reasons" for not returning to their home state. The IRO refugee definition did not, however, enable claimants to vindicate purely subjective concerns about impending harm, except insofar as the controlling states were prepared to classify such fears as objectively demonstrable.

The definitional structure of the IRO Constitution was the initial point of reference in formulating the Convention refugee definition.[15] Its dualistic central criterion — including either past persecution or prospective risk of persecution — was clearly the major influence on the three draft definitions submitted to the first session of the Ad Hoc Committee on Refugees and Stateless Persons. The United States' proposal,[16] for example, spoke of persons outside their country "because of persecution or fear of persecution";[17] the French[18] and British[19] advocated only the prospective branch

---

[13] Statement of the Secretary-General, U.N. Doc. A/C.3/527 at 7, October 26, 1949. *Accord* 1 A. Grahl-Madsen, *The Status of Refugees in International Law*, p. 175 (1966): "[I]t is apparent that the likelihood of becoming a victim of persecution may vary from person to person. For example, a well-known personality may be more exposed to persecution than a person who has always remained obscure. Also, some persons are more strong-willed or more outspoken than others, and therefore more susceptible to attract the attention of the authorities than other people."

[14] It was the coincidence of ideology between the refugees and the Western states which operated the International Refugee Organization that gave the appearance of a subjectively inspired protection system. The "valid reasons" criterion itself provided a means by which states could require objective evidence of harm before granting refugee status. *See* J. Hathaway, "The Evolution of Refugee Status in International Law: 1920-1950" (1984), 33 I.C.L.Q. 348, at 374-79.

[15] [T]he General Assembly had envisaged a definition of refugees corresponding to that contained in the Constitution of the IRO, on the understanding that that definition must not be static . . . ": Statement of Mr. Henkin of the U.S.A., U.N. Doc. E/AC.32/SR.5, at 3, January 30, 1950. *Accord* A. Grahl-Madsen, *supra*, note 13, at 173: " 'Well-founded fear' is a technical term, evolved by the drafters of the Refugee Convention from the clumsy phrase 'persecution, or fear based on reasonable grounds of persecution' employed in Part I, section C, of Annex I to the IRO Convention."

[16] U.N. Doc. E/AC.32/L.4, January 18, 1950.

[17] *Id.*, at Art. A(2).

[18] U.N. Doc. E/AC.32/L.3, January 17, 1950.

[19] U.N. Doc. E/AC.32/L.2, January 17, 1950.

of the test: "owing to a justifiable fear of persecution"[20] and "serious apprehension based on reasonable grounds . . . of . . . persecution"[21] respectively.

The compromise that emerged from the drafting process was to establish present or prospective assessment of risk as the norm for refugee protection, but to continue to honour the past persecution standard for persons within the scope of a pre-1951 refugee agreement. The Israeli and American delegates took the lead in insisting that the victims of Naziism and other refugees already protected under earlier accords should retain their entitlement to protection either because of anticipated harm were they to be returned, or as a result of "sentimental reasons"[22] based on past persecution. The propriety of extending protection to these refugees on the basis of their subjective concerns was explicitly argued as a justifiable exception to the norm of objective, prospective assessment:

> If the objective criteria of the first category were applied to such cases, an injustice would be committed. In point of fact, the reasons why some of the refugees did not return to their countries of origin were not objective but subjective. They were not being prevented from returning; in some cases they were even invited to return. But they no longer had the courage or desire to do so. Thus, persons who had left Germany, not of their own accord, but for reasons outside their own desires, could not refer to persecutions which no longer existed. It was their horrifying memories which made it impossible for them to consider returning.[23]

In the Convention as ultimately adopted, therefore, persons determined to be refugees under earlier arrangements are not required to demonstrate a well-founded fear of being persecuted,[24] and are not automatically subject to cessation of refugee status if conditions become safe in their homeland.[25]

It was the intention of the drafters, however, that all other refugees should have to demonstrate "a present fear of persecution"[26] in the sense that they "are or may in the future be deprived of the protection of their country of origin".[27] Thus, it was agreed that the first branch of the IRO test[28] which

---

[20] *Supra*, note 18, at Art. 1(1)(b).

[21] *Supra*, note 19, at Art. 1(2)(b).

[22] Statement of Mr. Henkin of the U.S.A., U.N. Doc. E/AC.32/SR.18, at 5, February 8, 1950.

[23] Statement of Mr. Robinson of Israel, U.N. Doc. E/AC.32/SR.18, at 4, February 8, 1950.

[24] *Convention, supra*, note 10, at Art. 1(A)(2).

[25] "This Convention shall cease to apply to any person (sic) falling under the terms of Section A if . . . [h]e can no longer, because the circumstances in connexion with which he has been recognized as a refugee have ceased to exist, continue to refuge to avail himself of the protection of the country of his nationality; [*p*]*rovided that this paragraph shall not apply to a refugee falling under section A(1) of this article* [*which lists refugees protected under earlier arrangements*] *who is able to invoke compelling reasons arising out of previous persecution for refusing to avail himself of the protection of the country of nationality*" [Emphasis added]: *Convention, supra*, note 10, at Art. 1(C)(6).

[26] Statement of Sir Leslie Brass of the United Kingdom, U.N. Doc. E/AC.32/SR.18, at 6, February 8, 1950.

[27] Statement of Mr. Rochefort of France, U.N. Doc. A/C.3/529, at 4, November 2, 1949.

[28] *Supra*, note 12.

focused on past persecution should be omitted in favour of the "well-founded fear of being persecuted" standard,[29] involving evidence of a present or prospective risk in the country of origin. The use of the term "fear" was intended to emphasize the forward-looking nature of the test, and not to ground refugee status in an assessment of the refugee claimant's state of mind. This interpretation is buttressed by the fact that the Convention provides for the cessation of refugee status upon the establishment of safe conditions in the country of origin, whether or not the refugee continues to harbour a subjective fear of return.[30] In consequence, it is not accurate to speak of the Convention definition as "containing both a subjective and an objective element":[31] it is rather an objective test to be administered in the context of present or prospective risk for the claimant.

3.1.2 The Practical Imperative for Prospective Assessment of Risk

In addition to the historical reasons why "fear" should be interpreted as mandating an anticipatory, objective assessment of risk rather than a subjective evaluation of the claimant's concerns, it would be anomalous to define international legal obligations in such a way that persons facing the same harm would receive differential protection. Why should states be expected to distinguish among persons similarly at risk on the basis of variations of individual temperament or tolerance? Why should an individual of stoic disposition be viewed as less worthy of protection than one who is easily scared, or who proclaims her concerns with great fervour?[32] Yet surely this is the implication of giving "substantial, if not primary weight to a claimant's own assessment of his or her own situation."[33]

Logic dictates that since the central issue is whether or not an individual can safely return to her state,[34] the claimant's anxiety level is simply not a

---

[29] *Convention, supra*, note 10, at Art. 1(A)(2).

[30] *Convention, supra*, note 10, at Art. 1(C)(5) and (6).

[31] *See*, e.g., G. Melander, *supra*, note 4; G. Gilbert, "Right of Asylum: A Change of Direction" (1983), 32 I.C.L.Q. 633, at 644.

[32] *Accord* A. Grahl-Madsen, *supra*, note 13, at 174: "[T]he frame of mind of the individual hardly matters at all. Every person claiming . . . to be a refugee has 'fear' . . . of being persecuted in the sense of the present provision, irrespective of whether he jitters at the very thought of his return to his home country, is prepared to brave all hazards, or is simply apathetic or even unconscious of the possible dangers."

[33] R. Sexton, *supra*, note 1, at 733. *Accord* P. Hyndman, "Refugees Under International Law with a Reference to the Concept of Asylum" (1986), 60 Australian L.J. 148, at 149; "The decision-maker must be satisfied that the person in question subjectively has a real fear."

[34] "Some member of Congress claim that the reason for the original decision to leave is the only critical issue — and that the prospect of persecution upon return is insufficient to qualify a person as a refugee. That argument, however, transforms language that focuses on why an individual 'is unable or unwilling to return' into a provision that places sole emphasis on reasons for departing": H. Fish, Jr., "A Congressional Perspective on Refugee Policy", [1983] World Refugee Survey 48, at 50. *Accord* D. Gross, "The Right of Asylum Under United States Law" (1980), 80 Columbia L. Rev. 1125, at 1134.

relevant consideration. This is in keeping with the basic nature of the international human rights undertaking, which binds states to respect objective indicators of human dignity as defined in universal terms.[35] These standards are common to all, and do not vary as a function of particularized perceptions or concerns.

3.1.3 Subjective Fear as a Negative Constraint on the "Objective Trump"

The experience of Canadian courts in attempting to "acknowledge . . . the applicant's subjective fear"[36] in the process of refugee determination demonstrates the need to dispense with this erroneous interpretation of the Convention's structure. Proof of an "irrepressible",[37] "inconquerable"[38] fear is asserted to be at the heart of the protection decision. The individuality of feelings and variations in their intensity are said to be recognized[39] in the context of a host of factors, including "age, education, physical and moral strength of the subject".[40] Indeed, several Canadian decisions have explicitly adopted the UNHCR's position:

> An evaluation of the subjective element is inseparable from an assessment of the personality of the applicant, since psychological reactions of different individuals may not be the same in identical conditions.[41]

In reality, though, the practical impediments[42] to the meaningful evaluation of the claimant's subjective assessment of concern have led courts to

---

[35] "The Universal Declaration not only reflects a consensus of world opinion on the nature of the fundamental rights and freedoms belonging to every individual, but also expresses a unanimity of belief in the principle that the inherent dignity and worth of the human person requires respect for and protection of that person's rights": V. Saari and R. Higgins Cass, "The United Nations and the International Protection of Human Rights: A Legal Analysis and Interpretation" (1977), Ca. W. Intl. L.J. 591, at 597.

[36] *Joseph Adjei v. Minister of Employment and Immigration* (1989), 7 Imm. L. Rev. (2d) 169 (F.C.A.), at 171.

[37] *Amjad Ali Chaudry*, Immigration Appeal Board Decision M82-1160, September 29, 1982, at 4; *Jose Mariano Aguilar Vides*, Immigration Appeal Board Decision M83-1009, February 3, 1983, at 2; *Rouzbeh Amjadishad*, Immigration Appeal Board Decision M85-1935, May 13, 1987, at 4.

[38] *Gilberto Chonta Gallegos*, Immigration Appeal Board Decision M83-1588, January 25, 1984, at 1.

[39] "Fear, even well-founded or reasonable fear, is a subjective feeling within the person who experiences it. Its compelling and constraining power can vary in intensity from one person to another and should be evaluated in the light of the particular circumstances of each case": *Louis-Paul Mingot* (1973), 8 I.A.C. 351, at 356. *Accord Marc Georges Sévère* (1974), 9 I.A.C. 42, at 46.

[40] *Lionel Medina Aragon*, Immigration Appeal Board Decision 77-1084, May 26, 1977, at 3.

[41] UNHCR, *supra*, note 7, p. 12. *See Ayadurai Gerard Ravindiran*, Immigration Appeal Board Decision V86-6067, March 26, 1987; *Sylvia Dytlow*, Immigration Appeal Board Decision V87-6361X, October 29, 1987, at 8, *per* A. Wlodyka; *Jorge Pizarro Parada*, Immigration Appeal Board Decision V87-6004, January 26, 1988, at 9, *per* A. Wlodyka; affirmed by Federal Court of Appeal Decision A-696-88, April 3, 1989.

[42] A sense of the awkwardness of the subjective assessment of risk can be gleaned from the

apply something of an "objective trump" which makes it unnecessary to examine subjective fear in most cases with a strong objective foundation, and which enables evidence that tends to deny the existence of risk to override even the most fervently stated fear of persecution. In the result, the two-pronged "subjective" and "objective" assessment has been functionally converted to a single objective standard, ironically bringing Canadian practice into line with the original intentions of the drafters of the Convention.[43]

In *Maria Beatriz Maldonado Verga*,[44] for example, the Board was confronted with a claimant who suffered from neurotic anxiety as a result of what she perceived to be a pattern of taunting, ridicule, and surveillance consequent to her opposition to the Chilean military dictatorship. The decision in the case did not question the sincerity of the applicant's subjectively held fears, but nonetheless dismissed her claim on the ground that in objective terms her concerns were "exaggerated".[45] In *Bakhshish Gill Singh*,[46] the Board examined the claim of a former Indian government official who testified that he was being pursued by authorities in that country in consequence of his work on behalf of the Sikh cause:

> The majority of the Board is of the view that Mr. Gill has a subjective fear of returning to India . . . . In the opinion of the majority, his demeanour suggested a genuine subjective fear. The hasty reaction to a statement by a friend regarding a possible arrest, namely leaving his job of 22 years, is in keeping with such a subjective fear by a highly strung and excitable person . . . . However, the question that remains is whether Mr. Gill's fear is rationally based, in other words, whether an examination of the facts presented at the hearing suggests that . . . there is an objective basis for Mr. Gill's subjective fear. In the opinion of the majority, there is no such objective basis.[47]

Both of these cases exemplify the generally accepted view that subjective fear "must and can be assessed objectively".[48]

---

guidelines prepared by the United Nations to assist states in the interpretation of the Convention definition: "It will be necessary to take into account the personal and family background of the applicant, his membership of a particular racial, religious, national, social or political group, his own interpretation of his situation, and his personal experiences — in other words, everything that may serve to indicate that the predominant motive for his application is fear. Fear must be reasonable. Exaggerated fear, however, may be well-founded if, in the circumstances of the case, such a state of mind can be regarded as justified": UNHCR, *supra*, note 7, p. 12.

[43] *See* text *supra* at Section 3.1.1, note 26 ff.

[44] Immigration Appeal Board Decision 79-9002, C.L.I.C. Notes 6.16, March 22, 1979.

[45] *Id.*, at 11. *See also Jorge Pizarro Parada*, Immigration Appeal Board Decision V87-6004, January 26, 1988, at 10, *per* A. Wlodyka; affirmed by Federal Court of Appeal Decision A-696-88, April 3, 1989.

[46] Immigration Appeal Board Decision V87-6246X, July 22, 1987.

[47] *Id.*, at 4, *per* D. Anderson.

[48] *Munir Mohamad Adem Suleiman*, Immigration Appeal Board Decision V81-6246, November 16, 1983, *per* G. Loiselle. *Accord Marc Georges Sévère*, (1974) 9 I.A.C. 42; *Guillermo Lautaro Diaz Fuentes* (1974), 9 I.A.C. 323; affirmed on other grounds at (1974), 52 D.L.R. (3d) 463 (F.C.A.); *Oscar Suarez Cleito*, Immigration Appeal Board Decision M81-1219, December 8,

How is this objective assessment of subjective fear to occur? In *Rouzbeh Amjadishad*[49] the Board held:

> . . . Subjective fear is capable of objective assessment; in other words, a person claiming refugee status must establish consistently, plausibly and credibly that specific events or designated persons intervened in his life so that there arose in him an almost irrepressible feeling of a physical or psychological threat against him or against his fundamental rights as a human being.[50]

This analysis thus equates the sincerity of the claimant's subjective fear with the coherence of her testimony.[51] On the one hand, this approach is factually flawed because persons suffering from genuine, post-traumatic anxiety are often unable adequately to recall information, much less relate it in an articulate manner.[52] Moreover, it represents a simple collapsing of the "subjective element" into the "objective element"[53] of the refugee definition, since the assessment of credibility is supposed to be a means of establishing with as much precision as possible the true extent of the objective risk faced by the refugee claimant — not of giving force to emotions or feelings.

The more pernicious interpretations of the "fear" criterion involve the disentitlement of persons whose claims to refugee status may have been otherwise objectively solid. First, the Board has sometimes ruled that persons who do not avail themselves of the earliest opportunity to flee their state of origin cannot reasonably be said to fear persecution in that country.[54] Second,

---

1981; *Seraq Bozkal Mehmet Mohamed*, Immigration Appeal Board Decision M83-1011, January 25, 1983; *Jagdish Gill Singh*, Immigration Appeal Board Decision V86-6351X, April 22, 1987; *Carlos Alberto Sanes Suarez*, Immigration Appeal Board Decision M86-1587X, September 30, 1987.

[49] Immigration Appeal Board Decision M85-1935, May 13, 1987.

[50] *Id.*, at 4 *per* M. Doré. *Accord Raul Garcia Zavala*, Immigration Appeal Board Decision 81-1222, C.L.I.C. Notes 45.10, June 29, 1982.

[51] This view is consistent with the position of the United Nations: "Due to the importance that the definition attaches to the subjective element, an assessment of credibility is indispensable where the case if not sufficiently clear from the facts of the record": UNHCR, *supra*, note 7, p. 12. The need to assess credibility is apparent, but it is not a means of giving force to subjective feelings. It is rather intended to test the objective plausibility of the testimony offered in evidence by the refugee claimant.

[52] *See* discussion of expert psychiatric evidence on this subject in *Mario Benito Fuentes Leiva*, Immigration Appeal Board Decision 79-9101, C.L.I.C. Notes 27.12, November 13, 1980, at 4-6.

[53] It is argued by some that this diminution of the role of a purely subjective element is part of an effort by states to minimize the influence of individual claimants in the refugee determination process: M. Chemille-Gendreau, *supra*, note 7, at 9.

[54] In *Oscar Manuel Diaz Duran*, the Board observed that " . . . the applicant alleged that for the period 1975 to 1979 he has had to move from friend to friend and never had an opportunity to work as he was afraid of being detained again as he was released by a friend, without authorization, and also because of the fact that he did not report for military service at age eighteen. The Board finds it incredible that after having suffered for all these years the applicant, after obtaining his passport on 18th January, 1979, waited until the 27th of May, 1979 to leave his country, a period of more than four months": Immigration Appeal Board Decision 80-9116, April 16, 1980, at 2-3, *per* U. Benedetti; affirmed on other grounds at (1980), 42 N.R. 342. *See generally* Section 2.3, *supra*.

claims have been denied on the ground that those who truly fear return to their state ought reasonably to claim protection in intermediate countries of potential refuge, rather than disclosing their fear only upon entry into Canada.[55] Third, and most frequently asserted, is the notion that genuinely fearful persons would not delay in making their need for protection known to Canadian authorities, and would in any event seek status before deportation is imminent.[56] In *Harjinder Dhillon Singh*,[57] for example, it was observed that the claimant

> . . . did not claim refugee status upon his arrival in Canada, . . . he worked illegally in Canada for a year and a half, using fraudulent documentation to do so, and only at the time of his arrest did he make a claim to refugee status. Is this the behaviour of a man with a well-founded fear of persecution? In the opinion of the Board, it is not.[58]

The conceptual difficulties in the drawing of these conclusions have been previously discussed,[59] but it must surely be conceded that whatever the relationship between delay in the presentation of a claim to refugee status and the genuineness of the need for protection, these concerns speak only to an objective evaluation of credibility, not to the assessment of subjective fear.[60]

---

[55] "It is hard to believe that a person in the grip of an uncontrollable fear of being persecuted for political or other reasons does not make any effort to eradicate this fear when the opportunity arises": *Luis Omar Reyes Ferrada*, Immigration Appeal Board Decision T81-9476, September 18, 1981, at 4, *per* J.-P. Houle. *Accord Jasbir Singh*, Immigration Appeal Board Decision T83-9400, April 14, 1983, at 5, *per* D. Davey: "Whereas the Board has consistently held that it is not necessary to seek refugee status in the first country reached, it is not supportive of a genuine fear of persecution for a person to travel by ship to fifteen or sixteen countries without seeking refugee status." The Federal Court of Appeal in *Marcel Simon Chang Tak Hue v. Minister of Employment and Immigration* has, however, recently confined this approach to situations where the objective need for protection has remained constant since departure from the state of origin: Federal Court of Appeal Decision A-196-87, March 8, 1988. *See generally* Section 2.3, *supra*.

[56] [H]e did not apply for [refugee status] on his arrival in Canada but waited until an Inquiry was convened by the Canadian Immigration authorities. The Board is of the opinion that the actions of the applicant are not those of a political refugee who is afraid of returning to his home country": *Tawfiq Mohammed Tawfiq Al-Shanti*, Immigration Appeal Board Decision 79-9055, April 5, 1979, at 7, *per* U. Benedetti. *Accord Yaw Opoku-Gyamfi*, Immigration Appeal Board Decision V80-6253, August 13, 1980; affirmed on other grounds by Federal Court of Appeal Decision 80-A-67; *Harbhajan Washir Singh*, Immigration Appeal Board Decision T79-9454, December 7, 1982.

[57] Immigration Appeal Board Decision T84-9049, October 21, 1985.

[58] *Id.*, at 5, *per* B. Suppa.

[59] *See* text *supra* at Section 2.4, note 137 ff.

[60] Serious questions should be raised about the utility of this type of evidence in the objective context as well: "The Board seemed to prefer form to substance in attempting to rank the honesty and openness of the applicant as the primary consideration . . . . With little knowledge of the Canadian immigration process, the individual may not even know of the existence of this privilege to claim protection as a refugee under the Act. The timeliness of the application does not make an individual any more or less of a refugee until all the facts are examined. That the applicant will demonstrate fear is expected; is it not logical that this fear will carry over

At most, then, delay in departure or the presentation of a refugee claim may need to be explained by a refugee claimant who wishes her testimony to be relied upon in support of her case.[61] It is entirely inappropriate, however, to equate delay with an absence of subjective fear, thereby giving unwarranted weight to one factor in the determination of a claimant's credibility.

3.1.4 Fear as an Aspect of the Objective Assessment of Risk

The recent decision of the British House of Lords in *Sivakumaran*[62] provides a thorough analysis of the meaning of the phrase "well-founded fear", drawing richly on the drafting history and internal context of the Convention. Lord Keith refutes the notion that the appropriate test is anything other than objective:

> . . . the general purpose of the convention is surely to afford protection and fair treatment to those for whom neither is available in their own country *and does not extend to the allaying of fears not objectively justified, however reasonable these fears may appear from the point of view of the individual in question . . . .* Fear of persecution, in the sense of the convention, is not to be assimilated to a fear of instant personal danger arising out of an immediately presented predicament . . . . *The question is what might happen if he were to return to the country of his nationality.* He fears that he might be persecuted there. Whether that might happen can only be determined by examining the actual state of affairs in that country. [Emphasis added][63]

In a concurring judgment, Lord Goff states succinctly:

> . . . the true object of the convention is not just to assuage fear, however reasonably and plausibly entertained, but to provide a safe haven for those unfortunate people whose fear of persecution is in reality well founded.[64]

These conclusions are historically and logically compelling, and are moreover consistent with practice in continental Europe.[65] Their explicit adop-

---

into dealings with governmental authorities generally?" C. Wydrzynski, "Refugees and the *Immigration Act*" (1979), 25 McGill L.J. 154, at 177.

[61] An example of the type of appropriately careful inquiry into delay in the presentation of a claim is provided by dissenting Board member A. Wlodyka in the decision of *Banta Dhaliwal Singh*: "The Board notes that the applicant did not immediately apply for refugee status status in Canada but rather remained some time here legally pursuant to his visa. However, the applicant did ultimately report voluntarily to Canada Immigration to make his refugee claim and the applicant has put forward an explanation of why he did so. His lack of success to obtain a visa from the American Embassy also explains some of his caution . . . . I am prepared to give the said applicant the benefit of the doubt in my finding that he has a subjective fear of persecution": Immigration Appeal Board Decision M87-6103X, April 30, 1987, at 12.

[62] *R. v. Secretary of State for the Home Department, ex parte Sivakumaran*, [1988] 1 All E.R. 193 (H.L.).

[63] *Id.*, at 196-97, *per* Lord Keith of Kinkel.

[64] *Id.*, at 202, *per* Lord Goff of Chieveley.

[65] In the Federal Republic of Germany, for example, "[s]eule compte . . . selon la jurispru-

tion in Canadian law would serve two purposes: first, it would end the lip service currently paid to the relevance of the claimant's emotional state to the determination of risk; and, second, it would establish clearly that negative inferences tending to show an absence of subjective fear are not a sufficient ground upon which to deny refugee status. The sole implication of the "fear" criterion of the definition is that the assessment of risk must occur within a *prospective* context. In other words, irrespective of what the claimant has or has not already experienced, the question to be asked is whether there is reason to believe that she requires safe haven from anticipated risk in her state of origin.

3.2 Well-Founded Assessment of Risk: Stating the Test

If the Convention is concerned only with the prospective assessment of risk, what then is the threshold of concern required to substantiate a claim to refugee status? Under what circumstances can it be said that refugee law ought to recognize the legitimacy of a claimant's professed need for protection?

The drafting history of the Convention itself is informative in only the most general terms. An individual is a refugee if she has a "justifiable"[66] case, "good reasons"[67] to flee, and "reasonable grounds"[68] for concern. While these formulations reinforce the objective nature of the test, they do not set a clear standard for determination. Nor does the explanation offered by the UNHCR advance this understanding very far. We are told only that a "well-founded" fear is one that is "supported by an objective situation",[69] and that ultimately this objective test is rooted in subjectivity:

> In general, the applicant's fear should be considered well-founded if he can establish, to a reasonable degree, that his continued stay in his country of origin has become *intolerable to him* for the reasons stated in the definition, or would for the same reasons be intolerable if he returned there. [Emphasis added][70]

This confusing formulation may be rooted in a well-meaning attempt to give priority to the claimant's subjective assessment of need and hence to expand the scope of refugee status. But if this is so, it is not in keeping with the

---

dence actuelle du Tribunal administratif fédéral, l'intention de persécution de l'Etat, indépendamment des convictions ou craintes subjectives du réfugié": P. Nicolaus, "La notion de réfugié dans le droit de R.F.A." (1985), 4 A.W.R. Bull. 158, at 160.

[66] Proposal of France, U.N. Doc. E/AC.32/L.3/Corr. 1, at 1.

[67] Statement of Sir Leslie Brass of the United Kingdom, U.N. Doc. E/AC.32/SR.18, at 6, February 8, 1950, adopted in the Report of the First Session of the Ad Hoc Committee on Statelessness and Related Problems, U.N. Doc. E/1618, at 39.

[68] Proposal of the United Kingdom, U.N. Doc. E/AC.32/L.2, at 1, January 17, 1950.

[69] UNHCR, *supra*, note 7, p. 12.

[70] *Id.*, at 12-13.

intentions of the drafters of the Convention.[71] Moreover, this failure of the international community to come to grips with the essence of the objective test of well-founded fear has forced states to devise their own, and at times unduly restrictive, standards of assessment.

In the United States, for example, the accepted approach for many years was to insist on proof of risk on a balance of probabilities:[72] recognition as a refugee could occur only where harm was "reasonably likely to occur".[73] The Supreme Court of Canada concurred in this standard in a somewhat distinct context in its decision in the case of *Kwiatkowsky v. Minister of Manpower and Immigration*.[74] Drawing on the reasoning of the Federal Court of Appeal in *Lugano v. Minister of Manpower and Immigration*[75] that harm must be "more likely than not"[76] before a refugee claim could proceed to a full hearing, the Supreme Court determined that "the test of balance of probabilities . . . is the correct one."[77]

The *Kwiatkowsky* "balance of probabilities" standard was explicitly binding only on an application to receive a full oral hearing from the Immigration Appeal Board,[78] and did not address the substantive test that should ultimately govern the determination of the claim itself. While there was a formal commitment to the application of the same standard at both levels, the courts in practice tended to impose a somewhat lower threshold at this second stage, repeatedly citing the need to "establish the credibility and plausibility"[79] of the claim in order to meet the objective standard of the

---

[71] "The objects of the convention . . . will surely be fulfilled if refugee status is afforded in cases where there is a real and substantial risk of persecution for a convention reason. The travaux préparatoires, which I have studied with care, do not appear to me to be inconsistent with [this] interpretation . . . . Paragraph 42 of the *Handbook* amounts to a statement of the point of view espoused by the High Commissioner but provides no justification for that point of view as a matter of construction": *Supra*, note 62, at 202, *per* Lord Goff.

[72] A. Evans, "Political Refugees and the United States Immigration Laws: Further Developments" (1972), 66 A.J.I.L. 571, at 575.

[73] D. Gross, *supra*, note 34, at 1134; *accord* P. Woods, "The Term 'Refugee' in International and Municipal Law: An Inadequate Definition in Light of the Cuban Boatlift" (1981), ASILS Intl. L.J. 39, at 44.

[74] (1982), 45 N.R. 116 (S.C.C.).

[75] [1976] 2 F.C. 438, 13 N.R. 322 (C.A.).

[76] *Id.*, at 439.

[77] *Supra*, note 74, at 123, *per* Wilson J.

[78] Under the *Immigration Act* as it existed prior to the decision of the Supreme Court of Canada in the case of *Singh*, a refugee claimant was not entitled to an oral hearing before a person authorized to decide her case. Rather, an immigration official presided over an examination under oath concerning the facts of her claim. The transcript of this examination was then studied by the Refugee Status Advisory Committee, which made a recommendation to the Minister of Employment and Immigration regarding the merits of the case. Those persons who were determined not to be a Convention refugee could seek leave for an oral redetermination hearing before the Immigration Appeal Board.

[79] *Marc Georges Sévère* (1974), 9 I.A.C. 42, at 47, *per* J.-P. Houle. *Accord*, e.g., *Miroslaw Henryk Siedmiogrodzki*, Immigration Appeal Board Decision 80-1100, June 19, 1980; *Oscar*

refugee definition. It was necessary to demonstrate a "cause and effect relationship which would show that the applicant has a genuine fear of returning to his country",[80] although there was no need to show that the claimant faced anything approaching certain persecution upon return.[81] The anomaly of a *de facto* insistence on a more stringent standard at the level of an application for leave than at the hearing on the merits was brought to an end by the Supreme Court of Canada's finding that the provisions of the *Immigration Act* upon which the first stage procedure was based were unconstitutional in that they failed to guarantee claimants the right to an oral hearing before the decision-maker.[82] As noted in a powerful dissenting opinion in *Robert Satiacum*,[83] "[n]ow that the language of the section has been struck down, it seems appropriate that the test which was based on that language also should be struck down".[84]

The creation of this opportunity in Canada for reconsideration of the standard of "well-founded" fear coincided with the issuance of pertinent judgments by each of the Supreme Court of the United States and the British House of Lords. In the case of *I.N.S. v. Cardoza-Fonseca*,[85] the American Supreme Court rejected the traditional "balance of probabilities" standard in favour of a more generous "reasonable possibility" test:

> There is simply no room in the United Nations definition for concluding that because an applicant has a 10% chance of being shot, tortured, or otherwise persecuted, that he or she has no 'well-founded fear' of the event happening . . . . [A] moderate interpretation of the 'well-founded fear' standard would indicate that so long as an objective situation is established by the evidence, it need not be shown that the situation will probably result in persecution, but it is enough that persecution is a reasonable possibility.[86]

Suarez Cleito, Immigration Appeal Board Decision M81-1219, December 8, 1981; *Cumhur Dembil*, Immigration Appeal Board Decision M82-1275, January 6, 1983.

[80] *Harri Chandra Persaud*, Immigration Appeal Board Decision T84-9035, May 30, 1984, at 3, *per* B. Howard. The notion of a preponderance of proof was frequently invoked. *See* e.g., *Mahmuour Rahman*, Immigration Appeal Board Decision M86-1507X, November 5, 1986; *Gabriel Sarfo Kantanka*, Immigration Appeal Board Decision M87-1598X, September 16, 1987; and *Charles Benhene*, Immigration Appeal Board Decision M87-1609X, January 20, 1988.

[81] "[I]t is my opinion that the Board erred in imposing on this applicant and his wife the requirement that they *would be* subject to persecution since the statutory definition required only that they establish a 'well-founded fear of persecution'. The test imposed by the Board is a higher and more stringent test than that imposed by the statute": *Re Naredo and Minister of Employment and Immigration* (1981), 130 D.L.R. (3d) 752, at 753, *per* Heald J.

[82] *Singh et al v. Minister of Employment and Immigration*, [1985] 1 S.C.R. 177.

[83] Immigration Appeal Board Decision V85-6100, July 10, 1987. The dissenting opinion was affirmed by the Federal Court of Appeal on judicial review of this case: *Minister of Employment and Immigration v. Robert Satiacum*, Federal Court of Appeal Decision A-554-87, June 16, 1989.

[84] *Id.*, at 42, *per* D. Anderson.

[85] 467 U.S. 407 (1987).

[86] *Id.*, at 453, *per* Stevens J. *See generally* M. Gibney, "A 'Well-Founded Fear' of Persecution" (1988), 10(1) Human Rts. Q. 109.

This progressive interpretation of the substantive threshold was considered by the House of Lords in the *Sivakumaran*[87] case. The context, however, was quite different. Whereas the American Supreme Court was in the process of liberalizing an exceedingly strict standard of objective proof,[88] the House of Lords was confronted with a decision of the Court of Appeal that had effectively eroded the objective nature of the "well-founded fear" test:

> Fear is clearly an entirely subjective state experienced by the person who is afraid. The adjectival phrase 'well-founded' qualifies, but cannot transform, the subjective nature of the emotion. The qualification will exclude fears which can be dismissed as paranoid, but we do not understand why it should exclude those which, although fully justified on the face of the situation as it presented itself to the person who was afraid, can be shown objectively to have been misconceived.[89]

The House of Lords unanimously rejected this formulation, and insisted on the primacy of the objective foundation of a claim to refugee status. Lord Keith of Kinkel quotes with approval the test adopted by the Supreme Court of the United States,[90] but goes on to posit an arguably more restrictive standard of determination:

> In my opinion the requirement that an applicant's fear of persecution should be well founded means that there has to be demonstrated a *reasonable degree of likelihood* that he will be persecuted for a convention reason if returned to his own country. [Emphasis added][91]

In their concurring judgments, both Lord Templeman and Lord Goff of Chieveley softened the notion of "likelihood" in favour of a test which inquires whether there is evidence of a "real and substantial danger of persecution".[92] Overall, though, the House of Lords standard appears to be somewhat more exacting than the American "reasonable possibility" test.

The first Canadian reference to these emerging views is found in the dissenting opinion of Immigration Appeal Board member David Anderson in *Robert Satiacum*.[93] The judgment rejects the "balance of probabilities" approach as anachronistic,[94] and adopts a "reasonable chance"[95] standard that is indistinguishable from the American test in *Cardoza-Fonseca*.[96] This conceptual breakthrough was explicitly endorsed by the Federal Court of

---

[87] [1988] 1 All E.R. 193 (H.L.)

[88] *See* text *supra* at notes 72-73.

[89] [1987] 3 W.L.R. 1047 (C.A.), at 1052-1053, *per* Sir John Donaldson M.R.

[90] *Supra*, note 87, at 197.

[91] *Supra*, note 62, at 197-98.

[92] *Supra*, note 62, at 199, *per* Lord Templeman, and at 202, *per* Lord Goff of Chieveley.

[93] *Supra*, note 83.

[94] *Supra*, note 83, at 41-42, *See also* text *supra* at notes 78-84.

[95] *Supra*, note 83, at 43.

[96] *Supra*, note 85. *See* text *supra* at notes 85-86.

Appeal in the case of *Joseph Adjei v. Minister of Employment and Immigration*[97] in which the parties agreed to renounce the *Kwiatkowsky*[98]-based "balance of probabilities" test in favour of a new "reasonable chance" standard. Mr. Justice MacGuigan went on to equate the "reasonable chance"[99] test with "good grounds for fearing persecution",[100] and "a 'reasonable' or even a 'serious possibility' as opposed to a mere possibility"[101] of persecution. Most important, the decision expresses clearly its disapproval of the more restrictive British "real and substantial danger" test derived from *Sivakumaran*:[102]

> Despite the terminology sanctioned by the House of Lords for interpreting the British legislation, we are nevertheless of the opinion that the phrase "substantial grounds for thinking" is too ambiguous to be accepted in a Canadian context. It seems to go beyond . . . "good grounds" . . . and even to suggest probability.[103]

In the final analysis, then, Canadian law has chosen to follow the more liberal American trend. Insofar as there is objective evidence to show that there is a reasonable possibility or chance of relevant persecution in the claimant's state of origin, the claim should be adjudged well-founded. In adopting this position, Canada has come clearly into line with dominant[104] scholarly opinion which has consistently rejected the "balance of probabilities" standard in favour of such formulations as "good reasons",[105] "plausible danger",[106] "some proof",[107] "reasonable in the circumstances",[108] "real chance",[109] or "serious possibility".[110] The "reasonable possibility" test is the appropriate compromise between respect for the Convention's commitment to anchor protection decisions in objectively observable risks and the need simultane-

---

[97] (1989), 7 Imm. L.R. (2d) 169 (F.C.A.), at 172.

[98] (1982), 45 N.R. 116 (S.C.C.).

[99] *Supra*, note 97, at 172.

[100] *Id.*

[101] *Supra*, note 97, at 173.

[102] [1988] 1 All E.R. 193 (H.L.)

[103] *Supra*, note 97, at 173-74, *per* MacGuigan J.

[104] For a contrary view, *see*, e.g., D. Martin in C. Sumpter, "Mass Migration of Refugees — Law and Policy" (1982), 76 A.S.I.L.P. 13, at 13.

[105] P. Weis, "The concept of the refugee in international law" (1960), J. de droit intl. 928, at 970.

[106] G. Melander, "The Protection of Refugees" (1974), 18 Scandinavian Studies in Law 153, at 158.

[107] S. Aga Khan, "Legal Problems Relating to Refugees and Displaced Persons" (1976), Recueil des cours 287, at 297.

[108] C. Wydrzynski, "Refugees and the *Immigration Act*" (1979), 25 McGill L.J. 154, at 170.

[109] A. Helton, "Persecution on Account of Membership in a Social Group as a Basis for Refugee Status" (1983), 15 Columbia Human Rts. L. Rev. 39, at 56.

[110] G. Goodwin-Gill, "Entry and Exclusion of Refugees: The Obligations of States and the Protection Function of the Office of the UNHCR" (1980), Michigan Y.B. Intl. L. Studies 291, at 299.

ously to avoid the establishment of an inappropriately high threshold of concern.

One potentially contentious issue that flows from this judicial shift to the "reasonable possibility" standard is that decision-makers may be inclined to set precise though arbitrary "percentage risk thresholds" short of the probability point as the minimum standard for refugee protection. Mr. Justice Stevens' reference to the sufficiency of a 10 per cent chance of persecution[111] should be viewed simply as an exhortation to abandon the rigidity of the "balance of probabilities" test, and not as an invitation to define new, equally rigid standards of attainment. Because the risk of persecution will never be definitively measurable, decision-makers should ask only whether the evidence as a whole discloses a risk of persecution which would cause a reasonable person in the claimant's circumstances to reject as insufficient whatever protection her state of origin is able and willing to afford her.

3.2.1 Relevance of General Evidence of Respect for Human Rights

The appropriate starting point for an analysis of objective conditions within the refugee claimant's state of origin is an examination of that country's general human rights record.[112] Because the insufficiency of state protection is the *sine qua non* for recognition as a refugee, persons who flee countries that are known to commit or acquiesce in persecutory behavior should benefit from a rebuttable presumption that they have a genuine need for protection.[113] The Federal Court made this point in overturning a negative decision involving a Ghanaian whose fear of persecution stemmed from the infamous activities of the Rawlings dictatorship:

> I have mentioned the Board's zeal to find instances of contradiction in the applicant's testimony. While the Board's task is a difficult one, it should not be

---

[111] *Supra*, note 86.

[112] *Nana Adoma Frimpong v. Minister of Employment and Immigration*, Federal Court of Appeal Decision A-765-87, May 12, 1989; *Charles Kofi Owusu Ansah v. Minister of Employment and Immigration*, Federal Court of Appeal Decision A-1265-87, May 19, 1989. *Accord* C. Pompe, "The Convention of 28 July 1951 and the International Protection of Refugees" (1956), Rechtsgeleerd Magazyn Themis 425, republished in English as U.N. Doc. HCR/INF/42, at 10; G. Melander, *supra*, note 106, at 158; K. Petrini, "Basing Asylum Claims on a Fear of Persecution Arising from a Prior Asylum Claim" (1981), 56 Notre Dame Lawyer 719, at 724; B. Tsamenyi, "The 'Boat People': Are They Refugees?" (1983), 5 Human Rts. Q. 348, at 365.

[113] "One reason why this rebuttable presumption can be so vital is that it is widely recognized by international bodies like the United Nations that the fleeing individual is often unable to gather and subsequently offer 'objective' evidence of the claimed persecution . . . . The rebuttable presumption suggested here, in a sense, *is* a form of objective evidence. What it does is to provide some information, some degree of probability, on the level of human rights violations in the claimant's homeland": M. Gibney, "A 'Well-Founded' Fear of Persecution" (1988), 10(1) Human Rights Q. 109, at 119. *Accord* G. Goodwin-Gill, "Non-Refoulement and the New Asylum Seekers" (1986), 26(4) Virginia J. Intl. L. 897.

over-vigilant in its microscopic examination of the evidence of persons who, like the present respondent, testify through an interpreter and tell tales of horror in whose objective reality there is reason to believe.[114]

Conversely, those claimants who come from states which have generally laudable human rights records face a tougher objective threshold: whether through their own testimony or whatever other evidence can be marshalled, they must counter the established perception that their country is one that can be relied upon to afford them meaningful protection.

An effort should be made to gather background human rights data from a broad cross-section of official and non-governmental sources[115] in order to supplement whatever evidence may be adduced by the claimant herself. It is critical that the process of garnering human rights information not be left solely to the refugee claimant: fact-finding is a responsibility that the applicant shares with the examining authority.[116] Moreover, all relevant information which comes to the attention of the determination authority must be shared with the refugee claimant in order that she may have "an opportunity to meet that evidence and to make representations thereon."[117]

In assessing the general human rights information, decision-makers must constantly be on guard to avoid implicitly recharacterizing the nature of the risk based on their own perceptions of reasonability. Simply because a par-

[114] *Benjamin Attakora v. Minister of Employment and Immigration*, Federal Court of Appeal Decision A-1091-87, May 19, 1989, at 4, *per* Hugessen J.; setting aside Immigration Appeal Board Decision T86-10336X, October 14, 1987.

[115] Strict reliance on official governmental reporting has been criticized in two recent Board decisions. In *Antonio Pereira Costa*, use of the U.S. *Country Reports on Human Rights Practices* was appropriately constrained: "The report of a department of government of a foreign state to its legislature can be of little weight, especially when the only purpose of the report is compliance with a named foreign law of which we know nothing and the provenance of the report and the qualifications of those who prepared it are nowhere disclosed": Immigration Appeal Board Decision T87-9107X, July 16, 1987, at 3-4, *per* G. Eglinton. A similar caution may apply with respect to reports generated by the Department of External Affairs: "The fact that no doubt conscientious, even distinguished, Canadian diplomats serving in West Africa have certain views about the nature of governance of Ghana and the legitimacy of the generality of refugee claims by Ghanaians . . . is of no relevance": *Joseph Manso Frimpong*, Immigration Appeal Board Decision T87-10043X, October 29, 1987, at 5, *per* G. Eglinton.

[116] "In most cases a person fleeing from persecution will have arrived with the barest necessities and very frequently even without personal documents. Thus, while the burden of proof in principle rests on the applicant, the duty to ascertain and evaluate all the relevant facts is shared between the applicant and the examiner. Indeed, in some cases it may be necessary for the examiner to use all the means at his disposal to produce the necessary evidence in support of the application": UNHCR, *supra*, note 7, p. 47. To assist this shared process of fact-finding in relation to human rights conditions, the Canadian Immigration and Refugee Board has established a national network of publicly accessible Documentation Centres, which collect and summarize all available sources of relevant information in relation to refugee-producing countries.

[117] *Leonel Eduardo Quinteros Hernandez v. Minister of Employment and Immigration*, Federal Court of Appeal Decision A-506-81, February 12, 1982, *per* Heald J. *Accord Swaran Singh v. Minister of Employment and Immigration*, Federal Court of Appeal Decision A-1346-83, December 3, 1984.

ticular state of affairs may be difficult to understand from the vantage point of the country of adjudication does not give licence to disregard relevant information. As the Immigration Appeal Board carefully observed in a case involving persecution based on family membership:

> We who live in a democratic society where order is maintained by peaceful means may find it hard to believe that the authorities would harass someone either directly or through his family simply because he bore a name that they held in abomination. However, we must keep our personal opinions to ourselves, and instead try to place the situation in its proper context . . . . It is not for me to judge this policy, and I am not about to do so. I am merely describing an internationally acknowledged phenomenon.[118]

Related to this point is the inherent political lens through which the human rights record of the country of origin is viewed.[119] As Goran Melander has noted, we have "a definition of the term 'refugee' which is applicable when political considerations do not prevent states from recognizing a person".[120] Because a finding that the claimant faces a risk of persecution is perceived to imply censure of the state of origin,[121] there is always a risk that concern for the protection of refugees may be subordinated to foreign policy concerns.[122] Where there is political antagonism between the states of origin and asylum, the political lens may result in an enhanced willingness on the part of decision-makers to emphasize negative aspects of the human rights profile.[123] Conversely, if the two states enjoy good relations, the generalized stereotype of the country of origin as an ally may stand in the way of an evenhanded assessment of the risk to a particular claimant.[124] Human rights

---

[118] *Luis Enrique Toha Seguel*, Immigration Appeal Board Decision 79-1150, C.L.I.C. Notes 28.8, November 13, 1980, at 4, *per* J.-P. Houle. *Accord Muhammad Shahidul Islam*, Immigration Appeal Board Decision M82-1278, C.L.I.C. Notes 72.5, June 4, 1984, at 3, *per* E. Chambers.

[119] *See* F. Krenz, "The Refugee as a Subject of International Law" (1966), 15, I.C.L.Q. 90, at 102; M. Iognat-Prat, "L'évolution du concept de réfugié: Pratiques contemporaines en France" (1981), 28 Pluriel 13, at 21; and P. Nicolaus, "La notion de réfugié dans le droit de R.F.A." (1985), 4 A.W.R. Bull. 158, at 160.

[120] G. Melander, *supra*, note 106, at 161.

[121] World Peace Through Law Centre, *Toward the Second Quarter Century of Refugee Law*, p. 11 (1976); P. Hyndman, "Refugees Under International Law with a Reference to the Concept of Asylum" (1986), 60 Australian L.J. 148, at 149.

[122] D. Rickard, "The Rhetoric and the Reality" (1986), Legal Services Bull. 214, at 216.

[123] "If there is political antipathy between the governments of the country of origin and of the country of refuge, it may not be too difficult to win recognition as a refugee. Failing this political constellation, the situation becomes much tougher for the individuals concerned. The different American attitudes to 'refugees' from Cuba and 'entrants' from Haiti may be a case in point": A. Grahl-Madsen, "International Refugee Law Today and Tomorrow" (1982), 20 Archiv des Völkerrechts 411, at 421.

[124] "But those determining eligibility are rather inclined to think in stereotypes, i.e. that a political situation in another country is such that the fear can be regarded as 'well-founded' and that in another country it is not, and here political considerations often play a role": P. Weis, "Convention Refugees and *De Facto* Refugees", in G. Melander and P. Nobel, eds., *African Refugees and the Law*, p. 16 (1978). *Accord* F. Marino-Menendez, "El concepto de

information must therefore be considered in as full and value-neutral a way as possible.[125] If the focus is genuinely to be the welfare of the involuntary migrant,[126] decision-makers must afford weight to inconvenient and politically awkward information that is demonstrative of the risk associated with return.

Finally, it is important to recognize that background human rights information, while important, is not determinative of a claim to refugee status. Its utility is to establish a *rebuttable presumption* of risk or the absence thereof, which must be tested against the whole of the evidence presented. In particular, the testimony of the claimant in relation to her circumstances must always be the central factor in the process of assessing the risk of persecution in the state of origin.[127]

3.2.2 Role of the Refugee Claimant's Testimony

The heart of the refugee determination process is the careful consideration of the claimant's own evidence, whether provided orally or in documentary form.[128] Both the Convention and the UNHCR guidelines are conspicuously silent on the issue of entitlement to an oral hearing.[129] Since the decision of the Supreme Court of Canada in *Singh et al v. Minister of Employment and Immigration*,[130] however, Canadian law has required that all applicants for refugee status receive an opportunity to be heard by the authority responsible for the adjudication of their case.[131] What is the weight,

---

refugiado en un contexto de derecho internacional general" (1983), 35(2) Revista española de derecho internacional 337, at 352.

[125] Given that political goals were arguably at the root of the conceptual framework incorporated in the Convention, there are real limits to the promotion of a neutral humanitarian or human rights based perspective. *See* J. Hathaway, "A Reconsideration of the Underlying Premise of Refugee Law" (1990), 31(1) Harvard Intl. L. J. 129; and M. Chemille-Gendreau, "Le concept de réfugié en droit international et ses limites" (1981), 28 Pluriel 3, at 9.

[126] "The humanitarian thrust of the refugee problem can be lost in a maze of political manoeuvres": C. Wydrzynski, *supra*, note 108, at 170.

[127] "Comment apprécier si la crainte est fondée? La seule solution consiste à mettre en parallèle l'histoire personnelle de l'intéressé et la situation politique dans le pays qu'il a été constraint de fuir": M. Iognat-Prat, *supra*, note 119, at 21. *Accord* K. Petrini, *supra*, note 112, at 724.

[128] "[T]he credibility of an applicant . . . is usually the main factor in establishing whether there exists a 'well-founded fear of persecution' ": *Leonel Eduardo Quinteros Hernandez*, Immigration Appeal Board Decision V80-6192, C.L.I.C. Notes 35.11, August 18, 1981, at 4, *per* F. Glogowski.

[129] "Due to the fact that the matter is not specifically regulated by the 1951 Convention, procedures adopted by States parties to the 1951 Convention and to the 1967 Protocol vary considerably": UNHCR, *supra*, note 7, p. 45. The guidelines prepared by the Executive Committee of UNHCR require only that "[t]he applicant should be given the necessary facilities . . . for submitting his case to the authorities concerned": U.N. Doc. A/32/12/Add.1, at para. 53(6)(e)(iv).

[130] [1985] 1 S.C.R. 177.

[131] Indeed, the Board has expressed its concern that failure to testify may preclude the proper assessment of the claim: *Ebrahim Zbedat*, Immigration Appeal Board Decision 86-9954, C.L.I.C. Notes 106.17, October 30, 1986; affirmed by Federal Court of Appeal Decision A-693-86, October

then, that should be attached to the claimant's own testimony in the assessment of the possibility of persecution?

In Canada, so long as the claimant's testimony is plausible, credible, and frank, it may constitute the whole of the evidence of objective risk necessary to support an affirmative finding of refugee status,[132] even where it consists largely of hearsay evidence.[133] There is no requirement of external corroboration of an uncontradicted credible account,[134] although the refugee claimant may reasonably be expected to address any apparently inconsistent evidence, including that which may be contained in general human rights reports.

In what circumstances will testimony be adjudged plausible, credible, and frank, and hence sufficient to establish the objective foundation of a claim to refugee status? The primary rule has been stated by the Federal Court of Appeal to be that "[w]hen an applicant swears to the truth of certain allegations, this creates a presumption that those allegations are true unless there be reason to doubt their truthfulness."[135] In view of this basic premise, two forms of caution are appropriate before any inferences are drawn that might discount the sworn testimony of a refugee claimant.[136]

First, the decision-maker must be sensitive to the fact that most refugees have lived experiences in their country of origin which give them good reason to distrust persons in authority. They may thus be less than forthright

---

8, 1987; *José Manuel Elias da Cruz*, Immigration Appeal Board Decision T87-9255X, October 27, 1987; *Ajit Singh*, Immigration Appeal Board Decision T81-9741, January 6, 1988; *Lottay Singh*, Immigration Appeal Board Decision V84-6176, February 11, 1988.

[132] C. Blum, 'Who Is a Refugee? Canadian Interpretation of the Refugee Definition" (1986), 1 Imm. J. 8, at 9.

[133] J. Grey, *Immigration Law in Canada*, p. 117 (1984).

[134] *Aram Ovakimoglu v. Minister of Employment and Immigration* (1983), 52 N.R. 67 (F.C.A.), at 6; *Juan Antonio Quereillac Acevedo*, Immigration Appeal Board Decision M85-1398, October 7, 1987. This view contrasts sharply with the traditional preoccupation of authorities in the United States with documentary evidence and the testimony of corroborative witnesses. *See*, e.g., G. Pick, "People Who Live on Hope — and Little Else" (1983), 11 Student Lawyer 12, at 35.

[135] *Ranjit Thind Singh v. Minister of Employment and Immigration*, Federal Court of Appeal Decision A-538-83, November 27, 1983, *per* Heald J.; *accord Alfredo Nelson Villarroel Salvatierra v. Minister of Employment and Immigration*, (1979), 31 N.R. 50 (F.C.A.); and *Pedro Enrique Juarez Maldonado v. Minister of Employment and Immigration*, [1980] 2 F.C. 302 (C.A.).

[136] The Immigration Appeal Board has frequently suggested that a more exacting test be applied in assessing credibility, including " . . . the witness' desire to be truthful; other motives; general integrity; general intelligence; relationship or friendship to other parties; opportunity for exact observations; capacity to observe accurately; firmness of his memory to carry in his mind the facts as observed; ability to resist the influence, frequently unconscious, to modify his recollection; capacity to express what is clearly in his mind; ability to reproduce in the witness box the facts observed; and his demeanour while testifying": *Graciano de Jesus de Almeida*, Immigration Appeal Board Decision T87-9819X, January 7, 1988, at 4, *per* L. Goodspeed. *Accord*, e.g., *Henrie Ezambe*, Immigration Appeal Board Decision M87-1106, June 9, 1987; *Jean Maxene Moly*, Immigration Appeal Board Decision M87-1836X, April 5, 1988.

in their dealings with immigration and other officials, particularly soon after their arrival in an asylum state. The past practice of the Board of assessing credibility on the basis of the timeliness of the claim to refugee status,[137] compliance with immigration laws,[138] or the consistency of statements made on arrival with the testimony given at the hearing[139] is thus highly suspect, and should be constrained in the contextually sensitive manner discussed previously in Chapter 2.[140]

Second, it is critical that a reasonable margin of appreciation be applied to any perceived flaws in the claimant's testimony.[141] A claimant's credibility should not be impugned simply because of vagueness or inconsistencies in recounting peripheral details, since memory failures are experienced by many persons who have been the objects of persecution.[142] Because an understandable anxiety affects most claimants compelled to recount painful facts

---

[137] *See*, e.g., *Jaime Vladimiro Colima Acuna*, Immigration Appeal Board Decision 80-9125, at 5, *per* U. Benedetti: "[T]he applicant decided to come as a visitor and only after being here approximately a week made a claim to refugee status." *But see Muhammad Shahidul Islam*, Immigration Appeal Board Decision M82-1278, C.L.I.C. Notes 72.5, June 4, 1984, at 4, *per* E. Chambers: "Much was made of the fact that Mr. Islam did not immediately, upon his arrival in Canada, declare himself as a refugee claimant to the immigration authorities. Again, we should not apply our standards to one who has lived in fear of uniformed authorities for so long a period. We cannot assume that the niceties of Canadian immigration law are well-known to the inhabitants of the bazaars and villages of Bangladesh." *Accord* C. Wydrzynski, "Refugees and the *Immigration Act*" (1979), 25 McGill L.J. 154, at 177; Minister of Employment and Immigration, "New Refugee Status Advisory Committee Guidelines on Refugee Definition and Assessment of Credibility" (1982), at Guideline 18(a): "A claim may be credible even though it was not made at the earliest possible opportunity. A genuine refugee may well wait until he is safely in the country before making a claim. He cannot, in every case, be expected to claim refugee status at the port of entry."

[138] *See*, e.g., *Ricknauth Mohan*, Immigration Appeal Board Decision T82-9251, May 4, 1982, at 3, *per* U. Benedetti: "On more than one occasion [the claimant] was not very honest in dealing with the immigration authorities . . . . "

[139] *See*, e.g., *Mario Benito Fuentes Leiva*, Immigration Appeal Board Decision 79-9101, April 5, 1979. *But see Abu Sayeed Mohammed Jabed Hossein*, Immigration Appeal Board Decision M87-1040X, April 30, 1987, at 4, *per* R. Julien: "The Board is of the opinion that it is acceptable for a person who had barely arrived in Canada and was in a precarious situation in which he did not know all the hazards of our system, strictly speaking, to answer only the questions asked, without providing further explanations": *Yim Shing Mak*, Immigration Appeal Board Decision V87-6640X, May 17, 1988; Minister of Employment and Immigration, *supra*, note 137, at Guideline 18(e).

[140] *See* Chapter 2, *supra*, at note 103 ff. This is particularly true where the allegedly inconsistent testimony was given through an interpreter. In *Abdi Mohamed Ali*, Immigration Appeal Board Decision T87-9585, February 14, 1989, at 3, member E. Rotman noted that ". . . the Board is satisfied that translation could be a factor in the inconsistencies in the account of events and dates. The Board believes that the claimant should be given the benefit of the doubt."

[141] *Benjamin Attakora v. Minister of Employment and Immigration*, Federal Court of Appeal Decision A-1091-87, May 19, 1989.

[142] This problem was explicitly acknowledged by the Board in *Mario Angel Molina Riquelme*, Immigration Appeal Board Decision 79-9363, C.L.I.C. Notes 22.6, July 9, 1980. In practice, however, the Board has sometimes imposed unwarranted expectations on claimants. In *Jagir Ghuman Singh*, for example, the Board found the applicant's testimony that he had been picked

in a formal and foreign environment, only significant concerns about the plausibility of allegations of direct relevance to the claim should be considered sufficient to counter the presumption that the sworn testimony of the applicant is to be accepted as true. As stated in *Francisco Edulfo Valverde Cerna*:[143]

> The Board does not expect an applicant for Convention refugee status to have a photographic memory for details of events and dates that happened a long time ago, but it is reasonable to expect that important events that happened as a consequence of other events should be found to have taken place in some consistent and logical order.[144]

Ultimately, however, even clear evidence of a lack of candour does not necessarily negate a claimant's need for protection:

> Even where the statement is material, and is not believed, a person may, nonetheless, be a refugee. "Lies do not prove the converse." Where a claimant is lying, and the lie is material to his case, the [determination authority] must, nonetheless, look at all of the evidence and arrive at a conclusion on the entire case. Indeed, an earlier lie which is openly admitted may, in some circumstances, be a factor to consider in *support* of credibility.[145]

Given the objective focus of the Convention definition, the purpose of eliciting evidence from the claimant herself is not to ascertain whether she harbours a subjective fear of return. Rather, it is to establish how circumstances in the homeland impact on her own security, and why she feels compelled to seek protection abroad.[146] Against the backdrop of human rights

---

up and beaten by the police on two or three occasions not to be credible because "[w]hen questioned regarding the alleged beatings, Mr. Singh could not elaborate nor could he support his contention that he would be picked up and jailed were he to return to India": Immigration Appeal Board Decision T82-9689, October 25, 1982, at 3, *per* E. Teitelbaum. *Accord Victor Manuel Trauco Arias*, Immigration Appeal Board Decision T84-9334, February 5, 1986, in which the claimant's confusion at hearing led to a negative assessment of credibility; and *Jaswant Singh*, Immigration Appeal Board Decision T87-9326, September 28, 1987, in which the claimant's inability to recall certain dates of national significance resulted in a finding of lack of credibility.

[143] Immigration Appeal Board Decision V87-6608X, March 7, 1988.

[144] *Id.*, at 4-5, *per* B. Howard.

[145] Minister of Employment and Immigration, *supra*, note 137, at Guideline 18(d). *Accord Oscar Roberto Cruz*, Immigration Appeal Board Decision V83-6807, June 26, 1986; *Monoranchitarasa Nalliah*, Immigration Appeal Board Decision M84-1642, October 20, 1987; and *Tacir Yaliniz v. Minister of Employment and Immigration* (1989), 7 Imm. L.R. (2d) 163 (F.C.A.), at 164, *per* Marceau J.: "While we agree that it is within the province of the Board to assess credibility, we are of the view that the Board's apparently complete rejection of the Applicant's statements was not justified. It seems to us that the Board should have asked itself whether, even assuming some exaggerations, the Applicant had not shown that he had undoubtedly been the victim of harassment of a variety of forms amounting to persecution, making thereby his fear to go back not only genuine but objectively founded."

[146] *See*, e.g., *Vidya Ajodhia*, Immigration Appeal Board Decision M85-1709, November 12, 1987, in which member P. Davey gives more weight to the applicant's account of the racially inspired risk in which she found herself in Guyana than to the official assessments of human rights conditions.

reports from the country of origin, the determination authority must decide whether the individual applicant faces a reasonable chance of serious harm if returned to her home.

3.2.3 Evidence of Individualized Past Persecution

Past persecution is in no sense a condition precedent to recognition as a refugee. The Convention is concerned with protection from prospective risk of persecution,[147] and does not require that an individual should already have been victimized. This principle was recognized in Canada[148] by the decision in *Guillermo Lautaro Diaz Fuentes*:[149]

> . . . he does not need to establish that there has already been persecution; what he is obliged to prove is that he has well-founded fear of being persecuted if he remains in or returns to the country of which he is a citizen or resident, and that owing to such fear he is unable or unwilling to avail himself of the protection of the country of which he is a national.[150]

While the Board's jurisprudence has at times exhibited an unhealthy fixation with past maltreatment,[151] the Federal Court of Appeal has consistently affirmed the propriety of a forward-looking assessment of risk, notably in the cases of *Waldeck Sylvestre v. Minister of Employment and Immigration*,[152] *Re Naredo and Minister of Employment and Immigration*,[153] and

---

[147] "[T]he word 'fear' refers not only to persons who have actually been persecuted, but also to those who wish to avoid a situation entailing the risk of persecution": UNHCR, *supra*, note 7, p. 13.

[148] This view is not shared throughout the community of states parties to the Convention. "A restrictive approach, espoused, for example, by Denmark and Norway, interprets 'well-founded fear' as requiring the applicant to show *prior* persecution at the hands of the oppressive government": A. Helton, "Persecution on Account of Membership in a Social Group as a Basis for Refugee Status" (1983), 15 Columbia Human Rts. L. Rev. 39, at 57. *See also* F. Marino-Menendez, "El concepto de refugiado en un contexto de derecho internacional general" (1983), 35(2) Revista española de derecho internacional 337, at 354.

[149] (1974), 9 I.A.C. 323.

[150] *Id.* at 341, *per* J.-P. Houle. *Accord* Minister of Employment and Immigration, *supra*, note 137, at Guideline 18(f): "A person may be credible claimant even though he has never been persecuted. The absence of actual detention or detection by the authorities or of wounds should not lead to the assumption of fabrication."

[151] *See*, e.g., *Lionel Medina Aragon*, Immigration Appeal Board Decision 77-1084, May 26, 1977 (" . . . in most cases fear can be proven only by substantial evidence e.g. former acts of active persecution"); *Hector Eduardo Contreras Guttierez*, Immigration Appeal Board Decision V80-6220, C.L.I.C. Notes 30.11, March 16, 1981 (concern expressed in majority opinion that claimant "was not disabled in any way in the alleged beatings and torture he received"); *Orhan Demir*, Immigration Appeal Board Decision M82-1274, January 6, 1983 (" . . . he has not produced any evidence that he was persecuted in any way for his religious opinions"); and *Seraq Bozkal Mehmet Mohamed*, Immigration Appeal Board Decision M83-1011, January 25, 1983 ("[T]he only persons who can be recognized as refugees within the meaning of the Convention and of the Act are those who meet the criteria set forth in the definition, and who can demonstrate in a consistent and credible manner that they were victims of acts committed by authorities in their country of nationality . . . .")

[152] Federal Court of Appeal Decision A-34-78, June 12, 1978.

[153] (1981), 130 D.L.R. (3d) 752 (F.C.A.).

Alfredo Manuel Oyarzo Marchant v. Minister of Employment and Immigration:[154]

> . . . the Board appears to have treated what happened to the applicant . . . as not amounting to persecution because it did not include arrest or detention. In so doing the Board . . . has failed to consider what happened not only as to whether it could be in itself a form of persecution, but also whether *it could be the basis*, along with the incidents of 1973 and 1974, of a well-founded *fear of future persecution* . . . . [Emphasis added][155]

It is thus unnecessary to establish past persecution in order to succeed on a claim to refugee status. Where evidence of past maltreatment exists, however, it is unquestionably an excellent indicator of the fate that may await an applicant upon return to her home. Unless there has been a major change of circumstances within that country that makes prospective persecution unlikely, past experience under a particular regime should be considered probative of future risk.[156] As the Federal Court of Appeal noted in the *Oyarzo Marchant*[157] decision:

> . . . since it is the foundation for a present fear that must be considered, such incidents in the past are part of the whole picture and cannot be discarded entirely as a basis for fear, even though what has happened since has left them in the background.[158]

The issue is not the fact of the past persecution, but rather whether "that which happened in the past may happen in the future".[159] As cogently stated in the guidelines employed by the now disbanded Refugee Status Advisory Committee:

> Past persecution is evidence to substantiate a well-founded fear. However, it is not the only evidence. A person may not have been persecuted in the past, and yet still be a refugee. Looking, as it does, to the future, the refugee definition is concerned with possibilities and probabilities rather than with certainties.[160]

In sum, evidence of individualized past persecution is generally a sufficient,[161] though not a mandatory, means of establishing prospective risk.

---

[154] [1982] 2 F.C. 779.

[155] *Id.* at 781, *per* Thurlow C.J.

[156] *See*, e.g., *Francisco Humberto Gonzalez Galindo*, [1981] 2 F.C. 781 (C.A.). In this decision, the Court set aside a judgment of the Immigration Appeal Board on the ground that it had failed to take due account of independent medical evidence that the claimant's condition was consistent with having already been a victim of torture. This evidence was deemed sufficient to override the Board's concern that the claimant's relatively minor political involvement was inconsistent with a well-founded fear of persecution.

[157] *Supra*, note 154.

[158] *Supra*, note 154, at 781, *per* Thurlow C.J.

[159] *Marek Musial*, Immigration Appeal Board Decision V80-6368, November 19, 1980, at 2, *per* B. Howard.

[160] Minister of Employment and Immigration, *supra*, note 137, at Guideline 4.

[161] C. Blum, "Who Is a Refugee? Canadian Interpretation of the Refugee Definition" (1986), 1 Imm. J. 8, at 9.

Where the claimant testifies that she has left her country in anticipation of serious harm, both the general human rights record of her state and the experiences of other similarly situated persons are appropriately considered as alternative means of establishing the objective risk associated with return.

3.2.4 Evidence of Harm to Persons Similarly Situated

Insofar as there is no evidence of past persecution of the claimant herself, the concrete foundation for a claim to refugee status may be established by circumstantial evidence[162] that persons similarly situated to the claimant are at risk in the state of origin. While an individual need not already have suffered harm in order to qualify as a refugee,[163] there must nonetheless be some evidence on the basis of which the decision-maker can reasonably judge whether or not the applicant faces a reasonable chance of persecution were she to be returned to her home state. The best circumstantial indicator of risk is the experience of those persons perceived by authorities in the state of origin to be most closely connected to the claimant, generally including persons who share the racial, religious, national, social, or political affiliation upon which the claimant bases her case.[164] This information may be gleaned from general human rights data, the claimant's testimony, or any other evidence adduced at the hearing.

An example of the application of this principle in Canadian law can be found in the decision of the Federal Court of Appeal in *Anthony Andre Williams v. Minister of Employment and Immigration*.[165] In that case the Court directed the Immigration Appeal Board to take cognizance of letters from the applicant's brother and mother in which the nature of the risk to family members was set out, and held that these forms of evidence could provide a sufficient objective basis for the claim to refugee status.

A similar position was taken in the case of *Chaudri v. Minister of Employment and Immigration*,[166] this time in the context of the experiences of friends

---

[162] "The adjective 'well-founded' was meant to signify that 'a person has either been actually a victim of persecution or can show why he fears persecution.' In other words, the contracting party has to agree that 'a well-founded fear' of persecution does exist on the basis of circumstantial evidence to corroborate a person's personal judgment derived from his state of mind": Y. Shimada, "The Concept of the Political Refugee in International Law" (1975), 19 Japanese Ann. Intl. L. 24, at 33-34.

[163] J. van der Veen, "Does Persecution by Fellow-Citizens in Certain Regions of a State Fall Within the Definition of 'Persecution' in the Convention Relating to the Status of Refugees of 1951?" (1980), 11 Netherlands Y.B. Intl. L. 167, at 168; G. Goodwin-Gill, "Entry and Exclusion of Refugees: The Obligations of States and the Protection Function of the Office of the UNHCR" (1980), Michigan Y.B Intl. L. Studies 291, at fn. 47.

[164] "He may well have a well-founded fear of persecution if relatives, friends, or other members of the same racial or social group have been persecuted": D. Anker and M. Posner, "The Forty Year Crisis: A Legislative History of the Refugee Act of 1980" (1981), 82 San Diego L. Rev. 1, at 67. *Accord* M. Ryan, "Political Asylum for the Haitians?" (1982), 14 Case Western Reserve J. Intl. L. 155, at 171.

[165] Federal Court of Appeal Decision A-57-81, June 16, 1981.

[166] (1986), 69 N.R. 114 (F.C.A.).

and associates. The claimant had been involved with political affairs in Pakistan before coming to Canada on a student visa. During his time in Canada, a violent political coup took place, and martial law was imposed. The Immigration Appeal Board found that because the applicant's political activities had been of a fairly minor nature, he was unlikely to be at risk if returned to Pakistan, and dismissed his claim to refugee status. The Federal Court of Appeal set this decision aside because *inter alia* the Board had failed to consider evidence that other persons who, like the claimant, had engaged in minor forms of political activism, were in fact experiencing severe problems in Pakistan:

> Neither the applicant's "minor" role nor the length of his absence from Pakistan were relevant in the light of the uncontradicted evidence which the Board had accepted, namely, that others who had played the same role had been persecuted and that political persecutions of former members of the P.P.P. were still current at the time of the appeal. In the circumstances, it appears to me that, if the Board had not committed the errors which I have indicated, it could only have come to the conclusion that the applicant had satisfied the definition of Convention Refugee.[167]

This decision demonstrates the importance of seeking out contextualized surrogate indicators of risk (what is *in fact* happening to persons like the claimant?)[168] rather than relying on generic or intuitive reasoning about the likelihood of harm (is it reasonable that persons who played minor roles in the past are in danger?). By defining the community of persons at the focus of the inquiry to coincide as closely as possible with the basis of the claim to refugee status, it is possible both to provide prospective protection and to reserve recognition for those persons who are genuinely at risk of serious harm.

3.2.5 Assessing Risk Within the Context of Generalized Oppression

In view of the probative value of the experiences of persons similarly situated to the claimant, it is ironic that courts have shown a marked reluctance to recognize as refugees persons whose apprehension of risk is borne out in the suffering of large number of their fellow citizens. Rather than looking to the fate of other members of the claimant's racial, social, or other group as the best indicator of possible harm, decision-makers have routinely disfranchised refugees whose concerns are based on generalized, group-defined oppression.

This problem is most often manifested in the assertion that the claimant must be able to show that she has been "personally singled out"[169] for perse-

---

[167] *Id.*, at 117, *per* Hugessen J.

[168] In *Carlos Alberto Sanes Suarez*, for example, the Board looked to the testimony of an expert witness to assess the risk of harm to persons similarly situated to the claimant: Immigration Appeal Board Decision M86-1587X, September 30, 1987.

[169] D. Martin in C. Sumpter, "Mass Migration of Refugees — Law and Policy" (1982), 76

cution, that is, that she fears something more than a generalized denial of human rights,[170] and can recount a "coherent program of opposition . . . or . . . personal histories of persecution".[171] Claims have been dismissed on the basis that "other suspects probably received the same treatment",[172] because the applicant "was only one of many thousands"[173] similarly situated, and where the country of origin is "a restless and violent society where racism and disorder are part of the human condition".[174] Typical of the oft-repeated particularized evidence rule is the decision in the case of Lebanese claimant *Mohammed Said Sleiman*:[175]

> . . . there is no evidence that he or any members of his family have ever suffered any persecution or faced any special difficulty . . . beyond the problems they would face in consequence of the generalized circumstances existing there. Further, there is no evidence . . . which would set [the claimant and his family] apart to the extent they would be selected for persecution.[176]

This approach confuses the requirement to assess risk on the basis of the claimant's particular circumstances[177] with some erroneous notion that refu-

---

A.S.I.L.P. 13, at 14; S. Lamar, "Those Who Stand at the Door: Assessing Immigration Claims Based on Fear of Persecution", (1983) 18 New England L. Rev. 395, at 410; K. Hailbronner, "Non-Refoulement and 'Humanitarian' Refugees: Customary International Law or Wishful Legal Thinking?" (1986), 26(4) Virginia J. Intl. L. 857, at 857.

[170] D. Roth, "The Right of Asylum Under United States Immigration Law" (1981), 33 U. Florida L. Rev. 530, at 549.

[171] G. Loescher and J. Scanlan, "Human Rights, U.S. Foreign Policy, and Haitian Refugees" (1984), 26(3) J. Interamerican Studies 313, at 327.

[172] *Julner Jean-Philippe*, Immigration Appeal Board Decision 75-1081, August 28, 1975, at 5, *per* R. Tremblay. *Accord Matija Sokol*, Immigration Appeal Board Decision 77-3022, April 29, 1977, and *Mohamed Anwar Hossan*, Immigration Appeal Board Decision M84-1277, November 14, 1984.

[173] *Jim Martin Kwesi Mensah*, Immigration Appeal Board Decision V79-6136, August 7, 1979, at 4, *per* C. Campbell; set aside on other grounds by Federal Court of Appeal Decision A-527-79, May 2, 1980; subsequently affirmed in Federal Court of Appeal (1981), 36 N.R. 332. *Accord Rashed Mohamed Mahmoud El Arabi*, Immigration Appeal Board Decision 74-10409, January 29, 1975; *Matija Sokol*, Immigration Appeal Board Decision 77-3022, April 29, 1977; and *Hector Ivan Olguin Herrera*, Immigration Appeal Board Decision T80-9358, October 14, 1980; affirmed by the Federal Court of Appeal at [1981] 2 F.C. 801.

[174] *Ramesh Mahadeo*, Immigration Appeal Board Decision T83-10420, December 20, 1983, at 5, *per* B. Howard. *Accord Fernando Alejandro Cordova Seguel*, Immigration Appeal Board Decision 76-1157, August 11, 1977, at 5, *per* J.-P. Houle: "[T]he definiton does not expand on what is to be understood by 'persecution' in an international society where it has been proven, or, at the very least, where it is public knowledge that large sectors of this society use denunciation, torture and detention as instruments of vengeance against political adversaries or, worse yet, as instruments of government."

[175] Immigration Appeal Board Decision V79-6125, C.L.I.C. Notes 18.13, April 10, 1980; affirmed by Federal Court of Appeal Decision A-437-80, September 30, 1980.

[176] *Id.*, at 2, *per* C. Campbell.

[177] "The collective aspect of the 'refugee' phenomenon thus ceased to be decisive in granting refugee status, the emphasis being placed henceforth on the situation of the individual": S. Aga Khan, "Legal Problems Relating to Refugees and Displaced Persons" (1976), Recueil des cours 287, at 297. *Accord* P. Hyndman, "The 1951 Convention Definition of Refugee" (1987),

gee status must be based on a completely personalized set of facts.[178] The issue to be addressed is whether the applicant for refugee status faces a reasonable chance of being persecuted because of who she is or what she believes,[179] not whether that chance is identifiable to her alone, or is supported by a unique dossier of experiences.[180] As the ministerial guidelines for the Refugee Status Advisory Committee[181] noted:

> A person is a refugee whether he is persecuted alone, or persecuted with others. A person need not be singled out for persecution in order to be a refugee. Each claim must be assessed individually. Once that assessment takes place, a claim cannot be rejected simply because a large number of others could also legitimately fear the same persecution.[182]

The tendency to reject claims based on broadly based phenomena may derive from a mistaken extrapolation of the principle that persons at risk of generalized, indiscriminate forms of harm are not refugees.[183] The rationale for considering the victims of natural disasters or widespread turmoil to be outside the scope of the Convention[184] is not, however, their adverse impact

---

9 Human Rts. Q. 49, at 51: "At the outset a point that needs to be emphasized is that the definition is worded in terms of individuals."

[178] "Under a strict reading of this definition, those fleeing wars, or those seeking refuge from mass slaughter, are often not considered bona fide refugees because they are not singled out for persecution . . . ": M. Gibney, "A 'Well-Founded Fear' of Persecution" (1988), 10(1) Human Rts Q. 109, at 114. The more desirable position is that "the alien should only be required to show a valid fear of generalized persecution, and not necessarily a fear of persecution which would be leveled at the alien as an individual": L. Wildes, "The Dilemma of the Refugee: His Standard for Relief" (1983), 4 Cardoza L. Rev. 353, at 372.

[179] "[I]f a person is subjected to any such measure as deprivation of life or physical freedom for political reasons, he is a victim of persecution. It does not alleviate his situation in the very least if the measure is part of a general policy or if the whole strata of the population are subjected to the same kind of measures": *Mauricio Eliseo Pacheco Martinez*, Immigration Appeal Board Decision M87-1506X, September 9, 1987, at 3, *per* P. Arsenault.

[180] "The definition of 'Convention refugee' does not necessarily require that the applicant be the sole target of acts of persecution. The fact that he suffers the same treatment as other inhabitants of his country does not affect the validity of his claim": *Joseph Vester Bellefleur*, Immigration Appeal Board Decision M87-1593X, September 1, 1987, at 2, *per* P. Arsenault. *Accord Helena Olearczyk v. Minister of Employment and Immigration* (1990), 8 Imm. L.R. (2d) 18.

[181] Minister of Employment and Immigration, *supra*, note 137.

[182] *Id.*, at Guideline 9.

[183] "[A] person fleeing his country because of a natural disaster such as a flood or earthquake is not covered; neither is a person fleeing his country because of war, foreign domination or occupation or civil disturbance, *if there is absent the fear of persecution*" [Emphasis added]: World Peace Through Law Centre, *Toward the Second Quarter Century of Refugee Law*, p. 4 (1976). *See generally* Chapter 5, *infra*.

[184] This general position should be qualified in two ways. First, institutional efforts under the auspices of the UNHCR and regional developments in Africa, Asia, and Latin America have moved toward enfranchising a greater range of the victims of natural and man-made disasters than does the Convention. With respect to UNHCR efforts, *see* S. Aga Khan, *supra*, note 177, at 348; and P. Hartling, "Concept and Definition of 'Refugee' — Legal and Humanitar-

on large numbers of persons, but is rather the non-discriminatory nature of the risk:

> The text . . . obviously did not refer to refugees from natural disasters, for it was difficult to imagine that fires, floods, earthquakes or volcanic eruptions, for instance, differentiated between their victims on the grounds of race, religion or political opinion. Nor did that text cover all man-made events. There was no provision, for example, for refugees fleeing from hostilities . . . . [185]

Because, as is discussed in detail in Chapter 5, refugee law is concerned only with protection from serious harm tied to a claimant's civil or political status, persons who fear harm as the result of a non-selective phenomenon are excluded. Those impacted by natural calamities,[186] weak economies,[187] civil unrest,[188] war,[189] and even generalized failure to adhere to basic standards of human rights are not, therefore, entitled to refugee status on that basis alone.

This having been said, refugee law does extend protection in even these situations where there is some element of differential intent or impact based on civil or political status.[190] The genuineness of claims grounded in a form of broadly based harm, like all others, is a function of two basic issues. First, is the anticipated state-tolerated harm of sufficient gravity to constitute persecution?[191] If so, is there a connection between the risk faced and the clai-

---

ian Aspects", paper given at Second Nordic Seminar on Refugee Law, Copenhagen, pp. 11-14 (1979, unpublished); regarding efforts in Africa, Asia, and Latin America respectively, *see* G. Coles, "Some Reflections on the Protection of Refugees from Armed Conflict Situations" (1984), In Defense of the Alien 78, at 79; J. Patrnogic, "Refugees — A Continuing Challenge" (1982), 30 Annuaire de droit international médical 73, at 77; and Note, "International Protection in Latin America" (1985), 14 Refugees 5, at 5. Second, as discussed in Section 1.5 *supra*, the position has recently been argued that customary international law recognizes a duty to a "third category" of humanitarian refugees. *See* G. Goodwin-Gill, "Non-Refoulement and the New Asylum Seekers" (1986), 26(4) Virginia J. Intl. L. 897, at 905.

[185] Statement of Mr. Robinson of Israel, U.N. Doc. A/CONF.2/SR.22, at 6, July 16, 1951.

[186] T. Le and M. Esser, "The Vietnamese Refugee and U.S. Law" (1981), 56 Notre Dame Lawyer 656, at 665-66.

[187] I. Foighel, "Legal Status of the Boat People" (1979), 48 Nordisk Tidsskrift Intl. Ret. 217, at 222.

[188] "The definition of Convention refugee does not include genuine fear, however well founded, of living in a country in a state of total unrest": *Geda Laguerre*, Immigration Appeal Board Decision M87-1511X, August 24, 1987, at 4, *per* D. Ange. *Accord* M. Schultheis, "A Continent in Crisis: Migrants and Refugees in Africa", paper prepared for conference on "The African Context of Human Rights", p. 11 (1987, unpublished).

[189] UNHCR, *supra* note 7, p. 39.

[190] "Membership in a minority group is in itself insufficient to establish refugee status. Government laws or policies that discriminate against persons because of their membership in a minority group, however, tend to create a *prima facie* case of persecution": D. Roth, *supra*, note 170, at 549.

[191] "Differences in the treatment of various groups do indeed exist to a greater or lesser extent in many societies. Persons who receive less favourable treatment as a result of such differences are not necessarily victims of persecution. It is only in certain circumstances that discrimination will amount to persecution. This would be so if measures of discrimination lead to conse-

mant's race, religion, nationality, social group, or political opinion?[192] If the harm is both sufficiently serious and has a differential impact based on civil or political status, then a claim to Convention refugee status is made out, however many people are similarly affected.

By way of example, the victims of a flood or earthquake are not *per se* Convention refugees,[193] even if they have fled to a neighbouring state because their own government was unable or unwilling to provide them with relief assistance. If, on the other hand, the government of the home state chose to limit its relief efforts to those victims who were members of the majority race, forcing a minority group to flee to another country in order to avoid starvation or exposure, a claim to refugee status should succeed because the harm feared is serious and connected to the state, and the requisite element of civil or political differentiation is present. Gilbert Jaeger provides a similar illustration in the context of economic oppression:

> Economic oppression and deprivation are unfortunately rife the world over. In a number of countries, they affect the population as a whole or its overwhelming majority (often with the exception of the privileged old or new class at the top and possibly of a more or less significant buffer group — the middle and lower middle classes — in between). In such cases, economic oppression and deprivation are not related to any of the five bases of persecution specified by the general definition and would not qualify the oppressed and deprived for refugee status.
>
> In countries which are more stratified socially or in societies segmented through ethnic or religious cleavage, economic oppression and deprivation may strike a specific group — whether through active measures or resulting from a policy of neglect. In such circumstances, any member of that group may individually qualify for refugee status, particularly if the economic oppression and deprivation are tantamount to destitution or otherwise of a serious nature.[194]

Similar examples would be the sheltering of only members of a particular political group during civil insurrection or war, the provision of core freedoms or entitlements to all but the adherents of a certain religion, or the

---

quences of a substantially prejudicial nature for the person concerned, e.g. serious restrictions on his right to earn his livelihood, his right to practise his religion, or his access to normally available educational facilities": UNHCR, *supra*, note 7, p. 15. *See generally* Chapter 4, *infra*.

[192] "[A] well-founded fear . . . is different from an apprehension about facts and circumstances that would be the result of a general situation which affects people indiscriminately, for example, poor economic conditions or war": *Ismail Hassan Dembil*, Immigration Appeal Board Decision M80-1018, March 7, 1980, at 2, *per* J.-P. Houle. *Accord* UNHCR, *supra*, note 7, p. 17.

[193] *Supra*, note 186. *Accord* A. Fragomen, "The Refugee: A Problem of Definition" (1970), 3 Case Western Reserve J. Intl. L. 45, at 58: "Applicants for refugee status may have difficulty coming within one of the enumerated grounds of persecution . . . . Frequently, [the applicant's] movements were the result of natural calamity, military operations, or civil war. None of these occurrences would result in the person being accorded refugee status."

[194] G. Jaeger, "The Definition of 'Refugee': Restrictive versus Expanding Trends", [1983] World Refugee Survey 5, at 7.

exclusion of members of a given nationality or social group from access to the general system of police or judicial protection. However many people may be affected, the relevant issues are the seriousness of the harm that may eventuate, and its linkage to civil or political status.

This rejection of the particularized evidence rule is supported by three auxiliary concerns, including the historical context in which the Convention was established, the logic of protection based on need, and the desirability of conformity with the "reasonable chance" test articulated by the Federal Court of Appeal in *Adjei*.[195]

First, the historical framework of the Convention makes clear that it was designed to protect persons within large groups whose fear of persecution is generalized, not merely those who have access to evidence of particularized risk. The primary intended beneficiaries of the Convention were the many displaced victims of the Second World War and the ideological dissidents from Eastern Europe,[196] virtually all of whom were assumed to be worthy of protection by reason of their group-defined predicament. When refugee law evolved through the Protocol[197] to protect refugees from outside Europe, no new conceptual limitations were added, as a result of which there is no basis in law for reading a particularized evidence rule into the Convention-based regime.[198]

Second, it is logically inconsistent from either a humanitarian or human rights perspective to refuse cases arising from broadly based persecution. To do so is to advantage the claims of the élite, as only "[a] few persons who have become prominent and who may have done well in their home country

---

[195] *See* Section 3.2, *supra*, at note 97 ff.

[196] "The proposed definition covered four groups of refugees . . . . In the first appeared the so-called refugees of the First World War . . . . The second group comprised the refugees of the period between the two wars, the victims of fascism and naziism . . . . That was a clearly defined group to whom the convention should apply . . . . Thirdly, there was the group of 'neo-refugees', the definition of which was broad enough to allow the inclusion of persons who had left their home since the beginning of the Second World War as the result of political, racial, or religious persecution, or those who might be obliged to flee from their countries for similar reasons in the future . . . . The fourth group covered displaced persons and unaccompanied children": Statement of Mr. Henkin of the U.S.A., U.N. Doc. E/AC.32/SR.3, at 10, January 26, 1950.

[197] 606 U.N.T.S. 8791, entered into force on October 4, 1967. *See generally* Section 1.3, *supra*.

[198] It is arguable that in the post-Protocol era, the conceptual scope of the Convention is roughly the equivalent of the Statute of the UNHCR. The Statute was intended to apply to the victims of broadly based persecution, as the following exchange from its drafting history demonstrates. The delegate of the United Kingdom enquired of his American counterpart, " . . . whether the United States definition would cover the case where, as the result of a revolutionary change of government . . . say for the sake of argument, in Great Britain, a large section of the population was vicitimized and found it necessary to flee the country?" Mr. Henkin of the United States replied that " . . . the definition would cover those who had to flee from the country to another as the result of a major political upheaval of the kind all had in mind. If the political changes were of a minor nature, the definition, he felt, would not cover them." U.N. Doc. E/AC.7/SR.173, at 5, August 12, 1950.

[will] be able to show that they have been the target of concrete measures amounting to persecution by the authorities."[199] Moreover, because many extremely heinous violations of human rights, including genocide,[200] are by their very nature aimed at groups rather than individuals, the particularized evidence rule would marginalize refugee law in the extreme:

> Consider, for example, the case of a black South African applying here for asylum, and assume that he would, upon return, be subject to no extra or particular persecution for having attempted to gain asylum. Surely a court . . . would be bound to consider evidence of the way that country's political system structurally persecutes blacks and, having considered such evidence, to hold that this structural persecution was sufficient to make out his asylum claim. It would betray not only the proper, but also the required, judicial role for a court to bar itself from assessing whether the systemic hardship inflicted on blacks in South Africa amounts to persecution . . . . [201]

Third, the notion of restricting refugee status to persons who have been "singled out" for persecution is inconsistent with the ruling of the Federal Court of Appeal[202] that a claimant need only demonstrate a "reasonable chance" or "serious possibility"[203] of persecution for her claim to be considered well-founded. Forcing an applicant to show that she has somehow been targeted for persecution goes substantially beyond this idea of "good grounds for fearing persecution",[204] and suggests instead a probability of harm,[205] the very standard that was rejected by the Court.[206] In the United States where the standard of determination is indistinguishable from that in Canada,[207] appellate courts have recognized the inappropriateness of the "singled out" standard, and have rejected its application in decisions involv-

---

[199] A. Grahl-Madsen, "International Refugee Law Today and Tomorrow" (1982), 20 Archiv des Völkerrechts 411, at 421.

[200] T. Cox, "Well-Founded Fear of Being Persecuted: The Sources and Application of a Criterion of Refugee Status" (1984), 10 Brooklyn J. Intl. L. 333, at 350.

[201] Note, "Political Legitimacy in the Law of Political Asylum" (1985), 99 Harvard L. Rev. 450, at 469.

[202] *Joseph Adjei v. M.E.I.* (1989), 7 Imm. L.R. (2d) 169 (F.C.A.).

[203] *Id.*, at 173, *per* MacGuigan J.

[204] *Id.*, at 174.

[205] " 'Good reasons' requires that some objective element be considered in the determination of refugee status, but this element cannot be construed so strictly as to conflict with the primary emphasis on the 'plausible account.' It cannot be demanded, as a prerequisite to the grant of refugee status, that an individual prove either the objective conditions existing in the country of origin or that he will be singled out for persecution": T. Cox, *supra*, note 200, at 350.

[206] "Despite the terminology sanctioned by the House of Lords for interpreting the British legislation, we are nonetheless of the opinion that the phrase 'substantial grounds for thinking' is too ambiguous to be accepted in a Canadian context. It seems to go beyond . . . 'good grounds' . . . and even to suggest probability": *Supra*, note 202, at 173-74, *per* MacGuigan J.

[207] The relevant phraseology is "reasonable possibility" of persecution, comparable to the Canadian "reasonable chance" of persecution. *See* Section 3.2, *supra*, at note 85 ff.

ing the generalized oppression of union members[208] and pervasive violence[209] in El Salvador. Indeed, in the case of *Bolanos Hernandez v. I.N.S.*,[210] the Court of Appeals (9th Circuit) not only reversed a finding that a refugee claim could be dismissed merely because the applicant came from a country where the lives and freedom of a large number of people are at risk, but went so far as to characterize reasoning of that sort as "turn[ing] logic on its head".[211]

In sum, while modern refugee law is concerned to recognize the protection needs of particular claimants, the best evidence that an individual faces a serious chance of persecution is usually the treatment afforded similarly situated persons in the country of origin. In the context of claims derived from situations of generalized oppression, therefore, the issue is not whether the claimant is more at risk than anyone else in her country, but rather whether the broadly based harassment or abuse is sufficiently serious to substantiate a claim to refugee status. If persons like the applicant may face serious harm in her country, and if that risk is grounded in their civil or political status, then in the absence of effective national protection she is properly considered to be a Convention refugee.[212] As Atle Grahl-Madsen has observed, "[o]nce a person is subjected to a measure of such gravity that we consider it 'persecution', that person is 'persecuted' in the sense of the Convention, irrespective of how many others are subjected to the same or similar measures."[213]

---

[208] *Zavala Bonilla v. I.N.S.*, 730 F. 2d 562 (9th Cir., 1984), cited in Note, *supra*, note 201, at 470.

[209] *Bolanos Hernandez v. I.N.S.*, 749 F. 2d 1316 (9th Cir. 1984), cited in Note, *supra*, note 201, at 470. *See also* D. Anker, "American Immigration Policy and Asylum" (1987), 38(4) Harvard L. Bull. 4, at 8.

[210] *Id.*

[211] *Id.*, at 1323, cited in Note, *supra*, note 201, at 470. This position has recently been codified in the United States: "In evaluating whether the applicant has sustained his burden of [proof] . . . the asylum officer or immigration judge shall not require the applicant to provide evidence that he would be singled out individually for persecution if . . . he establishes that there is a pattern or practice in his country of nationality or last habitual residence of persecution of groups of persons similarly situated to the applicant . . .; and he establishes his own inclusion in and identification with such group of persons such that his fear of persecution upon return is reasonable": 8 C.F.R. 208.13(b)(2)(i), July 27, 1990.

[212] The preceding formulation of the generalized circumstances test was adopted by the Federal Court of Appeal in *Vajie Salibian v. Minister of Employment and Immigration*, Federal Court of Appeal Decision A-479-89, May 24, 1990, at 9-10, *per* Decary J. Persons affected by broadly based oppression may be refugees "if it can be shown that such a regime is indeed dangerous for them": E. Huyck and L. Bouvier, "The Demography of Refugees" (1983), 467 The Annuals Am. Academy 39, at 41.

[213] 1 A. Grahl-Madsen, *The Status of Refugees in International Law*, p. 213 (1966). This quotation has been adopted by the Immigration Appeal Board in cases such as *Joseph Vester Bellefleur*, Immigration Appeal Board Decision M87-1593X, September 1, 1987; and *Mauricio Eliseo Pacheco Martinez*, Immigration Appeal Board Decision M87-1506X, September 9, 1987.

4

Persecution

The refugee claimant must apprehend a form of harm which can be characterized as "persecution". This chapter examines the basis for the choice of persecution as the key definitional criterion in the Convention, and attempts to sketch a framework for determining when particular forms of mistreatment are of sufficient gravity to be classified as persecutory. Whereas Chapter 3 focused on the evidentiary standard which should be applied in assessing a claim to refugee status, this chapter is concerned with the substantive nature of the harm that refugee law is intended to confront.

The persecution standard evolved from the legitimate concern first stated in the 1938 Convention concerning the Status of Refugees coming from Germany[1] to exclude from protection those persons who were leaving their country for "reasons of purely personal convenience."[2] The Constitution of the International Refugee Organization[3] rephrased this principle in positive terms, and required the putative refugee to show "valid objections" to returning to her country of origin, which might include fear of persecution.[4] The modern Convention, in turn, adopted the basic approach of the IRO precedent,[5] but made persecution the exclusive benchmark for international refugee status.[6]

---

[1] 192 L.N.T.S. 59.

[2] G. Melander, "The Protection of Refugees" (1974), 18 Scandinavian Studies in Law 153, at 159.

[3] G.A. Res. 62, U.N. Doc. A/64/Add. 1, at 97.

[4] The IRO also recognized as "valid objections" compelling family reasons arising out of prior persecution, infirmity or illness, and objections of a political nature: *supra*, note 3. In practice, IRO policy extended protection as well to persons who feared discrimination: T. Cox, "Well-Founded Fear of Being Persecuted: The Sources and Application of a Criterion of Refugee Status" (1984), 10 Brooklyn J. Intl. L. 333, at 339.

[5] "[The] definition of the term 'refugee' referred to those who were victims of persecution 'as a result of events' in Europe prior to 1 January 1951. That phrase was derived from the Constitution of the International Refugee Organization, and had a recognized meaning which everyone understood": Statement of Mr. Henkin of the U.S.A., U.N. Doc. E/AC.7/SR.173, at 5, August 12, 1950. *See also* Y. Shimada, "The Concept of the Political Refugee in International Law" (1975), 19 Japanese Ann. Intl. L. 24, at 35.

[6] The narrowing of the grounds for protection was noted by the Director-General of the International Refugee Organization, who argued that the exclusive reliance on fear of persecution, ". . . will exclude persons having IRO valid objections of [a] political nature and [who object to return] for compelling family reasons, thus militating against persons of undoubted political

While it is true that the persecution-based standard permitted the identification of the victims of Naziism,[7] it also spoke to the ideology-charged atmosphere which dominated the thinking of the Western states that prepared the Convention.[8] The malleable persecution-based standard could be interpreted to embrace most of the emigrant dissidents from adversary states in the East Bloc,[9] and would thus promote the immigration of Eastern Europeans to Western states then experiencing acute manpower shortages.[10] Moreover, because a finding that a refugee claimant faces the possibility of persecution implies censure of the state of origin, each recognition of refugee status would simultaneously support efforts to stigmatize as injurious the political systems in the Communist countries of origin.[11]

Our continuing reliance[12] on the persecution-based standard in an age when

---

sincerity. . .": Cable from the Director-General of the I.R.O., U.N. Doc. E/AC.32/L.16, at 1, January 30, 1950. In the result, the Convention definition ". . . clearly does not include everyone outside his or her country in a situation of distress and unable to return home": P. Hyndman, "The 1951 Convention Definition of Refugee: An Appraisal with Particular Reference to the Sri Lankan Tamil Claimants" (1987), 9 Human Rts. Q. 49, at 52.

[7] "These instruments center on a definition of 'refugee' that was designed to secure the humanitarian objective of relieving the victims of Nazi persecutions": J. Garvey, "Toward a Reformulation of International Refugee Law" (1985), 26 Harvard Intl. L.J. 483, at 483.

[8] K. Brill, "The Endless Debate: Refugee Law and Policy and the 1980 Refugee Act" (1983), 32 Cleveland State L.Rev. 117, at 137. *Accord* G. Melander, *supra*, note 2, at 160: "Owing to the boycotting by the East European states of the organs of the United Nations, . . . the Refugee Convention [was] drafted by Western states only. It was quite natural to claim persecution in the country of origin. All the refugees emanated from East European states. Countries of asylum, i.e. Western states, were not obliged to take any political considerations into account. The relations between Eastern and Western states at that time could hardly have been worse."

[9] It has been noted that the drafters "wished to create an instrument for the protection of persons who had escaped from, or did not wish to return to, specific countries in which, in the common opinion of the Parties, conditions of persecution prevailed at the time the Convention was concluded": C. Pompe, "The Convention of 28 July 1951 and the International Protection of Refugees" (1956), Rechtsgeleerd Magazyn Themis 425, published in English as U.N. Doc. HCR/INF/42, May 1958.

[10] "In establishing a legal and organizational framework to deal with the refugee problem, the Western powers were not only guided by a humanitarian concern for Europe's refugees. For ideological reasons, they had to identify anyone who had moved from Eastern Europe as a victim of communist rule. For economic and political purposes, they had to facilitate the removal of many refugees from the shattered states of Western Europe to the labour-hungry countries of the New World": Independent Commission on International Humanitarian Issues, *Refugees: The Dynamics of Displacement*, p. 32 (1986).

[11] "Neither was the judgemental and polemical character of such a definition. . . seen as posing a serious problem, since it was the time of the Cold War, when such an approach would serve from the Western point of view, as a useful means of stigmatising the Communist regimes of Eastern Europe as persecutors": G. Coles, "Approaching the Refugee Problem Today", in G. Loescher and L. Monahan, eds., *Refugees and International Relations*, pp. 374-75 (1989).

[12] "It could be argued that in practice the element of 'persecution' is no longer being regarded as an essential element in the definition of a 'refugee', and that while lip-service is still paid to this element, it is no longer considered by some States to be a *sine qua non*. . . . However, this may be an over-simplification": G. Coles, "Background Paper for the Asian Working Group on the International Protection of Refugees and Displaced Persons", p. 99 (1980, unpublished).

refugee states of origin and destination are frequently politically compatible has compromised the ability of refugee law to afford broadly based protection.[13] In contrast to the cold war assumption of valid reasons for departure, refugee recognition today may be denied for reasons of foreign policy,[14] or at least be conditioned by an unspoken view that an allied state is unlikely to act in a persecutory way. As Goran Melander has noted, "[r]ather than expose itself to the disapproval of the country of origin, a government may deny a person the status of refugee."[15] The challenge is to recast the notion of "persecution" in a manner which is consonant with modern political realities, and which genuinely enables governments to conceive of refugee protection as a humanitarian act which ought not to be a cause of tension between states.[16]

4.1 Persecution as the Sustained or Systemic Violation of Basic Human Rights Resulting from a Failure of State Protection

The traditional Canadian formulation of the persecution standard focuses on the existence of persistent harassment[17] by or with the knowledge of the authorities of the state of origin.[18] It involves the "constant infliction of some mental or physical cruelty",[19] "persistent or urgent efforts to harm or cause

---

[13] The Convention definition has been described as ". . . a definition partly stripped of political feeling though not yet raised to the purely humanitarian and politically neutral level where protection is afforded to the legally unprotected human being as such": C. Pompe, *supra*, note 9, at 13. *See generally* J. Hathaway, "A Reconsideration of the Underlying Premise of Refugee Law" (1990), 31(1) Harvard J. Intl. L. 129.

[14] "[G]ranting refugee status can be a delicate political matter. It can be seen as involving a comment upon the internal affairs of the country from which the person has fled, and to amount, in effect, to a statement that there may be reasons why people within the country fled could fear persecution. . . . Because of the negative imputation which this carries, and the possible detrimental effect upon the relationships existing between the country of refuge and that of origin, many States are hesitant to grant refugee status for considerations of a political nature": P. Hyndman, "Refugees Under International Law with a Reference to the Concept of Asylum" (1986), 60 Australian L.J. 148, at 149.

[15] *Supra*, note 2, at 159.

[16] "Expressing the wish that all States, recognizing the social and humanitarian nature of the problem of refugees, will do everything within their power to prevent this problem from becoming a cause of tension between States. . .": Preamble to the *Convention Relating to the Status of Refugees*, 189 U.N.T.S. 2545, entered into force April 22, 1954 ("*Convention*").

[17] "[T]he essential element is the harassment inflicted on the person by, or with the tacit or formal consent of, the authorities of the country of his nationality. . .": *Moise Danilo Bahamondes Peralta*, Immigration Appeal Board Decision 79-1082, C.L.I.C. Notes 18.9, December 12, 1979, at 3, *per* J.-P. Houle. *Accord Wladyslaw Zastawny*, Immigration Appeal Board Decision 77-1125, July 2, 1977; *Luis Enrique Toha Seguel*, Immigration Appeal Board Decision 79-1150, C.L.I.C. Notes 28.8, November 13, 1980; and *Arulvelrajah Rajanayagam*, Immigration Appeal Board Decision M84-1390, December 31, 1984.

[18] *Zahirdeen Rajudeen v. Minister of Employment and Immigration* (1985), 55 N.R. 129 (F.C.A.).

[19] *Marc Georges Sévère* (1974), 9 I.A.C. 42, at 47, *per* J.-P. Houle.

to suffer",[20] and "pursuit with enmity",[21] such as to provoke "an irrepressible fear of asking the authorities . . . for protection".[22] The Immigration Appeal Board succinctly stated the core of the test in its judgment in the case of *Gladys Maribel Hernandez*:[23]

> The criteri[on] to establish persecution is harassment, harassment that is so constant and unrelenting that the victims feel deprived of all hope of recourse, short of flight, from government by oppression.[24]

The equation of persecution with harassment highlights the need to show a sustained or systemic risk, rather than just an isolated incident of harm.[25] It does not, however, advance understanding of the nature of the harms within the scope of persecution.

It is generally acknowledged that the drafters of the Convention intentionally left the meaning of "persecution" undefined[26] because they realized the impossibility of enumerating in advance all of the forms of maltreatment which might legitimately entitle persons to benefit from the protection of a foreign state.[27] Bits and pieces of insight into the intended meaning of "persecution" can nonetheless be gleaned from the Convention's drafting history.

First, the drafters clearly viewed persecution as a sufficiently inclusive concept to capture the spectrum of phenomena which had induced involuntary migration during and immediately after the Second World War, ranging from

---

[20] *Shafiqur Mohammed Rahman,* Immigration Appeal Board Decision M84-1073, C.L.I.C. Notes 74.4, September 11, 1984, at 4, *per* G. Loiselle.

[21] *Mascime Mouryoussef*, Immigration Appeal Board Decision 80-1036, C.L.I.C. Notes 21.8, March 24, 1980, at 2, *per* J. Scott.

[22] *Jose Mariano Aguilar Vides,* Immigration Appeal Board Decision M83-1009, February 3, 1983, at 2, *per* J.-P. Houle. *Accord David Ignacio Casado Molina*, Immigration Appeal Board Decision M83-1028, April 13, 1983, at 1, *per* G. Loiselle, which defined as persecution "acts committed by or with the tacit consent of the authorities of [the] country of origin — actions that have given rise to an unconquerable fear of repression against which [the claimant] would not be able to seek protection from the government authorities. . . ."

[23] Immigration Appeal Board Decision M81-1212, January 6, 1983.

[24] *Id.,* at 5, *per* G. Loiselle.

[25] *Ana Vilma Irrarrazabal Olmedo*, Immigration Appeal Board Decision T80-9327, September 22, 1980; affirmed by Federal Court of Appeal Decision A-650-80, April 8, 1981; *Luis Omar Reyes Ferrada*, Immigration Appeal Board Decision T81-9476, September 18, 1981, affirmed by Federal Court of Appeal Decision A-572-81, May 3, 1982; *Shaugin Ajwal Singh*, Immigration Appeal Board Decision V87-6244X, June 16, 1987.

[26] "The term 'persecution' has nowhere been defined and this was probably deliberate": P. Weis, "The concept of the refugee in international law" (1960), 87 J. du droit intl. 928, at 970. *Accord* 1 A. Grahl-Madsen, *The Status of Refugees in International Law*, p. 193 (1966): "It seems as if the drafters have wanted to introduce a flexible concept which might be applied to circumstances as they might arise; or in other words, that they capitulated before the inventiveness of humanity to think up new ways of persecuting fellow men."

[27] *Id. See also* C. Fong, "Some Legal Aspects of the Search for Admission into Other States of Persons Leaving the Indo-Chinese Peninsula in Small Boats" (1981), 52 British Y.B. Intl. L. 53, at 92.

the deprivation of life and liberty inflicted by the Nazis,[28] to the ideological conformism imposed by the communist states.[29] From the beginning, there was no monolithic or absolute conceptual standard of wrongfulness, the implication being that a variety of measures in disregard of human dignity[30] might constitute persecution. Refugee status was premised on the risk of serious harm,[31] but not on the possibility of consequences of life or death proportions.[32] In addition to the Convention's acceptance of deprivation of basic civil and political freedoms as sufficient cause for international concern, serious social and economic consequences were also acknowledged to be within the purview of persecution.[33]

Second, the intention of the drafters was not to protect persons against any and all forms of even serious harm, but was rather to restrict refugee recognition to situations in which there was a risk of a type of injury that would be inconsistent with the basic duty of protection owed by a state to

---

[28] [I]n no case could the victims of racial persecution be compelled to resume their former nationality or resettle in the countries where they had suffered so bitterly": Statement of Mr. Rochefort of France, 11 ESCOR (406th mtg.) at 276, August 11, 1950.

[29] "As to refugees, both present and future, arriving in central and western Europe from eastern European lands, he considered that, having regard to the terms of the draft convention and the observations of the High Commissioner for Refugees, the non-governmental organizations need have no fear that such refugees would not be covered by the present text": Statement of Mr. Warren of the U.S.A., U.N. Doc. A/CONF.2/SR.21, at 15, July 14, 1951.

[30] [W]hat is persecution in the particular case is a question of fact. Other measures in disregard of human dignity might also constitute persecution": P. Weis, *supra*, note 26, at 970. *Accord* Y. Shimada, "The Concept of the Political Refugee in International Law" (1975), 19 Japanese Ann. Intl. L. 24, at 37; and M. Chemille-Gendreau, "Le concept de réfugié en droit international et ses limites" (1981), 28 Pluriel 3, at 9.

[31] "The word persecution is generally taken to exclude individuals who face discrimination or maltreatment other than of a very serious kind": R. Plender, "Admission of Refugees: Draft Convention on Territorial Asylum" (1977), 15 San Diego L.Rev. 45, at 53. *Accord* K. Petrini, "Basing Asylum Claims on a Fear of Persecution Arising from a Prior Asylum Claim" (1981), 56 Notre Dame Lawyer 719, at 723; and D. Gross, "The Right of Asylum Under United States Law" (1980), 80 Columbia L.Rev. 1125, at 1136, who characterizes persecution as involving more than "minor disadvantage or trivial inconvenience".

[32] "Because persecution is a factual question, the official must have broad latitude in making the determination as to whether the person claiming the benefit is in fact persecuted. It is clear, however, that 'persecution' is not restricted solely to physical abuse or incarceration": A. Fragomen, "The Refugee: A Problem of Definition" (1970), 3 Case Western Reserve J. Intl. L. 45, at 54.

[33] This point was established in an exchange between the representative of the American Federation of Labor and the delegate of France during the drafting of the Convention. Mr. Stolz of the AFL ". . . recalled that people sometimes left their country for social or economic reasons, an eventuality which was not specifically mentioned [in the Convention]". Mr. Rain of France replied that he ". . . thought that the nature of the persecution should be described in very broad terms. In actual practice he felt sure that the people referred to by the AF of L representative would be recognized as refugees": U.N. Doc. E/AC.32/SR.17, at 3-4, February 6, 1950. Indeed, European determination authorities readily recognized such claims in the early years of the Convention's life: *see* A. Grahl-Madsen, *supra*, note 26, at 201-09.

its own population.[34] As a holistic reading of the refugee definition demonstrates, the drafters were not concerned to respond to certain forms of harm *per se*, but were rather motivated to intervene only where the maltreatment anticipated was demonstrative of a breakdown of national protection.[35] The existence of past or anticipated suffering alone, therefore, does not make one a refugee, unless the state has failed in relation to some duty to defend its citizenry against the particular form of harm anticipated.[36]

These basic tenets — a liberal sense of the types of past or anticipated harm which might warrant protection abroad,[37] and a fundamental preoccupation to identify forms of harm demonstrative of breach by a state of its basic obligations of protection — are of continuing relevance today. For persecution to remain a meaningful concept, it must be interpreted in the light of these principles as they apply in modern context.[38] As noted by the Committee on Population and Refugees of the Council of Europe:

> . . . the concept of persecution should be interpreted and applied liberally and also adapted to the changed circumstances which may differ considerably from those existing when the Convention was originally adopted. . . . [A]ccount should be taken of the relation between refugee status and the denial of human rights as laid down in different international instruments.[39]

This approach will not eliminate the danger of political distortion inherent in the retention of the persecution standard,[40] but it may at least prevent the Convention from becoming a mere anachronism.

Drawing on these basic precepts, persecution may be defined as the sus-

---

[34] This concern is most clear in the early formulations of the generalized refugee definition. The British draft, for example, provided that the Convention would apply to "unprotected persons" (U.N. Doc. E/AC.32/L.2, at 1, January 17, 1950), while the French draft spoke of persons who were "unwilling or unable to claim the protection of [their] country" (U.N. Doc. E/AC.32/L.3, at 3, January 17, 1950). As finally agreed to, the Convention extends only to a person who is ". . . unable or. . . unwilling to avail himself of the protection" of his or her country of origin: *Convention, supra*, note 16, at Art. 1(A)(2).

[35] "This limitation on the definition of refugee owes its origin to the fact that the refugee is designated as a person who stands in need of international protection because he or she is deprived of that in his or her own country": R. Plender, *supra*, note 31, at 54.

[36] "The concept of persecution is usually attached to acts or circumstances for which the government . . . is responsible . . . [and which] leave the victims virtually unprotected by the agencies of the State": C. Fong, *supra*, note 27, at 92.

[37] "The term 'persecution', used in the Refugee Convention and Protocol as well as in the UNHCR Statute, has never been officially defined, but the drafters of the Convention clearly conceived it in a liberal way": A. Grahl-Madsen, "Identifying the World's Refugees" (1983), 467 Annals A.A.P.S.S. 11, at 15.

[38] "Motives for leaving home countries and seeking asylum have changed from the standard persecution arguments of European refugees; motives have become increasingly complex and mixed, not always linked to persecution in the European sense": M. Chamberlain, "The Mass Migration of Refugees and International Law" (1983), 7 Fletcher Forum 93, at 104.

[39] Cited in remarks by J. Thomas in A. Woods, ed., "Refugees: A New Dimension in International Human Rights", (1976) 70 A.S.I.L.P. 58, at 69.

[40] *See* text *supra* at note 12 ff.

tained or systemic violation of basic human rights[41] demonstrative of a failure of state protection.[42] A well-founded fear of persecution exists when one reasonably anticipates that remaining in the country may result in a form of serious harm[43] which government cannot or will not prevent,[44] including either "specific hostile acts or. . . an accumulation of adverse circumstances such as discrimination existing in an atmosphere of insecurity and fear".[45] The balance of this chapter examines the nature of basic human rights which constitute a state's duty of protection, the application of these standards in a number of specific contexts, and the circumstances in which a state may be said to have failed in its duty to ensure those basic human rights.

4.2 The Nature of a State's Duty of Protection

It is axiomatic that we live in a highly imperfect world, and that hardship and even suffering remain very much a part of the human condition for perhaps the majority of humankind. It is also true that there is no universally accepted standard of quality of life, nor of the role that a government should play in meeting the hopes and needs of its citizenry.[46] This plurality of

---

[41] The Preamble to the Refugee Convention commences with a specific reference to the interrelationships between refugee protection and international human rights law: "The High Contracting Parties, [c]onsidering that the Charter of the United Nations and the Universal Declaration of Human Rights . . . have affirmed the principle that human beings shall enjoy fundamental rights and freedoms without discrimination. . . . Have agreed as follows": *Convention, supra*, note 16, at Preamble. *Accord* S. Young, "Who is a Refugee? A Theory of Persecution" (1982), 5 In Defence of the Alien 38, at 46: "But before the law can infer an intent at harassment, a standard of duty by which we measure the misfeasance or nonfeasance is necessary. Fortunately such a standard exists in the International Covenant. . . ."

[42] "[T]he acts must be committed by the government (or the party) or organs at its disposal, or the behaviour must be tolerated by the government in such a way as to leave the victims virtually unprotected by the agencies of the State": C. Fong, *supra*, note 27, at 92. *See generally* Section 4.5, *infra*.

[43] "[P]ersecution is also very much a question of degree and proportion, requiring relation of the general notion to commonly accepted principles of human rights": G. Goodwin-Gill, "Entry and Exclusion of Refugees: The Obligations of States and the Protection Function of the Office of the UNHCR" (1980), Michigan Y.B. Intl. L. Studies 291, at 298.

[44] "[T]he intent necessary for a finding of persecution can be imputed to a government. Persecution would thus arise not only from a conscious intent to harm (malfeasance) but also from misfeasance or nonfeasance": S. Young, *supra*, note 41, at 45. *Accord* G. Goodwin-Gill, *supra*, note 43, at 298-99, in which the author notes that persecution comprehends "failure (voluntary or involuntary) on the part of the state authorities to prevent or suppress [private] violence".

[45] D. Anker and M. Posner, "The Forty Years Crisis: A Legislative History of the Refugee Act of 1980" (1981), 82 San Diego L.Rev. 1, at 67.

[46] "The way of achieving [the] assault on injustice has to be through a scheme of obligations under international law. The particulars of this accountability, however, must be drafted differently for different societies. Each government's acts are to be evaluated in terms of the conditions of its society as determined by that society's preferred values and structures of social organization": S. Sinha, "Human Rights: A Non-Western Viewpoint" (1981), 67 Archiv für Rechts und Sozial Philosophie 76, at 89-90.

experience and outlook restricts any attempt to define in absolute terms the nature of the duty of protection which a state owes to its people, as is clear from the deference that international law consistently pays to both cultural distinctiveness and sovereign autonomy.[47]

Nonetheless, the international community has recognized that there are certain basic rights, including both freedoms from interference and entitlements to resources, which all states are bound to respect as a minimum condition of legitimacy.[48] This recognition led to the adoption of common international standards of acceptable behaviour, which governments have agreed to accept as limitations on claims of cultural heterogeneity and autonomy of action. While it is true that international law binds sovereign states only to the extent that they agree to be bound,[49] the breadth of the emerging international law of human rights is unquestionably impressive.

Among the myriad treaties, declarations, rules and other standards adopted by states, the International Bill of Rights, consisting of the Universal Declaration of Human Rights,[50] the International Covenant on Civil and Political Rights,[51] and the International Covenant on Economic, Social, and Cultural Rights,[52] is central. More than any other gauge, the International Bill of Rights is essential to an understanding of the minimum duty owed by a state to its nationals. Its place derives from the extraordinary consensus achieved on the soundness of its standards, its regular invocation by states,

---

[47] "No matter how much one may vilify state sovereignty, the argument that a supranational legal authority is viable, or latent, is a very difficult one to make: One must first establish, in the context of United Nations law for example, that Article 2(7) of the Charter is invalid and no longer applies to human rights. . . . [T]his is no mean feat, involving as it does a wholesale redefinition of the sources of international obligation by substituting majority rule for state consent as the ultimate basis of legal validity in the system": J. Watson, "Legal Theory, Efficacy and Validity in the Development of Human Rights Norms in International Law" (1979), 3 U. Illinois L. Forum 609.

[48] "[T]he strict doctrine of national sovereignty has been cut down in two crucial respects. First, how a state treats its own subjects is now the legitimate concern of international law. Secondly, there is now a superior international standard, established by common consent, which may be used for judging the domestic laws and the actual conduct of sovereign States within their own territories and in the exercise of their internal jurisdictions, and may therefore be regarded as ranking in the hierarchy of laws even above national constitutions": P. Sieghart, *The International Law of Human Rights*, p. 15 (1983).

[49] *Supra*, note 47.

[50] U.N.G.A. Res. 217A (III), December 10, 1948 ("UDHR"). Article 14 of the UDHR provides for "the right to seek and enjoy in other countries asylum from persecution." In reliance on this provision, it may be argued that "[t]he asylum provision assures that where a member state fails to abide by the [other UDHR-based] standards, the individual at risk will be able to find sanctuary in another member state": A. Helton, "Persecution on Account of Membership in a Social Group as a Basis for Refugee Status" (1983), 15 Columbia Human Rts. L.Rev. 39, at 56.

[51] U.N.G.A. Res. 2200 (XXI), December 19, 1966, entered into force March 23, 1976 ("ICCPR").

[52] U.N.G.A. Res. 2200 (XXI), December 19, 1966, entered into force January 3, 1976 ("ICESCR").

and its role as the progenitor for the many more specific human rights accords.[53] Reference to the International Bill of Rights in deciding whether or not a state has failed to provide basic protection in relation to core, universally recognized values is moreover consistent with the Convention's own Preamble and General Assembly Resolution 2399 (XXIII).[54]

The use of a human rights standard for determining the existence of persecution is not accepted by all. The most conservative position, argued by Karl Zink, is that only a narrow subset of human rights violations can constitute persecution, namely, deprivation of life[55] or physical freedom.[56] This position is often inappropriately tied to a narrow and literal reading of Article 33 of the Convention, which prohibits the return of a refugee to "the frontiers of territories where his life or freedom would be threatened. . . ."[57] Atle

---

[53] "The Universal Declaration not only reflects a consensus of world opinion on the nature of the fundamental rights and freedoms belonging to every individual, but also expresses a unanimity of belief in the principle that the inherent dignity and worth of the human person requires respect for and protection of that person's rights. Since its adoption, the Declaration has achieved an international status far beyond the early expectations of its drafters. The Declaration has been referred to in numerous international instruments, and it has been made directly or indirectly a part of the constitutions of a number of states. . . . From an international law perspective, one is justified in maintaining that the Declaration, which technically has only the force of moral persuasion, has now become a part of customary international law and, thus, legally binding on all states": V. Saari and R. Higgins Cass, "The United Nations and the International Protection of Human Rights: A Legal Analysis and Interpretation", (1977) California W. Intl. L.J. 591, at 597. The two Covenants on Human Rights, which carry the precepts of the Universal Declaration forward in detailed and binding form, have now been ratified by 92 (ICESCR) and 87 (ICCPR) state parties: J.-B. Marie, "International Instruments Relating to Human Rights: Classification and Chart Showing Ratifications as of 1 January, 1989" (1989), 10 Human Rights L.J. 111-12.

[54] The Preamble to the Convention invokes the Universal Declaration of Human Rights as the means by which states "have affirmed the principle that human beings shall enjoy fundamental rights and freedoms without discrimination." As noted by the European Court of Human Rights in *Golder v. United Kingdom* (1975), 1 E.H.R.R. 524, at para. 34, the preamble of an international convention may be used to determine its object and purpose. This principled approach to refugee determination was endorsed in U.N.G.A. Res. 2399 (XXIII), December 6, 1968, which called on states to treat "new refugee situations in accordance with the principles and spirit of the Declaration on Territorial Asylum and the Universal Declaration of Human Rights." *Accord* P. Hyndman, "The 1951 Convention Definition of Refugee" (1987), 9 Human Rights Q. 49, at 61.

[55] This narrow view was advocated by the Swiss Government during the drafting of the Refugee Convention: "The Swiss Federal Government regarded as refugees all aliens whose lives are in danger for political reasons, and who, to escape that danger, were compelled to seek refuge in Switzerland": Statement of Mr. Schurch of Switzerland, U.N. Doc. A/CONF.2/SR.20, at 13, July 13, 1951.

[56] Zink interpreted persecution ". . . so as to mean only deprivation of life or of physical freedom. In the former category he includes enforced, protracted unemployment in the absence of other means of livelihood, but he excludes attacks on a person's physical integrity, unless such attacks may lead to the victim's death or implies loss of physical freedom": 1 A. Grahl-Madsen, *The Status of Refugees in International Law*, p. 193 (1966).

[57] *Convention, supra*, note 16, at Art. 33(1). Grahl-Madsen soundly refutes this view: "The quoted phrases were absolutely not conceived of as a more precise formulation of the concept

Grahl-Madsen adopts only a slightly more liberal view, arguing without explanation that the restriction or denial of such rights as freedom of thought, conscience and religion, freedom of opinion and expression, and freedom of peaceful assembly and association are outside the ambit of persecution.[58]

The dominant view, however, is that refugee law ought to concern itself with actions which deny human dignity in any key way, and that the sustained or systemic denial of core human rights is the appropriate standard.[59] This position has been specifically endorsed in the Canadian case law.[60] The judgment in *Luis Enrique Toha Sequel*,[61] for example, noted that in discussing persecution, ". . . we are not talking about physical torture alone, but about any act intended to deny or trample on a person's fundamental rights."[62] The Federal Court of Appeal has agreed, as is clear from the decision in *Alfredo Manuel Oyarzo Marchant v. Minister of Employment and Immigration:*[63]

> . . .the Board . . . appears to imply . . . that it defined "persecution" as necessarily requiring deprivation of the applicant's liberty. If this is so, then the Board erred in law, in my view, in applying such a restrictive definition.[64]

What rights are appropriately considered to be basic and inalienable? Within the International Bill of Rights, four distinct types of obligation exist.

---

of 'persecution.' It was apparently the intention of the Ad Hoc Committee that the words 'life and freedom' should be given a very broad interpretation. . . and that any kind of 'persecution' which may entitle a person to the status of Convention 'refugee' shall be considered a 'threat to life or freedom' in the sense of Articles 31 and 33. In other words, we may look to Article 1 in order to determine the scope of Articles 31 and 33, but not *vice versa*": A. Grahl-Madsen, *supra*, note 56, at 196.

[58] *Id.,* at 195.

[59] "I see human rights as the principal indices of human well-being, the recognition of which has been considered by the international community as the foundation of freedom, justice and peace. . . . Accordingly, the refugee problem, as any other political problem, should be approached from the perspective of human rights in order to determine the basic legal and moral nature of the problem and of the solution required": G. Coles, "The Human Rights Approach to the Solution of the Refugee Problem: A Theoretical and Practical Enquiry", in A. Nash, ed., *Human Rights and the Protection of Refugees Under International Law,* p. 196 (1988). *Accord,* e.g., J. Vernant, *The Refugee in the Post-War World,* p. 8 (1953); G. Melander, *Eligibility Procedures in Western European States,* p. 7 (1976); G. Goodwin-Gill, *The Refugee in International Law,* p. 38 (1983); and A. Ghoshal and T. Crowley, "Refugees and Immigrants: A Human Rights Dilemma" (1983), 5 Human Rts. Q. 327, at 329.

[60] *See, e.g., Felix Salatiel Nuñez Veloso,* Immigration Appeal Board Decision 79-1017, August 24, 1979 ("against his basic and inalienable human rights"); *Jose del Rosario Perez Gomez,* Immigration Appeal Board Decision M79-1179, June 2, 1980 ("a serious infringement of basic human rights and such infringement is equivalent to persecution"); and *Jose Mariano Aguilar Vides,* Immigration Appeal Board Decision M83-1009, February 3, 1983 ("flouting of his fundamental rights").

[61] Immigration Appeal Board Decision 79-1150, C.L.I.C. Notes 28.8, November 13, 1980.

[62] *Id.,* at 3, *per* J.-P. Houle.

[63] [1982] 2 F.C. 779 (C.A.).

[64] *Id.,* at 782, *per* Heald J. *Accord Luis Rene Amayo Encina v. Minister of Employment and Immigration,* [1982] 1 F.C. 520 (C.A.).

First in the hierarchy are those rights which were stated in the Universal Declaration, translated into immediately binding form in the ICCPR,[65] and from which no derogation whatsoever is permitted, even in times of compelling national emergency.[66] These include freedom from arbitrary deprivation of life,[67] protection against torture or cruel, inhuman, or degrading punishment or treatment,[68] freedom from slavery,[69] the prohibition on criminal prosecution for *ex post facto* offences,[70] the right to recognition as a person in law,[71] and freedom of thought, conscience, and religion.[72] The failure to ensure these rights under any circumstances is thus appropriately considered to be tantamount to persecution.

Second are those rights enunciated in the UDHR and concretized in binding and enforceable form in the ICCPR,[73] but from which states may derogate during a "public emergency which threatens the life of the nation and the existence of which is officially proclaimed".[74] These include freedom from arbitrary arrest or detention;[75] the right to equal protection for all,[76] including children[77] and minorities;[78] the right in criminal proceedings to a fair and public hearing and to be presumed innocent unless guilt is proved;[79] the protection of personal and family privacy and integrity;[80] the right to internal movement and choice of residence;[81] the freedom to leave and return to one's country;[82] liberty of opinion, expression, assembly, and association;[83]

---

[65] "Each State Party to the present Covenant undertakes to respect and to ensure to all individuals within its territory and subject to its jurisdiction the rights recognized in the present Covenant. . . . Where not already provided for by existing legislative or other measures, each State Party to the present Covenant undertakes to take the necessary steps. . . to adopt such legislative or other measures as may be necessary to give effect to the rights recognized in the present Covenant": ICCPR, *supra*, note 51, at Art. 2(1)-(2).

[66] "In time of public emergency which threatens the life of the nation and the existence of which is officially proclaimed, the State Parties to the present Covenant may take measures derogating from their obligations under the present Covenant. . . [but] [n]o derogation from Articles 6, 7, 8 (paragraphs 1 and 2), 11, 15, 16 and 18 may be made under this provision": ICCPR, *supra*, note 51, at Art. 4(1)-(2).

[67] ICCPR, *supra*, note 51, at Art. 6.

[68] Art. 7.

[69] Art. 8.

[70] Art. 15.

[71] Art. 16.

[72] Art. 18.

[73] *See* note 65, *supra*.

[74] ICCPR, *supra*, note 51, at Art. 4(1).

[75] Arts. 9-10.

[76] Arts. 3 and 26.

[77] Art. 24.

[78] Art. 27.

[79] Art. 14.

[80] Arts. 17 and 23.

[81] Art. 12(1).

[82] Art. 12(2)-(4).

[83] Arts. 19-22.

the right to form and join trade unions;[84] and the ability to partake in government,[85] access public employment without discrimination,[86] and vote in
periodic and genuine elections.[87] The failure to ensure any of these rights
will generally constitute a violation of a state's basic duty of protection, unless
it is demonstrated that the government's derogation was strictly required by
the exigencies of a real emergency situation, was not inconsistent with other
aspects of international law, and was not applied in a discriminatory way.[88]
Where, for example, the failure to respect a basic right in this category goes
beyond that which is strictly required to respond to the emergency (in terms
of scope or duration), or where the derogation impacts disproportionately
on certain subgroups of the population, a finding of persecution is warranted.[89]

Third are those rights contained in the UDHR and carried forward in the
International Covenant on Economic, Social, and Cultural Rights. In contrast to the ICCPR, the ICESCR does not impose absolute and immediately
binding standards of attainment, but rather requires states to take steps to
the maximum of their available resources to progressively realize rights[90] in
a non-discriminatory way.[91] The basic values protected are the right to work,[92]

---

[84] Art. 22.

[85] Art. 25(a).

[86] Art. 25(c).

[87] Art. 25(b).

[88] Permissible derogation is limited to acts which are ". . . strictly required by the exigencies
of the situation, provided that such measures are not inconsistent with [the state's] other obligations under international law and do not involve discrimination solely on the ground of race,
colour, sex, language, religion, or social origin": ICCPR, *supra*, note 51, at Art. 4(1). Moreover, emergency situations must be officially declared, and formal notice of derogation given
to the Secretary-General of the United Nations: *Id.*, at Art. 4(1)-(3).

[89] A group of experts in international law was convened by the International Commission
of Jurists in 1984 to draft *The Siracusa Principles on the Limitation and Derogation Provisions
in the International Covenant on Civil and Political Rights.* The consensus achieved was intended
to reflect the existing state of international law with respect to the scope of the limitation clauses,
and the type of situations which qualify as public emergencies: U.N. Doc. E/CN.4/1984/4,
reproduced at (1986), 36 I.C.J. Review 48.

[90] "Each State Party to the Covenant undertakes to take steps, individually and through international assistance and co-operation, especially economic and technical, to the maximum of
its available resources, with a view to achieving progressively the full realization of the rights
recognized in the present Covenant by all appropriate means, including particularly the adoption of legislative measures": ICESCR, *supra*, note 52, at Art. 2(1). This obligation has recently
been interpreted to mean, *inter alia*, that states must, regardless of their level of development,
ensure respect for minimum subsistence rights for all, and that in assessing the adequacy of
measures undertaken, "attention shall be paid to equitable and effective use of and access to
the available resources", including those available through international cooperation and
assistance: *The Limburg Principles*, Principles 0.10-0.13, reported at (1986), 37 I.C.J. Review 43.

[91] "The States Parties to the present Covenant undertake to guarantee that the rights enunciated in the present Covenant will be exercised without discrimination of any kind as to race,
colour, sex, language, religion, political or other opinion, national or social origin, property,
birth, or other status": ICESCR, *supra*, note 52, at Art. 2(2).

[92] ICESCR, *supra*, note 52, at Art. 6.

including just and favourable conditions of employment, remuneration, and rest;[93] entitlement to food,[94] clothing,[95] housing,[96] medical care,[97] social security,[98] and basic education;[99] protection of the family, particularly children and mothers;[100] and the freedom to engage and benefit from cultural, scientific, literary, and artistic expression.[101] While the standard of protection is less absolute than that which applies to the first two categories of rights, a state is in breach of its basic obligations where it either ignores these interests notwithstanding the fiscal ability to respond,[102] or where it excludes a minority of its population from their enjoyment.[103] Moreover, the deprivation of certain of the socio-economic rights, such as the ability to earn a living, or the entitlement to food, shelter, or health care will at an extreme level be tantamount to the deprivation of life or cruel, inhuman or degrading treatment,[104] and hence unquestionably constitute persecution.

Fourth, a few of the rights recognized in the Universal Declaration were not codified in either of the binding covenants on human rights, and may thus be outside the scope of a state's basic duty of protection. The right to own and be free from arbitrary deprivation of property[105] and the right to be protected against unemployment[106] are examples of rights which are included in this group, and which will not ordinarily suffice in and of themselves as the foundation for a claim of failure of state protection.

---

[93] Art. 7.

[94] Art. 11(1).

[95] *Id.*

[96] *Id.*

[97] Art. 12.

[98] Art. 9.

[99] Arts. 13-14.

[100] Art. 10.

[101] Art. 15.

[102] "[T]he available resources language should be read as establishing a priority for social welfare. Given the purposes of the Economic Covenant, it is hard to see how the alternative reading would make any sense. It is clear that the drafters of the Economic Covenant wished to impose obligations on states. Yet if the only obligation arising from the Economic Covenant was that a state could spend what it wanted on social welfare, then this would be no obligation at all and the drafters would have failed in their goal": D. Trubek, "Economic, Social, and Cultural Rights in the Third World: Human Rights Law and Human Needs Programs", in T. Meron, ed., *Human Rights in International Law*, p. 215 (1984).

[103] "Some obligations under the Covenant require immediate implementation in full by all States parties, such as the prohibition of discrimination in article 2(2) of the Covenant": *The Limburg Principles, supra*, note 90, at Principle 0.7.

[104] "To take a central example, that of the relationship between ICCPR 6(1) and ICESCR 11(1), the question is whether the 'right to life' can be interpreted to include a 'right to an adequate standard of living,' various aspects of the latter right thus falling to be adjudicated in the name of the former. If sustainable, such an interpretation generates an implicit overlap between the two articles. . .": C. Scott, "The Interdependence and Permeability of Human Rights Norms: Towards a Partial Fusion of the International Covenants on Human Rights" (1989), 27(4) Osgoode Hall L.J. 769, at 780.

[105] UDHR, *supra*, note 50, at Art. 17.

[106] Art. 23.

In sum, persecution is most appropriately defined as the sustained or systemic failure of state protection in relation to one of the core entitlements which has been recognized by the international community.[107] The types of harm to be protected against include the breach of any right within the first category, a discriminatory or non-emergency abrogation of a right within the second category, or the failure to implement a right within the third category which is either discriminatory or not grounded in the absolute lack of resources. The sections which follow examine the application of this general principle in specific contexts.

4.3 Risk to Civil and Political Rights

Under the human rights paradigm, the serious possibility of a violation of a first category right will always constitute a risk of persecution. Thus, the threat of execution,[108] assault,[109] torture,[110] slavery, or enforced conformity of belief[111] exemplifies failure by the state to protect core values.[112] As was cogently noted in the decision of *Philomene Lundy:*[113]

---

[107] *Accord* M. Gibney and M. Stohl, "Human Rights and U.S. Refugee Policy", in M. Gibney, ed., *Open Borders? Closed Societies? The Ethical and Political Issues*, p. 159 (1988): "Drawing the line on what is or is not persecution has been extremely difficult and politically charged. The position taken here is that there are different levels of persecution (and human rights violations) that are practiced in the world, and such levels ought to be recognized in making refugee admission determinations."

[108] This includes the threat of execution directed against a broadly defined group. In *Kidane Ghebreiyesus*, the Immigration Appeal Board held in relation to an Eritrean from Ethiopia that ". . . a civil war directed against a minority race inside a country, verging on genocide, is without doubt evidence of racial persecution": Immigration Appeal Board Decision 79-1137, C.L.I.C. Notes 20.3, March 21, 1980, at 3, *per* R. Tremblay. *Accord Adan Jeronimo Alvarenga*, Immigration Appeal Board Decision M87-1081, May 20, 1987.

[109] The threat of rape, for example, is a sufficient basis to fear persecution, as is noted in the decision of *Maria Veronica Rodriguez Salinas Araya*, Immigration Appeal Board Decision 76-1127, January 6, 1977, at 8, *per* J.-P. Houle: "[T]hreats such as these are degrading and constitute quite clearly an attack on the moral integrity of the person and, hence, persecution of the most vile sort." *Accord Philomene Lundy*, Immigration Appeal Board Decision M87-1496X, November 26, 1987.

[110] "[T]he right of persons not to be subjected to torture or inhuman or degrading treatment may be considered a peremptory rule of customary international law": K. Hailbronner, "Non-Refoulement and 'Humanitarian' Refugees: Customary International Law or Wishful Legal Thinking?" (1986), 26(4) Virginia J. Intl. L. 857, at 887.

[111] Guy Goodwin-Gill has argued that notwithstanding its non-derogable character, the denial of freedom of worship may be equated with persecution only in certain circumstances: *see* G. Goodwin-Gill, "Entry and Exclusion of Refugees" (1980), Michigan Y.B. Intl. L. 291, at 298-99.

[112] Persecution ". . . would encompass threats to life and liberty, so that execution, detention, and torture are readily included. . .": G. Goodwin-Gill, *supra*, note 111, at 298. *Accord* I. Foighel, "Legal Status of the Boat People" (1979), 48 Nordisk Tidsskrift for Intl. Ret. 217, at 221; F. Marino-Menendez, "El concepto de refugiado en un contexto de derecho internacional general" (1983), 35(2) Revista española de derecho internacional 337, at 354.

[113] Immigration Appeal Board Decision M87-1496X, November 26, 1987.

. . . Nothing can justify the use of violence against persons, for the purpose either of exercising or of retaining power. Oppression by all those who abuse their power will always be unacceptable and reprehensible, especially where the power is maintained by force. . . .[114]

Similarly, the real risk of a human rights violation of the second category — arbitrary arrest or detention,[115] denial of freedom of movement,[116] opinion, association, or privacy[117] for example — is usually to be equated with persecution. The only exception is short-term,[118] emergency derogation of a non-discriminatory nature from a second category right, which under international law is insufficient to establish the absence of state protection. In general, Canadian courts have recognized the need to view any sustained attack on one's physical, moral, or intellectual integrity as probative of persecution.[119] As stated in the decision of *Charles Kwado Amoah:*[120]

> . . . it is not necessary for an individual to be beaten or tortured for him to have a feeling of persecution. It is sufficient if his fundamental freedom, his feelings of membership in a particular social group or the expression of his opinions are threatened for a well-founded fear to arise in him.[121]

---

[114] *Id.,* at 1, *per* J. Blumer.

[115] "[T]he applicant stated under oath that on none of the occasions he was arrested and detained was he formally charged and he was never summoned for trial. This constitutes a serious infringement of basic human rights and such infringement is equivalent to persecution": *Jose del Rosario Perez Gomez*, Immigration Appeal Board Decision M79-1179, June 2, 1980, at 3, *per* J.-P. Houle. *Accord Fernando Alejandro Cordova Seguel*, Immigration Appeal Board Decision 76-1157, August 11, 1977; *Jose Mariano Aguilar Vides*, Immigration Appeal Board Decision M83-1009, February 3, 1983. On the other hand, the Board inexplicably chose to ignore evidence of arbitrary detention in an Indian case involving repeated mass arrests consequent to demonstrations of political opposition: *Harpal Gill Singh*, Immigration Appeal Board Decision T83-10185, December 12, 1983.

[116] This would include mass expulsions of minority groups, ". . . when the expelled minority is hostile to the belief system of the dominant group": G. Beyer, "The Political Refugee: 35 Years Later" (1981), 15 Intl. Migration Rev. 26, at 26.

[117] In the case of *Noe Aguillar Martinez*, it was decided that the illicit search of the family home on six occasions, in tandem with repeated questioning of the wife about her husband's whereabouts, was "tantamount to persecution": Immigration Appeal Board Decision M80-1145, November 20, 1980, at 4, *per* J.-P. Houle.

[118] Grahl-Madsen, for example, draws an arbitrary standard for determining when emergency detention is of sufficient duration to amount to persecution: "When it comes to threats to freedom, it is hoped that my old conclusion still holds good: that imprisonment or detention for a period of three months or more constitutes persecution": A. Grahl-Madsen, "International Refugee Law Today and Tomorrow" (1982), 20 Archiv des Völkerrechts 411, at 422.

[119] [P]ersecution does not consist solely in physical torture; an essential element of persecution is harassment. . . . Any repeated or sustained attack on not only a person's physical integrity, but also on his moral integrity, constitutes persecution. . .": *Juan Alejandro Araya Heredio*, Immigration Appeal Board Decision 76-1127, January 6, 1977, at 6-7, *per* J.-P. Houle. *Accord Fernando Alejandro Cordova Seguel*, Immigration Appeal Board Decision 76-1157, August 11, 1977, at 6; *Jose del Rosario Perez Gomez*, Immigration Appeal Board Decision M79-1179, June 2, 1980; *Andrzej Staniszewski*, Immigration Appeal Board Decision M87-1024X, April 22, 1987.

[120] Immigration Appeal Board Decision M87-1300X, November 2, 1987.

[121] *Id.,* at 2, *per* J. Blumer.

Three types of confusion exist in relation to the application of the human rights framework in the context of threats to life or freedom. On the one hand, theorists such as Paul Weis have taken an overly inclusive position, arguing that "[a] threat to life or freedom. . . will always be persecution. . . ."[122] This view overlooks the possibility of a constrained, non-discriminatory[123] abrogation of human rights of the second category during an emergency situation, such as the imposition of temporary restrictions on freedom of assembly or internal movement. As discussed above,[124] such a short-term suspension of rights may not be demonstrative of a failure of state protection, in which case it will not suffice as the basis for establishing a fear of persecution.

Second and conversely, a number of Canadian decisions have failed to recognize the rule that a threat to life or freedom is generally to be equated with persecution. In *Romilio Dictmart Aranda Diaz*,[125] for example, the Board dismissed a Chilean claim in which military personnel invaded the applicant's home and treated his family roughly, causing the claimant's wife to miscarry. This action, coupled with subsequent regular police visits and interrogations, was adjudged insufficient to establish refugee status. Fellow Chilean *Hector Eduardo Contreras Guttierez*[126] fared no better. Even though he had been badly beaten and tortured on several occasions during unlawful detentions, the Immigration Appeal Board characterized the incidents as merely part of "massive security measures",[127] and noted that the claimant ". . . was not disabled in any way in the alleged beatings and torture he received and admitted there were no scars"![128] A third example is the decision in *Raman Kumar Chopra,*[129] an Indian claimant who was twice beaten by police in addition to imprisonment and regular police harassment, but who in the Board's view was not persecuted. These cases illustrate a discomforting tendency to demand proof of impending harm substantially in excess of the limits established by international human rights norms.[130]

---

[122] P. Weis, "The concept of the refugee in international law" (1960), 87 J. du droit intl. 928, at 970. *Accord* I. Foighel, *supra*, note 112, at 221.

[123] UNHCR correctly confines Weis' principle to discriminatory situations: "[A] threat to life or freedom *on account of race, religion, nationality, political opinion or membership of a particular social group* is always persecution" [Emphasis added]: UNHCR, *Handbook on Procedures and Criteria for Determining Refugee Status*, p. 14 (1979).

[124] *See* text *supra* at notes 88-89.

[125] Immigration Appeal Board Decision V80-6225, C.L.I.C. Notes 23.7, July 30, 1980.

[126] Immigration Appeal Board Decision V80-6220, C.L.I.C. Notes 30.11, March 16, 1981.

[127] *Id.,* at 9, *per* W. Hlady.

[128] *Id.,* Member Bruce Howard authored a powerful dissenting opinion in which he found that the claimant had suffered in an "unspeakable manner" and was "systematically tortured in body, mind and spirit": *Id.,* at 15, *per* B. Howard.

[129] Immigration Appeal Board Decision M83-1196, November 7, 1983. *Accord Karthigesu Sivanesan*, Immigration Appeal Board Decision M84-1513, January 7, 1985, in which three arrests and detentions, one including torture, were considered to be insufficient evidence of persecution.

[130] *See, e.g.,* F. Marino-Menendez, *supra*, note 112, at 354.

Third, the Immigration Appeal Board has on occasion inappropriately dismissed claims of risk to civil and political rights because they were grounded in the advocacy of socio-economic welfare. For example, in *Meril Meryse,*[131] the risk of imprisonment or torture faced by the claimant in consequence of his lobbying for economic reform in Haiti was dismissed as merely a desire for "economic betterment";[132] evidence of possible military harassment of a Ghanaian because of his membership in a pressure group demanding better economic conditions led to a negative finding because "his protests were directed against economic rather than political considerations";[133] and fear of assault due to the claimant's withdrawal from "a vicious system of political patronage" in Guyana was deemed to raise economic concerns outside the scope of the refugee definition.[134] These judgments fail to focus on the central concern of risk to physical, moral, or intellectual integrity, and demonstrate an unhealthy predisposition to question the possibility of a need for protection where socio-economic issues are involved. To be preferred is the type of reasoning found in the decision of *Grimaldo Remigio Corcuera Guzman,*[135] involving a Peruvian claimant who was detained for organizing political demonstrations in support of the rights of the poor. The Immigration Appeal Board found the applicant to be ". . . in a category of persons subject to harassment in the form of attacks on his basic rights"[136] and determined him to be a Convention refugee.

Critics argue that the relative ease of establishing a risk of persecution on the basis of a threat to life or freedom privileges these aspects of human dignity in relation to social, economic, and cultural rights.[137] This observation, while correct, accurately reflects the current hierarchical state of the international law of human rights.[138] Rather than downgrading the seriousness with which we view risks to civil and political liberties, however, the more

---

[131] Immigration Appeal Board Decision M73-2608, April 30, 1975.

[132] *Id.*, at 24, *per* J. Scott.

[133] *Jim Martin Kwesi Mensah,* Immigration Appeal Board Decision V79-6136, August 7, 1979, at 3, *per* C. Campbell; initially set aside on other grounds by Federal Court of Appeal Decision A-527-79, May 2, 1980, but ultimately affirmed on other grounds subsequent to rehearing in Federal Court of Appeal: (1981), 36 N.R. 332.

[134] *Omar Khan,* Immigration Appeal Board Decision V80-6223, C.L.I.C. Notes 25.9, July 24, 1980, at 3, *per* C. Campbell.

[135] Immigration Appeal Board Decision M82-1265, September 30, 1983.

[136] *Id.,* at 4, *per* R. Tremblay.

[137] F. Marino-Menendez, *supra*, note 112, at 354.

[138] "[O]f the Universal Declaration's 25 paragraphs dealing with specific rights, 6 were devoted to economic, social, and cultural rights. In principle the emphasis attached to these rights by the socialist and some other countries had been recognized. . . . In practice, however, the UN was to neglect economic, social, and cultural rights as a serious field of endeavour for the next two decades. . . . While the recent development of concern with economic rights has been interpreted by some commentators as resulting in 'the elimination of civil and political rights from serious international consideration,' an attempt to restore balance into the treatment of the two sets of rights had in fact been long overdue": P. Alston, "The Universal Declaration at 35: Western and Passé or Alive and Universal?" (1983), 31 I.C.J. Rev. 60.

constructive direction for reform would seem to be the broadening of our perspective on those socio-economic rights which, like issues of life and freedom, ought reasonably to be considered central to a state's basic duty of protection.

4.4 Risk to Economic, Social, and Cultural Rights

Just as the serious risk of violation of civil and political liberties indicates a lack of state protection, so too does failure to respect social, economic, and cultural rights. This position is often misunderstood to imply that everyone who is poor, or who leads a life with few material advantages, can successfully advance a claim to refugee status. For example, Scott Burke has challenged the propriety of refugee claims grounded in the denial of socio-economic rights on the basis that ". . . hundreds of millions of people, including the entire Third World . . . suffer the deprivation of the 'rights' set forth in the Covenant [on Economic, Social, and Cultural Rights],"[139] thus implying a right to asylum "for anyone from an economically backward society."[140] Kenneth Brill has pointedly observed that "[o]ne of the main reasons for not expanding the refugee definition to encompass others besides political persecutees is that this would open the floodgates to the kind of economic migrants that our immigration system has sought to exclude."[141] These characterizations demonstrate a fundamental misperception of the nature of economic, social, and cultural human rights.

Unlike the Civil and Political Covenant,[142] the International Covenant on Economic, Social, and Cultural Rights[143] does not create obligations that states are required to fulfil immediately upon accession. Rather, the duty of each state party is simply "to take steps, individually and through international assistance and co-operation, especially economic and technical, to the maximum of its available resources, with a view to achieving progressively the full realization of the rights recognized",[144] and to "guarantee that the rights enunciated. . . will be exercised without discrimination of any kind. . . ."[145] Thus, the Covenant creates two kinds of duty. First, a government must marshal national and international resources[146] and give priority

---

[139] S. Burke, "Compassion Versus Self-Interest: Who Should Be Given Asylum in the United States?" (1984), 8 Fletcher Forum 311, at 320.

[140] *Id.,* at 319.

[141] K. Brill, "The Endless Debate" (1983), 32 Cleveland State, L. Rev. 117.

[142] *Supra*, note 51.

[143] *Supra*, note 52.

[144] ICESCR, *supra*, note 52, at Art. 2(1).

[145] Art. 2(2).

[146] "[I]n evaluating the performance of any state under the principle of progressive realization, would it not be proper to take into account a decision not to use available international assistance to meet social needs?. . . [T]he legislative history of the Economic Covenant indicates that the broader meaning of 'available resources' was intended: the official history explicitly

to the expenditure of those resources in achieving the full realization of human rights.[147] Second, and more commonly related to refugee claims, states must implement socio-economic rights on a non-discriminatory basis, and may not, for example, limit basic educational opportunities to members of certain minority groups, or deny the right to work to members of an opposition political party. It must be emphasized, however, that the persistence of non-discriminatory poverty or hardship does not constitute *per se* a violation of the Covenant.[148]

In addition to this carefully circumscribed duty, the substantive scope of most socio-economic rights is far from a guarantee of prosperity for all. By way of example, the mandatory scope of the right to health only obligates states to work to reduce infant mortality, improve hygiene, control diseases, and establish basic medical services.[149] Similarly, the right to education requires universal access only to primary education, with further opportunities conditioned by circumstances.[150]

Taken together, these carefully crafted qualifications within the ICESCR mean that an absence of state protection can be said to exist only where a government fails to ensure the non-discriminatory allocation of available resources to meet the most basic of socio-economic needs. It is in this context that refugee protection becomes relevant — not as a means of guaranteeing access to "the good life", but rather only to vindicate the right of everyone to those social, economic, and cultural attributes which are essential to human dignity.

4.4.1 Persecution Distinguished from Hardship

A line is therefore drawn between migration for reasons of "personal convenience"[151] or in search of improved living conditions, and migration driven by fear of a human rights violation tantamount to persecution. Because economic hardship is not necessarily a contravention of human rights norms, it is correct to exclude from refugee protection persons whose sole motivation for migration is the desire to leave generalized, difficult economic conditions, or who only wish the opportunity to build a more economically secure life.[152] Such persons are economic migrants, not refugees:

---

says that this clause was meant to include international aid": D. Trubek, "Economic, Social and Cultural Rights in the Third World", in T. Meron, ed., *Human Rights in International Law*, pp. 215-16 (1984).

[147] *Id.*

[148] "[R]efugees are challenging a policy . . . and a conception of refugeehood that denies special consideration to persons fleeing civil war or mass poverty attributable in part to policies of friendly authoritarian regimes": K. Brill, *supra*, note 141, at 126.

[149] ICESCR, *supra*, note 52, at Art. 12.

[150] Art. 13.

[151] This distinction can be traced to the 1938 *Convention concerning the Status of Refugees coming from Germany*, 192 L.N.T.S. 59, which excluded from refugee status those persons who had left Germany for "reasons of purely personal convenience."

[152] "Clearly a person is not a refugee if that person is outside his or her own country simply

> The apprehension or calculation of the hardships which may be the lot of an entire group of people; and the reasonable desire to improve one's condition in life, either psychologically, socially or morally, are not sufficient. . . .[153]

This principle is, however, subject to two major qualifications.

First, economic deprivation which is discriminatory in the sense of being directed against or experienced only by a minority within a state can be demonstrative of persecution. As discussed in more detail in the next section, it is clear that where economic suffering has a political, racial, or otherwise disfranchising impact, its victims may qualify as refugees.[154] As noted by Michael Schulteis:[155]

> . . . economic depression or persecution may also find expression in poverty, both absolute and relative, but they are a consequence of the system itself. For example, in some developing countries political and economic policies marginalize and impoverish local populations by depriving them of economic resources and political voice.[156]

In circumstances of this sort, where serious economic hardship is specific in its oppressive impact, a violation of human rights in the nature of persecution is established.[157]

The second qualification relates to persons who have a genuine fear of persecution, but who may *also* wish to improve their economic position or live in a country which enjoys conditions of prosperity. They need to leave their own country because their basic human rights are genuinely at risk, but they choose to seek protection in a country of social or economic opportunity. While the Immigration Appeal Board has occasionally appeared determined to deny such claims,[158] the fact of this auxiliary motivation is quite

---

because he or she is able to earn a better living in the new country'': P. Hyndman, ''Refugees Under International Law with a Reference to the Concept of Asylum'' (1986), 60 Australian L.J. 148, at 149.

[153] *Louis-Paul Mingot* (1973), 8 I.A.C. 351, at 367, *per* J.-P. Houle. *See also Marc Michel Cylien*, Immigration Appeal Board Decision 73-12462, March 21, 1974 (''desire to find better economic conditions''); set aside on other grounds by Federal Court of Appeal Decision A-163-80, September 30, 1980.

[154] M. Posner, ''Who Should We Let In?'' (1981), 9 Human Rts. 16, at 18.

[155] M. Schulteis, ''A Continent in Crisis: Migrants and Refugees in Africa'', paper prepared for Conference on ''The African Context of Human Rights'' (1987, published).

[156] *Id.*, at 10.

[157] G. Jaeger, ''The Definition of 'Refugee': Restrictive versus Expanding Trends'', [1983] World Refugee Survey 5, at 7. *Accord* D. Anker and M. Posner, ''The Forty Year Crisis'' (1981), 82 San Diego L. Rev. 1, at 67.

[158] *See, e.g., Harbhajan Washir Singh*, Immigration Appeal Board Decision T79-9454, December 7, 1982, in which the Board commented adversely on the claimant's desire to seek employment in Canada; *Christolene Permaul*, Immigration Appeal Board Decision T83-9310, April 13, 1983, which pointed out the high rate of unemployment in the claimant's country of origin before dismissing her claim; and *Munir Mohamad Adem Suleiman*, Immigration Appeal Board Decision V81-6246, November 16, 1983, which recounts a series of serious threats against the claimant, a member of the Eritrean Liberation Front, but rejects his claim after noting that he wished the opportunity to go to school in Canada.

irrelevant to the issue of refugee status, as was eloquently stated in the decision of *Guillermo Lautaro Diaz Fuentes:*[159]

> A superficial examination of the appellant's testimony both at the special inquiry and at the appeal hearing might suggest that the appellant is seeking material security above all, and that he might be what is called. . . an "economic migrant". . . . But we must not consider this testimony out of context; on the contrary, what we must find out is whether behind apparent personal and economic motives there exists a fear of persecution. . . . The distinction between an economic migrant and a refugee is not always easy to establish, but what is important to keep in mind is that if a person is a refugee, the fact that he also is or may be an economic migrant does not deprive him of his status as a refugee.[160]

This position has been approved by the Federal Court of Appeal decision in *Abeba Teklehaimanot v. Immigration Appeal Board,*[161] in which Mr. Justice Pratte held that there is no incompatibility in law between refugee status and the desire to establish oneself as a permanent resident of Canada.

In sum, while the rule that economic migrants are to be distinguished from refugees is well-recognized, care must be taken to ensure that both the victims of economic oppression and refugees who seek the assistance of states of relative economic prosperity are not excluded from protection.

4.4.2 Defining a Breach of Economic, Social, or Cultural Rights

Thus far the argument has been that persecution may result from breach of a core social, economic, or cultural right; that socio-economic human rights are abrogated only where a state either neglects their realization in the face of adequate resources, or implements them in a discriminatory way; and that the existence of generalized hardship is neither a sufficient nor a disqualifying factor in defining the existence of socio-economic persecution. It remains, then, to examine in more detail the circumstances in which a threat to basic economic, social, or cultural rights is tantamount to persecution.

First, purely financial grievances do not constitute persecution,[162] this principle being a subset of the rule that core principles of human rights do not include a right to private property.[163] The case of *Jose Salvador Ficciella Munizaga*[164] involved a wealthy pro-Allende Chilean businessman whose opportunities and patronage had evaporated after the *coup d'état,* leading him to claim that he was being economically punished by the new regime.

---

[159] (1974), 9 I.A.C. 323.

[160] *Id.,* at 343.

[161] Federal Court of Appeal Decision A-730-79, September 8, 1980.

[162] *See* C. Wydrzynski, *Canadian Immigration Law and Procedure,* p. 320 (1983). In some earlier international refugee accords, however, a threat against freedom, life or property was deemed to be of sufficient gravity to warrant protection: *see* Y. Shimada, "The Concept of the Political Refugee in International Law" (1975), 19 Japanese Ann. Intl. L 24, at 36.

[163] *See* text *supra* at note 105.

[164] Immigration Appeal Board Decision 79-1222, C.L.I.C. Notes 14.14, December 13, 1979.

The Board correctly observed that it would not ". . . look into all business transactions of the applicant in his native country and pronounce whether he has real financial grievances. . . [because] [e]ven if he has, it is not equivalent to persecution".[165] Similarly, a claim grounded solely on the actual or anticipated confiscation of property or damage to goods, without any attendant risk to personal security or basic livelihood, is not of sufficient gravity to warrant the granting of refugee status.

Second, and also incapable of establishing persecution, are circumstances in which the rights at risk are related to core entitlements, but the threat does not go to the heart of the right as elaborated in international law. For example, the Board regularly characterized as insufficient the concerns of non-communist Eastern Europeans who were relegated to inferior accommodation and were denied access to the full range of food and other amenities available to adherents of the ruling party. These claims have been accurately assessed as raising the spectre of discrimination short of persecution.[166] Polish claimant *Helena Olearczyk,*[167] for example, had been a member of Solidarity, and refused to join the ruling Communist Party. The Board found that

> . . . indeed she has been the victim of some harassment. Her superiors exercised some control over her union activities and it is probable that she was denied promotions and employment benefits. However, this harassment cannot be considered persecution in the sense of the Convention.[168]

This judgment was affirmed on judicial review, the Federal Court of Appeal noting that it agreed with the Board's view "that the harassment described was not sufficiently serious to amount to persecution".[169] Because socio-economic rights are intentionally defined in international law in terms of minimally acceptable standards, not every instance of unfairness broadly related to an enumerated right will support a finding of persecution.[170] While,

[165] *Id.,* at 2, *per* F. Glogowski.

[166] *See* R. Howard, "Contemporary Canadian Refugee Policy: A Critical Assessment" (1980), 6 (2) Cdn. Public Policy 361, at 363. *See also Josef Ligas,* Immigration Appeal Board Decision 75-10390, December 19, 1975; *Tadeusz Jakubowski,* Immigration Appeal Board Decision V79-6197, October 4, 1979; *Zdzislaw Liedtke,* Immigration Appeal Board Decision V80-6383, December 10, 1980; *Henryk Stanley Komisarski,* Immigration Appeal Board Decision V81-6162, May 28, 1981; *Jaroslaw Jozef Litwinski,* Immigration Appeal Board Decision V81-6322, October 8, 1981.

[167] Immigration Appeal Board Decision M87-1897X, February 9, 1988.

[168] *Id.,* at 2, *per* J. Cardinal. *Accord Andrzej Matuszewski,* Immigration Appeal Board Decision V80-6058, at 2, *per* C. Campbell; reversed on other grounds by Federal Court of Appeal Decision A-163-80, September 30, 1980.

[169] *Helena Olearczyk v. Minister of Employment and Immigration* (1990), 8 Imm. L.R. (2d) 18, at 19, *per* Hugessen J.

[170] In the United States, for example, only "*substantial economic disadvantage* caused by the foreclosure of economic opportunity constitutes persecution under the refugee statutes" [Emphasis added]: Note, "Political Legitimacy in the Law of Political Asylum" (1985), 99 Harvard L.Rev. 450, at 460. *Accord* A. Fragomen, "The Refugee: A Problem of Definition" (1970), 3 Case Western Reserve J. Intl. L. 45, at 54; D. Gross, "The Right of Asylum Under United

for example, the rights to food and shelter are among those recognized in the ICESCR,[171] it is only an "adequate standard of living"[172] that is guaranteed by law, not access to the full range of desirable commodities and services.

The third category includes those claims which evince a serious risk to core human rights, and hence justify a finding of fear of persecution. The classic example is economic proscription,[173] the fundamental breach of the right to work established by Article 23 of the Universal Declaration[174] and Articles 6 and 7 of the ICESCR.[175] Even the most conservative theorists agree that the sustained or systemic denial of the right to earn one's living is a form of persecution,[176] which can coerce or abuse as effectively as imprisonment or torture.[177] This has been recognized by the Federal Court of Appeal in judgments such as *Luis Rene Amayo Encina v. Minister of Employment and Immigration,*[178] involving a Chilean socialist who was subjected to constant surveillance at work following the military coup, ultimately fired from his job, and blocked by a system of official clearances from obtaining other employment. The Federal Court found the claimant to be a Convention refugee, noting that ". . . over a period of years [he] suffered persecution from various sources at his place of work and, after his discharge therefrom, during his period of unemployment prior to coming to Canada, all as a result of his former political activities and beliefs".[179]

Traditionally, however, the economic proscription principle has been nar-

---

States Law" (1980), 80 Columbia L. Rev. 1125, at 1135. *But see Kovac v. I.N.S.,* 407 F. 2d 102, at 107 (9th Cir. 1969) in which the claim of a Yugoslavian chef forced to work as an unskilled cook was recognized as evincing a fear of persecution.

[171] ICESCR, *supra*, note 52, at Art. 11(1).

[172] *Id.*

[173] *See generally* J. Hathaway and M. Schelew, "Persecution by Economic Proscription: A New Refugee Dilemma" (1980), 28 Chitty's L.J. 190.

[174] *Supra*, note 50.

[175] *Supra*, note 52.

[176] Zink, for example, recognized "protracted forced unemployment" as a form of persecution: B. Roberts, "Can the Boat People Assert a Right to Remain in Asylum?" (1980), 4 U. Puget Sound L.R. 176. *Accord* A. Grahl-Madsen, "International Refugee Law Today and Tomorrow" (1982), 20 Archiv des Völkerrechts 411, note 118, at 422: "States may still be prepared to regard economic proscription (on an individual basis and for clearly political reasons) — so severe as to deprive a person of all means of livelihood — as persecution in the sense of the Convention. . . ."

[177] "[P]ersecution. . . should include forms of economic harassment that make it impossible for certain minorities to earn a living. Being prevented from earning a living is just as great a persecution as imprisonment": G. Gilbert, "Right of Asylum: A Change of Direction" (1983), 32 I.C.L.Q. 633, at 645. In the United States, it has been recognized that the impairment of an individual's ability to earn a livelihood amounts to political persecution: *Desir v. Ilchert*, 840 F. 2d 723 (9th Cir. 1988).

[178] Federal Court of Appeal Decision A-720-80, February 27, 1981; setting aside Immigration Appeal Board Decision T80-9349, October 2, 1980. The claim was ultimately rejected on reconsideration by the Immigration Appeal Board on July 9, 1981. *Accord Alfredo Manuel Oyarzo Marchant*, [1982] 2 F.C. 779 (C.A.).

[179] *Id.*, at 2, *per* Urie J.

rowly defined to focus on situations of total exclusion from remunerative employment. In the well-known case of *Jan Piotr Kwiatkowsky*,[180] for example, the claimant alleged a fear of return to Poland on the basis *inter alia* that his religious beliefs and opposition to Communism had resulted in his exclusion from career progress as a teacher. Noting that his dissident status had resulted only in demotion, and not in a denial of his right to work as a teacher, his complaint was characterized as discrimination falling short of persecution.[181] Conversely, forced submission to grossly inappropriate forms of work has been characterized as persecution, as noted in the decision in *Juan Alejandro Araya Heredio:*[182]

> The Convention does not define persecution . . . but it is quite certain that persecution does not consist solely in physical torture; an essential element of persecution is harassment, so much so that real persecution would be present in the case of a person who was denied all opportunity to work or even one who, in order to survive, was forced to accept work manifestly incompatible with his occupational training.[183]

The decision of the Federal Court of Appeal in *Aram Ovakimoglu v. Minister of Employment and Immigration*[184] has adopted this broad reading. The Court characterized the testimony of the Armenian Christian Turkish claimant as "uncontradicted evidence of harassment and persecution which cried out for further exploration"[185] by the Immigration Appeal Board, noting his "difficulties in obtaining and in retaining his employment"[186] and indeed "the lack of possibility for his advancement either in the army or

---

[180] Immigration Appeal Board Decision M79-1220, C.L.I.C. Notes 18.10, December 13, 1979; affirmed on other grounds by Federal Court of Appeal Decision at (1981), 34 N.R. 237, and the Supreme Court of Canada at (1982), 45 N.R. 116.

[181] *Id.*, at 6. *Accord Tomasz Gozdalski*, Immigration Appeal Board Decision M87-1027X, April 23, 1987.

[182] Immigration Appeal Board Decision 76-1127, January 6, 1977. *Accord* I. Foighel, "Legal Status of the Boat People" (1979), 48 Nordisk Tidsskrift for Intl. Ret. 217, at 221, in which persecution is said to include "lost work, imminent risk of not being able to earn a livelihood, and reduced possibilities of work in relation to qualification."

[183] *Id.*, at 6-7, *per* J.-P. Houle. *But see* the extremely narrow conceptualization of economic proscription applied in the case of *Hua Kien Hui*, Immigration Appeal Board Decision V87-6081X, July 21, 1987, at 6, *per* D. Anderson: "[E]ven though Mr. Hui was classed by the authorities to be of landowner and [Kuo Min Tang] class background, and was consequently required to work on a farm for four years in hard and unpleasant jobs, discrimination of this type does not, in itself, constitute a basis for a well-founded fear of persecution. Political re-education through manual labour, combined with indoctrination classes, is carried on, unfortunately, in many countries and for many large social groups."

[184] (1983), 52 N.R. 67 (F.C.A.); setting aside Immigration Appeal Board Decision T82-9976, January 25, 1983. The claim was rejected on reconsideration by the Immigration Appeal Board in its decision of January 6, 1984.

[185] *Id.*, at 69, *per* Urie J.

[186] *Id.*

in civilian life''.[187] This decision takes a holistic view of the substance of the right to work, including both the right to access employment and the right to "just and favourable conditions of work", established by Articles 6 and 7 respectively of the Covenant.[188] Persecution may therefore be established where an individual is prevented from securing any employment, or where the only work which she is permitted to access is, for example, of an extremely dangerous nature or grossly out of keeping with her qualifications and experience.

A problem in applying the economic proscription doctrine can arise where it is difficult to distinguish with precision between the impact of the persecutory acts of the state and the effects of a generally depressed economy. Particularly in the case of refugees from less developed countries, the inability to obtain employment may be the combined result of a general scarcity of work and the efforts of the government or its agent to ensure that whatever minimal opportunities may exist are denied to the refugee. In such circumstances, it is inappropriate to dismiss the claim, as the refugee has still been effectively disfranchised by the state. The fact that initial opportunities were limited is not pertinent to the issue of whether the claimant has been disadvantaged beyond the norm because of the government's persecutory acts.

In contrast, the Immigration Appeal Board has sometimes refused such claims. In the case of *Pedro Ignacio Vera Jiminez,*[189] for example, the Board did not "find it credible that the *sole barrier to employment* for [the claimant] was his political involvement. High unemployment and his lack of work experience are major factors that cannot be discounted as reasons for his lack of success. . . ." [Emphasis added] In the decision of *Ghouse Mahmood Khan Arshad,*[190] the claim was dismissed because "[t]he difficulty in finding work, in this particular case, may be attributable *just as much* to the economic situation in India as to discrimination by the party in power." [Emphasis added] These decisions do not deny that state action was exerted to foreclose economic opportunities, but instead avoid the issue on the ground that conditions would have been difficult even absent governmental interference. Such analysis misses the central issue of whether or not persecution occurred, and results in discrimination against claimants from economically depressed countries.

Forms of economic persecution not related to the right to work enjoy a more ambiguous position thus far in the Canadian jurisprudence. While the decision of the Immigration Appeal Board in *Luis Enrique Toha Seguel*[191] is vague authority for the proposition that the discriminatory denial of educa-

---

[187] *Id.*

[188] ICESCR, *supra*, note 52.

[189] Immigration Appeal Board Decision 81-9344, November 12, 1981.

[190] Immigration Appeal Board Decision 81-9474, September 18, 1981.

[191] Immigration Appeal Board Decision 79-1150, C.L.I.C. Notes 28.8, November 13, 1980.

tional or health facilities is a form of persecution,[192] other decisions are less encouraging. In *Naresh Persaud Ramsarran,*[193] for example, evidence of racially differentiated access to basic school supplies and emergency hospital care in Guyana was characterized as "drastic discrimination",[194] but not persecution. Similarly, the case of *Urszula Grochowska*[195] portrayed Polish denial of schooling and medical insurance to Gypsies as "extensive discrimination. . . [which] does not constitute persecution within the meaning of the definition of a Convention refugee".[196] These precedents take an overly narrow view of the meaning of persecution, and warrant reconsideration in the light of the human rights paradigm set out above. More in keeping with a holistic notion of human rights is the decision in *Vidya Ajodhia,*[197] involving the state-condoned racially discriminatory allocation of basic foodstuffs in Guyana. In accepting the claim to refugee status of an Indo-Guyanese citizen, the Board noted:

> It may be argued that the unfair distribution of food to Indo-Guyanese is a situation of discrimination rather than persecution. However, in my opinion, the withholding of essential food on a daily basis is clearly indicative of persecution.[198]

4.5 Failure of the State's Duty to Protect Basic Human Rights

Not all persons who have left their country because of risk to basic human rights are refugees. As noted in the introduction to this chapter,[199] refugee law is designed to interpose the protection of the international community only in situations where there is no reasonable expectation that adequate national protection of core human rights will be forthcoming. Refugee law is therefore "substitute protection"[200] in the sense that it is a response to disfranchisement from the usual benefits of nationality.[201] As Guy Goodwin-Gill puts it, ". . . the degree of protection normally to be expected of the government is either lacking or denied".[202]

---

[192] *Id.,* at 4, *per* J.-P. Houle. *Accord* G. Goodwin-Gill, "Entry and Exclusion of Refugees" (1980), Michigan Y.B. Intl. L. Studies 291, at 298-99: "Depending on the circumstances, persecution may thus comprise less overt measures such as the imposition of serious economic disadvantage, denial of access to employment, to the professions or to education. . . ."

[193] Immigration Appeal Board Decision T83-9371, April 25, 1983 and February 4, 1985.

[194] *Id.,* at 4, *per* J.-P. Houle.

[195] Immigration Appeal Board Decision V84-6217, October 24, 1984.

[196] *Id.,* at 5, *per* D. Anderson.

[197] Immigration Appeal Board Decision M85-1709, November 12, 1987.

[198] *Id.,* at 4, *per* P. Davey.

[199] *See* text *supra* at notes 34-36.

[200] J. Patrnogic, "Refugees — A Continuing Challenge" (1982), Annuaire de droit international médical 73, at 75.

[201] Memorandum from the Secretary-General, U.N. Doc. E/AC.32/2, at 13, January 3, 1950.

[202] G. Goodwin-Gill, "Non-Refoulement and the New Asylum Seekers" (1986), 26 (4) Virginia J. Intl. L. 897, at 901.

This means that in addition to identifying the human rights potentially at risk in the country of origin, a decision on whether or not an individual faces a risk of "persecution" must also comprehend scrutiny of the state's ability and willingness effectively to respond to that risk. Insofar as it is established that meaningful national protection is available to the claimant, a fear of persecution cannot be said to exist. This rule derives from the primary status accorded to the municipal relationship between an individual and her state,[203] and the principle that international human rights law is appropriately invoked only when a state will not or cannot comply with its classical duty to defend the interests of its citizenry.[204] Andrew Shacknove has helpfully phrased this principle in terms of a breakdown of the protection to be expected of the minimally legitimate state:

> Persecution is but one manifestation of the broader phenomenon: the absence of state protection of the citizen's basic needs. It is this absence of state protection which constitutes the full and complete negation of society and the basis of refugeehood.[205]

The balance of this part examines the application of this general rule. First, how does one assess state accountability for the actions of non-governmental groups or private individuals,[206] the impact of which may be to undermine access to national protection? And second, does an individual have a right to protection in her region of origin, or does the state meet its duty by providing adequate protection in some other part of the country?

4.5.1 Agents of Persecution

The most obvious form of persecution is the abuse of human rights by organs of the state, such as the police or military.[207] This may take the form of either pursuance of a formally sanctioned persecutory scheme, or nonconforming behaviour by the official agents which is not subject to a timely and effective rectification by the state.[208] In such cases, it is clear that the

---

[203] 1 A. Grahl-Madsen, *The Status of Refugees in International Law*, pp. 97-101 (1966).

[204] "The general definition must be seen as a product of the legal and political philosophy of the 18th, 19th and early 20th centuries in the western countries. The major terms of this philosophy were the State and the Individual, and the respective rights and duties of the State and the Individual. . .": P. Hartling, "Concept and Definition of 'Refugee' — Legal and Humanitarian Aspects" (1979, unpublished).

[205] A. Shacknove, "Who is a Refugee?" (1985), 95 Ethics 274, at 277.

[206] The *travaux préparatoires* of the Convention do not establish any distinction between persecution at the hands of the government and persecution by private citizens: J. van der Veen, "Does Persecution by Fellow-Citizens in Certain Regions of a State Fall Within the Definition of 'Persecution' in the Convention Relating to the Status of Refugees of 1951?" (1980), 11 Netherlands Y.B. Intl. L. 167, at 170.

[207] "The source of the persecution is not limited. It may emanate from the government or a third party. Obviously, it will be much easier to show that the fear of persecution is well-founded if the government of the State of origin is perpetrating it. . . ": G. Gilbert, "Right of Asylum: A Change of Direction" (1983), 32 I.C.L.Q. 633, at 645.

[208] In *Jit Dhaliwal Singh*, for example, the claimant's father-in-law, who had been an active

citizen can have no reasonable expectation of national protection, since the harm feared consists of acts or circumstances for which governmental authorities are responsible.[209] As noted in the decision of *Ganganee Janet Permanand:*[210]

> The abuse of power by agents of the State or their unwillingness to discharge their duties in respect to a particular citizen or group of citizens could indeed constitute persecution. However, to be so, such practices must be carried out systematically and with the overt or covert concurrence of the state.[211]

Similarly, there is no meaningful protection when a government supports[212] or condones[213] privately inflicted violations of core human rights. But for this notion of vicarious responsibility, ill-willed states could deprive their victims of recourse to refugee protection simply by contracting out their agenda of harm to unofficial instrumentalities. Thus, the actions of thugs linked to the government[214] or of party members acting in concert with those in

---

Akali Dal supporter, died after being beaten by police; the claimant's wife was subsequently murdered by thugs from the opposition political party, with no adequate police response. In the circumstances, the Board held that the claimant ". . . had every reason to fear that if he was set upon by supporters of the Congress Party on his way home he could not expect to invoke successfully the protection of the police": Immigration Appeal Board Decision T85-9358, June 8, 1987, at 5, *per* E. Townshend.

[209] C. Wydrzynski, "Refugees and the *Immigration Act*" (1979), 25 McGill L.J. 154, at 181.

[210] Immigration Appeal Board Decision T87-10167, August 10, 1987.

[211] *Id.*, at 6, *per* P. Ariemma.

[212] "Clearly, direct government encouragement of private oppression will sustain an asylum claim": D. Gross, "The Right of Asylum Under United States Law" (1980), 80 Columbia L. Rev. 1125, at 1139.

[213] "If the atrocities which cause persons to flee are of relatively short duration only, for example, just an episode, and they are effectively put to an end by the government, there may hardly be any reason for considering the persons concerned political refugees. . . . If, on the other hand, the disturbances continue over a protracted period, without the government being able to check them effectively, this may be considered such a 'flaw' in the organization of the State that it may justify . . . recognition of refugee status. . .": A. Grahl-Madsen, *supra*, note 203, p. 192.

[214] The claim of an Indian citizen was based on beatings he received at the hands of "thugs representing the Congress Party" who assaulted him by reason of his membership in the Janta Party. His application was initially dismissed on the ground that "[t]he threats and beatings Mr. Verma described were not from the police but from 'various thugs' some of whom he identified as being members of the Congress Party": Immigration Appeal Board Decision M82-1115, March 28, 1983, at 5, *per* D. Davey. The decision was reversed in the Federal Court of Appeal, which noted that ". . . the Board erred in law in not addressing the effect of the return to power of the Congress Party in 1980 as relevant to the applicant's fear of political persecution", thus acknowledging the sufficiency of toleration of private behaviour as the basis for a fear of persecution: *Surinder Kumar Verma v. Immigration Appeal Board et al.,* Federal Court of Appeal Decision A-481-83, October 27, 1983, at 2, *per* LeDain J. *Accord Fritz Roland*, Immigration Appeal Board Decision M87-1587X, November 9, 1987, at 3, in which member M. Dore ascribed accountability to the Haitian government for the actions of the Tontons Macoutes, in that they were "in the service of the persons in power".

power[215] have been appropriately characterized as persecutory, based on the notion that persecution comprehends actions "by, or with the tacit approval of the government".[216]

Beyond these acts of commission carried out by entities with which the state is formally or implicitly linked,[217] persecution may also consist of either the failure or inability of a government effectively to protect the basic human rights of its populace.[218] Specifically, there is a failure of protection where a government is *unwilling* to defend citizens against private harm, as well as in situations of objective *inability* to provide meaningful protection. This is a somewhat more complex notion, derived from the principle that the legitimacy of a government is inextricably linked to the sufficiency of the protection it affords its citizenry. As argued and accepted in the decision of the French Conseil d'Etat in *Esshak Dankha:*[219]

---

[215] While some decisions of the Immigration Appeal Board dismissed claims of persecution at the hands of members of the governing party (*see,* e.g., *Nankisore Mangal*, Immigration Appeal Board Decision T82-9141, April 22, 1982, and *Harbhajan Washir Singh*, Immigration Appeal Board Decision T79-9454, December 7, 1982), Federal Court authority appears to accept the propriety of such claims. In *Anthony Andre Williams*, the Immigration Appeal Board dismissed the claim of a St. Lucian who alleged that he had been seriously threatened by members of the governing Labour Party by reason of his work for the opposition United Workers' Party. The Board dismissed the claim, noting that the "threats to which he referred to were [made] by . . . 'rousters' of the Labour Party and not by persons authorized by the Labour Party to carry out these actions": Immigration Appeal Board Decision 81-9029, January 28, 1981, at 1-2, *per* A. Weselak. The Federal Court of Appeal set the decision aside, noting simply that "[i]n light of the Board's statement . . . that there was no evidence of persecution, we cannot be satisfied that the Board did consider the entire record . . . or that if it had, it would necessarily have reached the same conclusion": Federal Court of Appeal Decision A-57-81, June 16, 1981, at 1-2, *per* Heald J.

[216] *Charles Polak*, Immigration Appeal Board Decision 81-3009, April 23, 1981, *per* J. Scott. *Accord,* e.g., *Munir Mohamad Adem Suleiman*, Immigration Appeal Board Decision V81-6246, July 23, 1981; *Juan de la Cruz Cuevas Fuente*, Immigration Appeal Board Decision 79-1117, August 28, 1979; *Nezihi Yilmaz*, Immigration Appeal Board Decision 80-9123, C.L.I.C. Notes 18.14, April 16, 1980.

[217] To the contrary, where the harm feared is strictly private in nature, and the government in the country of origin is both willing and able to afford protection, the requisite degree of state involvement is not established. In *Daniel Cripaul*, for example, the Board correctly denied the claim of a Guyanan Christian whose parents had been the targets of rocks and bottles thrown by other East Indians who objected to their religion. Because there was no evidence of state awareness of the incident, much less complicity or inability to act, the claim of fear of persecution was not made out: Immigration Appeal Board Decision M81-1106, June 4, 1981.

[218] The case of Sri Lankan Tamil *Saam Yagasampanthar Murugesu* was initially refused by the Immigration Appeal Board on the ground that evidence that a person is "discriminated or even persecuted by the religious or racial majority group" cannot establish a fear of persecution: Immigration Appeal Board Decision M82-1142, July 13, 1982, at 3, *per* F. Glogowski. After reversal by the Federal Court of Appeal, the Immigration Appeal Board accepted the claim, noting that ". . . too many persons, especially Tamils, were not given the benefit [of the] legal system. . .": Immigration Appeal Board Decision M82-1142, September 30, 1983, at 8, *per* G. Loiselle.

[219] Decision No. 42.074, May 27, 1983.

. . . the existence and the authority of the State are conceived and justified on the grounds that it is the means by which members of the national community are protected from aggression, whether at the hands of fellow citizens, or from forces external to the State. [Unofficial translation][220]

Thus, the state which ignores or is unable to respond to legitimate expectations of protection[221] fails to comply with its most basic duty,[222] thereby raising the prospect of a need for surrogate protection.[223] Intention to harm on the part of the state is irrelevant:[224] whether as the result of commission, omission, or incapacity, it remains that people are denied access to basic guarantees of human dignity, and therefore merit protection through refugee law.[225]

The Federal Court of Appeal indicated its support for this comprehensive standard in the decision of *Aram Ovakimoglu v. M.E.I.,*[226] involving a Christian Armenian citizen of Turkey. The Immigration Appeal Board had dismissed the claim because there was no proof of direct harassment by Turkish authorities, although there was evidence that the government had failed to protect the claimant from mob violence inflicted by reason of his nationality and religion.[227] The Federal Court referred the case back to the Board, noting *inter alia* that "the lack of protection available to [the claimant], in common with his fellow Armenians, by the authorities, from harassment,

---

[220] Conclusions of M. Genevois, Commissaire du Gouvernement, in *Esshak Dankha, supra*, note 219. Reported in F. Julien-Laferrière, "Bulletin de jurisprudence française" (1984), 3 Clunet 119, at 122.

[221] "Persecution may include behaviour tolerated by government in such a way as to leave the victim virtually unprotected by the agencies of the state": Minister of Employment and Immigration, "New Refugee Status Advisory Committee Guidelines on Refugee Definition and Assessment of Credibility" (1982), at Principle 6. *Accord* C. Fong, "Some Legal Aspects of the Search for Admission into Other States of Persons Leaving the Indo-Chinese Peninsula in Small Boats" (1981), 52 British Y.B. Intl. L. 53, at 92.

[222] "The fact therefore must be that the individuals themselves, each in his own personal and sovereign right, entered into a compact with each other to produce a Government. . . founded on a moral theory, on a system of universal peace, on the indefeasible hereditary Rights of Man. . . [and] this is the only mode in which Governments have a right to arise, and the only principle on which they have a right to exist": T. Paine, *Rights of Man* 47 and 154 (1915). *See also* R. Hofman, "Refugee-Generating Policies and the Law of State Responsibility" (1985), 45 Zeitschrift Auslandisches Offentliches 694, at 700.

[223] *Accord* A. Grahl-Madsen, *supra*, note 203, at 192.

[224] "Thus, if groups of citizens perpetrate acts of persecution against other groups, and if the government of the country is either unable or unwilling to provide protection to the victimized, the victims nonetheless will be considered to be the objects of persecution. The fact that the government wishes to provide protection will not alter this situation": P. Hyndman, "The 1951 Convention Definition of Refugee" (1987), 9 Human Rts. Q. 49, at 67.

[225] "Since asylum law is designed to protect those who are unable to protect themselves in their native country, any retrenchment from the 'unable or unwilling' standard would be unwarranted": D. Gross, "The Right of Asylum Under United States Law" (1980), 80 Columbia L. Rev. 1125, at 1139.

[226] (1983), 52 N.R. 67 (C.A.).

[227] Immigration Appeal Board Decision T82-9976, January 25, 1983.

both mental and physical, by Moslem Turks, all because he and others were Armenian Christians''[228] ought to have been taken into consideration.

This holistic standard of state obligation was clearly elaborated in the landmark decision in *Zahirdeen Rajudeen v. Minister of Employment and Immigration.*[229] The evidence at the hearing established that the Sri Lankan claimant was at risk because he was a Tamil Muslim in a society dominated by Sinhalese Buddhists, and that the police were either unwilling or unable to protect him from violence at the hands of Sinhalese mobs. In the Federal Court, Heald J. found that the requisite degree of state complicity was established by evidence of official indifference to the protection of Tamils.[230] The concurring judgment of Stone J. provides a clear statement of the test of the adequacy of state protection:

> . . . an individual cannot be considered a "Convention refugee" only because he has suffered in his homeland from the outrageous behaviour of his fellow citizens. To my mind, in order to satisfy the definition the persecution complained of must have been committed or been condoned by the state itself and consist either of conduct directed by the state toward the individual or in it knowingly tolerating the behaviour of private citizens, *or refusing or being unable to protect the individual from such behaviour.* [Emphasis added][231]

In applying the *Rajudeen* principle, the Immigration Appeal Board has defined four situations in which there can be said to be a failure of state protection:

1. Persecution committed by the state concerned;
2. Persecution condoned by the state concerned;
3. Persecution tolerated by the state concerned;
4. Persecution not condoned or not tolerated by the state concerned but nevertheless present because the state either refuses or is unable to offer adequate protection.[232]

This approach was confirmed in *Surujpal v. M.E.I.,*[233] involving failure by Guyanese authorities to protect members of the People's Progressive Party from politically motivated violence.

---

[228] *Supra*, note 226, at 69.

[229] (1985), 55 N.R. 129 (F.C.A.).

[230] *Id.*, at 134.

[231] *Id.*, at 135.

[232] *Tezcan Ozdemir,* Immigration Appeal Board Decision M83-1304, C.L.I.C. Notes 77.12, December 18, 1984, at 6, *per* F. Glogowski. On the other hand, the Board has at times reverted to a focus on intentional wrongdoing. In *Arulvelrajah Rajanayagam*, for example, it was inaccurately stated that persecution ". . . implies a deliberate seeking out of an individual or group for mistreatment": Immigration Appeal Board Decision M84-1390, December 31, 1984, at 5, *per* D. Anderson.

[233] "In our view it is not material whether the police directly participated in the assaults or not. What is relevant is whether there was police complicity in a broader sense. . . . It is not required that State participation in persecution be direct; it is sufficient that it is indirect, provided that there is proof of State complicity": (1985) 60 N.R. 73 (F.C.A.), at 75-76.

Obviously, there cannot be said to be a failure of state protection where a government has not been given an opportunity to respond to a form of harm in circumstances where protection might reasonably have been forthcoming:

> A refugee may establish a well-founded fear of persecution when the official authorities are not persecuting him if they refuse or are unable to offer him adequate protection from his persecutors. . . however, he must show that he sought their protection when he is convinced, as he is in the case at bar, that the official authorities — when accessible — had no involvement — direct or indirect, official or unofficial — in the persecution against him.[234]

The Federal Court's decision in *M.E.I. v. Robert Satiacum*[235] further defined the notion of failure of protection by establishing that persecution cannot be said to exist where the absence of protection is remediable through federal control over local inaction or the intervention of a fair and independent judicial process.[236] The test of the sufficiency of protection in Canadian law is thus defined in terms of practical realities: Whatever the formal position of the state, is there a *de facto* failure of protection, grounded in intention, indifference, or incapacity?

Some degree of ambiguity regarding this test is demonstrated in the recent decision of the Federal Court of Appeal in *Attorney General of Canada v. Patrick Francis Ward*.[237] This decision involved a former member of the Irish National Liberation Army (I.N.L.A.), who was unable effectively to secure protection from Irish authorities against the vengeance of his former colleagues after he became an informer for the government. The Immigration Appeal Board had recognized the claim, stating:

> Fear of persecution and lack of protection are also related elements. Persecuted persons clearly do not enjoy the protection of their country of origin and evidence of the lack of protection may create a presumption as to the likelihood of persecution and to the well-foundedness of any fear.[238]

On appeal by the government, the majority decision in the Federal Court of Appeal rejected this reasoning, and held:

---

[234] *Jose Maria da Silva Moreira*, Immigration Appeal Board Decision T86-10370, April 8, 1987, at 4, *per* V. Fatsis.

[235] Federal Court of Appeal Decision A-554-87, June 16, 1989.

[236] "*Rajudeen* and *Surujpal v. Minister of Employment and Immigration* . . . both involved the illegal and violent harassment of refugee claimants by intolerant majorities, with police acquiescence or indifference which amounted to State complicity in the persecution. Neither country, Sri Lanka (*Rajudeen*) nor Guyana (*Surujpal*) is a federal state, and in neither case was the judicial system of the country in play. Both cases clearly deal with the kind of law enforcement which may amount to persecution. Neither relates in any way to the judicial process, let alone to a fair and independent judicial process": *Id.*, at 8, *per* MacGuigan J.

[237] Federal Court of Appeal Decision A-1190-88, March 5, 1990; leave to appeal granted by the Supreme Court of Canada on November 8, 1990: Supreme Court Bulletin 2347.

[238] Immigration Appeal Board Decision, T89-10967X, December 2, 1988.

No such presumption arises. The determination can only be made after an assessment and weighing of the evidence to ascertain whether or not the claimant [has] . . . a well-founded fear of persecution for one of the reasons set out in the definition. Thereafter, the other aspects of inability or unwillingness must be addressed.[239]

While the majority decision employs the language of "state complicity",[240] it would appear that the real concern was the Board's assertion of a *presumption* of fear of persecution in circumstances where state protection is absent. Rather, such a decision is to be made only after "an assessment and weighing of the evidence" to ensure that the absence of protection is attributable to a form of civil or political status protected under the Convention (thereby excluding claims from situations of generalized, undifferentiated violence).[241] In this case, the majority on the Federal Court misconstrued the evidence of a linkage between the harm feared and the claimant's civil or political status,[242] resulting in an unfortunate application of an otherwise valid principle.

Moreover, the carefully reasoned concurring judgment of Mr. Justice Mac-Guigan lends support to the traditional broad view of the failure of state protection:

> . . . it seems to me to be begging the question to read into the concept of a well-founded fear of persecution that it must emanate from the state or at least involve state complicity. . . . [T]aking into account (1) the literal text of the statute, (2) the absence of any decisive Canadian precedents, and (3) the weight of international authority, the Board's interpretation of the statutory definition is the preferable one. No doubt this construction will make eligible for admission to Canada claimants from strife-torn countries whose problems arise, not from their nominal governments, but from various warring factions, but

---

[239] *Supra*, note 237, at 15, *per* Urie J.

[240] "The record here clearly shows that the Respondent does not allege state complicity as playing a part in his fear of seeking the protection of the police in either part of Ireland. Rather, he fears that by the very nature of the I.N.L.A. and its methods of operation, the police would be unable to afford that protection": *Supra*, note 237, at 14, *per* Urie J.

[241] *See* Section 5.6.3, *infra*.

[242] "I am unable to conceive that Parliament in adopting the definition of Convention refugee intended it to extend to persons belonging to organizations whose sole raison d'être is by force to overthrow the duly and democratically constituted authority in countries such as the United Kingdom and the Republic of Ireland where unquestionably the rule of law continues to prevail. If that is so the Respondent cannot be a refugee. Mere protestations of repentance are not enough to obviate the incidence of membership. If there is any way he can be legally admitted to this country, it is not, in my opinion, by the device of claiming refugee status": *supra*, note 237, at 20-21, *per* Urie J. This passage completely misconstrues the nature of the case, in that the basis of claim was *not* the claimant's advocacy of terrorism, but rather his explicit *rejection* of the I.N.L.A. The same error is apparent in the majority's definition of the social group to which the claimant belongs: in their view, it is the I.N.L.A. (*supra*, note 237, at 8), whereas in fact his status is more appropriately defined as membership in a class of persons who have renounced the I.N.L.A. in order to lend their support (at great personal risk) to the "democratically constituted authority".

I cannot think that this is contrary to "Canada's international legal obligations with respect to refugees and. . . its humanitarian tradition with respect to the displaced and the persecuted."[243]

Read in conjunction with the majority decision, this clarification ensures that claims from strife-torn countries should be considered on their merits, but does not suggest admission on that ground alone.[244]

This holistic approach to state protection is mirrored in the case law of the United States,[245] which defines agents of persecution to include "forces the government cannot or will not control".[246] In international human rights fora, too, a failure of national protection has been found in circumstances where there was no evidence of active culpability. For example, the views of the United Nations Human Rights Committee in *Rubio v. Colombia*[247] held a breach of Article 6 of the ICCPR (right to life) to be established due to the state's failure to take appropriate measures to prevent the disappearance and subsequent killing of two persons, and to investigate effectively the responsibility for their murders. The European Court of Human Rights in *Plattform 'Artze Fur Das Legen' v. Austria*[248] found that freedom of peaceful assembly could not be reduced to a mere duty on the part of the state not to intervene, but rather imposed an affirmative obligation on the state to protect lawful demonstrations from those wishing to interfere with or disrupt them. And similarly, in its first judgment, the Inter-American Court of Human Rights held in *Velasquez Rodriguez v. Honduras*[249] that the decisive factor in determining whether or not a state has adequately respected human rights is whether a particular violation of human rights has occurred with the support or connivance of the public authorities, or whether their attitude has enabled the infringement to occur because of the absence of adequate preventive or punitive measures. The duty in Canadian law to assess

---

[243] *Supra*, note 237, at 13-15, *per* MacGuigan J.

[244] *See* Section 5.6.3, *infra*.

[245] *See in particular McMullen v. I.N.S.*, 658 F. 2d 1312 (9th Cir. 1981.). "Under the *McMullen* standard, an alien must demonstrate not only that he is subject to persecution, but that in some way his native government is responsible for or is unable to prevent the harm threatened": C. Tompkin, "A Criminal at the Gate: A Case for the Haitian Refugee" (1982), 7 Black L.J. 387, at 399. *Accord* D. Gross, *supra*, note 225, at 1139.

[246] *Id.*, at 1315.

[247] Communication 161/1983, November 2, 1987, reported at (1987), 2(3/4) Interights Bulletin 36.1.

[248] Series A, No. 139, June 21, 1988, reported at (1988), 3(2) Interights Bulletin 19.

[249] Series C, No. 4, July 29, 1988, reported at (1989), 28 I.L.M. 291. Indeed, the Court went so far as to hold the state liable to pay compensation to the victim's family: *see* (1989), 4(2) Interights Bulletin 21. This decision is consistent with positions taken earlier by the Inter-American Commission on Human Rights. In *Rubin v. Paraguay*, for example, the Commission held the government responsible because "either through inaction or ineffective actions, [it] had not been able to identify, much less punish, those responsible for the attacks and arbitrariness, thereby leaving the company in a legally defenceless position and virtually bankrupting it": Case No. 9642, March 29, 1987, reported at (1987), 2(3/4) Interights Bulletin 34.

the sufficiency of state protection on the basis of the *de facto* viability of effective recourse to national authorities, rather than looking to specific forms of active culpability, is thus fully consistent with the general international trend.

4.5.2 Regionalized Failure to Protect

A person cannot be said to be at risk of persecution if she can access effective protection in some part of her state of origin. Because refugee law is intended to meet the needs of only those who have no alternative to seeking international protection,[250] primary recourse should always be to one's own state.

The surrogate nature of international protection is clear from the text of the Convention definition itself, which limits refugee status to a person who can demonstrate inability or legitimate unwillingness "to avail himself of the protection of [the home] *state*".[251] That is, the focus of analysis is the relationship between the claimant and her national government. Where there is no *de facto* freedom from infringement of core human rights in a particular region (for example, due to the actions of an errant regional government or forces which make the exercise of national protection unviable), but the national government provides a secure alternative home to those at risk,[252] the state's duty is met and refugee status is not warranted.

The drafting history of the Convention and its companion UNHCR Statute support this interpretation by their insistence on the exclusion of internally protected persons. The French delegate, for example, expressed the view that "there was no general definition covering [internal] refugees, since any such definition would involve an infringement of national sovereignty"[253] and that "[i]t was certain that the United Nations did not intend to apply the provisions of the Convention to national refugees. . . ."[254] Mrs. Roosevelt of the United States noted:

> All credit was due to the governments which bore the heavy burdens of those moves of people unilaterally, but those problems should not be confused with the problem before the General Assembly, namely, the provision of protection for those outside their own countries, who lacked the protection of a

---

[250] "[R]efugees are, in essence, persons whose basic needs are unprotected by their country of origin, who have no remaining recourse other than to seek international restitution of their needs, and who are so situated that international assistance is possible": A. Shacknove, "Who Is a Refugee?" (1985), 95 Ethics 274, at 277.

[251] *Convention, supra,* note 16, at Art. 1(A)(2).

[252] The rhetoric of protection may not, of course, square with reality: "The public expression by a Minister of a sincere humanitarian conviction is small comfort to an individual refugee who is dodging bullets in the bush": A. Simmance, "Refugees and the Law", [1981] New Zealand L.J. 550, at 550.

[253] Statement of Mr. Rochefort of France, U.N. Doc. E/AC.7/SR.172, at 4, August 12, 1950.

[254] Statement of Mr. Rochefort of France, U.N. Doc. A/CONF.2/SR.24, at 17, July 17, 1951.

Government and who required asylum and status in order that they might re-build lives of self-dependence and dignity.[255]

The underlying assumption in the debate was therefore that the existence of sufficient national protection[256] was inconsistent with status as an internationally recognized refugee.

The primacy of domestic protection has been recognized in Canadian jurisprudence as well. In *Karnail Singh*,[257] the claim of a Sikh from the Punjab region of India was denied because of his admission that he could avoid police harassment by moving to a different region of the country. The Immigration Appeal Board enunciated the principle that "[i]f the applicant is able to live in security in some other area of his own country, he is not a refugee from that country."[258] In both *Jainarine Jerome Ramkissoon*[259] and *Bènto Rodrigues da Silva*,[260] the Board applied the internal protection principle to situations where uncontrollable private violence was limited in scope to certain regions of the state of origin, with safety available elsewhere in the country.

The logic of the internal protection principle must, however, be recognized to flow from the absence of a need for asylum abroad. It should be restricted in its application to persons who can *genuinely access* domestic protection, and for whom the reality of protection is *meaningful*.[261] In situations where, for example, financial, logistical, or other barriers prevent the claimant from reaching internal safety; where the quality of internal protection fails to meet basic norms of civil, political, and socio-economic human rights; or where internal safety is otherwise illusory or unpredictable, state accountability for the harm is established and refugee status is appropriately recognized.

---

[255] Statement of Mrs. Roosevelt of the U.S.A., 4 UNGAOR (264th plen. mtg.) at 473, December 2, 1949.

[256] Even the advocates of a more liberal refugee definition focused on the absence of *de facto* protection in the state of origin as a condition precedent to international protection. *See,* e.g., Draft Proposal for Article 1 submitted by the United Kingdom, U.N. Doc. E/AC.32/L.2, at 1, January 17, 1950.

[257] Immigration Appeal Board Decision M83-1189, C.L.I.C. Notes 62.4, November 14, 1983.

[258] *Id.,* at 3, *per* B. Howard.

[259] Immigration Appeal Board Decision T84-9057, June 21, 1984.

[260] Immigration Appeal Board Decision T86-9740, December 10, 1986.

[261] "The fear of being persecuted need not always extend to the *whole* territory of the refugee's country of nationality. Thus in ethnic clashes or in cases of grave disturbances involving civil war conditions, persecution of a specific ethnic or national group may occur in only one part of the country. In such situations, a person will not be excluded from refugee status merely because he could have sought refuge in another part of the same country, if under all the circumstances it would not have been reasonable to expect him to do so": UNHCR, *supra,* note 123, pp. 21-22.

5

Nexus to Civil or Political Status

Refugee law exists in order to interpose the protection of the international community in situations where resort to national protection is not possible. Because it is fundamentally a form of surrogate or substitute protection, the beneficiaries of refugee law have always been defined to exclude those who enjoy the basic entitlements of membership in a national community, and who ought reasonably to vindicate their basic human rights against their own state.[1] Refugees are unprotected persons, not just in the sense that their basic liberties or entitlements are in jeopardy, but more fundamentally because it is impossible for them to work within or even to restructure the national community of which they are nominally a part in order to exercise those human rights.[2] Their position within the home community is not just precarious; there is also an element of fundamental marginalization[3] which distinguishes them from other persons at risk of serious harm. As stated by Rogers Smith:[4]

> The refugee has been cast adrift, usually because his religion, ethnicity, economic aspirations, political beliefs or political alliances in some way stand opposed to his putative government's efforts to create and sustain a strong nation state.[5]

The early refugee accords did not articulate this notion of disfranchisement or breakdown of basic membership rights, since refugees were defined simply by specific national, political, and religious categories, including anti-Communist Russians, Turkish Armenians, Jews from Germany, and others.[6] The *de facto* uniting criterion, however, was the shared marginalization of

---

[1] "There must be a rupture of normalcy of relations between him and his state, which rupture must derive from events which are political in nature": B. Tsamenyi, "The 'Boat People': Are They Refugees?" (1983), 5 Human Rts. Q. 348, at 360.

[2] "The events which are the root-cause of a man's becoming a refugee derive from the relations between the State and its nationals": J. Vernant, *The Refugee in the Post-War World*, p. 5 (1953).

[3] P. Woodward, "Political Factors Contributing to the Generation of Refugees in the Horn of Africa" (1987), 9(2) Intl. Relations 111, at 112.

[4] R. Smith, "Refugees, immigrants and the claims of the nation-state", [1987] Times Literary Supplement 1422 (December 25-31, 1987).

[5] *Id.*

[6] *See* Chapter 1, *supra*, in particular at notes 18 and 21.

the groups in their states of origin, with consequent inability to vindicate their basic human rights at home. These early refugees were not merely suffering persons, but were moreover persons whose position was fundamentally at odds with the power structure in their home state. It was the lack of a meaningful stake in the governance of their own society which distinguished them from others, and which gave legitimacy to their desire to seek protection abroad.[7]

The modern refugee definition[8] gave voice to this premise by moving away from protection on the basis of named, marginalized groups, and toward a more generic formulation of the membership principle.[9] Given the prevailing primacy of the civil and political paradigm of human rights,[10] it was contextually logical that marginalization should be defined by reference to norms of non-discrimination: a refugee was defined as a person at risk of serious harm *for reasons of* race, religion, nationality, membership of a particular social group, or political opinion.[11] The rationale for this limitation was not that other persons were less at risk, but was rather that, at least in the context of the historical moment, persons affected by these forms of fundamental socio-political disfranchisement were less likely to be in a position to seek effective redress from within the state.[12]

Under the Convention, then, if the peril a claimant faces — however wrongful it may be — cannot somehow be linked to her socio-political situation

---

[7] The means of denying membership during the period 1920-1950 may be classified in terms of juridical, social, and individuated disfranchisement. *See* Chapter 1, *supra*, at notes 9-28.

[8] The 1951 Convention follows the model of a 1938 resolution of the Intergovernmental Committee for Refugees which moved away from a list of eligible categories to embrace "persons . . . who must emigrate on account of their political opinions, religious beliefs and racial origin": Resolution of the Committee, I.C.R. Doc., July 14, 1938.

[9] "[T]he history of the cognizable categories of persecution illustrates that they were intended to serve a liberal purpose, by creating a universally applicable and acceptable standard to replace ad hoc, situational responses to disparate refugee crises": D. Gagliardi, "The Inadequacy of Cognizable Grounds of Persecution as a Criterion for According Refugee Status" (1987-88), 24 Stanford J. Intl. L. 259, at 267-68. "The grounds of persecution set forth by the Convention are sufficiently broad so that the major grounds for discrimination or oppression have been included": A. Fragomen, "The Refugee: A Problem of Definition" (1970), 3 Case Western Reserve J. Intl. L. 45, at 54.

[10] "Americans were prominent among the architects and builders of international human rights, and American constitutionalism was a principal inspiration and model for them. As a result, most of the provisions of the Universal Declaration of Human Rights, and later of the International Covenant on Civil and Political Rights, are in their essence American constitutional rights projected around the world": L. Henkin, "International Human Rights and Rights in the United States", in T. Meron, ed., *Human Rights in International Law: Legal and Policy Issues*, p. 39 (1984).

[11] *Convention relating to the Status of Refugees*, 189 U.N.T.S. 2545, entered into force on April 22, 1954, at Art. 1(A)(2) ("*Convention*").

[12] L. Holborn, *The International Refugee Organization: A Specialized Agency of the United Nations: Its History and Work, 1946-1952*, pp. 47-48 (1956).

and resultant marginalization,[13] the claim to refugee status must fail. Put succinctly, refugee law requires that there be a nexus between who the claimant is or what she believes and the risk of serious harm in her home state.[14]

Critics of the membership principle argue that refugee law should embrace, for example, persons in flight from natural disaster, civil strife, war, or economic calamity simply as a response to their human misery.[15] It is suggested by some that refugee law is essentially coterminous with international human rights law, or even with humanitarianism, such that any person whose basic dignity is jeopardized should be entitled to seek protection abroad.[16] This generous perspective collides with the implicit assumption of conventional refugee law that unless excluded from the national community, one should vindicate claims to liberties and entitlements from within the state.[17] So long as the victims of a generalized disaster are not denied membership in the body politic, they are expected to work to address their needs through existing structures or by creating or rebuilding internal mechanisms for redress.

The dilemma, though, is that while the membership principle itself remains meaningful, its precise formulation in terms of civil or political status (race, religion, nationality, membership of a particular social group, or political opinion) may be unduly anchored in a particular era. These categories were seen by the drafters of the Convention as sufficiently inclusive to meet the claims of all known European refugees at the close of the Second World

---

[13] "It can hardly be expected for the applicant to specify the ground, as he may himself sometimes not be aware why he was subjected to persecution or threatened with persecutionary measures": P. Weis, "The concept of the refugee in international law" (1960), 87 J. du droit intl. 928, at 970.

[14] "All other reasons are irrelevant, unless used to augment a claim of persecution, or to show the circumstances that the alien would face at home": K. Petrini, "Basing Asylum Claims on a Fear of Persecution Arising from a Prior Asylum Claim" (1981), 56 Notre Dame Lawyer 719, at 724.

[15] The civil or political status criterion ". . . has created the greatest division and ferment, for there would seem to be little difference between suffering arising from one of those five sources and any other form of suffering. The results are the same; the human cost is incalculable. Nevertheless, the last requirement has been the sticking point in the debate over the adequacy of asylum law to protect victims of all types of calamities": M. Heyman, "Redefining Refugee: A Proposal for Relief for the Victims of Civil Strife" (1987), 24 San Diego L.Rev. 449, at 453.

[16] "Precisely *why* an individual is persecuted is largely irrelevant — the *existence* of persecution is the only essential question. Because the definition of persecution is not dependent upon the enumeration of certain cognizable grounds, their presence within the definition of refugee is inappropriate. Their inclusion invites inquiry into factors that are tangential to the notion of persecution itself and the humanitarian purpose of providing relief to victims of persecution. The spirit of domestic and international refugee policy is lost in the shuffle": D. Gagliardi, *supra*, note 9, at 272.

[17] Rather than supplanting domestic responsibility for human rights, the purpose of the Refugee Convention was to assist only persons who "lacked the protection of a government": Statement of Mrs. Roosevelt of the U.S.A., 5 UNGAOR at 473, December 2, 1949.

War,[18] but are seen by some as inadequate to capture the spectrum of forms of disfranchisement in existence today.[19]

On the one hand, it remains strikingly true that racism, religious intolerance and other forms of socio-political disfranchisement continue to pose important barriers to national protection that refugee law can meaningfully address.[20] Developments since 1951, however, have suggested ways in which states might be inclined to expand the list of marginalizing phenomena. In particular, a clear majority of the nations in attendance at the abortive 1977 United Nations Conference on Territorial Asylum would have been prepared to recognize "foreign occupation or domination" as an additional valid ground for claiming refugee status.[21] At the regional level, the OAU Convention already recognizes claims grounded in "external aggression, occupation, foreign domination or events seriously disturbing public order",[22] and the Latin American Cartagena Declaration recommends status for persons in flight from "generalized violence, foreign aggression, internal conflicts, massive violations of human rights or other circumstances which have seriously disturbed public order".[23] There is a certain logical appeal in this

---

[18] "The United States delegation had said before, and must say again, that in its opinion all persons in need of protection at the present time were fully covered by the definition provided in article 1 of the draft Convention": Statement of Mr. Henkin of the U.S.A., U.N. Doc. E/AC.7/SR.166, at 14, August 22, 1950.

[19] "By singling out certain grounds for persecution, the refugee definition (at least a narrow reading of it) might well exclude persecution on other grounds, or persecution for no apparent reason at all": M. Gibney and M. Stohl, "Human Rights and U.S. Refugee Policy", in M. Gibney, ed., *Open Borders? Closed Societies? The Ethical and Political Issues*, p. 157 (1988). *Accord* D. Gagliardi, *supra*, note 9, at 281: "While tradition alone may be a substantial argument for maintaining cognizable categories of persecution, the problems of modern refugees frequently defy traditional analysis. The situations in El Salvador and Haiti illustrate the point. In the early part of the twentieth century, concepts of race, religion or political belief may have been sufficient to distinguish persons genuinely deserving of asylum from displaced persons, or from economic migrants seeking a more comfortable existence. However, these categories are hopelessly inadequate for the protection of persons fleeing random oppression and violence perpetrated by governments upon their populations".

[20] "Communal violence is one of the most frightening forms of conflict. When the members of one ethnic, religious or linguistic group clash with the neighbouring members of another, atrocities are almost inevitable. Even when governments do not have discriminatory policies, their inability to protect their own minorities or a threatened social group can indirectly cause the flight of large numbers of people": Independent Commission on International Humanitarian Issues, *Winning the Human Race?*, p. 98 (1988).

[21] Other amendments agreed to were essentially clarifications of the existing five grounds, e.g., specific mention of struggles against colonialism, apartheid, and racism (forms of political opinion); reference to colour, national origin, and ethnic origin (variants of race and nationality); and family status (arguably within the scope of a particular social group). *See* F. Leduc, "L'Asile territorial et la Conférence des Nations Unies de Genève, Janvier 1977" (1977), 23 Ann. française de droit intl. 221, at 247-48.

[22] Organization of African Unity, *Convention governing the specific aspects of refugee problems in Africa*, U.N.T.S. 14,691, entered into force June 20, 1974, at Art. I(2). *See generally* Section 1.4.3, *supra*.

[23] *Declaracion de Cartagena*, Doc. OEA/Ser.L/II.66, doc. 10, rev. 1, at Conclusion 3. *See generally* Section 1.4.4, *supra*.

type of evolution, since these phenomena may result in fundamental marginalization as effectively as civil or political discrimination. The grounding of refugee claims in the existence of violence or occupation would continue the Convention's focus on factors which undermine the political relationship between citizen and state, and is in that sense qualitatively distinct from proposals (never adopted at either the universal or regional level) to grant refugee status to the victims of natural disaster or economic hardship.[24]

Even though conceptually logical, this kind of liberalization of the Convention's grounds of claim is unlikely to receive universal support because of its practical implications. Whereas reliance on the demonstration of civil or political discrimination normally presupposes that only a minority of the population of any state can access refugee status, a move toward recognition of claims based on generalized oppression *per se* would have the effect (at least in theory) of putting whole populations in the position of claiming refugee status. This would seem to be quite fundamentally at odds with both the fairly narrow conceptualization of the drafters of the Convention[25] and the trend to restrictionism in northern countries.[26]

In Canada, the Convention-based list of civil and political grounds for refugee status ". . . is exhaustive and must be applied strictly and objectively".[27] Since persons who may have good reason to fear persecution for some other reason are thus excluded,[28] the link between fear of persecution and civil or political status needs to be clearly established.[29]

---

[24] "This condition excludes victims of natural disasters from the definition of the refugee known to international law; to put it more precisely, the events which are the root-cause of a man's becoming a refugee are always of a political nature": J. Vernant, *The Refugee in the Post-War World*, p. 5 (1953).

[25] "In the light of the nature of the draft Convention, it was probable that if a global definition were adopted some countries might be reluctant to adhere to this Convention; there were persons who might be considered as refugees, for example those fleeing from a revolution, for whom countries might not wish to provide a blank cheque of protection in advance; there were also other persons, admittedly refugees, in respect of whom the question would arise as to whether or not they should enjoy, or needed, the protection of an international convention": Statement of Mr. Henkin of the U.S.A., U.N. Doc. E/AC.7/SR.158, at 14, August 15, 1950.

[26] "[M]any states in the developed world are now expressing alarm at the number of people arriving at their borders, seeking refuge from intolerable conditions in their own country. Their tradition of offering asylum as a positive act of state policy and international solidarity is coming under mounting pressure. The steady process of expressing this solidarity through formal legal instruments has been halted, and is in danger of being reversed": Independent Commission on International Humanitarian Issues, *Refugees: Dynamics of Displacement*, pp. 31-32 (1986).

[27] *Marc Georges Sévère* (1974), 9 I.A.C. 42, at 47, *per* J.-P. Houle.

[28] "The already liberal interpretation of the Geneva Convention Relating to the Status of Refugees is not, however, sufficiently flexible to apply to all persons who, for good reason, run the risk of imprisonment": *Antonio Correia*, Immigration Appeal Board Decision 75-10245, April 5, 1976, at 2, *per* G. Legare. This decision, however, may exemplify an unwarranted strictness of interpretation of the notion of civil or political status, as the claim of a former member of the Portuguese internal security service was denied in relation to both membership of a particular social group and political opinion.

[29] "These grounds must relate directly to the appellant, upon whom the burden of proof falls":

Essentially, Canadian law prescribes a "but for" test: Would the claimant be similarly at risk of serious harm but for her civil or political status? First, there must be some causal connection between civil or political status and risk.[30] Where an applicant belongs to a minority group, but there is no demonstrable nexus between that fact and her fear of persecution, the claim cannot succeed. Thus, applications have been dismissed where the denial of employment was the result of incapacity rather than coincidental adverse political opinion;[31] where the claimant's religion could not be related to his fear of assault;[32] and where detention occurred at a time when the state could not have known of the applicant's ideology.[33]

On the other hand, it is not required that the totality of the risk faced by the claimant be specific to persons of her civil or political status. As discussed in Chapter 3, persons already at generalized risk may nonetheless succeed on a claim to refugee status if some element of differential intent or impact based on civil or political status is demonstrated.[34] The landmark decision of the Federal Court in *Zahirdeen Rajudeen*[35] rejected the Immigration Appeal Board's finding that the Sri Lankan claimant was not a refugee because the harassment he faced was simply the product of generalized civil unrest.[36] While acknowledging the context of generalized violence, the Federal Court nonetheless found for the claimant because he faced a heightened risk as a result of being both Tamil and a Muslim. The "but for" test thus requires only that the particular level of jeopardy faced by the applicant be linked to civil or political status, not that the whole of the risk be uniquely associated with that status.

The particular historical context which led to the linkage between refugeehood and civil or political status notwithstanding, the analysis which follows will show that it is largely possible for a liberal interpretation of the five enumerated grounds to sustain the Convention's vitality.[37] By contour-

---

Manuel Jesus Torres Reyes, Immigration Appeal Board Decision 75-1063, October 23, 1975, at 6, *per* R. Tremblay; set aside on other grounds by the Federal Court of Appeal on October 28, 1976; claim ultimately rejected by the Immigration Appeal Board on December 20, 1976.

[30] The recent decision of the Federal Court of Appeal in *Attorney General of Canada v. Patrick Francis Ward* underscores the importance of a linkage between fear of persecution and the enumerated grounds in the Convention: Federal Court of Appeal Decision A-1190-88, at 15, *per* Urie J.; leave to appeal granted by the Supreme Court of Canada on November 8, 1990: Supreme Court Bulletin 2347.

[31] *Fernando Alfonso Naredo Arduengo*, Immigration Appeal Board Decision T80-9159, C.L.I.C. Notes 27.13, November 20, 1980, at 3; set aside on other grounds by the Federal Court of Appeal at (1981) 130 D.L.R. (3d) 752, December 18, 1981; claim ultimately rejected by the Immigration Appeal Board on April 15, 1985.

[32] *Dionisio Nunes Esteves*, Immigration Appeal Board Decision T87-9304X, September 15, 1987.

[33] *Ajit Singh*, Immigration Appeal Board Decision T83-9208, October 15, 1987, at 3.

[34] *See* text *supra* at Section 3.2.5, especially at note 175 ff.

[35] *Rajudeen v. Minister of Employment and Immigration* (1985), 55 N.R. 129 (F.C.A.).

[36] Immigration Appeal Board Decision V83-6091, C.L.I.C. Notes 57.10, July 20, 1983, at 4.

[37] "[T]hese criteria of grounds for persecution were drafted with special reference to the situation created by the Second World War, but have, however, been found acceptable also

ing the bases for claim so as to identify instances of fundamental disfranchisement in which deference to national remedies for human rights violations is not viable, refugee law can remain meaningful to the modern victims of socio-political marginalization.[38]

5.1 Race

The first form of disfranchisement within the scope of refugee law is that based on race. While the drafters of the Convention did not specifically define the term, the historical context makes clear that their intent was to include those Jewish victims of Naziism who had been persecuted because of their ethnicity, whether or not they actively practised their religion.[39] This historical rationale is important, because it legitimizes the attribution of a broad social meaning to the term "race" which includes all persons of identifiable ethnicity.[40] As Atle Grahl-Madsen has observed, the Convention's notion of race includes not only persons at risk by reason of their membership in a particular scientific category, but also other groups such as Jews and Gypsies whose physical or cultural distinctiveness has caused them to suffer social prejudice.[41] The possibility of overlap between race and other enumerated factors such as religion, nationality, and membership of a particular social group is thus clear, but presents no real problem since claims may be based on one or a combination of forms of civil or political disfranchisement.[42]

---

in our times. . .'': I. Foighel, "Legal Status of the Boat People" (1979), 48 Nordisk Tidsskrift for Intl. Ret. 217, at 222.

[38] "Although the Convention seems to limit considerably the scope of refugees by enumerating five factors for their persecution, in fact it establishes rather broad categories": Y. Shimada, "The Concept of the Political Refugee in International Law" (1975), 19 Japanese Ann. Intl. L. 24, at 33.

[39] Grahl-Madsen suggests that the reference to "race" is derived from SHAEF Administrative Memorandum Number 39 which was "aimed at helping the Jewish victims of Nazi persecution, of whom some were persecuted because of their Jewish race, some because of their Jewish religion, and some for both reasons": 1 A. Grahl-Madsen, *The Status of Refugees in International Law*, pp. 217-18 (1966). *Accord* P. Hyndman, "The 1951 Convention Definition of Refugee: An Appraisal with Particular Reference to the Sri Lankan Tamil Applicants" (1987), 9 Human Rts. Q. 49, at 69.

[40] "[E]thnicity is probably the background of the more dubious term 'race'": I. Foighel, *supra*, note 37, at 222.

[41] "The origin of the phrase makes it quite clear that the word 'race' in the present context denotes not only the major ethnic groups, such as Europeans ('the white race'), Africans ('the black race'), Mongols ('the yellow race'), Red Indians, etc., but also groups which are less easily differentiated, such as Jews, gipsies [sic], etc. In the present context the word 'race' is therefore referring to social prejudice rather than to a more or less scientific division of mankind. In other words, the term 'race', as used in Article IA(2), is a social more than an ethnographic concept, and is applicable whenever a person is persecuted because of his ethnic origin": A. Grahl-Madsen, *supra*, note 39, p. 218.

[42] "It is immaterial whether the persecution arises from any single one of these reasons or from a combination of two or more of them. Often the applicant himself may not be aware of the reasons for the persecution feared. It is not, however, his duty to analyse his case to such an extent as to identify the reasons in detail": United Nations High Commissioner for Refugees, *Handbook on Procedures and Criteria for Determining Refugee Status*, p. 17 (1979).

A broad interpretation of race is not only historically defensible, but is moreover consistent with modern international usage.[43] The widely accepted International Convention on the Elimination of All Forms of Racial Discrimination,[44] for example, defines "racial discrimination" as including differential treatment based on "race, colour, descent, or national or ethnic origin".[45] In the refugee context, the clear majority of delegates to the Conference on Territorial Asylum similarly agreed to extend protection to persons persecuted for reasons of "race, colour, national or ethnic origin".[46] The Executive Committee of the UNHCR adopted this perspective, and has recommended a comprehensive definition of race to states:

> Race, in the present connexion, has to be understood in its widest sense to include all kinds of ethnic groups that are referred to as "races" in common usage. Frequently, it will entail membership of a specific social group of common descent forming a minority within a larger population.[47]

This UNHCR-derived interpretation has been explicitly adopted into Canadian law in a series of decisions commencing with *Boleslaw Dytlow*,[48] as well as in immigration policy guidelines.[49] The relevant case law has equated race with "ethnic background",[50] "heritage",[51] and "distinct minority" status.[52]

---

[43] "Given legal developments affecting this topic over the last thirty years, the broad meaning can be considered valid also for the purposes of the 1951 Convention": G. Goodwin-Gill, *The Refugee in International Law,* p. 27 (1983). Among those Goodwin-Gill considered as within this broad meaning are Asian Ugandans, the Hutu from Burundi, ethnic Chinese from Vietnam, and blacks from South Africa.

[44] G.A. Res. 2106 A (XX), December 21, 1965, entered into force January 4, 1969. This Convention has been adhered to by 127 states, including Canada: J.-B. Marie, "International Instruments Relating to Human Rights: Classification and Chart Showing Ratifications as of 1 January, 1989" (1989), 10 Human Rts. L.J. 103.

[45] *Id.,* at Art. 1(1).

[46] U.N. Doc. A/CONF.78/12, at Art. 2(1)(a). This amendment was co-sponsored by Algeria, Egypt, Iraq, Jordan, Kuwait, Libya, Morocco, Saudi Arabia, Somalia, Syria, and Yemen, and was adopted by a vote of 50 in favour, 19 opposed, and 12 abstaining: F. Leduc, "L'Asile territorial et la Conférence des Nations Unies de Genève, Janvier 1977" (1977), 23 Ann. française de droit intl. 221, at 248.

[47] UNHCR, *supra,* note 42, p. 18.

[48] Immigration Appeal Board Decision V87-6040X, July 7, 1987, at 1-2, *per* A. Wlodyka; affirmed without comment by Federal Court of Appeal Decision A-569-87, April 13, 1988. *See also Sylvia and Patrycya Dytlow*, Immigration Appeal Board Decision V87-6361X, October 29, 1987; *Stanislaw Dytlow and Krystyna Pawlowksa,* Immigration Appeal Board Decision V86-6268/6270, December 28, 1988.

[49] Race is said to denote "not only major ethnic groups such as black, white, European, African, etc., but also embraces the social concept e.g. Jews, Gypsies, a particular tribe or minority, racial or ethnic": Canada Employment and Immigration Commission, *Immigration Manual,* at I.S. 13.07(1)(a)(i), June 1990.

[50] *Pierre Katanku Tshiabu Tshibola*, Immigration Appeal Board Decision M84-1074, May 30, 1985, at 4, *per* P. Davey.

[51] *Ganganee Janet Permanand,* Immigration Appeal Board Decision T87-10167, August 10, 1987, at 1, *per* P. Ariemma.

[52] *Boleslaw Dytlow*, Immigration Appeal Board Decision V87-6040X, July 7, 1987, at 2, *per* A. Wlodyka.

Among those whose claims have been dealt with on the basis of race are Ibos from Nigeria,[53] the Mohajirs of Pakistan,[54] the Baganda from Uganda,[55] Guyanese of East Indian descent,[56] Tamils from Sri Lanka,[57] the Baluba from Zaire,[58] and Gypsies of Polish origin.[59] The primary notion which unites these groups is their exclusion from state protection based on identifiable ethnicity.

The equation of race with minority status must be viewed in the context of effective political power, not just numbers. Since refugee law is concerned with the absence of protection rather than with minority status *per se*, the members of a country's ethnic majority may be protected as racially defined refugees if they are disfranchised in terms of respect for core human rights. In *Pierre Katanku Tshiabu Tshibola*,[60] for example, the Immigration Appeal Board accepted the claim of a Baluba from Zaire. It noted that while the Baluba constitute half the population of that state, the Ngwandi ethnic group holds effective power, thereby creating a risk of oppression for the Baluba. Similarly, in the case of *Ganganee Janet Permanand*[61] the Board observed:

> The Indo-Guyanese community to which the claimant belongs is the largest in number in Guyana. The numerical majority, of course, does not necessarily guarantee immunity from persecution by a minority holding the power of the State.[62]

One can similarly imagine the extension of this principle to blacks in South Africa,[63] and to other ethnic groups denied effective political voice within their country of origin. Majority status alone does not negate a claim to racially defined refugee status if discernible ethnicity gives rise to a genuine risk of serious harm not remediable by national protection.

---

[53] *Jones Adeniji Adetuyi*, Immigration Appeal Board Decision 79-9057, March 5, 1979.

[54] *Owais Uddin Ahmad*, Immigration Appeal Board Decision 79-1197, November 21, 1979.

[55] *Joseph Maria Mpagi*, Immigration Appeal Board Decision V80-6254, August 13, 1980.

[56] *Benaiserie Mangra*, Immigration Appeal Board Decision T83-10491, January 5, 1984; *Oumar Baksh*, Immigration Appeal Board Decision T83-10588, January 18, 1984; *Jainarine Jerome Ramkissoon,* Immigration Appeal Board Decision T84-9057, June 21, 1984; *Ganganee Janet Permanand,* Immigration Appeal Board Decision T87-10167, August 10, 1987.

[57] *Krishnapillai Easwaramoorthy,* Immigration Appeal Board Decision T82-9736, June 18, 1984. *Accord* P. Hyndman, *supra*, note 39, at 69.

[58] *Pierre Katanku Tshiabu Tshibola*, Immigration Appeal Board Decision M84-1074, May 30, 1985.

[59] *Boleslaw Dytlow*, Immigration Appeal Board Decision V87-6040X, July 7, 1987, affirmed without comment in Federal Court of Appeal Decision A-569-87, April 13, 1988; *Sylvia and Patrycya Dytlow*, Immigration Appeal Board Decision V87-6361X, October 29, 1987; *Robert Dytlow*, Immigration Appeal Board Decision V87-6521X, January 5, 1988; *Stanislaw Dytlow and Krystyna Pawlowska,* Immigration Appeal Board Decision V86-6268/6270, December 28, 1988.

[60] Immigration Appeal Board Decision M84-1074, May 30, 1985.

[61] Immigration Appeal Board Decision T87-10167, August 10, 1987.

[62] *Id.*, at 7, *per* P. Ariemma.

[63] Z. Rizvi, "Causes of the Refugee Problem and the International Response", in A. Nash, ed., *Human Rights and the Protection of Refugees under International Law*, p. 111 (1988).

5.2 Nationality

Closely linked to the notion of race or ethnicity is the concept of nationality. As in the case of race, the drafting history of the Convention offers no specific definition of nationality.[64] The early commentators assumed a narrow meaning of the term, roughly equivalent to formal citizenship, leading to the obvious question of why a state would choose to persecute its own citizens merely by reason of their status as citizens.[65] A slightly more expansive interpretation of citizenship, however, suggests a number of situations in which disfranchisement on the basis of formal political status is conceivable.

First, resident internationally unprotected persons, such as refugees and stateless persons,[66] might be the objects of human rights abuse by reason of their status as "foreigners". While inhabitants who retain the formal and effective citizenship of another state could not advance a claim to refugee status in relation to the state of domicile,[67] those who cannot enjoy meaningful protection elsewhere are properly assessed as refugees in accordance with the concept of state of former habitual residence.[68] Second, persons who are denied full citizenship in their own state (such as Palestinians in Israel) could qualify as nationally defined refugees insofar as their inferior political status can be shown to put them at risk of persecution. Third, some states may disfranchise a portion of their population by ascribing a different nationality to them (as in the case of the black "homelands" in South Africa), and establishing regimes which fail to guarantee basic human rights to those assigned the new "nationality". Fourth, persecution based on nationality might arise in the context of a state composed of previously sovereign territories (such as the U.S.S.R.), where measures are directed against those who define their nationality in terms of allegiance to the predecessor state.

In addition to notions of formal nationality, it is generally suggested that nationality encompasses linguistic groups and other culturally defined

---

[64] N. Robinson, *Convention relating to the Status of Refugees: Its History, Contents and Interpretation*, p. 53 (1953).

[65] *Id. Accord* C. Pompe, "The Convention of 28 July 1951 and the International Protection of Refugees", [1956] Rechtsgeleerd Magazyn Themis 425, published in English as U.N. Doc. HCR/INF/42, May 1958, at 9: "How persecution on grounds of nationality comes in is not quite clear, as the refugee either possesses (or did possess) the nationality of the country in which he fears persecution, or was settled there as a stateless person."

[66] "Persecution for 'reasons of nationality' is also understood to include persecution for lack of nationality, that is: persecution of stateless persons": 1 A. Grahl-Madsen, *The Status of Refugees in International Law*, p. 219 (1966).

[67] Such persons would not have a well-founded fear of persecution in relation to their country of nationality, and would therefore fail to meet the alienage requirements of the Convention definition. *See* Section 2.4, *supra*.

[68] *See* Section 2.5.2, *supra. Accord* G. Goodwin-Gill, *The Refugee in International Law*, p. 29 (1983).

collectivities,[69] thus overlapping to a significant extent with the concept of race.[70] Because many such groups share a sense of political community distinct from that of the nation state, their claims to refugee protection may reasonably be determined on the basis of nationality as well as on race.

5.3 Religion

Religion as defined in international law[71] consists of two elements. First, individuals have the right to hold or not to hold[72] any form of theistic, non-theistic, or atheistic belief.[73] This decision is entirely personal: neither the state nor its official or unofficial agents may interfere with an individual's right to adhere to or to refuse a belief system,[74] nor with a decision to change one's beliefs.[75] Second, an individual's right to religion implies the ability to live in accordance with a chosen belief, including participation in or absten-

---

[69] "The term 'nationality' in this context is not to be understood only as 'citizenship.' It refers also to membership of an ethnic or linguistic group. . .": UNHCR, *supra*, note 42, p. 18. *Accord* A. Grahl-Madsen, *supra*, note 66, p. 218; G. Goodwin-Gill, *supra*, note 68, p. 29; B. Tsamenyi, "The 'Boat People': Are They Refugees?" (1983), 5 Human Rts. Q. 348, at 366; C. Wydrzynski, *Canadian Immigration Law and Procedure*, p. 327 (1983).

[70] "The term 'nationality' generally receives a broad interpretation and can overlap with some of the other grounds. It is usually taken to include, as well as citizenship, members of specific ethnic or linguistic groups and may occasionally overlap with the term 'race'": P. Hyndman, "The 1951 Convention Definition of Refugee" (1987), 9 Human Rts. Q. 49, at 70. *Accord* UNHCR, *supra*, note 42, p. 18.

[71] *See* in particular *Universal Declaration of Human Rights*, U.N.G.A. Res. 217A (III), December 10, 1948 (*"UHDR"*), at Art. 18; *International Covenant on Civil and Political Rights*, U.N.G.A. Res. 2200 (XXI), December 19, 1966, entered into force March 23, 1976 (*"ICCPR"*), at Art. 18; *Declaration on the Elimination of All Forms of Intolerance and of Discrimination Based on Religion or Belief*, U.N.G.A. Res. 36/55, November 25, 1981 (*"Declaration"*).

[72] The resurgence of religious fundamentalism in many parts of the world will undoubtedly give rise to refugee claims grounded in reprisals for failure to adopt the official ideology. *See* Z. Rizvi, *supra*, note 63, p. 111.

[73] *Draft International Convention on the Elimination of All Forms of Intolerance and of Discrimination based on Religion or Belief*, U.N. Doc. E/1980/13 (*"Draft Convention"*), at Art. I(a). This draft convention received overwhelming support in the United Nations Commission on Human Rights, but has not been adopted.

[74] "No one shall be subject to coercion which would impair his freedom to have or to adopt a religion or belief of his choice": ICCPR, *supra*, note 71, at Art. 18(2). *Accord* Declaration, *supra*, note 71, at Art. I(2). In contrast, some Canadian decisions have held that the application of official pressure to renounce a religion is not sufficient to constitute a claim to refugee status: *Lech Jankowski*, Immigration Appeal Board Decision V80-6410, C.L.I.C. Notes 26.11, January 5, 1981; *Radovan Sumera*, Immigration Appeal Board Decision V81-6161, May 28, 1981.

[75] Draft Convention, *supra*, note 73, at Art. III(a). The issue of apostasy was considered by the Immigration Appeal Board in the case of *Adel Mohammed Bakr Mohamed*, an Egyptian who had converted from Islam to Christianity. While evidence of genuine risk was found lacking in the particular circumstances, the Board appears to have accepted the principle that refugee protection could appropriately be extended to persons with an apprehension of persecution due to their decision to change religion: Immigration Appeal Board Decision V87-6168, November 18, 1988, at 3.

tion from formal worship and other religious acts, expression of views, and the ordering of personal behaviour.[76]

Because religion encompasses both the beliefs that one may choose to hold and behaviour which stems from those beliefs, religion as a ground for refugee status similarly includes two dimensions.[77] First is the protection of persons who are in serious jeopardy because they are identified as adherents of a particular religion.[78] It is not necessary that a claimant have taken any kind of active role in the promotion of her beliefs, nor even that she be particularly observant of its precepts or rituals. In the case of *Francisco Jorge Carvalho Penha*,[79] for example, the Immigration Appeal Board remarked that "[t]he fact that [the claimant] had not received baptism does not detract from the . . . claim since he was perceived by members of his community as being a Jehovah's Witness."[80] This decision contrasts favourably with other cases in which protection on the ground of religion was limited to objectively defined religious practitioners.[81] The central issue must be whether there is a linkage between the threat of persecution and the claimant's self-defined or externally ascribed religious beliefs, in which case refugee protection is warranted.

Alternatively, because religion includes also behaviour which flows from belief, it is appropriate to recognize as refugees persons at risk for choosing to live their convictions. This proposition is constrained only by the limitation expressed in the International Covenant on Civil and Political Rights:

---

[76] The Universal Declaration refers to the right "either alone or in community with others and in public or private, to manifest [one's] religion or belief in teaching, practice, worship and observance": UDHR, *supra*, note 71, at Art. 18. *Accord* ICCPR, *supra*, note 71, at Art. 18. The Declaration elaborates this notion to include the right of parents to determine their children's moral education, and the freedoms to maintain and assemble in places of worship, to establish charitable and humanitarian institutions, to acquire and use religious articles and materials, to write and disseminate religious information, to teach religion, to solicit funds, to establish a religious leadership, to observe holidays and ceremonies, and to communicate with others at the national and international levels on matters of religion: Declaration, *supra*, note 71, at Arts. 5 and 6.

[77] *See* A. Grahl-Madsen, *supra*, note 66, p. 218; and G. Goodwin-Gill, *supra*, note 68, pp. 27-28.

[78] For example, "[t]he present century has . . . seen large-scale persecution of Jews under the hegemony of Nazi and Axis powers up to 1945, while more recent targets have included Jehovah's Witnesses in Africa, Moslems in Burma, Baha'is in Iran and believers of all persuasions in totalitarian and self-proclaimed atheist states": G. Goodwin-Gill, *supra*, note 68, pp. 27-28.

[79] Immigration Appeal Board Decision T87-9305X, December 16, 1987.

[80] *Id.*, at 2, *per* P. Ariemma.

[81] *See*, e.g., *Joseph Maria Mpagi*, Immigration Appeal Board Decision V80-6254, August 13, 1980, in which nominal membership in the Roman Catholic Church was adjudged insufficient to bring the claim within the scope of the Convention. *Accord Tadeusz Adamusik*, Immigration Appeal Board Decision 75-10405, January 15, 1976; affirmed on other grounds by the Federal Court of Appeal at (1976), 12 N.R. 262; *Teresa Augustyn*, Immigration Appeal Board Decision T81-9103, March 18, 1981; *Leczek Franciszek Bala*, Immigration Appeal Board Decision V81-6136, May 11, 1981.

Freedom to manifest one's religion or beliefs may be subject only to such limitations as are prescribed by law and are necessary to protect public safety, order, health, or morals or the fundamental rights and freedoms of others.[82]

While the scope of this restriction is arguably broad, the assertion in one Board decision that "[g]iven the applicant's religious attitude . . . one might reasonably expect that he will 'keep his mouth shut' "[83] is simply wrong. The peaceful expression of one's beliefs, including engaging in worship,[84] playing an active role in religious affairs,[85] and proselytizing[86] may give rise to a genuine need for protection. Religious behaviour includes more than just formal acts of worship, and may encompass, for example, conscientious objection to military service.[87]

In its decision in *Bento Rodrigues da Silva*,[88] the Immigration Appeal Board developed the unhelpful notion that a religiously defined claim is to be dismissed if the applicant is not prevented from practising her religion. This principle has been taken to mean that the form of harm feared in religiously grounded cases must be specifically religious.[89] *Boota Bilaspuri Singh*,[90] for example, involved the claim of a Sikh preacher whose frequent addresses on Indian radio and television dealt with the political implications of his religious beliefs. He was arrested, detained, and ordered to refrain from "preaching on controversial topics".[91] Without even considering whether the claimant's arrest, detention, and denial of free speech (all arguably in con-

---

[82] ICCPR, *supra*, note 71, at Art. 18(3).

[83] *Orhan Demir*, Immigration Appeal Board Decision M82-1274, January 6, 1983, at 4, *per* J.-P. Houle.

[84] *Teresa Augustyn,* Immigration Appeal Board Decision T81-9103, March 18, 1981; *Leczek Franciszek Bala*, Immigration Appeal Board Decision V81-6136, May 11, 1981; *Radovan Sumera*, Immigration Appeal Board Decision V81-6161, May 28, 1981; *Mikieal L. Dankha,* Immigration Appeal Board Decision V82-6160, C.L.I.C. Notes 46.10, August 12, 1982; *Bento Rodrigues da Silva*, Immigration Appeal Board Decision T86-9740, December 10, 1986; *Joao Machado da Silva*, Immigration Appeal Board Decision T87-9612X, October 5, 1987.

[85] *Joseph Maria Mpagi*, Immigration Appeal Board Decision V80-6254, August 13, 1980; *Mikieal K. Dankha*, Immigration Appeal Board Decision V82-6160, C.L.I.C. Notes 46.10, August 12, 1982.

[86] *Orhan Demir*, Immigration Appeal Board Decision M82-1274, January 6, 1983, at 3. *But see Panagiotis Billias*, Immigration Appeal Board Decision 79-1166, C.L.I.C. Notes 27.10, July 7, 1980.

[87] In the case of a Salvadoran draft evader, "the Board [found] a systematic persecution by reason of religion. It is the failure of the recruiting system to make allowances for the convictions of the conscientious objector that forms the basis of the fear. Such a failure amounts to fear of persecution within the meaning of the Act": *Luis Alberto Mena Ramirez*, Immigration Appeal Board Decision V86-6161, May 5, 1987, at 5, *per* D. Anderson. *Accord Theodosios Drouskas*, Immigration Appeal Board Decision 79-1055, C.L.I.C. Notes 11.18, October 11, 1979, at 6. *See* discussion of draft evasion and desertion *infra* at Section 5.7.

[88] Immigration Appeal Board Decision T86-9740, December 10, 1986.

[89] *See*, e.g., *Jiwan Kaur Kang*, Immigration Appeal Board Decision V86-6183, April 13, 1987; *Kinder Sangha Singh*, Immigration Appeal Board Decision V87-6263X, September 23, 1987.

[90] Immigration Appeal Board Decision V87-6150X, May 19, 1987.

[91] *Id.*, at 3.

travention of international human rights law[92]) were sufficiently serious to constitute persecution, the Board concluded that

> Although Mr. Bilaspuri was prevented on several occasions from speaking on political topics, there was no evidence led which would indicate that he was prevented from practicing his religion. In the case of *da Silva*, the Board concluded that where there [is] no evidence that the claimant [is] precluded from practicing his faith, he [is] unable to establish a well-founded fear of persecution by reason of his religion.[93]

This assumption that only specifically religious forms of persecution are relevant in religiously based claims is misguided, since our concern is to identify situations where there is a genuine risk of any kind of serious harm consequent upon a choice or exercise of one's belief system. In some circumstances, the serious harm may indeed consist of the suppression of the right to religious choice or expression, clearly within the scope of persecution.[94] Indeed, as the Board noted in *Tomasz Gozdalski*,[95] indirect prevention of religious practice is sufficient to establish a claim to refugee status:

> Mr. Gozdalski is a devout Catholic, citizen of an atheist country, Poland. The State, however, tolerates the practice of religion officially, but it seems that very often the army or the corporations (which are all state owned) schedule *compulsory* meetings for communist propaganda on Sunday morning, when a good Catholic would attend mass, thus a disguised way of preventing freedom of religion. For a deeply religious person, this could amount to persecution.[96]

Alternatively, however, a claim is also established where an individual is allowed to adopt or exercise a belief system, but other serious human rights consequences flow from such a decision or action. For example, in *Abdul Rashid*[97] the Immigration Appeal Board looked to evidence of the socio-economic victimization of the Ahmadi claimant to substantiate his claim to refugee status, and in *Jorge Marcal Baltazar*[98] the Board was willing to consider evidence of religiously inspired interference with the claimant's livelihood. Any form of anticipated harm within the scope of persecution[99] suffices, so long as it is linked to a decision to hold or exercise a particular form of belief.

---

[92] *See* Section 4.4, *supra*.

[93] *Supra*, note 90, at 6, *per* J. MacLeod.

[94] *Boguslaw Buk*, Immigration Appeal Board Decision V80-6188, June 12, 1980; *Darshan Singh*, Immigration Appeal Board Decision T84-9443, October 3, 1984; *Rajmati Singh*, Immigration Appeal Board Decision T84-9608, November 15, 1984.

[95] Immigration Appeal Board Decision M87-1027X, April 23, 1987.

[96] *Id.*, at 1, *per* M. Durand. *But see Jan Waclaw Zariczniak,* Immigration Appeal Board Decision T81-9160, C.L.I.C. Notes 31.11, April 24, 1981.

[97] Immigration Appeal Board Decision M87-1023X, April 16, 1987.

[98] Immigration Appeal Board Decision T87-9226X, October 1, 1987.

[99] *See* Chapter 4, *supra*.

5.4 Political Opinion

The notion of persecution on account of political opinion was conceived in liberal terms. The Convention's drafters noted that in addition to "diplomats thrown out of office" and persons "whose political party had been outlawed", even "individuals who fled from revolutions" ought to be encompassed by the political opinion category.[100] That is, protection on the ground of political opinion was to be extended not only to those with identifiable political affiliations or roles, but also to other persons at risk from political forces within their home community. Contemporary Canadian jurisprudence mirrors this historical conceptualization in most respects.

5.4.1 Unexpressed Political Opinion

Because the Convention definition refers to "political opinion" rather than to the arguably more constrained notion of "political activity", there is no requirement that a claimant have acted upon her beliefs prior to departure from her country in order to qualify for refugee status.[101] As stated in the landmark decision of *Juan Alejandro Araya Heredio:*[102]

> . . . the Convention speaks not of political activities but of political opinions. Opinions are often, but not necessarily, expressed in action, and history has taught us that some political regimes. . . persist in pursuing some of their nationals simply because the latter supported a former regime or collaborated with it, or simply because they oppose or, owing to their former loyalties, constitute a challenge to the authority now in power.[103]

In some circumstances, the expression of a non-conforming political belief while in the home state may simply have been a practical impossibility,[104] while in other cases the applicant may not have held or felt as strongly about the particular belief at the time of departure.[105] Because the refugee defini-

---

[100] U.N. Doc. E/AC.7/SR.172, August 12, 1950, at 18-23, and U.N. Doc. E/AC.7/SR.173, August 12, 1950, at 5.

[101] "A person is a political refugee if he has a well-founded fear based on political opinion. He need not have a well-founded fear based on political activity": Minister of Employment and Immigration, "New Refugee Status Advisory Committee Guidelines on Refugee Definition and Assessment of Credibility", at Rule 11 (1982).

[102] Immigration Appeal Board Decision 76-1127, January 6, 1977. *Accord.*, e.g., *Akrimul Huque Chowdhury v. Deputy Attorney General of Canada*, Federal Court of Appeal Decision A-468-87, May 12, 1988, at 2, *per* MacGuigan J.: "[T]he definition of Convention Refugee in the Act refers not to 'political activities' but to 'political opinion'. . . ."

[103] *Id.*, at 7, *per* J.-P. Houle.

[104] "Because the applicants are fleeing from totalitarian states in which there are limited opportunities for political expression and great risks accompanying political dissent, it seems unreasonable for the Board to equate political motivation with political activism": D. Roth, "The Right of Asylum Under United States Immigration Law" (1981), 33 U. Florida L.Rev. 539, at 551.

[105] "[T]he fear of bad-faith claims does not justify an inflexible rule. . . many of these asylum applicants are students, who may never before have had the opportunity or the critical ability to compare political conditions in their homeland with those in other countries": D. Gross, "The Right of Asylum Under United States Law" (1980), 80 Columbia L.Rev. 1125, at 1142.

tion requires a forward-looking assessment of risk,[106] the issue to be addressed
is whether there is reason to believe that the claimant's decision to exercise
her right to form an opinion "on any matter in which the machinery of state,
government, and policy may be engaged"[107] would place her in jeopardy upon
return to her home state.[108]

First, there must be evidence that potential persecutors in the home state
either are or could reasonably become aware of the claimant's views. In the
case of *Emil Pers,*[109] for example, the Board dismissed the claim of a Polish
farmer and Solidarity sympathizer, who had illicitly sold crops directly to
the public:

> The applicant testified that he had not given any public expression to his polit-
> ical opinions. His political actions — selling his produce on the black market
> and distributing pamphlets on behalf of Solidarity — were clandestine and,
> consequently, unknown to any authorities. . . . The claim therefore fails essen-
> tially because the Board finds it improbable in the extreme that one could
> reasonably develop a fear of persecution by reasons of political opinions which
> are officially non-existent.[110]

Where home authorities have no actual knowledge of a claimant's convictions, it is sufficient to show that her views could reasonably lead to a clash
with those in positions of power:

> Due to the strength of his convictions, however, it may be reasonable to assume
> that his opinions will sooner or later find expression and that the applicant
> will, as a result, come into conflict with the authorities. Where this can reasona-
> bly be assumed, the applicant can be considered to have fear of persecution
> for reasons of political opinion.[111]

Since political expression is a core human right, the claimant must enjoy
a reasonable expectation of tolerance of peacefully articulated views. It is
therefore inappropriate simply to discount the risk of harm on the ground
that the claimant could avoid detection by keeping silent. This position has
yet to be fully acknowledged in the Canadian case law.[112] In the recent case

---

[106] *See* Section 3.1, *supra.*

[107] G. Goodwin-Gill, *The Refugee in International Law*, p. 31 (1983).

[108] With respect to the issue of post-departure statements of political opinion designed to secure
access to asylum abroad, *see* Section 2.1.2, *supra.*

[109] Immigration Appeal Board Decision M86-1634X, February 17, 1987; affirmed on other
grounds by Federal Court of Appeal Decision A-123-87, January 12, 1988.

[110] *Id.*, at 4-5, *per* E. Brown.

[111] UNHCR, *supra*, note 42, p. 20. *Accord* Minister of Employment and Immigration, *supra*,
note 101, at Guideline 11: "A person who is disposed to clash politically with authorities from
his country and who will probably or possibly suffer persecution because of that disposition
may be a refugee."

[112] In *Marina Galvis de Cardona*, the Board dismissed the claim of a Colombian student,
noting that her participation in a peaceful protest march was an "imprudent action taken know-
ingly and deliberately": Immigration Appeal Board Decision 77-1120, August 2, 1978, at 12,
per J.-P. Houle. Similarly, the Federal Court of Appeal in *Mauricio Esteban Lemoine Guajardo
v. Minister of Employment and Immigration* suggested that voluntary self-identification as a

of *Wai Chee Lee,*[113] for example, the Board dismissed the claim of a Chinese national who would face serious consequences for the expression of his pro-capitalist political views:

> The Board rejects the contention that the fear of the consequences of expressing political opinions is synonymous with a fear of persecution for political opinion. . . . Mistreatment by reason of political activity or fear of mistreatment if political views were to be expressed are not, *ipso facto*, grounds under the Convention or the Act for claiming refugee status. The United Nations Convention and the *Immigration Act, 1976*, are not charters of political rights.[114]

This reasoning is at odds with the human rights context within which refugee law was established, and is inexplicably unsympathetic to persons who demonstrate the courage to challenge the conformism of authoritarian states.[115] Since the purpose of refugee law is to protect persons from abusive national authority, there is no reason to exclude persons who could avoid risk only by refraining from the exercise of their inalienable human rights.[116] As Kenneth Brill has argued,

> . . . refugee status is not restricted to martyrs. If an individual can demonstrate that flight was a manifestation of an opinion that would have resulted in persecution if expressed, should he be denied asylum if persecution would ensue upon deportation?[117]

In addition to actual or possible future government knowledge of the claimant's political opinion, there must be reason to believe that dissent will not be tolerated.[118] The mere holding of a dissident perspective, therefore, in

---

Socialist would in some sense undercut the case of the Chilean claimant: Federal Court of Appeal Decision A-623-30, April 2, 1981, at 2, *per* Pratte J.; setting aside Immigration Appeal Board Decision V80-6284, C.L.I.C. Notes 41.9, December 1, 1981.

[113] Immigration Appeal Board Decision V87-6512X, December 21, 1987.

[114] *Id.*, at 7, *per* D. Anderson.

[115] To be preferred is the dissenting view of member Bruce Howard in the decision of *Hector Eduardo Contreras Guttierez*, who characterized the Chilean union activist as ". . . a young man with a cause whose actions at times are both heroic and foolish but at all times consistent with what some men have always done in such circumstances [of political oppression]": Immigration Appeal Board Decision V80-6220, C.L.I.C. Notes 30.11, March 16, 1981, at 17.

[116] "In view of the fact that the first paragraph of the Preamble to the Refugee Convention contains a direct reference to the Universal Declaration and the principle which thereby has been affirmed, 'that human beings shall enjoy fundamental rights and freedoms without discrimination', it seems reasonable to infer that a person may justly fear persecution 'for reason of political opinion' in the sense of the Refugee Convention if he is threatened with measures of a persecutory nature because of his exercise of or his insistence on certain of the 'rights' laid down in the Universal Declaration": 1 A. Grahl-Madsen, *The Status of Refugees in International Law*, p. 227 (1966).

[117] K. Brill, "The Endless Debate: Refugee Law and Policy and the 1980 Refugee Act" (1983), 32 Cleveland State L. Rev. 117, at 135.

[118] "Holding political opinions different from those of the Government is not in itself a ground for claiming refugee status, and an applicant must show that he has a fear of persecution for holding such opinions. This pre-supposes that the applicant holds opinions not tolerated by the authorities, which are critical of their policies or methods": UNHCR, *supra*, note 42, p. 19.

the absence of evidence of a consequential risk of persecution, is not sufficient to establish a claim to refugee status.[119] In the case of anti-Communist
Polish claimant *Adam Bohdan Moszczynski*,[120] for example, the Board ruled
that "[m]erely holding opinions, contrary to the policies of the government,
does not entitle a person to status as a Convention refugee. It is the fear
of persecution for holding those opinions which is relevant to the refugee
status determination."[121]

5.4.2 Political Opinion Implicit in Conduct

An alternative to grounding a claim on adherence to a political opinion
per se is to rely on evidence of engagement in activities which imply an adverse
political opinion, and which would elicit a negative governmental response
tantamount to persecution.[122] As the UNHCR notes, threats of persecution

> . . . have only rarely been based expressly on "opinion". . . . It will, there-
> fore, be necessary to establish the applicant's political opinion, which is at the
> root of his behaviour, and the fact that it has led or may lead to the persecu-
> tion that he claims to fear.[123]

Delegates to the Conference on Territorial Asylum, for example, were prepared to accept that participation in "the struggle against colonialism and
apartheid" was a valid expression of political opinion which could lead to
a grant of refugee status.[124] As Atle Grahl-Madsen has noted, subject only
to a neutrally applied criminality exclusion:[125]

> The Convention seeks to protect persons who would be subject to political perse-
> cution through no fault of their own. In this connexion the struggle for certain
> political convictions is not to be regarded as a fault but as a right founded in
> the Law of Nature.[126]

Traditionally it was thought that only those who enjoyed formal membership in a political party,[127] or indeed only those in political leadership roles

---

[119] *See*, e.g., *Marc Michel Cylien*, Immigration Appeal Board Decision 73-12462, March 21,
1974; *Meril Meryse*, Immigration Appeal Board Decision M73-2608, April 30, 1975; *Gladys
Maribel Hernandez*, Immigration Appeal Board Decision M81-1212, January 6, 1983.

[120] Immigration Appeal Board Decision V87-6285, March 7, 1988.

[121] *Id.*, at 5, *per* N. Singh.

[122] A. Grahl-Madsen, *supra*, note 116, p. 129.

[123] UNHCR, *supra*, note 42, p. 20. *Accord* C. Wydrzynski, *Canadian Immigration Law and
Procedure*, p. 331 (1983).

[124] U.N. Doc. A/CONF.78/12, at Art. 2(1)(a), adopted by the Committee of the Whole on
a 45-15-22 vote. *See* R. Plender, "Admission of Refugees: Draft Convention on Territorial Asylum" (1977), 15 San Diego L.Rev. 45, at 57; and E. Lentini, "The Definition of Refugee in
International Law: Proposals for the Future" (1985), 5 Boston College Third World L.J. 183,
at 192.

[125] *See* Section 6.3.2, *infra*.

[126] A. Grahl-Madsen, *supra*, note 116, p. 223.

[127] *See*, e.g., *Marc Georges Sévère* (1974), 9 I.A.C. 42, at 55; *Jim Martin Kwesi Mensah*,
Immigration Appeal Board Decision V79-6136, August 7, 1979, at 3; set aside on other grounds
by Federal Court of Appeal Decision A-527-79, May 2, 1980, and by Federal Court of Appeal
Decision A-524-80, March 10, 1981 ("[H]e held no office and in fact never took out a member-

within a party,[128] could qualify for refugee status on the basis of political opinion. However, as was cogently observed by dissenting Board member N. Singh in *Bakhshish Gill Singh:*[129]

> While one might expect the authorities to arrest and persecute the leaders and the high profile members of an organization, more often than not, to avoid adverse publicity and political ramifications, the leaders are left alone and the brunt of the persecution is borne by the rank and file members whose rights are easily violated.[130]

The excessive formalism of earlier judgments on actions which imply a political opinion has thus given way to a new jurisprudence which focuses on the attitudes and proclivities of the government in the applicant's state of origin:

> Nowhere in the Convention does it say that to be considered a refugee an applicant must have been prominent in the political life of his country of origin. The crucial test is that certain behaviour or actions on the part of the applicant are or have been perceived by the authorities in power as political opposition. For the purposes of applying this test, the Board cannot ignore the reputation a particular political regime has for intolerant suppression of any form of opposition. . . .[131]

---

ship card"); *Manuel Jesus Torres Quinones,* Immigration Appeal Board Decision V81-6153, May 11, 1981, set aside on other grounds by the Federal Court of Appeal at (1982), 45 N.R. 602 ("[H]e took no active part in election propaganda, or public service campaigns and restricted his involvement to doing government business in his garage and supporting [Socialist Party] social functions").

[128] *See,* e.g., *Azam Faceed Narine,* Immigration Appeal Board Decision V79-6140, C.L.I.C. Notes 15.15, December 5, 1979, at 5 ("There is no evidence he was a central political figure, that he held office of any kind or enjoyed or possessed power"); *Gyeabour Stephen Obeng Fosu,* Immigration Appeal Board Decision V80-6032, February 14, 1980, at 2; affirmed without out reasons by Federal Court of Appeal Decision 81-A-12, October 20, 1981 (". . . there is no evidence of any militant involvement or leadership role of any kind. . ."); *Romilio Dictmart Aranda Diaz,* Immigration Appeal Board Decision V80-6225, C.L.I.C. Notes 23.7, July 30, 1980, at 2; affirmed on other grounds by Federal Court of Appeal Decision A-588-80, March 20, 1981 (". . . Mr. Aranda held no important position in the [Chilean Socialist] party. He was just one of the members"); *Christolene Permaul,* Immigration Appeal Board Decision T83-9310, April 13, 1983; previously considered by the Federal Court of Appeal at (1983), 53 N.R. 323 ("Mrs. Permaul was a member of the P.P.P. with no specific functions or duties to perform other than attend meetings about once a month and sometimes distribute pamphlets"); *Leonel Eduardo Quinteros Hernandez,* Immigration Appeal Board Decision V80-6192, January 31, 1985, at 9 ("He never was a leader or executive member of the M.E.R.S. . ."); *Jatinder Singh,* Immigration Appeal Board Decision T83-10505, February 26, 1986, at 3 ("Mr. Singh himself was never an officer of the party but was just a member of the Akali Dal as are about 80% of the farmers in the rural area of the Punjab").

[129] Immigration Appeal Board Decision V87-6246X, July 22, 1987.

[130] *Id.,* at 12, *per* N. Singh. *Accord* C. Wydrzynski, *supra,* note 123, p. 331: "[T]he extent of political involvement or activity is not determinative of the claim, but, rather, most important is the treatment that the claimant has received or is likely to receive for the political activities. Minimal political activity can give rise to a well-founded fear of persecution. . . ."

[131] *Raul Rodolfo Lira Pastene,* Immigration Appeal Board Decision M79-1132, March 28, 1980, at 4, *per* J.-P. Houle.

Essentially any action which is perceived to be a challenge to governmental authority is therefore appropriately considered to be the expression of a political opinion.

This standard derives from a trilogy of decisions of the Federal Court of Appeal, all involving citizens of Chile. In *Re Ricardo Andres Inzunza Orellana and Minister of Employment and Immigration,*[132] the Court considered the application of a member of a Chilean church group who had organized anti-government theatrical performances. While the Immigration Appeal Board rejected the claim on the ground that "the applicant was never involved in any political activities",[133] the Federal Court noted in *obiter* that

> . . . the crucial test in this regard should not be whether the Board considers that the applicant engaged in political activities, but whether the ruling government of the country from which he claims to be a refugee considers his conduct to have been styled as political activity.[134]

Three months later, the Federal Court released its decision in the case of *Leonardo Arturo Espinosa Astudillo v. Minister of Employment and Immigration,*[135] involving a young man who had been the president of his school's sports club in Chile. Applying the dictum from the *Inzunza Orellana* decision, the Court found that ". . . in view of the considerable evidence referred to. . . to the effect that the government of Chile considered his activities in the Sports Club as being political, I hold the view that the Board erred in law in not giving due and proper consideration to the very relevant and cogent evidence."[136] This principle was further defined by the Federal Court in *Angel Eduardo Jerez Spring v. Minister of Employment and Immigration:*[137]

> . . . the Board should not forget that an activity which might have no political significance to us, if it had taken place in Canada, might be seen by a foreign government as having such significance.[138]

This notion of "political opinion" as a relative concept has been regularly applied by both the Immigration Appeal Board[139] and the Federal Court

---

[132] (1979), 103 D.L.R. (3d) 105 (F.C.A.).

[133] Immigration Appeal Board Decision T78-9213, December 19, 1978, at 6, *per* U. Benedetti.

[134] *Supra,* note 132, at 109, *per* Kelly D.J. Commenting on this decision, Wydrzynski writes that "[t]his principle seems to make the interpretive process somewhat more objective, and to benefit the claimant by recognizing that persecution is an irrational activity which may be a response to expression or activity considered harmless, or within the scope of recognized fundamental freedoms. . .": *supra,* note 123, p. 330.

[135] (1979), 31 N.R. 121 (F.C.A.); setting aside Immigration Appeal Board Decision 78-9178, November 16, 1978.

[136] *Id.,* at 122-23, *per* Heald J.

[137] Federal Court of Appeal Decision A-361-80, December 4, 1980; affirming Immigration Appeal Board Decision M79-1170, C.L.I.C. Notes 21.9, May 26, 1980.

[138] *Id.,* at 2, *per* LeDain J.

[139] *See,* e.g., *Moise Danilo Bahamondes Peralta,* Immigration Appeal Board Decision M79-1082, C.L.I.C. Notes 18.9, December 12, 1979, at 3, *per* J.-P. Houle ("The particular circumstances of an individual in relation to the situation in the country of his nationality must

of Appeal.[140] Among those acts which have been construed as expressions of political opinion are the unwillingness of an Iranian woman to wear the chador and attend Islamic functions,[141] the decision of Salvadoran parents to remove their son from the possibility of forced conscription,[142] a Tunisian soldier's alleged betrayal of his military oath,[143] engagement in espionage by a Syrian on behalf of the United States,[144] and even the refusal of a Guatemalan to declare a political opinion to local authorities.[145] The focus is always to be the existence of a *de facto* political attribution by the state of origin, notwithstanding the objective unimportance of the claimant's polit-

---

be taken to include the perception the authorities in power in that country have or could have of the individual's political activities"); *Saam Yagasampanthar Murugesu*, Immigration Appeal Board Decision M82-1142, September 30, 1983, at 9, *per* G. Loiselle ("[T]he crucial test in interpreting political activities is whether the ruling government in the country from which refuge is sought considers the conduct in question as political activity"); *Paul Valdez Schwarz*, Immigration Appeal Board Decision 84-9787, C.L.I.C. Notes 84.8, March 17, 1986; *Mario Arturo Fernandez Ortigoza*, Immigration Appeal Board Decision V83-6704, January 26, 1987; *Shahram Nassiribake*, Immigration Appeal Board Decision V87-6134, April 23, 1987; affirmed on procedural grounds by Federal Court of Appeal Decision A-272-87, April 14, 1988.

[140] *See, e.g., Francisco Humberto Gonzalez Galindo v. Minister of Employment and Immigration,* [1981] 2 F.C. 781 (C.A.); *Luis Rene Amayo Encina v. Minister of Employment and Immigration,* Federal Court of Appeal Decision A-720-80, February 27, 1981; *Alfredo Manuel Oyarzo Marchant v. Minister of Employment and Immigration,* [1982] 2 F.C. 779 (C.A.); *Yaw Owusu Adjei*, Federal Court of Appeal Decision A-498-81, February 25, 1982; *Akrimul Huque Chowdhury v. Deputy Attorney General of Canada*, Federal Court of Appeal Decision A-468-87, May 12, 1988.

[141] "[W]hile her family did not engage in overtly political acts, her actions and those of her relatives and friends would be construed by the authorities as anti-government": *Modjgan Shahabaldin*, Immigration Appeal Board Decision V85-6161, March 2, 1987, at 6, *per* J. MacLeod.

[142] "It is possible for an applicant who has never participated in the political life of his country to fear persecution because he has been wrongly associated with a political movement for one reason or another. The basic criterion is to determine whether the government running the country attributes political activities to the applicant": *Maria Alva Rina Rivera*, Immigration Appeal Board Decision M85-1453, September 22, 1987, at 2, *per* J. Blumer.

[143] *Mohamed Heidi Mahouachi,* Immigration Appeal Board Decision M84-1036, September 11, 1986.

[144] "[E]spionage against the Syrian Government for the benefit of a country whose democratic institutions are the same as those of Canada may be considered a political act for which the claimant can be given refugee status": *Tayshir Dan-Ash*, Immigration Appeal Board Decision M86-1420, October 20, 1986, at 10, *per* J. Cardinal; set aside on procedural grounds by Federal Court of Appeal Decision A-655-86, June 21, 1988. This characterization is a good example of the "ethnocentric gloss" often placed upon the concept of political opinion: *see* M. Ryan, "Political Asylum for the Haitians?" (1982), 14 Case Western Reserve J. Intl. L. 155, at 171.

[145] "It is apparent that the applicant has gone out of his way to avoid expressing a dangerous political opinion, but nevertheless, because of his refusal to respond to the Judiciales' questions, he has been deemed by them to hold political opinions antagonistic to the regime": *Mario Roberto Gudiel Medina*, Immigration Appeal Board Decision V83-6313, C.L.I.C. Notes 69.2, March 28, 1984, at 4-5, *per* B. Howard. *Accord Bolanos Hernandez v. I.N.S.,* 767 F. 2d 1277 (9th Cir. 1985), at 1286: "Choosing to remain neutral is no less a political decision than is choosing to affiliate with a particular political faction."

ical acts,[146] her own inability to characterize her actions as flowing from a particular political ideology,[147] or even an explicit disavowal of the views ascribed to her by the state.[148]

The equivalent evolution of the notion of political opinion in the United States[149] has been criticized by Donald Gagliardi as agreeable, though unwise because it is potentially over-inclusive:

> It is unwise to presume that persecution practiced by a government is necessarily political and based on disagreement. . . . It is not unheard of for a government attempting to suppress internal dissent to proceed with a purposefully over-inclusive program of oppression, especially where the government is unable to distinguish dissenters from the surrounding population adequately. . . . To regard this form of oppression as persecution based on political opinion. . . would substitute a rule that the politics of an alien need not be considered in asylum or deportation proceedings where the alien's government has engaged in random oppression.[150]

---

[146] "Neither the applicant's minor role nor the length of his absence from Pakistan were relevant in the light of the uncontradicted evidence which the Board had accepted, namely, that others who had played the same role had been persecuted. . .": *Tahir Ahmad Nawaz Chaudri v. Minister of Employment and Immigration* (1986), 69 N.R. 114 (F.C.A.), at 117, *per* Hugessen J.; setting aside Immigration Appeal Board Decision T82-10012, October 23, 1984. *See also Leonel Eduardo Quinteros Hernandez*, Immigration Appeal Board Decision V80-6192, January 31, 1985, at 3, *per* E. Chambers: "While those fortunate enough to live in a free and democratic society may attribute no political offence to his action, we cannot substitute our opinion for that of the military government of his native land."

[147] "A person claiming refugee status. . . because of political opinion does not have to be in conflict with the government of his nationality because of deeply held ideological differences. His controversy can result from actions which the government considers captious and, therefore, worthy of oppression": *Fernando Alfonso Naredo Arduengo*, Immigration Appeal Board Decision T80-9159, C.L.I.C. Notes 27.13, November 20, 1980, at 8-9, *per* D. Davey.

[148] *Maria Alva Rina Rivera*, Immigration Appeal Board Decision M85-1453, September 22, 1987, at 2.

[149] *See Hernandez Ortiz v. I.N.S.,* 777 F. 2d 509 (9th Cir. 1985); *Coriolan v. I.N.S.,* 559 F. 2d 993 (5th Cir. 1977); *Bolanos Hernandez v. I.N.S.,* 767 F. 2d 1277 (9th Cir. 1985); *Arqueta v. I.N.S.,* 759 F. 2d 1395 (9th Cir. 1985); *Desir v. Ilchert,* 840 F. 2d 723 (9th Cir. 1988). This position has not always been adhered to by the Board of Immigration Appeals, as evinced in the decision of *Matter of Acosta*, Interim Decision 2986, March 1, 1985, at 32: "[P]ersecution means the infliction of suffering or harm in order to punish an individual for possessing a particular belief or characteristic the persecutor seeks to overcome. . . . Thus, the requirement of persecution on account of political opinion refers not to the ultimate political end that may be served by persecution, but to the belief held by an individual that causes him to be the object of persecution." Appellate courts have recently paid some deference to this view: *see, e.g., Perlera-Escobar v. E.O.I.R.,* 884 F. 2d 1292 (11th Cir. 1990). *See generally* D. Anker and C. Blum, "New Trends in Asylum Jurisprudence" (1989), 1 Intl. J. Refugee L. 67, at 76 ff.

[150] D. Gagliardi, "The Inadequacy of Cognizable Grounds of Persecution as a Criterion for According Refugee Status" (1987-88), 24 Stanford J. Intl. L. 259, at 279. *Accord* M. Heyman, "Redefining Refugee: A Proposal for Relief for the Victims of Civil Strife" (1987), 24 San Diego L.Rev. 449, at 460: "The Ninth Circuit has probably incomprehensibly distorted the concept of political opinion. It has become something that may be nonideological and neutral, held for whatever reason (since motivation is irrelevant), and may be expressed in only 'silent' conduct, indeed may not be expressed at all. By this thinking, literally anyone — and therefore everyone — possesses political opinion. . . ."

This reasoning, however, assumes that the rationale for refugee law is in some sense the protection of persons on the basis of personal merit, e.g., those who possess a particular political opinion,[151] rather than the establishment of a surrogate protection system for those whose membership in the national community has been fundamentally denied.[152] Viewed from the latter perspective, the broad characterization of political opinion is an important means of maintaining the Convention's vitality in circumstances where the basis for oppression may not be readily ascertainable.

5.5 Membership of a Particular Social Group

The fifth enumerated ground for persecution, membership of a particular social group, was introduced with little explanation by the Swedish delegate as a last minute amendment to the Refugee Convention:

> . . . experience had shown that certain refugees had been persecuted because they belonged to particular social groups. . . . Such cases existed, and it would be as well to mention them explicitly.[153]

Who were the intended beneficiaries of this provision? On the one hand, it is argued that membership of a particular social group should be seen as "clarifying certain elements in the more traditional grounds for persecution",[154] those being race, religion, nationality, and political opinion. This was Canadian practice for some years, resulting in the recognition of social group claims only when the social group could be defined on the basis of one of the other four forms of civil or political status:

> Either the group must be political and proclaim and exhibit dissidence with the regime or be a religious sect which has been persecuted by the civil authorities because of its religious beliefs. In a multinational state, a racial minority might also constitute such a group.[155]

Under this approach, the notion of membership of a particular social group became largely superfluous,[156] since the groups which were recognized —

---

[151] "The 'syllogistic' reasoning. . . operates as follows: every extraditee or deportee who can establish certain acts or conditions as legitimately 'political' is entitled to asylum; therefore, offenders considered unworthy of asylum, or refugees considered inexpedient to accept, must be classified as nonpolitical": Note, "Political Legitimacy in the Law of Political Asylum", 99 Harvard L.Rev. 450, at 451.

[152] *See* text *supra* at note 1 ff.

[153] Statements of Mr. Petren of Sweden, U.N. Doc. A/CONF.2/SR.3, at 14, November 19, 1951; and U.N. Doc. A/CONF.2/SR.19, at 14, November 26, 1951. The Swedish amendment (incorporated in U.N. Doc. A/CONF.2/9) was adopted without discussion by a vote of 14-0-8.

[154] G. Goodwin-Gill, "Entry and Exclusion of Refugees: The Obligations of States and the Protection Function of the Office of the UNHCR" (1980), Michigan Y.B. Intl. L. Studies 291, at 297.

[155] *Obertz Belfond* (1975), 10 I.A.C. 208, at 222, *per* J.-P. Houle.

[156] "[T]he more narrow construction that IAB opinions have accorded the term 'social group' has effectively eliminated the term's use as an independent ground for finding persecution": R. Sexton, "Political Refugees, Nonrefoulement and State Practice: A Comparative Study"

illegal expatriates,[157] human rights activists,[158] and various anti-government associations — could already be protected under the rubric of one of the other four categories.[159] The inappropriateness of this neutering of the social group criterion was noted by the Federal Court of Appeal in *Attorney General of Canada v. Patrick Francis Ward:*[160]

> It was the contention of counsel for the Respondent that any reasonably definable organization *engaged in political activity* may be included in the definition [of a particular social group]. If that were so, I find it difficult to understand why it was necessary to include in the definition the term "a particular social group" when the term "political opinion" is part of the definition.[161]

Alternatively, the plea has been made to interpret membership of a particular social group as an essentially all-embracing "safety net",[162] requiring only some recognizable similarity of background among group members.[163] The position is most forcefully put by Arthur Helton,[164] who argues:

> The delegates intended to guarantee security from persecution to all refugees, without invidious or unnecessary distinctions. The "social group" category, designed to reaffirm this commitment, was adopted in the U.N. Convention without dissent, extending the protection of refugees far beyond what had previously been the norm. . . . The intent of the framers of the Refugee Convention was not to address prior persecution of social groups, but rather to save individuals from future injustice. The "social group" category was meant to

---

(1985), 18 Vanderbilt J. Transntl. L. 731, at 788. *Accord* C. Wydrzynski, "Refugees and the Immigration Act" (1979), 25 McGill L.J. 154, at 180.

[157] "It may be argued that when the punishment for illegal departure is excessive, all illegal expatriates constitute a special group and are persecuted for membership in that group": T. Le and M. Esser, "The Vietnamese Refugee and U.S. Law" (1981), 56 Notre Dame Lawyer 656, at 664.

[158] In *Emeline Gabriel*, the Immigration Appeal Board held participation in the Haitian "Ligue des droits de l'homme" to qualify as membership in a particular social group: Immigration Appeal Board Decision M86-1128, C.L.I.C. Notes 105.13, March 10, 1987, at 6, *per* R. Julien.

[159] *See* Section 5.4, *supra*.

[160] Federal Court of Appeal Decision A-1190-88, March 5, 1990; leave to appeal granted by the Supreme Court of Canada on November 8, 1990: Supreme Court Bulletin 2347.

[161] *Id.*, at 8, *per* Urie J.

[162] Foighel has argued that the social group criterion ". . . came into existence, inter alia, as a type of safety net in that this category was to include also race and ethnicity and, furthermore, was to operate as a kind of comprehensive provision for the categories of persons who had a legitimate claim upon being considered refugees in the international sense, although they were not clearly included in the categories specifically mentioned": I. Foighel, "Legal Status of the Boat People" (1979), 48 Nordisk Tidsskrift for Intl. Ret. 217, at 222.

[163] "[I]t seems appropriate to give the phrase a liberal interpretation. Whenever a person is likely to suffer persecution merely because of his background, he should get the benefit of the present provision": 1 A. Grahl-Madsen, *The Status of Refugees in International Law*, p. 220 (1966). *See also* G. Goodwin-Gill, *The Refugee in International Law*, p. 30 (1983), and P. Hyndman, "The 1951 Convention Definition of Refugee" (1987), 9 Human Rts. Q. 49, at 71.

[164] A. Helton, "Persecution on Account of Membership in a Social Group as a Basis for Refugee Status" (1983), 15 Columbia Human Rts. L.Rev. 39.

be a catch-all which could include all the bases for and types of persecution which an imaginative despot might conjure up.[165]

Helton goes on to suggest that all groups protected under any U.N. human rights convention, whether defined in statistical, societal, social, or associational terms, should be considered within the scope of the Convention.[166]

The notion of social group as an all-encompassing residual category is seductive from a humanitarian perspective, since it largely eliminates the need to consider the issue of a linkage between fear of persecution and civil or political status. Yet this is precisely the reason that Helton's analysis cannot stand. The drafters of the Convention did not wish to avoid drawing distinctions among various types of putative refugees, but rather intended to establish a demarcation between those whose fear was attributable to civil or political status (refugees) and those whose concern to flee was prompted by other concerns (not refugees).[167] Moreover, their purpose was anything but the creation of a regime to address new, future injustices, as Helton suggests. It is clear from the comments of the Swedish proponent of the social group category[168] and others that the Convention was designed simply as a means of identifying and protecting refugees from known forms of harm,[169] not of anticipating future, distinct types of state abuse. The liberal attempt to give life to the notion of social group has therefore gone too far, effectively disregarding the fourth element of the Convention definition. This trend has nonetheless been endorsed in some Canadian case law,[170] including in recent comments of the Federal Court of Appeal[171] which seem to define

---

[165] *Id.*, at 41-42 and 45.

[166] *Id.*, at 44-46 and 51 ff.

[167] "The different categories of refugees to which the proposed convention should apply must be clearly indicated; it would be difficult for the Governments to ratify a convention which otherwise would amount to a kind of document signed in blank to which could be subsequently added new categories of beneficiaries without number": Statement of Mr. Cha of China, U.N. Doc. E/AC.32/SR.5, at 2, January 30, 1950. *Accord*, e.g., Mr. Henkin of the U.S.A.: "[T]he obligations of signatory States must be accurately defined and that could not be done unless the categories to benefit were fixed at a given date. The States concerned could subsequently extend the scope of their obligations, but they could not undertake unlimited obligations in advance": U.N. Doc. E/AC.32/SR.3, at 13, January 26, 1950.

[168] *See* text *supra* at note 153.

[169] The United States successfully argued that the Convention should concern itself with " 'neo-refugees', the definition of which was broad enough to allow the inclusion of persons who had left their home since the Second World War as a result of political, racial or religious persecution, or those who might be obliged to flee from their countries for similar reasons in the future": Statement of Mr. Henkin of the U.S.A., U.N. Doc. E/AC.32/SR.3, at 10, January 26, 1950.

[170] "The Board is of the opinion that the ground 'membership in a particular social group' is a ground which must be given a broad and liberal interpretation in order to protect groups or individuals who do not necessarily have political, religious or racial ties at the root of their fear of persecution. Otherwise, this ground of 'social group' would be of very little value": *Richard Cid Requena Cruz*, Immigration Appeal Board Decision T83-10559, C.L.I.C. Notes 95.10, April 8, 1986, at 5, *per* G. Vidal.

[171] *Attorney General of Canada v. Patrick Francis Ward,* Federal Court of Appeal Decision

a particular social group simply as a group of persons "associated, allied, combined"[172] and "united in a stable association with common purposes",[173] with the possible caveat that its goals must not challenge "democratically constituted authority".[174]

A middle ground position which avoids reading "membership of a particular social group" as either redundant or all-inclusive was defined by the United States Board of Immigration Appeals in its decision in *Matter of Acosta:*[175]

> We find the well-established doctrine of *ejusdem generis*, meaning literally, "of the same kind," to be most helpful in construing the phrase "membership in a particular social group". That doctrine holds that general words used in an enumeration with specific words should be construed in a manner consistent with the specific words. . . . The other grounds of persecution. . . listed in association with "membership in a particular social group" are persecution on account of "race", "religion", "nationality", and "political opinion". Each of these grounds describes persecution aimed at an immutable characteristic: a characteristic that either is beyond the power of an individual to change or is so fundamental to individual identity or conscience that it ought not be required to be changed. . . . Thus, the other four grounds of persecution enumerated. . . restrict refugee status to individuals who are either unable by their own actions, or as a matter of conscience should not be required, to avoid persecution. Applying the doctrine of *ejusdem generis*, we interpret the phrase "persecution on account of membership in a particular social group" to mean persecution that is directed toward an individual who is a member of a group of persons all of whom share a common, immutable characteristic. The shared characteristic might be an innate one such as sex, color, or kinship ties, or in some circumstances it might be a shared past experience such as former military leadership or land ownership. The particular kind of group characteristic that will qualify under this construction remains to be determined on a case-by-case basis. However, whatever the common characteristic that defines the group, it must be one that the members of the group either cannot change, or should not be required to change because it is fundamental to their individual identities or conscience. Only when this is the case does the mere fact of group membership become something comparable to the other four grounds of persecution. . . .[176]

A-1190-88, March 5, 1990; leave to appeal granted by the Supreme Court of Canada on November 8, 1990: Supreme Court Bulletin 2347.

[172] *Id.*, at 10, *per* Urie J.

[173] *Id.*, at 4, *per* MacGuigan J.

[174] *Id.*, at 7, 20-21, *per* Urie J. The Court's exclusion of groups dedicated to the overthrow of "democratically constituted authority" from the scope of the social group category is an unfortunate amalgam of the fourth and fifth elements of the refugee definition. Rather than recasting the Convention's notion of social group to bar anti-democratic factions, such concerns ought to be addressed under the rubric of the Convention's exclusion clauses, adopted into Canadian law in 1989 (*see* Chapter 6, *infra*).

[175] Interim Decision 2986, March 1, 1985.

[176] *Id.*, at 37-39.

This formulation includes within the notion of social group (1) groups defined by an innate, unalterable characteristic; (2) groups defined by their past temporary or voluntary status, since their history or experience is not within their current power to change; and (3) existing groups defined by volition, so long as the purpose of the association is so fundamental to their human dignity that they ought not to be required to abandon it. Excluded, therefore, are groups defined by a characteristic which is changeable or from which dissociation is possible, so long as neither option requires renunciation of basic human rights.

By basing the definition of "membership of a particular social group" on application of the *ejusdem generis* principle, we respect both the specific situation known to the drafters — concern for the plight of persons whose social origins put them at comparable risk to those in the other enumerated categories[177] — and the more general commitment to grounding refugee claims in civil or political status. Beyond that, the linkage between this standard and fundamental norms of human rights correlates well with the human rights-based definition of "persecution".[178] Most important, the standard is sufficiently open-ended to allow for evolution in much the same way as has occurred with the four other grounds, but not so vague[179] as to admit persons without a serious basis for claim to international protection. As observed in the American decision of *Sanchez Trujillo v. I.N.S.*,[180] ". . . the term does not encompass every broadly defined segment of a population, even if a certain demographic division does have some statistical relevance".[181] Rather, a "particular social group" must be definable by reference to a shared characteristic of its members which "is fundamental to their identity".[182]

The balance of this part examines the application of the social group criterion so construed, as it relates to issues of gender, sexual orientation, family, class or caste, and voluntary associations.

---

[177] "The addition was intended to ensure that the Convention would embrace those — particularly in Eastern Europe during the Cold War — who were persecuted because of their social origins": R. Plender, "Admission of Refugees" (1977), 15 San Diego L.Rev. 45, at 52.

[178] *See* Section 4.2, *supra*.

[179] In his concurring judgment in *Attorney General of Canada v. Patrick Francis Ward*, Mr. Justice MacGuigan warned that the notion of a "particular" social group excludes groups which can only be defined in "nebulous" terms: *supra*, note 171, at 8, fn. 3.

[180] 801 F. 2d 1571 (9th Cir. 1986).

[181] *Id.*, at 1576, *per* Beezer J.

[182] *Id.* The Court goes on to make an unfortunate reference to the importance of a particular social group being defined by reference to a "voluntary associational relationship", although that comment is immediately contradicted by the recognition of the family (an obviously non-voluntary association) as "a prototypical example" of a particular social group: *Id.*, at 1576. In any event, Mr. Justice MacGuigan's decision in *Attorney General of Canada v. Patrick Francis Ward* makes clear that in Canada, a particular social group may be either natural or "non-natural": *supra*, note 171, at 4.

5.5.1 Gender

Gender-based groups are clear examples of social subsets defined by an innate and immutable characteristic. Thus, while gender is not an independent enumerated ground for Convention protection, it is properly within the ambit of the social group category.[183] The Executive Committee of the UNHCR endorsed this approach in its 1985 conclusion on "Refugee Women and International Protection":

> . . . States, in the exercise of their sovereignty, are free to adopt the interpretation that women asylum-seekers who face harsh or inhumane treatment due to their having transgressed the social mores of the society in which they live may be considered as a "particular social group" within the meaning of Article 1(A)(2) of the 1951 United Nations Refugee Convention.[184]

The decision in *Zekiye Incirciyan*[185] offered the first clear indication that Canadian law would follow the international lead. This case involved a Turkish widow, who had no close family in that country. She was harassed on a daily basis by young men, was sexually assaulted, and was the object of an abduction attempt. The Immigration Appeal Board found that the government was unwilling to protect the claimant because, in the authorities' view, it was inappropriate for her to be living without the protection of a male relative. Accordingly, the Board determined Mrs. Incirciyan to be a refugee by reason of her membership of a particular social group composed of "single women living in a Moslem country without the protection of a male relative."[186] This category meets the test for a particular social group, since gender and the absence of male relatives are not within the control of group members, and choice of marital status is a freedom guaranteed under core norms of international human rights law.[187] Early decisions of the Immigration and Refugee Board have similarly recognized the appropriateness of the social group designation for women in Lebanon[188] and for Tamil women in Sri

---

[183] *See*, e.g., D. Indra, "Gender: A Key Dimension of the Refugee Experience" (1987), 6(3) Refuge 3; and J. Greatbatch, "The Gender Difference: Feminist Critiques of Refugee Discourse" (1989), 1(4) Intl. J. Refugee L. 518.

[184] U.N. Doc. HCR/IP/2/Rev. 1986, at Conclusion No. 39 (XXXVI), para. (k), July 8, 1985. The Executive Committee adopted additional conclusions which addressed the special needs of women refugees in each of 1987 and 1988. *See generally* A. Johnson, "The International Protection of Women Refugees: A Summary of Principal Problems and Issues" (1989), 1(2) Intl. J. Refugee L. 221.

[185] Immigration Appeal Board Decision M87-1541X, August 10, 1987.

[186] *Id.*, at 1, *per* P. Davey.

[187] UDHR, *supra*, note 71, at Art. 16; ICCPR, *supra*, note 71, at Art. 23.

[188] Immigration and Refugee Board Decision T89-00260, July 1989, R.L.R.U. Cat. Sig. 10143, at 3, *per* G. Carson: "The Immigration Appeal Board decision in *Incirciyan* was brought to the attention of the Refugee Division. The decision, which is not binding on the Refugee Division, refers to single Moslem women living in a Moslem country without the protection of a male relative, as constituting members of a particular social group. The Refugee Division agrees with the basic concept as set out in *Incirciyan*."

Lanka.[189] Men, too, have occasionally benefitted from gender-specific interpretations of the social group category, as in *Oscar Roberto Cruz*[190] where the Board noted that the Salvadoran claimant was "a young man, a member of the broad social group that is the primary target of military and guerrilla alike".[191] While some have expressed reservations about the broad ambit of gender-defined social groups,[192] adherence to the *ejusdem generis* principle defeats such concerns, since race, nationality, religion, and even political opinion are also traits which are shared by large numbers of people.

5.5.2 Sexual Orientation

Homosexual and bisexual women and men constitute a second group defined by a fundamental, immutable characteristic. The Federal Administrative Court of Germany addressed the potential for homosexuality to define a "particular social group" in a 1986 decision involving the alleged persecution of an Iranian male by reason of his sexual orientation.[193] Noting the persecution of homosexuals in the Nazi concentration camps, the Court recognized the viability of considering sexual orientation as the basis for a claim to refugee status, assuming it to be an irreversible personal characteristic.

While the precise issue has not yet been adjudicated in Canada, the basis for treating sexual orientation as an immutable characteristic capable of defining a social group was established by the decision of the Federal Court Trial Division in *Timothy Veysey v. Commissioner of the Correctional Service of Canada*.[194] The applicant in that case alleged a breach of his right to equality by reason of the refusal of prison officials to extend the conjugal visitation policy in force for heterosexual spouses to include also homosexual spouses. In finding a violation of the equality rights provision of the Char-

---

[189] Immigration and Refugee Board Decision M89-01213, June 1989, R.L.R.U. Cat. Sig. 10240; Immigration and Refugee Board Decision M89-00407, July 1989, R.L.R.U. Cat. Sig. 10147; Immigration and Refugee Board Decision M89-01225, July 1989, R.L.R.U. Cat. Sig. 10017.

[190] Immigration Appeal Board Decision V83-6807, June 26, 1986.

[191] *Id.*, at 2, *per* B. Howard. *Accord*, e.g., *Marco Antonio Valladares Escoto*, Immigration Appeal Board Decision T87-9024X, July 29, 1987, at 6, *per* D. Davey: "[I]f the allegations were well-founded, the Board could find Mr. Escoto to be a Convention refugee by reason of his having belonged to a particular social group, young men of eligible age for military duty, who were subject to mistreatment after indiscriminate recruitment, a distinct group which made it the object of persecution."

[192] In reference to the notion of young, urban class Salvadoran males as constituting a particular social group, the U.S. Court of Appeals for the Ninth Circuit noted that ". . . such an all-encompassing grouping. . . is not that type of cohesive, homogenous group to which the term 'particular social group' was intended to apply": *Sanchez Trujillo v. I.N.S.,* 801 F. 2d 1571 (9th Cir. 1986), at 1577.

[193] Verwaltungsgerichthof Hessen, August 21, 1986, Ref. 10 OE 69/83, reported as IJRL/004 in (1989), 1(1) Intl. J. Refugee L. 110.

[194] (1989), 29 F.T.R. 74 (T.D.); appeal against this judgment dismissed by Federal Court of Appeal Decision A-557-89, May 31, 1990.

ter of Rights and Freedoms, Mr. Justice Dubé applied the *ejusdem generis* test to define the scope of non-enumerated heads of equality. His conclusions are unmistakably pertinent to the definition of "particular social group" in refugee law:

> Most of the grounds enumerated in s. 15 of the Charter as prohibited grounds of discrimination connote the attribute of immutability, such as race, national or ethnic origin, colour, age. One's religion may be changed, but with some difficulty; sex and mental or physical disability, with even greater difficulty. Presumably, sexual orientation would fit within one of these levels of immutability. Another characteristic common to the enumerated grounds is that the individuals or groups involved have been victimized and stigmatized throughout history because of prejudice, mostly based on fear or ignorance, as most prejudices are. This characteristic would also clearly apply to sexual orientation, or more precisely to those who have deviated from accepted sexual norms, at least in the eyes of the majority.[195]

5.5.3 Family

In view of the recognition in international law of the family as "the natural and fundamental group unit of society [which] is entitled to protection by society and the State",[196] it is not surprising that refugee claims based on family affiliation have been recognized as within the scope of the social group category, both in Canada and elsewhere.[197] Indeed, one of the few provisions which delegates to the unsuccessful Conference on Territorial Asylum were able to agree upon was the inclusion of "kinship" as a proper basis for the recognition of refugee status.[198]

The first Canadian decision to raise the possibility that one's family might constitute a particular social group within the meaning of the Convention definition was the 1979 judgment of the Federal Court of Appeal in *Astudillo v. Minister of Employment and Immigration.*[199] There followed a series of judgments of the Immigration Appeal Board which impliedly accepted this

---

[195] *Id.*, at 78, *per* Dubé J.

[196] UDHR, *supra*, note 71, at Art. 16(3); ICCPR, *supra*, note 71, at Art. 23(1).

[197] *See*, e.g., C. Blum, "Legal Perspectives on U.S. Jurisprudence Regarding Central American Refugee Claims" (1987), 7(1) Refuge 12. In Decision 16 A 10001/88 of the German Obeverwaltungsgericht (High Administrative Court), May 23, 1988, it was observed that "[p]ersecution of kin. . . is an objective reason which can be compared to the persecution of members of a specific social group, as in both cases one reason for the threat of political persecution is the persecution others suffer": Reported as IJRL/0021 in (1989), 1(3) Intl. J. Refugee L. 394.

[198] The Committee of the Whole adopted the Australian proposal, U.N. Doc. A/CONF.78/C.1/L.10, on a vote of 40-24-15: *see* A. Grahl-Madsen, *Territorial Asylum*, p. 209 (1980). The draft convention, however, was not adopted. *See* Section 1.4.2, *supra*.

[199] "While there may be some question as to whether his immediate family can be said to be 'a social group' within the meaning of the definition, there can be no doubt that the 'Sports Club' was a 'social group' as that term is used in the definition": (1979), 31 N.R. 121 (F.C.A.), at 123, *per* Heald J.

premise by recognizing the claims of siblings[200] and children[201] of activists, as well as those made by members of politically prominent families more generally.[202] It was not until the case of *Richard Cid Requena Cruz,*[203] however, that family was clearly stated to be a part of the concept of particular social group. In response to the petition of a young Peruvian who was the object of police harassment in consequence of the escape from the country of his father, the Board observed:

> The application, based on social group, raises the question as to whether or not a family can be considered a social group for the purposes of the *Immigration Act, 1976.* The answer to that question is a qualified yes. In some cultures, including Latin America, certain African nations and some others, for example, it is quite likely that an individual will be assumed to be a supporter of specific social, religious or political ideas merely because a father, uncle or other prominent family member is a known advocate of those ideas. This is not always so, however, and each case must be decided on its own merits on the basis of evidence presented.[204]

The *Requena Cruz* doctrine has been applied in a variety of circumstances, including the claims of the wife of a Chilean socialist,[205] the cousin of an opponent of the Guyanese government,[206] and the son of the organizer of a coup in Ghana.[207] As a rule, therefore, whenever there is an indication that the status or activity of a claimant's relative[208] is the basis for a risk

---

[200] *Bernarda Lucia Ramirez Cordero,* Immigration Appeal Board Decision M79-1211, C.L.I.C. Notes 28.10, December 12, 1980.

[201] *Askale Asnake,* Immigration Appeal Board Decision M80-1020, C.L.I.C. Notes 31.10, February 23, 1981.

[202] "We who live in a democratic society where order is maintained by peaceful means may find it hard to believe that the authorities would harass someone either directly or through his family simply because he bore a name that they held in abomination. However, we must keep our personal opinions to ourselves, and instead try to place the situation in its proper context": *Luis Enrique Toha Seguel,* Immigration Appeal Board Decision 79-1150, C.L.I.C. Notes 28.8, November 13, 1980, at 4, *per* J.-P. Houle.

[203] Immigration Appeal Board Decision T83-10559, February 8, 1984.

[204] *Id.,* at 3, *per* B. Howard.

[205] "Her claim was based largely on the claim of her husband, Mr. Pizarro. The Board held in *Requena Cruz* that a family does constitute a social group and that a claim based on family affiliation was within the purview of the definition of Convention refugee. Therefore, the Board is also prepared to consider her claim on the basis of her family relationship with Mr. Pizarro": *Maria Angelica Jiminez Ormeno Pizarro,* Immigration Appeal Board Decision V87-6004, January 26, 1988, at 2, *per* A. Wlodyka, affirmed without comment by the Federal Court of Appeal at (1990), 8 Imm. L.R. (2d) 223.

[206] This case recognized the sufficiency of a "family connection to an outspoken highly visible political opponent of the government": *Cleopatra Ramsingh,* Immigration Appeal Board Decision M86-1138, September 15, 1987, at 9, *per* P. Davey.

[207] *Morgan Otuo Acheampong,* Immigration Appeal Board Decision T84-9275, C.L.I.C. Notes 68.4, May 29, 1984.

[208] *See,* e.g., D. Gross, "The Right of Asylum Under United States Law" (1980), 80 Columbia L.Rev. 1125, at 1146-47.

of persecution, a claim grounded in family background[209] is properly receivable under the social group category. Moreover, as the decision in *Maria Mabel de la Barra Velasquez*[210] suggests, the notion of family is culturally relative, and may extend significantly beyond nuclear and blood relationships.

5.5.4 Class or Caste

A fourth form of particular social group encompasses immutable forms of class and caste. While it is often suggested that notions of class and social group are essentially coterminous,[211] the general definition posited above[212] excludes a social class defined by a changeable characteristic of a non-essential nature. For example, the members of a privileged social class who resist renunciation of economic privilege are not protected, since it is within their ability voluntarily to renounce their property, an interest which is not protected under core human rights norms.[213]

The exclusion would not apply, however, if the members of the privileged class were forever stigmatized for their origins even after renouncing their property, since past status is an immutable characteristic. In the case of *Luis Folhadela Carneiro de Oliveira,*[214] for example, the Board examined the claim of a Portuguese millionaire industrialist whose vast holdings had been nationalized and confiscated by the government which came to power in 1974. While this fact alone ought not to constitute the basis for a refugee claim, the Board was of the view that the claimant's fear of reprisals for his *past* social status, including the possibility of arrest without trial, was sufficient to bring him within the definition of membership of a particular social group.

In contrast to wealth or even middle class status, both of which can ordinarily be the subject of voluntary alienation, poverty as an economic class may

---

[209] *See* G. Goodwin-Gill, *The Refugee in International Law*, p. 30 (1983).

[210] Immigration Appeal Board Decision V80-6300, C.L.I.C. Notes 39.7, April 29, 1981. This case recognized a Chilean claim grounded on the activities of the applicant's mother's sister's husband and his brother.

[211] "A social group is essentially a social class": A. Fragomen, "The Refugee: A Problem of Definition" (1970), 3 Case Western Reserve J. Intl. L. 45, at 59. *Accord* B. Tsamenyi, "The 'Boat People': Are They Refugees?" (1983), 5 Human Rts. Q. 348, at 366: "This concept [of a particular social group] may therefore be understood to cover situations in which a person suffers persecution merely because of his background. This may include a person's being a member in a class within a society, for example, as a bourgeois, landowner, or civil servant."

[212] *See* text *supra* at note 176 ff.

[213] *But see* T. Le and M. Esser who argue that the Vietnamese "who left as a result of government action (such as the creation of 'New Economic Zones' or the promulgation of decrees eliminating private ownership)" qualify within the social group category: "The Vietnamese Refugee and U.S. Law" (1981), 56 Notre Dame Lawyer 656, at 664-65. This would not be so under the framework suggested here, unless the stigma of past status persisted in the face of a renunciation of wealth. The opportunity to own private property and to engage in the full range of wealth-generating activities are not fundamental, internationally recognized human rights. *See* Section 4.5.2, *supra*.

[214] Immigration Appeal Board Decision 75-10382, April 20, 1976.

constitute a particular social group, since membership cannot always voluntarily be given up:

> . . . the poor as a class. . . may constitute a persecuted "social group" when the economic conditions underlying their poverty are attributable to the exercise or maintenance of political power. If in a given country the poor are kept poor by those in power in order to maintain the current political structure — if all or substantially all economic opportunity is foreclosed — a victim of such poverty suffers "substantial economic disadvantage" on account of his membership in the lower class.[215]

Similarly, an economic class is within the scope of a particular social group where membership, though nominally voluntary, is the only means of ensuring basic subsistence, an interest protected under core norms of human rights law.[216] In the case of *Joseph Alexis Manasse,*[217] the Immigration Appeal Board correctly held membership in the Haitian peasant landowning class to be a form of particular social group, since in the context of a poor, agrarian society, membership in the class represents a means of access to basic needs. The central question, therefore, in examining wealth-based categories or classes is whether the group's defining characteristic is either innate or unchangeable, or if subject to voluntary alienation, whether it is premised on the realization of basic human rights. In all other cases, it would be reasonable to expect an applicant to accommodate herself to less privileged circumstances as an alternative to the invocation of international protection.

Beyond economics, class may also be defined in purely social terms, as in the context of a feudal or caste system,[218] or on the basis of education or occupation. In the case of Haitian *Jean Robert Amazan,*[219] for example, the Board concluded that the applicant's membership in "a threatening social group, [namely] educated young persons"[220] was sufficient to bring him within the ambit of the Convention definition. Insofar as class designations are inalienable, or can be disclaimed only at the expense of basic human rights, they may therefore appropriately be seen as defining a particular social group.

5.5.5 Voluntary Associations

Perhaps the most contentious aspect of the social group concept relates to membership in associations from which voluntary alienation is possible. Normally, the social group designation is concerned with the protection of

---

[215] Note, "Political Legitimacy in the Law of Political Asylum" (1985), 99 Harvard L.Rev. 450, at 461.

[216] *See* Section 4.5.2, *supra.*

[217] Immigration Appeal Board Decision M87-1634X, September 9, 1987.

[218] *See,* e.g., Z. Rizvi, "Causes of the Refugee Problem and the International Response", in A. Nash, ed., *Human Rights and the Protection of Refugees under International Law,* p. 112 (1988).

[219] Immigration Appeal Board Decision M87-1502X, December 7, 1987.

[220] *Id.,* at 2, *per* M. Durand.

persons from abuse based on characteristics which are beyond their control — gender, sexual orientation, family, and most forms of class or caste. However, as the decision in *Matter of Acosta*[221] suggests, immutability should be interpreted to include "a characteristic that either is beyond the power of an individual to change *or is so fundamental to individual identity or conscience that it ought not be required to be changed. . . .*" [Emphasis added][222] Thus, membership in a voluntary association defined by a non-fundamental purpose, such as recreation or personal convenience, would normally be seen to be outside the scope of the notion of a particular social group.[223] Conversely, where the purpose of the voluntary association is essential to individual identity or conscience, it is reasonable that members should have access to international protection where there is a risk of persecution for failure to renounce such basic interests. This approach is consistent with the decision of the Federal Court of Appeal in *Attorney General of Canada v. Patrick Francis Ward*,[224] in which an attempt was made to define the social group concept as applied to voluntary associations by examining the legal acceptability of their goals.[225]

Students are thus logically included within the social group category, since the pursuit of education is a basic international human right.[226] This characterization was raised as a possibility by the Federal Court of Appeal's decision in *Gladys Maribel Hernandez,*[227] and has been adopted by the Immigration Appeal Board in *Jesus Antonio Miranda Cuellar.*[228] More generally, groups defined by employment or profession fall within the social group category, since freedom to choose one's occupation is also a basic right.[229]

---

[221] Interim Decision 2986, March 1, 1985.

[222] *Id.*, at 38. This notion is in keeping with interpretation based on the *ejusdem generis* principle, since religion and political opinion are similarly subject to alienation, though at a cost inconsistent with core notions of human rights.

[223] *But see* Grahl-Madsen, who argues for the inclusion within the concept of particular social group of "certain associations, clubs or societies": 1 A. Grahl-Madsen, *The Status of Refugees in International Law*, p. 219 (1966).

[224] Federal Court of Appeal Decision A-1190-88, March 5, 1990; leave to appeal granted by the Supreme Court of Canada on November 8, 1990: Supreme Court Bulletin 2347.

[225] *Id.*, at 20-21, *per* Urie J. While the Court arguably draws the line too narrowly by its reference to respect for "the rule of law" as a distinguishing factor, the basic approach of enfranchising voluntary associations the purposes of which conform to basic legal norms is helpful.

[226] UDHR, *supra*, note 71, at Art. 26; *International Covenant on Economic, Social and Cultural Rights*, U.N.G.A. Res. 2200 (XXI), December 19, 1966, entered into force January 3, 1976 ("*ICESCR*"), at Art. 13. *Accord* G. Goodwin-Gill, *The Refugee in International Law*, p. 30 (1983); D. Anker, "Defining a 'Social Group'" (1983), 6 Immigration J. 15, at 15.

[227] Federal Court of Appeal Decision, May 20, 1982, at 2-3.

[228] Immigration Appeal Board Decision 80-9204, C.L.I.C. Notes 26.9, November 20, 1980.

[229] UDHR, *supra*, note 71, at Art. 23; ICESCR, *supra*, note 226, at Art. 6. *Accord* A. Grahl-Madsen, who includes "civil servants, businessmen, professional people, farmers, workers" within the social group category: *supra*, note 223, p. 219. As Angela Botelho notes, "A social group based on occupational criteria certainly falls within the parameters of the use of the term [social group] in sociological literature. . . . The advantage of an occupationally-based defini-

Trade union membership has also been accepted as the basis for refugee status in decisions such as *Wilfredo Alejandro Zubieta*[230] and *Oscar Trujillo Barraza*.[231] In all of these examples, voluntary participation is appropriately protected because of its linkage to core principles of human rights. The interests which underlie membership in the associations are so fundamental that international protection is in keeping with the underlying rationale for the social group category.

5.6 Other Grounds for Claiming Refugee Status

In determining whether there is a nexus between the claimant's fear of persecution and her civil or political status, care must be taken to examine the substantive, rather than the merely formal, grounds for seeking protection. In particular, claims which are based on activity which is criminalized in the country of origin, which relate to failure to perform military service, or which involve escape from war or violence may, under some circumstances, fall within the scope of the Convention definition, the absence of an obvious link to one of the five enumerated grounds notwithstanding. Under the veneer of a protection need apparently unrelated to civil or political status, there is often a political or other cause which is sufficient to establish a claim to refugee status.

5.6.1 Criminal Status: Prosecution or Persecution?

It is clear that refugee status may not be invoked by an individual solely on the basis that she is at risk of legitimate prosecution or punishment for breach of the ordinary criminal law.[232] As the UNHCR has noted:

---

tion lies in its limited and clearly delineated contours, and in its susceptibility to certain evidentiary requirements at the proof stage of asylum proceedings": A. Botelho, "Membership in a Social Group: Salvadoran Refugees and the 1980 Refugee Act" (1985), 8 Hastings Intl. Comp. L.Rev. 305, at 335. *See Manuel Jesus Torres Reyes et al v. Minister of Manpower and Immigration*, Federal Court of Appeal Decision, October 28, 1976, in which Mr. Justice Pratte noted the possibility that one's status as a former civil servant might be a basis for the recognition of refugee status; also *Emeline Gabriel*, Immigration Appeal Board Decision M86-1128, C.L.I.C. Notes 105.13, March 10, 1987, at 5, regarding persecution by reason of the political opinions of the applicant's employer.

[230] "The next question is whether the applicant has been persecuted because of his membership in such a particular social group. In my opinion, the fact of having been fired for union activities, arbitrarily labelled as a terrorist, considered along with the other fact that the applicant had been constantly harassed (according to the evidence which was not refuted) in his search for a living for himself and his family, constitutes persecution which interferes with the right to work and the dignity of a human being as we understand these in Canada": Immigration Appeal Board Decision 79-1034, C.L.I.C. Notes 14.10, October 31, 1979, at 2-3, *per* J.-P. Houle.

[231] Immigration Appeal Board Decision 77-9449, March 23, 1978. *Accord* UDHR, *supra*, note 71, at Art. 23(4); ICESCR, *supra*, note 226, at Art. 8; ICCPR, *supra*, note 71, at Art. 22(1).

[232] *See*, e.g., A. Grahl-Madsen, *supra*, note 223, p. 192.

Persecution must be distinguished from punishment for a common law offence. Persons fleeing from prosecution or punishment for such an offence are not normally refugees. It should be recalled that a refugee is a victim — or potential victim — of injustice, not a fugitive from justice.[233]

This proposition was propounded as part of Canadian law in the decision of *Louis-Paul Mingot*,[234] in which it was held that "[f]ear of being legally prosecuted before regular courts. . . [cannot] *in se* and *per se*, constitute a fear of persecution as defined in the Convention".[235] This is so even if the justice system in the country of origin fails to meet generalized standards of fairness, or the range of penalties ordinarily imposed in that nation seems out of line with the norms in other states. The case of Ghanaian *Anthony Appiah Asamoah,*[236] for example, raised the issue of an individual at risk of prosecution under very stringent laws for having allowed fire to destroy another's crops, who claimed refugee status on the basis of the inappropriateness of summary prosecution and severe penalties for offences of this kind. In rejecting his claim, the Board noted:

> . . . he has shown that he fears prosecution for an economic offence in Ghana, an offence which indeed may carry severe penalties with it and may not proceed entirely in accordance with Canada's criminal justice and evidentiary rules. . . [but] this offence is not directed solely against the applicant himself, but rather is applied to the population of Ghana in general. How this can be characterized as persecution is a question which has not been answered. . . .[237]

Such claims are outside the scope of the Convention because the risk faced by the claimant is only the potential criminal liability of every citizen, and is therefore not linked to a form of civil or political status enumerated in the definition. Insofar as an examination of both the nature of the criminal offence and its prosecution and punishment confirms that the offence is politically neutral in substance and application, then it cannot serve as the basis for a claim to refugee status.

On the other hand, Richard Plender has observed that while persecution and prosecution are not coterminous, neither are they mutually exclusive.[238] Because both the content and implementation of the criminal law are within the control of the state of origin,[239] it is possible for a government with persecutory intent to use the criminal law as a means of oppressing its opponents.[240] In such circumstances, it makes no sense to treat those at risk of

---

[233] UNHCR, *supra*, note 42, at 15.

[234] (1975), 8 I.A.C. 351.

[235] *Id.*, at 356, *per* J.-P. Houle.

[236] Immigration Appeal Board Decision T87-9902, January 19, 1988.

[237] *Id.*, at 3-4, *per* J. Weisdorf.

[238] R. Plender, "Admission of Refugees" (1977), 15 San Diego L.Rev. 45, at 54.

[239] K. Kawahara, "Analysis of Results of the First Session of the International Conference on Territorial Asylum", in International Institute of Humanitarian Law, ed., *Round Table on Some Current Problems of Refugee Law* 23 (1978).

[240] G. Goodwin-Gill, *supra*, note 226, p. 34.

politically inspired abuse of the criminal law as fugitives from justice; they are rather potentially at risk of persecution, and may properly be assessed as refugees.[241] This perspective is consistent with the internal structure of the Convention, the exclusion clauses of which[242] deny refugee status not to all "criminals" *per se*, but only to a person who "has committed a serious *non-political* crime outside the country of refuge. . ." [Emphasis added].[243] Similarly, the Draft Convention on Territorial Asylum provides for a clarification of the refugee definition to embrace persons at risk of "prosecution or punishment for reasons directly related to. . . persecution".[244]

Canadian law has only recently begun to examine critically the context of alleged criminality in a comprehensive way. In *Ethem Ictensev*,[245] the Board posed the question,

> When is a political action permissible although forbidden by law? Clearly, for our purposes, the fact that a political action is taken outside of the law is in itself not sufficient to invalidate a claim. However, the question posed cannot be answered in a simplistic fashion, for it involves the consideration of a large number of issues ranging from human rights to state security; from natural justice to emergency measures.[246]

A turning point was reached in the decision of Ghanaian *Godfred Appiah Kubi*,[247] involving an individual charged with the "criminal offence" of distributing anti-government pamphlets. After conducting a thorough review of the conflicting Canadian jurisprudence, the Board concluded that ". . . the commission of an offence should not *automatically* lead to the conclusion that the claimant's fear is of prosecution and punishment".[248] Looking beyond the alleged illegality of the act, the Board in this case noted that "[d]istributing pamphlets is often the only means of expressing contrary opinions in countries where there are restrictions on freedom of expression, a fundamental human right,"[249] and accordingly determined the criminal characterization of the claimant's actions to be without foundation.

---

[241] "It is now, in effect, recognized by all civilised states that ordinary criminals are to be extradited and that persons who fear punishment for political reasons may be granted protection by the receiving State": F. Krenz, "The Refugee as a Subject of International Law" (1966), 15 I.C.L.Q. 90, at 101. *Accord* D. Roth, "The Right of Asylum Under United States Immigration Law" (1981), 33 U. Florida L.Rev. 539, at 553-54: "The Board is therefore required to distinguish between violations of law that are essentially criminal and those which are political."

[242] *See* Section 6.3.2, *infra*.

[243] Convention, *supra*, note 11, at Art. 1(F)(b).

[244] A. Grahl-Madsen, *Territorial Asylum*, p. 208 (1980). *Accord* R. Plender, *supra*, note 238, at 58.

[245] Immigration Appeal Board Decision T87-9494X, October 19, 1987.

[246] *Id.*, at 13, *per* P. Ariemma.

[247] Immigration Appeal Board Decision T87-9053, June 10, 1987.

[248] *Id.*, at 4, *per* E. Townshend.

[249] *Id.*, at 6.

In what circumstances is it appropriate to give careful scrutiny to an allegation that a claimant is outside the scope of the definition because her fear derives only from genuine criminality? One set of concerns relates to the nature of the offence on the basis of which the claimant has been charged or convicted: Is it either an inherently political offence, or an ordinary criminal offence applied in politically suspicious circumstances? As noted by Gerard LaForest in relation to the law of extradition:

> . . . although the terminology of "political offence" is widespread, a satisfactory definition remains to be formulated. The term embraces two concepts: first, the purely political offence (e.g. treason, sedition, espionage, etc.), which is an act directed against the political organization or government of a state and contains no element of common crime, and secondly, what is described. . . as an offence of a political character, one that is a common crime but is so closely integrated with political acts or events that it is regarded as political.[250]

Alternatively, even if the offence itself is apparently a legitimate exercise of criminal law authority, has the enforcement of an otherwise proper law been somehow distorted to achieve a persecutory end? Where, for example, the decision to prosecute, the process under which the charge is heard, or the nature of the sentence imposed is politically manipulated, the refugee claim should not be dismissed as raising a simple issue of "fear of prosecution or punishment", but should instead be examined on its merits.

The notion of an "absolute political offence"[251] is based on the proposition that there is a range of activity which is outside the proper scope of the criminal law.[252] In the result, any "criminal" prosecution grounded in an illegitimate exercise of criminal law authority cannot be relied upon to exclude a claimant from refugee status.[253] The most readily recognizable form of absolute political offence is an attempt to criminalize the exercise of a fundamental human right,[254] at least insofar as the criminal prohibition applies in circumstances not recognized as emergency exceptions under international human rights law.[255] While Canadian law has shown a marked reluctance to apply this concept, for example in regard to freedom of political expression[256] and

---

[250] G. LaForest, *Extradition to and from Canada,* p. 63 (1977).

[251] *See generally* G. Goodwin-Gill, *The Refugee in International Law,* p. 38 (1983).

[252] K. Petrini, "Basing Asylum Claims on a Fear of Persecution Arising from a Prior Asylum Claim" (1981), 56 Notre Dame Lawyer 719, at 727.

[253] *Rebecca Fogel v. Minister of Manpower and Immigration,* (1976) 7 N.R. 172 (F.C.A.), at 175, *per* Thurlow J.

[254] 1 A. Grahl-Madsen, *The Status of Refugees in International Law,* p. 83 (1966); K. Petrini, *supra,* note 252, at 727. With regard to freedom of political speech in particular, *see* D. Gross, "The Right of Asylum Under United States Law" (1980), 80 Columbia L.Rev. 1125, at 1142.

[255] *See* Section 4.2, *supra,* particularly at note 73 ff.

[256] *See,* e.g., *Anil Kapur,* Immigration Appeal Board Decision T81-9450, August 26, 1981, at 3, *per* E. Teitelbaum ("His fear of returning to India derives from the warrant out for his arrest for having violated a prohibition order rather than from a substantiated fear of political persecution"); *Mahibur Rahman Chowdhury,* Immigration Appeal Board Decision T83-10497, C.L.I.C. Notes 90.8, February 13, 1986 (in which the claim of an individual sought under a

the right to leave one's country,[257] it is clearly unreasonable to accept at face value the state of origin's characterization of the exercise of a core human right not only as illegitimate, but as just cause for punishment.

The case of Chilean *Hector Eduardo Contreras Guttierez*[258] illustrates this point. The claimant was a union organizer at the national transportation company. While the right to form and join labour unions is unequivocally recognized in international human rights law,[259] the Chilean government outlawed such activities, and inflicted severe punishment on those suspected of supporting the trade union movement. The majority of the Board noted simply that "[s]uch activities are understood by the Court to be illegal",[260] and dismissed the claim. In a stirring dissent, member Bruce Howard underscored the importance of refusing to disallow claims grounded in an absolute political offence:

> Were the union activities illegal, as my colleague says? Of course they were, but we are not asked to judge legality and illegality in Chile. We are judging *persecution* as defined in the Act.[261]

---

warrant issued in consequence of participation in a political demonstration was dismissed on the basis of criminality); *Karnail Heer Singh*, Immigration Appeal Board Decision V87-6167X, June 3, 1987, at 10, *per* F. Wright; affirmed by Federal Court of Appeal Decision A-474-87, April 13, 1988 ("The applicant may be afraid of being arrested by the police again if he returns to India and engages in similar demonstrations. . . . In the opinion of the Board, this fear of prosecution does not represent a well-founded fear of persecution"); *George Goka Darko*, Immigration Appeal Board Decision T87-9173X, June 16, 1987, at 7, *per* C. De Morais ("Is the applicant fleeing persecution because he organized and participated in one demonstration. . . or prosecution for organizing and participating in an illegal march and destroying private property?").

[257] This issue is discussed in detail at Section 2.2.1, *supra. See*, e.g., *Maria Sandor*, Immigration Appeal Board Decision 79-9145, C.L.I.C. Notes 9.16, May 14, 1979, at 2, *per* A. Weselak ("She further states that should she return to Hungary now she would be put in jail because she refused to go back to Hungary from Austria. . . . [W]hile she may be subject to prosectuion upon her return, this is not a matter which can be considered to be persecution"); *Lech Jankowski*, Immigration Appeal Board Decision V80-6410, January 5, 1981, at 4-5, *per* B. Howard ("Unfortunately the definition. . . contains no reference to fear of punishment for a crime against the ordinary laws of the applicant's country. Moreover it is not reasonable that a person may place himself in jeopardy with the laws of his country by desertion and thereby claim special status if it is that act itself which creates the claim for refugee status"); *Henryk Stanley Komisarski*, Immigration Appeal Board Decision V81-6162, May 28, 1981, at 2, *per* C. Campbell, regarding a Pole who abandoned ship in Canada ("[V]iolating the laws of one's country and having to face the consequences does not make one a refugee"). *But see* the slightly more liberal judgment in *Stanislaw Julian Jodlowski*, Immigration Appeal Board Decision V81-6166, June 18, 1981, at 6-7, *per* D. Davey ("A person who flees his country [for a Convention reason]. . . is justified in placing before the Board his additional fear of reprisal for leaving his country in an unlawful manner. Such action, by itself, does not make a person a Convention refugee").

[258] Immigration Appeal Board Decision V80-6220, C.L.I.C. Notes 30.11, March 16, 1981.

[259] UDHR, *supra*, note 71, at Art. 23(4); ICCPR, *supra*, note 71, at Art. 22; ICESCR, *supra*, note 226, at Art. 8.

[260] *Supra*, note 258, at 4, *per* W. Hlady.

[261] *Id.*, at 12, *per* B. Howard.

In addition to "criminal" offences which are fundamentally illegitimate, a second category of concern is comprised of "relative political offences", which Atle Grahl-Madsen defines as

> . . . "common crimes" such as murder, robbery, burglary, etc. committed not for personal gain, but out of political motives. . . . [I]t is often considered right to classify perpetrators of such crimes as political offenders and not as common criminals. . . .[262]

While some argue that political intent does not take away from the common law character of such crimes,[263] both Grahl-Madsen[264] and Guy Goodwin-Gill[265] recognize that in appropriate circumstances, politically motivated common crime should not bar access to refugee protection. It would, of course, be appropriate to consider the genuineness of the political purpose of the act (as distinguished from more typically criminal motives such as personal gain); the extent of the linkage between the act committed and the political purpose being pursued; and, perhaps most important, the proportionality of the good sought to be attained in relation to the harm inflicted through the crime.[266] Where the motivation is genuine, the strategy credible, and the incidental harm tolerable in relation to the goal sincerely pursued, it is reasonable to view the action as more fundamentally political than criminal,[267] and hence to assess the refugee claim on its merits.[268]

---

[262] A. Grahl-Madsen, *supra*, note 254, p. 84.

[263] *See*, e.g., C. Pompe, "The Convention of 28 July 1951 and the International Protection of Refugees", [1956] Rechtsgeleerd Magazyn Themis 425, published in English as U.N. Doc. HCR/INF/42, May 1958, at 9; K. Zink, quoted in A. Grahl-Madsen, *supra*, note 254, p. 221; and F. Marino-Menendez, "El concepto de refugiado en un contexto de derecho internacional general" (1983), 35(2) Revista española de derecho intl. 337, at 355-56.

[264] "The Convention seeks to protect persons who would be subject to political persecution through no fault of their own. In this connexion, the struggle for a certain political conviction is not to be regarded as a fault but as a right founded in the Law of Nature": A. Grahl-Madsen, *supra*, note 254, p. 223.

[265] "The international community does not exist for the purpose of preserving established governments, and the political offence exception may be considered valuable for its dynamic quality": G. Goodwin-Gill, *The Refugee in International Law*, p. 38 (1983).

[266] *Id.*, at 60-61. On the susceptibility of politically motivated terrorism to this analysis, *see McMullen v. I.N.S.*, 788 F. 2d 591 (U.S.C.A., 9th Cir. 1986), at 597: "Such acts are beyond the pale of a protectable 'political offense.' These actions were directed solely at bringing about social chaos, with the eventual demise of the state intended only as an indirect result. . . . There is a meaningful distinction between terrorist acts directed at the military or official agencies of the state, and random acts of violence against ordinary citizens that are intended only 'to promote social chaos.'" *Quaere* the appropriate margin of appreciation where targeted assaults prove an insufficient incentive to abandon repression.

[267] "To fall within the [notion of a political offence], the act charged must have been committed as an incident or in furtherance of a political end": G. LaForest, *supra*, note 250, p. 63. *Accord Schtraks v. Government of Israel*, [1964] A.C. 556 (H.L.), in which purpose and motive are held to be key concerns in describing an offence as political in nature.

[268] There is a range of opinion among states on this issue. The Board of Immigration Appeals in the United States, for example, has rejected the appropriateness of this form of balancing:

The traditional Canadian view has been hostile to the notion of relative political offences. In *Musial v. Minister of Employment and Immigration,*[269] the Federal Court of Appeal held:

> A person who is punished for having violated an ordinary law of general application, is punished for the offence he has committed, *not for the political opinions that may have induced him to commit it.* [Emphasis added][270]

Similarly, in *Surujpal v. Minister of Employment and Immigration,*[271] the Federal Court examined the claim of a Guyanese citizen who, opposed to the one-party dominance in his country, defaced government election posters, and was consequently incarcerated for a week in unsanitary and unhealthy prison conditions. The Court dismissed the political significance of this event:

> Since this was by the applicant's own admission an arrest and imprisonment according to law (although he may not have realized it at the time), it could not establish a well-founded fear of persecution.[272]

The Immigration Appeal Board has similarly rejected the relative political offence concept on a number of occasions, resulting in the failure fully to assess the merits of the claims of a Salvadoran revolutionary,[273] an opponent of the Pinochet dictatorship in Chile found in possession of illicit weapons,[274] and even a naïve young Guyanan who believed that he could disrupt a corrupt election by stealing a ballot box![275] While each of these cases raises *prima facie* issues of criminality, the underlying political premise of the claimants' actions brings them within the relative political offence category, thus warranting a full examination of the merits of the refugee claim.

The relative political offence notion does enjoy something of a toehold

---

Matter of Rodriguez-Coto, Interim Decision 2985, February 21, 1985, at 3. *See*, e.g., G. Goodwin-Gill, *supra*, note 265, pp. 31 ff.

[269] (1981), 38 N.R. 55 (F.C.A.).

[270] *Id.*, at 60, *per* Pratte J.

[271] (1985), 60 N.R. 73 (F.C.A.).

[272] *Id.*, at 74, *per* MacGuigan J.

[273] "Apart from his account of his activity as a militant revolutionary, Mr. Lazo Cruz gave no evidence of his political philosophy or opinions. . . . If he is fearful of returning to El Salvador. . . then that fear flows from violent criminal activity which is beyond the definition of a 'refugee'. . .": *Jose Antonio Lazo Cruz*, Immigration Appeal Board Decision V80-6004, C.L.I.C. Notes 18.12, January 16, 1980, at 3, *per* C. Campbell.

[274] "He knew that the authorities had called for the surrender of all firearms and he had ample opportunity to do so. . . . His excuse for not doing so, namely, his perception that the coup would be short lived, and secondly, his fear that the weapons may have been previously used in some illegal activity indicates a fear of prosecution for possession of illegal firearms and not a well-founded fear of persecution": *Jorge Pizarro Parada*, Immigration Appeal Board Decision V87-6004, January 26, 1988, at 12, *per* A. Wlodyka; affirmed on other grounds by Federal Court of Appeal Decision A-696-88, April 3, 1989.

[275] "When the election was over he stole the ballot box, and whatever the justification is in his mind, this was a criminal act for which he must expect to answer": *Azam Faceed Narine*, Immigration Appeal Board Decision V79-6140, C.L.I.C. Notes 15.15, December 5, 1979, at 5, *per* C. Campbell.

in Canadian law. In 1982, the Immigration Appeal Board recognized in *Mohammad Mushtaq*[276] that the existence of a warrant for the claimant's arrest in Pakistan for disturbing the public peace could be probative of a risk of persecution, rather than simply a fear of prosecution. Similarly, an affirmative decision was rendered in the case of *Nana Kwasi Yeboah,*[277] involving a Ghanaian accused of the offence of "smuggling" for his part in spiriting opponents of the Rawlings dictatorship out of that country. Perhaps most significant is the decision in *Tayshir Dan-Ash:*[278]

> Prosecution for the commission of a crime under the laws of a given country does not correspond to persecution under the terms of the Convention. However, if such a crime is committed for political purposes, its punishment may be considered as persecution. . . . Whether prosecution and punishment amount to persecution in the sense of the Convention depends on the following factors: the object and purpose of the law, the precise motivation of the individual who breaches such law, the "interest" which such individual asserts and the extent of the punishment.[279]

In reviewing this decision, the Federal Court of Appeal left the door open to the evolution of a relative political offence concept in Canadian law, without in fact endorsing such a development:

> The Board was of the view that the respondent's admitted espionage against the Syrian government was a political act inspired by his political opinions and that this qualified him for refugee status. Assuming, without deciding, that this could be so and given the fact that the espionage, for which he was well paid, was the only apparent manifestation of [the] respondent's alleged political opinions, the Board's position is clearly dependent upon its finding that he was a credible witness. . . .[280]

Beyond instances in which the criminal substance of the offence is doubtful in either absolute or relative terms, it is also possible for the procedure in an otherwise legitimate and appropriate prosecution to be politically subverted. Insofar as this interference or bias results in a differential level of risk to persons defined by civil or political status, it may also remove the "prosecution" to the realm of persecution. The subversion may be of three kinds.

---

[276] Immigration Appeal Board Decision M81-1122, C.L.I.C. Notes 47.6, October 26, 1982.

[277] "Although the smuggling of two people out of Ghana could be considered by that country as a criminal offence, in the situation that prevails today in that country under a non-democratic government, it could be possible that the applicant would face serious consequences if returned to his home country": Immigration Appeal Board Decision T81-9165, C.L.I.C. Notes 42.9, May 11, 1982, at 4-5, *per* U. Benedetti.

[278] Immigration Appeal Board Decision M86-1420, October 20, 1986.

[279] *Id.*, at 10, *per* J.-P. Cardinal. The test cited is derived from G. Goodwin-Gill, *supra*, note 265, p. 35. This formulation does not explicitly raise the issue of proportionality of means to end, a critical concern in determining the acceptability of the breach of criminal law standards in the interest of advancing political goals.

[280] *Minister of Employment and Immigration v. Tayshir Dan-Ash*, Federal Court of Appeal Decision A-655-86, June 21, 1988, at 3, *per* Hugessen J.

First, Canadian law recognizes the illegitimacy of politically selective prosecution.[281] As Douglas Gross explains:

> . . . an alien known to his government as a dissident may claim that he was punished for [a] crime, while others, equally culpable, were not. . . . [In such circumstances] it is fair to presume that the alien is really being persecuted for his political opinion.[282]

In the case of *Saam Yagasampanthar Murugesu*,[283] for example, the Board discounted the alleged criminality of the claimant, implying that he may have been inappropriately implicated by the local authorities as retribution for his political activism.[284] A similar concern was expressed in the decision of *So Wo Li*:[285]

> Were she to return or be returned [to China], her previous tormenters, with their access to the officials in power, might well use their position to have Ms. Li treated with extreme severity for this offence [of illegal departure]. While such treatment might, at first glance, be considered prosecution for a criminal offence, such a singling out of Ms. Li for vigorous prosecution by reason of her past refusal to collaborate with her tormenters would, in my opinion, constitute actual persecution.[286]

In addition to selective prosecution, the legitimacy of the criminal law process can also be undermined by a process of adjudication which ignores basic standards of fairness in order to effect or support political repression. As Atle Grahl-Madsen states:

> If actual or alleged perpetrators of political offences and other persons who for some reason or other have attracted the wrath of public officials are not brought to trial in judicial proceedings, but subjected to "administrative measures". . . it is hardly appropriate to try to distinguish between those who have actually committed a political offence. . . and those who are completely innocent. . . . In cases where the government resorts to such extra-legal, or at least extra-judicial, measures, it seems fitting to speak of political persecution rather than prosecution for political offences. The same may apply if the courts have lost their independence and are in fact only a prolonged arm of the executive.[287]

---

[281] "[P]ersons who would fear punishment for any non-political offence of general application. . . will normally be rejected [as refugees]. Of course, this interpretive principle is not absolute, and where it is shown that criminal prosecution. . . was used as a form of selective punishment by a State based on [an enumerated ground], a successful claim might be established on this basis": C. Wydrzynski, *Canadian Immigration Law and Procedure*, p. 323 (1983).

[282] D. Gross, "The Right of Asylum Under United States Law" (1980), 80 Columbia L.Rev. 1125, at 1146.

[283] Immigration Appeal Board Decision M82-1142, July 13, 1982 and September 30, 1983.

[284] *See id.*, at 3-4 (judgment of September 30, 1983).

[285] Immigration Appeal Board Decision V88-00066X, September 23, 1988.

[286] *Id.*, at 9, *per* D. Anderson.

[287] 1 A. Grahl-Madsen, *The Status of Refugees in International Law*, p. 84 (1966). *Accord* K. Petrini, "Basing Asylum Claims on a Fear of Persecution Arising from a Prior Asylum Claim" (1981), 56 Notre Dame Lawyer 719, at 727.

This proposition meshes well with traditional Canadian concern to exclude from refugee status only persons who fear "being *legally prosecuted* before *regular courts*" [Emphasis added].[288] In the decision of *Shane Gregory Brannson*,[289] for example, the Board went to great lengths to respond clearly to allegations of differential prosecution in the United States based on race. Similarly, in *Krishnapillai Easwaramoorthy*,[290] the Board held that the Sri Lankan claimant was actually in fear of prosecution only after satisfying itself of the adequacy of the judicial procedures which would be brought to bear in hearing the charge against him.[291] The principle was perhaps most poignantly stated in the case of Chilean *Jesus Enrique Retamal Sanchez*,[292] in which the Board vindicated the claimant since no weight could be attached to his failure to answer criminal charges in a judicial system which lacked political independence:

> Being a victim of a glaring, absurd and iniquitous parody, and knowing as a result that he was condemned in advance, the applicant decided to leave his country and seek asylum elsewhere.[293]

The third type of political interference sufficient to undercut the legitimacy of a criminal prosecution consists of the imposition of differential punishment upon conviction as a means of persecuting the government's opponents. Richard Plender suggests:

> . . . the current test is to determine whether the punishment that the fugitive can expect in consequence of his crime is any greater than that which would be meted out to an individual of different political or religious opinion who has committed a similar offence in the same country and at the same time.[294]

In Canada, general support for this proposition can be surmised from the judgment in *David Eugene Thomas*:[295]

> The [Refugee] Convention was not created to protect foreigners who are fugitives from justice and neither can the criminal sentence which the claimant

---

[288] *Louis-Paul Mingot* (1973), 8 I.A.C. 351, at 356, *per* J.-P. Houle.

[289] Immigration Appeal Board Decision 80-9078, March 3, 1980; affirmed by Federal Court of Appeal Decisions A-213-80, June 5, 1980, A-161-80, October 9, 1980, and A-537-80, October 29, 1980; ultimately dismissed by the Immigration Appeal Board on October 30, 1980.

[290] Immigration Appeal Board Decision T82-9736, June 18, 1984; affirmed by Federal Court of Appeal Decision A-874-84, February 7, 1986; application for leave to appeal to the Supreme Court of Canada refused May 26, 1986.

[291] "[I]n the case at hand, the authorities issued a summons to the applicant to appear in court to answer allegations. The procedure that was adopted was far superior to the previous arrests and detentions of Mr. Easwaramoorthy in which the judicial system was conspicuously ignored": *Id.*, at 7, *per* D. Anderson.

[292] Immigration Appeal Board Decision 79-1110, C.L.I.C. Notes 19.7, April 23, 1980.

[293] *Id.*, at 7, *per* J.-P. Houle.

[294] R. Plender, "Admission of Refugees" (1977), 15 San Diego L.Rev. 45, at 56. *Accord* M. Posner, "Who Should We Let In?" (1981), 9 Human Rts. 16, at 18.

[295] (1974), 10 I.A.C. 44.

received be considered as a measure of persecution in the sense of the Geneva Convention *since this sentence was of a non-political character.* [Emphasis added][296]

In sum, the exclusion of refugee claims which appear to be based on criminal prosecution must be carefully constrained. While it is true that genuine criminality is not a form of civil or political status which attracts protection, the criminal law is not infrequently manipulated as a tool of persecution. In such cases, involving subversion of the substantive purposes of the criminal law — absolute and relative political offences — or interference with an otherwise legitimate criminal process by selective prosecution, punitive denial of procedural fairness, or politically inspired sentencing, it cannot accurately be said that the claimant faces a risk of prosecution, rather than persecution. Claims of this sort should thus be assessed in accordance with the definition, and without consideration of their allegedly criminal context.

5.6.2 Refusal to Perform Military Service

Persons who claim refugee status on the basis of a refusal to perform military service are neither refugees *per se* nor excluded from protection. In general terms:

> A person is clearly not a refugee if his only reason for desertion or draft-evasion is his dislike of military service or fear of combat. He may, however, be a refugee if his desertion or evasion of military service is concomitant with other relevant motives for leaving or remaining outside his country, or if he otherwise has reasons, within the meaning of the definition, to fear persecution.[297]

In this sense, the determination of a refugee claim grounded in refusal to perform military service is comparable to the issue of criminality just examined: the crucial question is whether the claimant can show that desertion or evasion is grounded in civil or political status, failing which the claim cannot succeed.

The insufficiency of a non-specific desire to escape a military service obligation is established by cases such as *Tadeusz Adamusik,*[298] in which the Immigration Appeal Board dismissed the claim of a Polish draft evader, noting simply that "[t]o serve in the armed forces is a duty of all Polish citizens and, therefore, the Board cannot consider Mr. Adamusik to be a refugee just for this reason".[299] This general position is derived from the notion,

---

[296] *Id.*, at 47, *per* A. Weselak.

[297] UNHCR, *supra*, note 42, at 40.

[298] Immigration Appeal Board Decision 75-10405, January 15, 1976; affirmed by the Federal Court of Appeal at (1976), 12 N.R. 262.

[299] *Id.*, at 3, *per* U. Benedetti. *Accord Teresa del Carmen Opazo Opazo*, in which the Chilean claimant was told that she could not "be classified as a refugee merely because she wants to escape [her] military commitment": Immigration Appeal Board Decision V81-6067, March 5, 1981, at 2, *per* B. Howard; affirmed by Federal Court of Appeal Decision A-170-81, September 24, 1981.

noted in *Victor Fathy Kamel,*[300] that "[t]he Convention does not contain any sections dealing [specifically] with army deserters or conscientious objectors".[301] Simply put, the nexus between the harm feared and civil or political status is absent.

The first exception to the exclusion of military evasion and desertion from the scope of the Convention involves claims based on the fact that conscription for engagement in a legitimate and lawful purpose is conducted in a discriminatory manner, or that prosecution or punishment for evasion or desertion is biased in relation to one of the five Convention-based grounds of protection.[302] This is essentially the parallel of the distortion of the general criminal law for a discriminatory purpose discussed above:[303] where a form of state-sanctioned harm is inflicted through the subversion of an otherwise lawful system, the differential nature of the risk based on discriminatory administration may remove the claim from the realm of ordinary military conscription. Where, for example, only members of a particular racial group are subject to conscription, where the military service obligation is enforced more rigorously against persons of a particular political perspective, or where the penalty for evasion or desertion is applied differently to members of a given religious group, the refugee claim should be fully examined on its merits.

A second qualification to this rule arises when desertion or evasion reflects an implied political opinion as to the fundamental illegitimacy in international law of the form of military service avoided. As Gilbert Jaeger writes,

> . . . a broad perception in democratic countries is that there is considerable difference between military service by consent, instituted according to democratic legislative process and called upon to defend the life of a democratic society, on the one hand, and on the other hand, military service in a dictatorial or quasi-dictatorial regime called upon to defend institutions and policies unrelated to accepted human rights standards or, even worse, utilized for internal or external aggression. . . . [T]he right to refuse military service on account of its illegitimate political purpose. . . is formally acknowledged by the UN General Assembly; such refusal qualifies an individual for the grant of asylum and refugee status.[304]

As in the case of an absolute political offence,[305] there is a range of military activity which is simply never permissible, in that it violates basic international standards. This includes military action intended to violate basic human rights, ventures in breach of the Geneva Convention standards for

---

[300] Immigration Appeal Board Decision 79-1104, C.L.I.C. Notes 15.11, August 1, 1979.

[301] *Id.*, at 5, *per* R. Tremblay.

[302] *See* UNHCR, *supra*, note 42, at 40.

[303] *See* text *supra* at note 281 ff.

[304] G. Jaeger, "The Definition of 'Refugee': Restrictive versus Expanding Trends", [1983] World Refugee Survey 5, at 7.

[305] *See* text *supra* at note 251 ff.

the conduct of war,[306] and non-defensive incursions into foreign territory.[307] Where an individual refuses to perform military service which offends fundamental standards of this sort, "punishment for desertion or draft evasion could, in the light of all other requirements of the definition, in itself be regarded as persecution".[308]

This exception has been specifically recognized by the General Assembly of the United Nations in its Resolution 33/165, dealing with the status of persons refusing service in military or police forces used to enforce apartheid in South Africa.[309] Because such service is inherently violative of basic human rights, the General Assembly agreed to call upon states to

> . . . grant asylum or safe transit to another State, in the spirit of the Declaration on Territorial Asylum, to persons compelled to leave their country of nationality solely because of a conscientious objection to assisting in the enforcement of *apartheid* through service in military or police forces; [and urged] Member States to consider favourably the granting to such persons of all the rights and benefits accorded to refugees under existing legal instruments. . . .[310]

While the adoption of this principle into American law has recently been overturned,[311] Canadian law continues to acknowledge that refusal to perform military service inconsistent with international legal obligations is a sufficient basis for a claim to refugee status. In *Jorge Ardon Abarca*,[312] involving a Salvadoran who deserted the army because of its persecution of civilians, the Board recognized the merit of avoiding behaviour in breach of the rules designed to protect civilian non-combatants:

> Mr. Abarca does not blindly reject the thought of compulsory military service. In fact, he has shown a willingness to serve in the armed forces in his country. However, he is not willing to serve further if it means having to become part of a government force that is systematically killing innocent people just to instill fear and terror into the general public. He strongly objects to serving

---

[306] *See* International Committee of the Red Cross, *The Geneva Conventions of August 12, 1949* (1983). The first convention deals with the protection of the wounded and the sick; the second with rules of maritime warfare; the third with fair treatment of prisoners of war; and the fourth with the protection of civilians.

[307] "All Members shall refrain in their international relations from the threat or use of force against the territorial integrity or political independence of any state, or in any other manner inconsistent with the Purposes of the United Nations": *Charter of the United Nations*, 59 Stat. 1031, T.S. No. 993, June 26, 1945, entered into force October 24, 1945, at Art. 2(4). This duty is subject to the right of self-defence stated in Art. 51.

[308] UNHCR, *supra*, note 42, at 40.

[309] U.N.G.A. Res. 33/165, December 20, 1978.

[310] *Id.*, at paras. 2-3.

[311] In *M.A. A26851062 v. I.N.S.*, it had been held that a refugee claim based on failure to perform military service could be established if ". . . the military engages in internationally condemned acts of violence with which the asylum-seeker sincerely does not wish to be associated. . .": 858 F. 2d 210, at 216 (4th Cir. 1989); reversed *en banc* at 899 F. 2d 304 (4th Cir. 1990).

[312] Immigration Appeal Board Decision V86-4030W, March 21, 1986.

in his country's military force because he would probably be forced to participate in violent acts of persecution against non-combatant civilians, which is
contrary to recognized basic international principles of human rights.[313]

This same approach is applied in the decision of *Zacarias Osorio Cruz,*[314]
in which the Mexican claimant deserted his army unit because he did not
wish to continue to be involved with the summary execution of political
prisoners:

> The applicant is not a refugee because he deserted, but rather because he has
> demonstrated that he has a well-founded fear of persecution because of his
> political opinions, which prevent him from taking part in a type of military
> action that is contrary to the most basic international rules of conduct.[315]

The third exception to the exclusion of claims based on refusal to engage
in military service relates to persons who raise principled objections to such
activity. As Guy Goodwin-Gill argues,

> Objectors may be motivated by reasons of conscience or convictions of a reli-
> gious, ethical, moral, humanitarian, philosophical, or other nature. . . . Mili-
> tary service and objection thereto, seen from the point of view of the state,
> are issues which go to the heart of the body politic. Refusal to bear arms, how-
> ever motivated, reflects an essentially political opinion regarding the permissi-
> ble limits of state authority: it is a political act. The "law of universal
> application" can thus be seen as singling out or discriminating against those
> who hold certain political views.[316]

In contrast to a claim based on refusal to participate in military activity contrary to international law, the notion of conscientious objection to military
service speaks to the predicament of individuals whose own beliefs conflict
with participation in legally permissible military activities.

The right to conscientious objection is an emerging part of international
human rights law, based on the notion that "[f]reedom of belief cannot be
truly recognized as a basic human right if people are compelled to act in ways
that absolutely contradict and violate their core beliefs".[317] Drawing on this
right to freedom of thought, conscience, and religion contained in both the
Universal Declaration of Human Rights[318] and the International Covenant
on Civil and Political Rights,[319] the United Nations Commission on Human
Rights has expressly recognized the right to conscientious objection as "a

---

[313] *Id.*, at 6, *per* G. Vidal.

[314] Immigration Appeal Board Decision M88-20043X, C.L.I.C. Notes 118.6, March 25, 1988.

[315] *Id.*, at 3, *per* P. Arsenault.

[316] G. Goodwin-Gill, *The Refugee in International Law*, pp. 33-34 (1983). While some writers distinguish religiously and politically motivated refusal to engage in military service, Grahl-Madsen refutes the logic of such a differentiation: 1 A. Grahl-Madsen, *The Status of Refugees in International Law*, p. 238 (1966).

[317] B. Frelick, "Conscientious Objectors as Refugees", in V. Hamilton, ed., *World Refugee Survey: 1986 in Review*, p. 31 (1987).

[318] UDHR, *supra*, note 71, at Art. 18.

[319] ICCPR, *supra*, note 71, at Art. 18.

legitimate exercise of the right of freedom of thought, conscience and religion", and appealed to states to provide for alternative service of a civilian and non-combatant nature.[320] This view is shared within the Council of Europe, where the right to an alternative to military service is recognized for persons who express compelling reasons of conscience against bearing arms.[321] Thus, insofar as a state fails to make provision for the accommodation of conscientious objectors, a principled claim to refugee status may be established.

Conscientious objection as an exception to the exclusion of refugee claims based on failure to perform military service was tentatively raised in Canada by the 1979 Immigration Appeal Board Decision in *Felix Salatiel Nuñez Veloso*.[322] Shortly thereafter, however, the Federal Court of Appeal issued its landmark decision of *Marek Musial v. Minister of Employment and Immigration*,[323] involving the claim of a Pole who wished to "avoid military service which [was] abhorrent to him on moral grounds",[324] because it involved "subjugating the Afghan people to communist domination".[325] The majority decision of the Court totally ignored the issue of conscientious objection:

> . . . the Board was right in assuming that a person who has violated the laws of his country by evading ordinary military service. . . cannot be said to fear persecution for his political opinions even if he was prompted to commit that offence by his political beliefs.[326]

In contrast, the concurring judgment of Chief Justice Thurlow left the possibility open that conscientious objection would be recognized in Canadian law:

> . . . I do not read the [Immigration Appeal Board's] reasons as meaning more than that army deserters and conscientious objectors are not, as such, within the definition. That is, as I see it, far from saying that because a person is an army deserter or a conscientious objector he cannot be a Convention refugee. . . .[327]

The majority view in *Marek Musial* enjoyed currency for some years, until questioned by a trilogy of Board decisions in 1987, commencing with the

---

[320] U.N. Doc. E/CN.4/1989/L.10/Add.15, March 9, 1989.

[321] Recommendation R(87)8, Committee of Ministers of the Council of Europe, April 9, 1987; *see also* Council of Europe Doc. 88.C55 (1988).

[322] "[T]he applicant. . . was forced by repeated threats to commit acts and take part in courses of action contrary to human dignity and totally opposed to her moral, religious and political convictions": Immigration Appeal Board Decision 79-1017, C.L.I.C. Notes 11.15, August 24, 1979, at 3, *per* J.-P. Houle.

[323] (1981), 38 N.R. 55 (F.C.A.); affirming Immigration Appeal Board Decision V80-6368, November 19, 1980.

[324] Immigration Appeal Board, *id.*, at 4, *per* B. Howard.

[325] Federal Court of Appeal, *id.*, at 57, *per* Thurlow C.J.

[326] *Id.*, at 60, *per* Pratte J.

[327] *Id.*, at 59, *per* Thurlow C.J.

case of Salvadoran *Luis Alberto Mena Ramirez*.[328] The claimant was a Jehovah's Witness who had resisted forced conscription on the ground that he was opposed to war and killing. There was no opportunity for Mr. Mena Ramirez to voice his conscientious objection, as a result of which he was labelled by the military as a guerilla sympathizer for refusing to join the army. In recognizing him as a Convention refugee, the Board noted:

> . . . a person with such deep seated scruples may very well have a subjective fear of persecution for no other reason than the possibility of being required to take part in military activities. It matters little that he is subjected to the same conscription laws and practices as other young men of military age who are without such scruples; the issue is not equal treatment, but fear of persecution. . . . [T]he Board finds a systematic persecution by reason of religion. It is the failure of the recruiting system to make allowances for the convictions of the conscientious objector that forms the basis of the fear. Such a failure amounts to fear of persecution within the meaning of the Act.[329]

The issue of conscientious objection was further resuscitated in the same year by *obiter* comments in *Marco Antonio Valladares Escoto*,[330] a young Honduran who claimed to be at risk of forcible conscription:

> A person is not a refugee if his *only* reason for making a claim is his dislike of military service or fear of combat. There may be instances where the objection against service is lodged in a genuine religious or moral conviction. If the Board were to find that his alleged fear of mistreatment following indiscriminate recruitment was based on a set of credible facts, the Board could find him to be a Convention refugee. . . .[331]

The culmination of this move away from the absolutist position adopted by the majority in *Marek Musial*[332] was the decision of the Board in *Basir Ahmad Ahmaddy*,[333] involving a citizen of Afghanistan who objected on principle to bearing arms in the service of the communist government of that state. At the conclusion of an extremely detailed judgment, the Board cited with approval the *concurring* judgment of Chief Justice Thurlow in *Marek Musial*,[334] and found the claimant to be a Convention refugee based on conscientious objection:

> He has a conscientious objection, both personally and due to his Islamic beliefs, to killing his brothers in a war in which he does not believe, a war which seems to be using mere children to systematically kill innocent civilians. His act of refusing to serve is one which could not be allowed to go "unpunished" by the authorities. It would be interpreted by them as an expression of political opinion contrary to their own. . . . This thereby brings him within the defini-

---

[328] Immigration Appeal Board Decision V86-6161, C.L.I.C. Notes 110.15, May 5, 1987.

[329] *Id.*, at 4-5, *per* D. Anderson.

[330] Immigration Appeal Board Decision T87-9024X, July 29, 1987.

[331] *Id.*, at 5-6, *per* D. Davey.

[332] *Supra*, note 323.

[333] Immigration Appeal Board Decision T86-10392, December 1, 1987.

[334] *See* text *supra* at note 327.

tion of Convention refugee as a conscientious objector. . . .[335]

This evolution is consistent with the international standards adopted in the years since the drafting of the Convention, while simultaneously respecting the internal structure of the Convention by linking conscientious objection to an implied political challenge to the legitimacy of the state.

In sum, claims which involve failure to perform military service, while not routinely within the scope of the Convention definition, may nonetheless lead to a recognition of refugee status in three circumstances. First, discrimination in the establishment or administration of a military service system may serve as a means of particularized social disfranchisement, thereby undercutting its political legitimacy, and opening the door to closer scrutiny. Second, the specific form of military service objected to may be fundamentally illegitimate, as when it contemplates violation of basic precepts of human rights law, humanitarian law, or general principles of public international law. Where the service is itself politically illegitimate, refusal to enlist or remain in service cannot be construed as a bar to refugee protection. Third, the failure to recognize the legitimacy of conscientious objection, and to provide for an appropriate and proportionate non-combatant alternative, may in and of itself constitute a sufficient threat to human rights to ground a claim to refugee status based on implied political opinion.

5.6.3 Victims of War and Violence

While the Refugee Convention was conceived as a response to the victims of war, it was not intended that all those displaced by violent conflict should enjoy refugee status:

> The text . . . obviously did not refer to refugees from natural disasters, for it was difficult to imagine that fires, flood, earthquakes or volcanic eruptions, for instance, *differentiated between their victims* on the grounds of race, religion, or political opinion. Nor did the text cover all man-made events. There was no provision, for example, for refugees fleeing from hostilities *unless* they were otherwise covered by Article 1 of the Convention. [Emphasis added][336]

This extract from the drafting history of the Convention makes clear two essential points. First, victims of war and conflict are not refugees *unless* they are subject to differential victimization based on civil or political status.[337] Second, it follows that it is incumbent on decision-makers to examine

---

[335] *Supra*, note 333, at 41, *per* S. Bell.

[336] Statement of Mr. Robinson of Israel, U.N. Doc. A/CONF.2/SR.22, at 6, July 16, 1951.

[337] "This [Convention] definition. . . leaves out many persons commonly thought of as refugees. For example, it does not cover most of those who flee the scene of an armed conflict, and armed conflict is a conspicuous source of many influxes that reach massive proportions": D. Martin, "Large-Scale Migrations of Asylum Seekers" (1982), 76 A.J.I.L. 598, at 607. *Accord*, e.g., D. Hull, "Displaced Persons: 'The New Refugees'" (1983), 13 Georgia J. Intl. Comp. L. 755, at 757; J. Starke, "Major Trans-Frontier 'Flows' of Refugee-Type Civilians" (1983), 57 Australian L.J. 366, at 366; R. Hofman, "Refugee-Generating Policies and the Law of State Responsibility" (1985), 45 Zeitschrift Auslandisches Offentliches 694, at 702; M. Gibney, "A 'Well-Founded Fear' of Persecution" (1988), 10(1) Human Rts. Q. 109, at 114.

the claims of persons in flight from violence in order to ascertain whether their particular circumstances disclose any evidence of a link between the harm feared and their civil or political status.[338]

Concern about the inappropriateness of this selective approach to the protection of war refugees[339] has led to the drafting of regional standards in both Africa[340] and Latin America[341] which provide for the general enfranchisement of the victims of violence. UNHCR has provided assistance to the victims of war, and it is arguable that a customary norm of providing temporary refuge to the victims of generalized violence is evolving from the practice of states.[342] Nonetheless, the Convention today remains firmly anchored in the notion of elevating only a subset of those at risk of war and violent conflict to the status of refugee.

This general proposition is well-established in Canadian law by a variety of cases involving the victims of violence in Lebanon,[343] Ethiopia,[344] and

---

[338] "A majority of today's refugees are victims of the military factor which although not enough in itself to satisfy eligibility criteria, plays an important complementary role in refugee flows": Z. Rizvi, "Causes of the Refugee Problem and the International Response", in A. Nash, ed., *Human Rights and the Protection of Refugees under International Law,* p. 112 (1988).

[339] "Rather early after the adoption of the 1951 Convention it became obvious that there existed groups and categories of persons who found themselves generally speaking in a similar position to that of refugees, without necessarily meeting the criteria of the general definition. In some cases these persons had left their country of origin for reasons other than those contained in the general definition, particularly war or civil war": G. Jaeger, "Status and International Protection of Refugees", in International Institute of Human Rights, ed., *Lectures Delivered at the Ninth Study Session of the International Institute of Human Rights,* p. 7 (1978). *Accord* J. Starke, *supra,* note 337, at 336: "It is obvious also that one lesson from this crisis of massive trans-frontier flows of civilians is that international refugee law needs to be overhauled, and a bridge built between it and the seemingly more generic international law of human rights."

[340] "The OAU definition is not simply wider; it is also qualitatively different. Whereas the earlier definitions contemplate situations of fear and danger created essentially by deliberate acts and policies, often of a discriminatory character and normally of the authorities of the country, the OAU definition contemplates also a state of affairs generally where the qualities of deliberateness and discrimination need [not] exist. It is generally agreed that this additional eligibility covers armed conflict situations, whether international or internal. . .": G. Coles, "Some Reflections on the Protection of Refugees from Armed Conflict Situations" (1984), 7 In Defense of the Alien 78, at 79. *See generally* Section 1.4.3, *supra.*

[341] "The 'Cartagena Declaration'. . . takes up the broadened definition of the term 'refugee' stated in the 1969 OAU Convention Governing the Specific Aspects of Refugee Problems in Africa, i.e. victims of 'violence' and 'conflicts' and not merely victims of 'persecution'. . .": Note, "International Protection in Latin America" (1985), 14 Refugees 5, at 5. *See generally* Section 1.4.4, *supra.*

[342] *See* Section 1.5, *supra.*

[343] "[H]e is a refugee from a civil war, and is not a 'Convention refugee'. . .": *Zohrab Khoren Meghdessian,* Immigration Appeal Board Decision 79-1204, C.L.I.C. Notes 14.12, November 21, 1979, at 5, *per* J. Scott. *Accord Mohammed Said Sleiman,* Immigration Appeal Board Decision V79-6125, C.L.I.C. Notes 18.13, April 10, 1980, at 2, *per* C. Campbell: "[T]here is no evidence that he or any members of his family have ever suffered persecution or faced any special difficulty in that country as a result of their race, religion, nationality, membership of a particular social group, or political opinion, beyond the problems they would face in consequence of the general circumstances existing there."

[344] "[A]lthough a well-founded fear is difficult to identify in each individual case, it is different

Chile.[345] Moreover, as the decision in *Elias Iskandar Ishac*[346] makes clear, the mere fact that the conflict escaped is based on religion or politics is not relevant unless persons of a particular religion or political perspective are differentially at risk. In this case, the Board found the risk to be roughly equivalent for persons of all beliefs, and hence refused the claim of a citizen of Lebanon attempting to escape the civil war in that country:

> If the appellant is a refugee at all, he is a refugee from civil war in his country, and not a refugee protected by the Convention. . . . A civil war, even on religious grounds, is not persecution as contemplated by the Convention.[347]

This general rule, however, admits of two important exceptions.

First, persons may be differentially at risk where the civil war or violence is directed at a particular social subgroup. This principle derives from the decision in *Tekeste Kifletsion,*[348] in which an Eritrean from Ethiopia was determined to be a Convention refugee on the basis of the genocidal conflict directed against members of his race by the Ethiopian government:

> . . . a civil war against a minority race inside a country, verging on genocide, is without doubt evidence of racial persecution.[349]

Here, it could not truly be said that the claimant was at risk only of an undifferentiated harm affecting all members of his society, but was rather specifically at risk by reason of his race.[350] This exception was affirmed by the Board in *Adan Jeronimo Alvarenga:*[351]

> Civil war in itself does not constitute persecution as contemplated by the Con-

---

from an apprehension about facts and circumstances that would be the result of a general situation which affects people indiscriminately, for example, poor economic conditions or war'': *Ismail Hassan Dembil,* Immigration Appeal Board Decision M80-1018, March 7, 1980, at 2, *per* J.-P. Houle; set aside by Federal Court of Appeal Decision A-163-80, September 30, 1980 on other grounds. *Accord Mahmoud Saddo,* Immigration Appeal Board Decision M80-1123, July 24, 1980.

[345] "He said he came to Canada because he feared there might be a war between Chile and Argentina. Even if that fear was well-founded, it would not entitle him to claim refugee status under the definition of refugee because a fear of war is not persecution for any of the reasons stated in the definition'': *Pedro Enrique Juarez Maldonado v. Minister of Employment and Immigration* (1979), 31 N.R. 34, at 42, *per* McKay D.J. (in dissent).

[346] Immigration Appeal Board Decision M77-1040, April 25, 1977.

[347] *Id.,* at 2, *per* J. Scott. *Accord Hassan Darwich,* Immigration Appeal Board Decision 77-3038, May 20, 1977; affirmed by the Federal Court of Appeal at (1978), 25 N.R. 462; *Elias El Chedraoui,* Immigration Appeal Board Decision M81-1296, February 10, 1982, at 2-3, *per* R. Tremblay: "The main reason given by the applicant to support his claim to refugee status are the horrors of the civil war. Although we have great sympathy for peoples who have to live in such a hell and we understand the trauma caused by such events, there is no provision in the Convention for determining that victims of internal wars between rival factions for religious reasons are refugees."

[348] Immigration Appeal Board Decision 79-1136, C.L.I.C. Notes 20.3, February 29, 1980.

[349] *Id.,* at 3, *per* R. Tremblay.

[350] *Accord Kidane Ghebreiyesus,* Immigration Appeal Board Decision 79-1137, C.L.I.C. Notes 20.3, March 21, 1980; *Isaak Afework,* Immigration Appeal Board Decision 79-1139, C.L.I.C. Notes 20.3, May 21, 1980.

[351] Immigration Appeal Board Decision M87-1081, May 20, 1987.

vention; however, a civil war directed against a religious group in particular or a social group would be persecution within the definition in the Convention.[352]

Second, even within the context of generalized violence or war, there may exist a risk of serious harm specific to persons defined by a particular form of civil or political status. While early Canadian decisions preferred simply to adopt an absolutely dismissive view of claims derived from situations of conflict,[353] the decision of the Federal Court of Appeal in *Zahirdeen Rajudeen v. Minister of Employment and Immigration*[354] marked a watershed in the approach to this issue. This case involved a Sri Lankan Tamil whose need for protection from Sinhalese thugs had been ignored by the authorities. The Immigration Appeal Board dismissed the claim as nothing more than a reflection of the generalized violence in Sri Lanka.[355] The Federal Court, however, found that the harm faced by the claimant was in fact due to the unwillingness of authorities to protect him because of his race and religion:

> The applicant was not mistreated because of civil unrest in Sri Lanka but because he was a Tamil and a Muslim.[356]

This decision underscores the critical importance of inquiring into all of the circumstances of a claimant coming from an area which suffers from generalized violence in order to discern whether or not the risk faced by a particular individual or group is in fact rooted in civil or political status, in which case refugee status may follow.

Thus, while the general proposition is that the victims of war and violence are not by virtue of that fact alone refugees, it is nonetheless possible for persons coming from a strife-torn state to establish a claim to refugee status. This is so where the violence is not simply generalized, but is rather directed toward a group defined by civil or political status; or, if the war or conflict is non-specific in impact, where the claimant's fear can be traced to specific forms of disfranchisement within the society of origin.

---

[352] *Id.*, at 3, *per* G. Loiselle.

[353] *See*, e.g., *Hassan Darwich*, Immigration Appeal Board Decision 77-3038, May 20, 1977; affirmed by the Federal Court of Appeal at (1978), 25 N.R. 462, at 463, in which the Lebanese claimant had in fact been targeted as a Moslem sympathizer, and was thus more particularly at risk; and *Muhieddine Abdul Wahab Jomaa*, Immigration Appeal Board Decision T79-9032, C.L.I.C. Notes 7.17, May 8, 1979, where the Lebanese claimant was acutely at risk by reason of his political neutrality. Both claims were dismissed as reflecting simply the risk associated with generalized violence.

[354] (1985), 55 N.R. 129 (F.C.A.).

[355] "Whether events in Sri Lanka can be classed as 'civil war' or not, there is certainly civil unrest, but the nature of that unrest and the resulting harassment of Mr. Rajudeen is not such that he can be classed as a Convention refugee": Immigration Appeal Board Decision V83-6091, C.L.I.C. Notes 57.10, July 20, 1983, at 4, *per* B. Howard.

[356] *Supra*, note 354, at 134, *per* Heald J.

6

Cessation and Exclusion

The Convention conceives of refugee status as a transitory phenomenon, which expires when a refugee can either reclaim the protection of her own state or has secured an alternative form of enduring protection.[1] Because refugee law is intended simply to afford surrogate protection pending the resumption or establishment of meaningful national protection, the Convention explicitly defines the various situations in which the cessation of refugee status is warranted.[2]

Similarly, refugee status was not envisaged as the entitlement of every person genuinely at risk of persecution. Serious criminals[3] and persons whose actions have exhibited flagrant disregard for the purposes of the United Nations[4] may face the possibility of persecution in their state of origin, but they are outside the scope of the refugee definition. The Convention's exclusion clauses[5] are framed so as to bar persons who pose a critical risk to the receiving state, or whose own breach of fundamental standards of humane conduct renders them unworthy of protection.

Issues of cessation of and exclusion from refugee status may arise in two contexts. First, since the incorporation into Canadian law in 1989 of Arti-

---

[1] "It is the return of refugees to their own community or their integration in a new one which constitutes a permanent or durable solution. . . . [I]nternational protection is of an essentially temporary nature and is the sum of all action which seeks to achieve the admission of a refugee into, and his secure stay in, a country where he or she is not in danger of *refoulement* and can enjoy basic rights and humane treatment until the above objective is achieved — that of renewed belonging in a community": Executive Committee of the High Commissioner's Programme, "Note on International Protection", U.N. Doc. A/AC.96/680, July 15, 1986, at 3.

[2] *Convention relating to the Status of Refugees*, 189 U.N.T.S. 2545, entered into force April 22, 1954 ("*Convention*"), at Art. 1(C). While Arts. 1(D) and 1(E) of the *Convention* are phrased in the language of exclusion, substantively they speak to the fact of surrogate protection and are thus more appropriately comparable to Art. 1(C)(3) than to the primary exclusion clause, Art. 1(F). "It is generally agreed that the enumeration of cessation clauses in Article 1C of the Refugee Convention. . . is exhaustive. In other words, once a person has become a refugee as defined in Article 1 of the Convention. . . he continues to be a refugee until he falls under any of those cessation clauses": 1 A. Grahl-Madsen, *The Status of Refugees in International Law*, p. 369 (1966).

[3] *Convention, supra,* note 2, at Art. 1(F)(a)-(b).

[4] *Id.*, at Art. 1(F)(c).

[5] Arts. 1(D) and (E) are treated herein as substantively analogous to cessation clauses: *see* note 2, *supra.*

cles 1(C),[6] (E) and (F)[7] of the Convention, the Immigration and Refugee
Board may determine that a person who otherwise meets the refugee definition is, as of the date of the hearing of the claim, within the scope of a cessation or exclusion clause.[8] Such a person is not a Convention refugee[9] and
is subject to removal.[10] Alternatively, a cessation hearing may be convened
before the Board subsequent to the recognition of refugee status.[11] If the
case for cessation is made out at this level, the refugee not already landed
as a permanent resident[12] is subject to removal. If landing has already taken
place, the individual ought not to continue to benefit from Convention-based
rights,[13] such as protection against *refoulement*,[14] but should nonetheless be
subject to the ordinary rules which govern loss of permanent resident status.[15]

This chapter considers the scope of the Convention's cessation and exclusion clauses, with a view to identifying the limited situations in which even

---

[6] *Immigration Act*, R.S.C. 1985, c. I-2, ss. 2(1), 2(2), and 2(3) [ss. 2(1) and (2) re-en., (3)
en. 1985, c. 28 (4th Supp.), s.1], hereafter referred to as the *Immigration Act*. The language
of Art. 1(C) of the *Convention* is not reproduced exactly in the *Immigration Act*, although it
is substantively indistinguishable.

[7] *Immigration Act,* at s. 2(1) [am. 1985, c. 28 (4th Supp.), s. 1] and Schedule [en. 1985, c. 28
(4th Supp.), s. 34]. It is noteworthy that the exclusion of persons in receipt of assistance from
a United Nations agency (other than UNHCR) established by Art. 1(D) of the *Convention,*
supra, note 2, has not been incorporated into Canadian law.

[8] *See,* e.g., *Fernando Ferreyra,* Immigration Appeal Board Decision M83-1097, C.L.I.C. Notes
68.5, July 18, 1984, at 19, *per* F. Glogowski: "[I]f at the time of the hearing, a refugee claimant, for any reason, can no longer fulfil the requirements to be characterized as a Convention
refugee, he will not be given such status by the Board. A change in government can be such
a reason in given circumstances."

[9] At the initial hearing before an adjudicator and a member of the Refugee Division, the claimant need only establish that there is at least some "credible or trustworthy evidence on which
the Refugee Division might determine the claimant to be a Convention refugee": *Immigration
Act,* at s. 46.01(6) [en. 1985, c. 28 (4th Supp.), s. 14]. In contrast, at the full hearing before
the Refugee Division, s. 69.1(9) [en. 1985, c. 28 (4th Supp.), s. 18] of the *Immigration Act* requires
a determination as to "whether or not the claimant is a Convention refugee", the latter term
being defined in s. 2(1) of the *Immigration Act* to require consideration of the issues of cessation and exclusion.

[10] "If a person falls under a cessation clause before he has been formally recognized as a
refugee, this has been considered a bar to his recognition. . .": A. Grahl-Madsen, *supra,* note
2, p. 370.

[11] "The Minister may make an application to the Refugee Division for a determination whether
any person who was determined under this Act or the regulations to be a Convention refugee
has ceased to be a Convention refugee": *Immigration Act,* at s. 69.2(1) [en. 1985, c. 28 (4th
Supp.), s. 18].

[12] Under s. 46.04(1) [en. 1985, c. 28 (4th Supp.), s. 14] of the *Immigration Act,* "[a]ny person who is finally determined under this Act to be a Convention refugee may, within the prescribed
period, apply to an immigration officer for landing of that person and any member of that
person's family who is in Canada at the time of the application", subject to certain exceptions
where the refugee retains status in a non-persecutory state.

[13] *Convention, supra,* note 2, at Arts. 3-34.

[14] *Id.,* at Art. 33(1).

[15] *Immigration Act,* at ss. 24, 27(1) [am. 1985, c. 30 (3rd Supp.), s. 4].

persons who are or have been genuinely at risk of serious harm grounded in civil or political status may not qualify as refugees. Because these clauses are to be applied only in relation to persons who otherwise present a *prima facie* need for protection, they ought reasonably to be strictly construed.[16] Nonetheless, it is clear that a state's duty under international refugee law extends neither to persons who benefit from sufficient protection elsewhere, nor to those whose own actions are inconsistent with the basic human rights undertaking.

The discussion here is divided into three parts. First, when can it be said that a refugee has regained the protection of her state of origin, such that she no longer requires refugee status? Second and alternatively, under what circumstances is surrogate national or international protection sufficient to meet the refugee's needs? Finally, which categories of persons are genuinely unworthy of international protection as refugees?

6.1 Persons Who Have Regained the Protection of Their State of Origin

It is a truism that the happiest solution to involuntary migration is the resumption of protection within a refugee's state of origin, such that she can return home in safety.[17] Under the Convention, the sufficiency of national protection may be manifested in either of two ways. First, the refugee herself may elect to entrust her safety to the state of origin by way of re-availment of its formal protection, re-acquisition of its nationality, or re-establishment in its territory.[18] Behaviour of this sort is deemed inconsistent with the refugee's professed need for protection, and gives rise to an objectively rebuttable presumption of cessation of status.[19] Second, the authorities in the

---

[16] "The cessation clauses are negative in character and are exhaustively enumerated. They should therefore be interpreted restrictively, and no other reasons may be adduced by way of analogy to justify the withdrawal of refugee status": United Nations High Commissioner for Refugees, *Handbook on Procedures and Criteria for Determining Refugee Status*, p. 27 (1979).

[17] "Both the facilitation and the promotion of voluntary repatriation fall within the province of UNHCR, and the right to return to one's own country locates such efforts squarely in a human rights context. To ignore this dimension, and other legal implications arising from the concept of nationality would be to condone the institutionalization of exile at the expense of fundamental human rights": G. Goodwin-Gill, "Refugees: The Functions and Limits of the Existing Protection System", in A. Nash, ed., *Human Rights and the Protection of Refugees under International Law,* p. 163 (1988).

[18] *Convention, supra,* note 2, at Art. 1(C)(1), (2), and (4).

[19] " '[W]ell-founded fear'. . . may exist irrespective of the state of mind of the individual concerned. It is the likelihood of his being persecuted upon his eventual return to his home country which matters. . . . It seems reasonable to apply. . . objective criteria with respect to Article 1(C)(1). It is not a 'penal' provision, and it should not operate against a person who has realized that his re-availment of protection was a mistake, and who is able to show that he — still or again — has well-founded fear of persecution": A. Grahl-Madsen, *supra,* note 2, at 390-91. *Accord* C. Pompe, "The Convention of 28 July 1951 and the International Protection of Refugees", [1956] Rechtsgeleerd Magazyn Themis 425, published in English as U.N.

country of reception may determine that human rights conditions in the country of origin have improved to such an extent that the once-present genuine risk of persecution is no longer a reality, thus opening the way for the refugee's return.[20]

6.1.1 Voluntary Re-availment of National Protection

Cessation based on re-availment of national protection[21] generally involves the consideration of efforts by a refugee to secure diplomatic or consular protection from the authorities of the state of which she is formally a citizen. Typically, the refugee will seek the issuance or renewal of a passport or other identity document, although a minority of cases centres on more formal requests for intervention or representation of the claimant's interests.[22] Because actions of this sort are technically viewed as implying protection, it is arguable that the refugee exhibits a willingness to entrust her welfare to the state of origin, and hence no longer requires protection under international law.[23]

Such an interpretation of this cessation clause represents a formal view of the notion of protection. As Atle Grahl-Madsen points out, ". . . a person may seldom have well-founded fear of being persecuted by the members of the foreign service of his home country; the pertinent fact is therefore that he fears persecution in the case of his return to his country of origin".[24] It is simply a legal fiction to assume that more than an exceedingly small percentage of persons who avail themselves of a state's consular facilities do so as a demonstration of either political loyalty or trust. Rather, the practical exigencies of life — travel, enrolment in school, professional accreditation, etc. — may simply require a person genuinely at risk of persecution to contact the external office of her state of origin to secure essential documentation. Too, many persons renew identity documents as a matter of routine, with no thought to the legal ramifications of their act. The disparity between the legal formalism familiar to the drafters of the Convention and the com-

---

Doc. HCR/INF/42, May 1958, at 10-11: "This provision is complementary to the concept of 'well-founded fear'. . . the decisive factor being [the adjudicating body's] judgment concerning the actual conditions in another country."

[20] *Convention, supra,* note 2, at Art. 1(C)(5)-(6).

[21] "This Convention shall cease to apply to any person falling under the terms of Section A if. . . [h]e has voluntarily re-availed himself of the protection of the country of his nationality. . .": *Convention, supra,* note 2, at Art. 1(C)(1). This provision parallels s. 2(2)(a) [re-en. 1985, c. 28 (4th Supp.), s. 1] of the *Immigration Act.*

[22] C. Wydrzynski, *Canadian Immigration Law and Procedure,* p. 337 (1983).

[23] *See,* e.g., G. Goodwin-Gill, *The Refugee in International Law,* p. 48 (1983): "In other cases of application for and obtaining a national passport or the renewal of a passport, it may be presumed, in the absence of evidence to the contrary, that reavailment of protection is intended. . . . Possession of a national passport and a visit to the country of origin would seem conclusive as to cessation of refugee status."

[24] 1 A. Grahl-Madsen, *The Status of Refugees in International Law,* p. 379 (1966).

mon understandings of most people has required the strict construction of this clause in order to avoid undercutting the protective mandate of refugee law.

First, the request for formal protection must be made voluntarily.[25] As noted by the French delegate who introduced the clause, ". . . a person lost his status of refugee only if he expressly wished to do so and, for that purpose, performed a number of voluntary acts. . .".[26] The request is not voluntary if, as in the case of *Wilfredo Alejandro Zubieta*,[27] the refugee is seeking only to comply with an administrative directive issued by the country of reception,[28] or indeed is under the mistaken impression that the maintenance of a valid passport or other status is expected of him.

Second, the diplomatic request must be made as an act of re-availment of protection, thus implying an intention to have one's interests defended by the issuing state.[29] In contrast, most ordinary, purely practical forms of diplomatic contact, such as requests for the certification of educational or occupational qualifications, or access to personal birth, marital, and other records, are dictated by practical necessity, rather than by a desire for protection.[30] Canadian decisions have usually acknowledged this principle, even if sometimes failing to apply it. A case in point is *Carlos Antonio Muñoz Munizaga*,[31] in which Chairman Scott explicitly juxtaposed principle and practice:

> Adopting the view of the [French] Commission des Recours that the motive for obtaining a passport must be examined — an eminently sensible approach since it relates directly to the aspect of "well-founded fear" which is an essential part of the definition of refugee — we ask, why did Muñoz obtain a Chilean passport in Vancouver? To go to Sweden. In the circumstances of this case, he was benefitting from his national status by applying for, obtaining, and using,

---

[25] P. Weis, "The concept of the refugee in international law" (1960), 87 J. de droit international 928, at 974-76.

[26] Statement of Mr. Rochefort of France, U.N. Doc. E/AC.7/SR.160, at 9, August 18, 1950.

[27] Immigration Appeal Board Decision 79-1034, C.L.I.C. Notes 14.10, October 31, 1979.

[28] *Accord* G. Goodwin-Gill, *supra*, note 23, at 48: "Sometimes, however, a refugee may be unwillingly obliged to seek a measure of protection from [his country of origin], as where a passport or travel document is essential to obtain the issue of a residence permit in the country of asylum. Being involuntary, the protection obtained should not bring refugee status to an end."

[29] "[W]hat seems to be determinative, as to whether there was a willingness on the part of the claimant to accept protection of the country of origin, is his motivation in obtaining or renewing the passport": C. Wydrzynski, *supra*, note 22, at 338. *Accord* A. Grahl-Madsen, "Protection of Refugees by Their Country of Origin" (1986), 11(2) Yale J. Intl. L. 362, at 393: "If the person still fears persecution and does not understand that obtaining a passport normally means availing oneself of the protection of the issuing state, it would obviously be difficult to withdraw refugee status on the basis of such a confused act."

[30] A. Grahl-Madsen, *supra*, note 24, p. 388.

[31] Immigration Appeal Board Decision 79-9358, C.L.I.C. Notes 13.11, November 1, 1979. *Accord Boguslawa Florkowski*, Immigration Appeal Board Decision 79-9375, C.L.I.C. Notes 19.6, April 14, 1980.

a document entitling him to the protection of his own country in his travels abroad. He has therefore lost any refugee status he may have had.[32]

Yet the reason Muñoz sought the passport was because he had been advised that his chances of securing asylum were better in Sweden than in Canada, in consequence of which he initially elected to travel onward — surely a motive which is the antithesis of a desire to secure Chile's protection! A similarly inappropriate application of the notion of re-availment is found in the decision of *Tarek Mohamed Shafey Wahba*,[33] involving an Egyptian claimant who reported the loss of his Egyptian passport to that country's embassy in Ottawa. Even though he did not apply for a replacement passport and secured a World Services Authority passport for his travel needs, the Board viewed the simple act of reporting the loss of the passport as indicating "that he was not unwilling to avail himself of the protection of his country".[34]

These decisions fail to come to grips with the *real* reasons which cause refugees to contact the diplomatic authorities of their country of origin. In particular, decision-makers have often relied on an inaccurate assumption that receipt of travel documentation is inherently a means of securing national protection:

> . . . it seems high time to dispel an idea that is all too prevalent — and, what is more, false — of exactly what a passport is. A passport is no more, in fact and in law, than a travel document issued by a country's proper authorities to allow one of its nationals to travel abroad and, if necessary, to call upon the services of its consular authorities in the foreign countries visited to provide the holder of the document with proper protection. The fact of holding a passport, even if it is valid and issued legally, in no way constitutes a guarantee that protection will be provided. . . .[35]

This position was acknowledged during the Convention's drafting,[36] and is generally recognized in public international law:

> . . . there is no duty on the part of a State to exercise protection over its citizens abroad; whether or not to exercise protection remains in the absolute discretion of the state. . . . The municipal law of the issuing state may provide that

---

[32] *Id.*, at 15, *per* J. Scott.

[33] Immigration Appeal Board Decision V80-6033, C.L.I.C. Notes 17.9, February 14, 1980.

[34] *Id.*, at 7, *per* F. Glogowski.

[35] *Felix Salatiel Nuñez Veloso*, Immigration Appeal Board Decision 79-1017, C.L.I.C. Notes 11.15, August 24, 1979, at 4-5, *per* J.-P. Houle. *Accord Roberto Luciano Perez Medina*, Immigration Appeal Board Decision M80-1078, C.L.I.C. Notes 38.10, September 9, 1981; and *Wilfredo Alejandro Zubieta*, Immigration Appeal Board Decision 79-1034, C.L.I.C. Notes 14.10, January 31, 1979.

[36] "It was extremely difficult to determine what would constitute a claim for protection. . . . [A] passport might be needed only for the purpose of travelling to resettle in a third country, and application for a passport should not, therefore, be necessarily regarded as an indication that the person concerned was no longer afraid of persecution": Statement of Mr. Henkin of the U.S.A., U.N. Doc. E/AC.7/SR.165, at 19, August 19, 1950.

the issuance of a passport to one of its nationals will be a guarantee that the state will protect the bearer while abroad. Nevertheless, the state can breach that guarantee without violating international law.[37]

Since there is no automatic linkage between the issuance or renewal of a passport and the granting of protection, it is critical that the real reason it is being sought form part of the determination authority's considerations. Unless the refugee's motive is genuinely the entrusting of her interests to the protection of the state of her nationality, the requisite intent is absent.

Third, the clause does not apply unless diplomatic or consular protection is actually given. As originally introduced by the French delegate, the clause provided that any person who attempted to secure diplomatic or consular protection from her state of origin would lose her refugee status,[38] whether or not protection was actually granted.[39] This strict approach was forcefully rejected by the British,[40] American,[41] and Peruvian[42] delegates, leading to intervention by the Chairman in favour of an interpretation which would limit cessation to circumstances in which formal protection was in fact forthcoming:

> . . . the opening words. . . namely "This Convention shall not apply to any refugee enjoying the protection of a government", made it clear that whatever claims he had made, such claims had been successful, otherwise he would not be enjoying the protection of a government.[43]

An American amendment substituting the final language, "has voluntarily re-availed himself of", in place of the original French version, "he volun-

---

[37] D. Turack, *The Passport in International Law*, p. 232 (1972).

[38] "Cette Convention ne s'appliquera pas à tout réfugié qui jouit de la protection d'un gouvernement parce que: (1) il s'est volontairement réclamé à nouveau de la protection du gouvernement du pays dont il avait la nationalité. . .": U.N. Doc. E/L.82, July 29, 1950.

[39] "The French delegation considered that it was for a refugee to make up his mind. He could not run with the fox and hunt with the hounds by seeking to retain his refugee status and yet at the same time claim the protection of the government of his nationality. The very fact that a refugee asked his Consul for protection was proof that he could return to his own country without fear, and such a step should suffice to deprive him of the status of refugee, even if it did not meet with a favourable reception": Statement of Mr. Rochefort of France, U.N. Doc. E/AC.7/SR.160, at 22, August 18, 1950.

[40] "[T]he provision did not mean that the mere fact that a refugee sought the protection of his government should be sufficient to deprive him of the status of refugee. It would no doubt be necessary, in addition, for his request to have met with a favourable reception": Statement of Mr. Fearnley of the United Kingdom, U.N. Doc. E/AC.7/SR.160, at 22, August 18, 1950.

[41] "A person should not automatically lose his status as a refugee just because he had made a claim which might not be granted": Statement of Mr. Henkin of the U.S.A., U.N. Doc. E/AC.7/SR.165, at 18, August 19, 1950.

[42] "He thought that the words 'he voluntarily claims anew the protection' should be replaced by the words 'he has once more secured the protection', since the important point was, not the application for protection, but the fact of obtaining it": Statement of Mr. Cabada of Peru, U.N. Doc. E/AC.7/SR.165, at 19, August 19, 1950.

[43] Statement of the Chairman, U.N. Doc. E/AC.7/SR.165, at 20, August 19, 1950.

tarily claims anew", was then adopted to give effect to the Chairman's ruling that the receipt of protection is key.[44]

The requisite elements of voluntarism, specific intent, and consummation constrain the frequency with which cessation based on voluntary re-availment of protection is likely to occur. This cautious confining of the clause's application is, however, appropriate in view of the risk that a purely formal or practical contact with foreign diplomatic personnel might otherwise put a refugee at risk of return to persecution.

6.1.2 Voluntary Re-acquisition of Nationality

While the legal import of availing oneself of diplomatic or consular services may be ambiguous, the decision to secure anew the citizenship of the state in which persecution was feared raises more poignantly the refugee's continuing need for protection.[45] Because nationality is widely understood to imply a bond of allegiance between state and citizen,[46] the refugee who resumes the citizenship of her state of origin must rebut the presumption that she may return to that country in safety.[47] Specific intent, therefore, is not requisite to cessation under this clause, although the requirements of voluntarism and consummation discussed in the preceding part apply here as well:

> Like the provision of Article 1(C)(1), the provision presently considered has its principal *raison d'être* as a means to bring about the termination of refugee status for those who wilfully or for no good reason take a positive step in order to normalize their relations with the authorities of their country of origin or in order to reap the benefits due to nationals of that country under international law or comity. Article 1(C)(2) should be applied very reluctantly indeed

---

[44] U.N. Doc. E/AC.7/SR.165, at 22, August 19, 1950. Some degree of ambiguity on this point remains, however, for two reasons. First, while there was agreement to change the French text from "se réclamer" to "se prévaloir" to reflect the amendment to the English text (U.N. Doc. E/AC.7/SR.165, at 22, August 19, 1950), the final version approved at the Conference of Plenipotentiaries maintained the original language. Second, the opening words upon which the Chairman relied to formulate his ruling were ironically deleted prior to adoption of the Convention at the Conference of Plenipotentiaries (*see* the report of an informal working party, U.N. Doc. A/C.3/L.131, at 2, November 30, 1950). Nonetheless, there was no further discussion of disfranchising refugees who were not in fact successful in securing the protection of their state of nationality.

[45] "The Convention shall cease to apply to any person falling under the terms of Section A if. . . [h]aving lost his nationality, he has voluntarily re-acquired it. . .": *Convention, supra*, note 2, at Art. 1(C)(2). The Canadian legislation refers simply to a "person [who] voluntarily reacquires his nationality", a more succinct formulation of the same principle, since *re*-acquisition implies that the nationality had been lost: *Immigration Act*, at s. 2(2)(b) [re-en. 1985, c. 28 (4th Supp.), s. 1].

[46] *See* R. Plender, *International Migration Law*, p. 39 (1988).

[47] "There is less scope for explanation or extenuating circumstances: the intention of the individual and the effectiveness of the act will suffice in most cases": G. Goodwin-Gill, *The Refugee in International Law*, p. 50 (1983).

to other categories of refugees, the continued existence of well-founded fear of persecution being the overriding consideration in cases of doubt.[48]

Thus, for example, re-acquisition of nationality through operation of law upon marriage or otherwise may fail to meet the requirement of voluntarism,[49] and hence not suffice to deprive a refugee of her status.[50] Nor is it enough to show that the refugee could have re-acquired her former citizenship but failed to do so, since there is no consummation of the act of protection.[51] The overriding concern is whether there is an act of re-acquisition of citizenship which is truly indicative of a normalization of relations between the refugee and her state of origin.

The scope of this cessation clause is also textually limited to a narrow subset of refugees. Persons who have continued to be formal citizens of their state of origin during their time as refugees are obviously not in a position to *acquire* the nationality of that country. Too, because it speaks to *re-acquisition* of nationality, this cessation clause does not apply to persons who are stateless from birth, but only to those who have at some point been denationalized or who have successfully renounced their citizenship, and who then go on to have their status as citizens reinstated.

6.1.3 Voluntary Re-establishment in the Country in Which Persecution was Feared

Re-establishment in the state of origin is perhaps the clearest indication that a refugee no longer views herself as being at risk.[52] In voluntarily taking up residence in the country which induced her flight, the refugee is in the most direct way possible signalling her willingness to entrust her welfare to that state.

The Convention requires freely chosen re-establishment, not mere return, before cessation ensues. The original draft of this clause, which would have revoked the refugee status of any person who "returns to his country of

---

[48] 1 A. Grahl-Madsen, *The Status of Refugees in International Law*, p. 395 (1966).

[49] "The granting of nationality by operation of law or by decree does not imply voluntary re-acquisition, unless the nationality has been expressly or impliedly accepted. . . . If such former nationality is granted by operation of law, subject to an option to reject, it will be regarded as a voluntary re-acquisition if the refugee, with full knowledge, has not exercised this option; unless he is able to invoke special reasons showing that it was not in fact his intention to re-acquire his former nationality": UNHCR, *supra*, note 16, p. 30.

[50] *See* A. Grahl-Madsen, *supra*, note 48, at 393-95.

[51] "A person does not cease to be a refugee merely because he could have re-acquired his former nationality by option, unless this option has actually been exercised": UNHCR, *supra*, note 16, p. 30.

[52] "This Convention shall cease to apply to any person falling under the terms of Section A if. . . [h]e has voluntarily re-established himself in the country which he left or outside which he remained owing to fear of persecution. . .": *Convention, supra*, note 2, at Art. 1(C)(4). The Canadian cessation clause is substantively identical: *Immigration Act*, at s.2(2)(d) [re-en. 1985, c. 28 (4th Supp.), s. 1].

former nationality",[53] was rejected by the Ad Hoc Committee on the ground that it might bar persons who had been forcibly repatriated to their state of origin, as well as those who had chosen to return to their country of origin only temporarily.[54] The substitute language which sets the cessation threshold at voluntary re-establishment in the country in which persecution was feared[55] was thus intended to ensure that only persons who have willingly resettled in their state of origin are subject to cessation of refugee status. As Paul Weis notes,

> If a person returns to his country of origin for a temporary stay without re-establishing himself, and then returns to the country where he was recognized as a refugee, this should not lead to *ipso facto* loss of refugee status.[56]

Re-establishment requires more than mere physical presence,[57] and a greater commitment to the country of origin[58] than is evinced, for example, by a temporary return to visit an ailing parent[59] or to bring out relatives, friends, or property.[60] Careful scrutiny of more prolonged and frequent visits for such purposes as holidays or business is warranted, however, since at some point the degree of attachment may qualify as re-establishment. While an occasional visit of up to a few weeks is too transitory to sustain the cessation of status,[61] a regular presence in the state of origin[62] for a significant part

---

[53] U.N. Doc. E/AC.32/L.4, at 3, January 18, 1950.

[54] *See*, e.g., Statement of the Director of the International Refugee Organization, U.N. Doc. E/AC.32/L.16, at 2, January 30, 1950.

[55] Statement of Mr. Henkin of the U.S.A., U.N. Doc. E/AC.7/SR.165, at 16, August 19, 1950. The amendment was adopted on a vote of 13-0-2: U.N. Doc. E/AC.7/SR.165, at 18, August 19, 1950, and was intended to speak to the situations of both persons with formal nationality and stateless persons.

[56] P. Weis, "The concept of the refugee in international law" (1960), 87 J. du droit international 928, at 978.

[57] A. Grahl-Madsen, *supra*, note 48, p. 371; G. Goodwin-Gill, *supra*, note 47, p. 51.

[58] "It is probably correct to define 're-establishment'. . . as residence with the explicit or implicit intention of remaining in the country, and to infer that a prolonged stay (a couple of years or more) implies such an intention": A. Grahl-Madsen, *supra*, note 48, p. 372.

[59] *But see* Immigration and Refugee Board Decision V89-00618, August 1989, R.L.R.U. Cat. Sig. 10395, at 5, *per* H. Neufeld, involving a Lebanese claimant who was summoned home due to his grandfather's illness. Notwithstanding this clearly valid reason for temporary return, the Board held that "[b]y returning to Lebanon and living there from June to August, 1987, it is reasonable to infer, in the absence of evidence to the contrary, that the claimant did not fear persecution at that time."

[60] P. Weis, *supra*, note 56, at 978; A. Grahl-Madsen, *supra*, note 48, p. 372.

[61] "Something more than a visit or mere presence is required; the individual must have settlement on a permanent basis in view, with no evident intention of leaving": G. Goodwin-Gill, *supra*, note 47, p. 51. *Accord* A. Grahl-Madsen, *supra*, note 48, p. 371: "A short visit abroad, for business or for pleasure, will not alter the picture." *But see* Immigration and Refugee Board Decision T89-00565, May 1989, R.L.R.U. Cat. Sig. 10016, in which a Salvadoran claimant returned to his country for a period of six months in order to visit his family and friends, and was held in consequence to have demonstrated a willingness to rely on El Salvador's protection. In view of the singular nature of this visit, it is questionable that the regularity of presence inherent in the notion of re-establishment was in fact present.

[62] *See*, e.g., *Jose Raul Morales*, Immigration Appeal Board Decision V86-6277, April 16,

of the year is *prima facie* inconsistent with a continued need for protection.[63] The claimant should bear the onus in such circumstances to demonstrate that she is objectively unable to benefit from protection of basic human rights in her country of origin, and thus continues to be a refugee.

It is not appropriate, however, to construe this cessation clause effectively to penalize refugees who return to "test the waters" in their state of origin.[64] If refugees are to be encouraged to attempt voluntary repatriation, generally viewed as the most desirable solution to refugeehood,[65] they must have some assurance that they can resume refugee status in the event that actual conditions at home prove unsafe.[66] Before a finding of cessation based on voluntary re-establishment is made, therefore, both the facts underlying the original, successful claim to refugee status and post-re-establishment factors should be taken into account. If the totality of the evidence demonstrates a forward-looking, genuine risk of persecution, this cessation clause is not a bar to continued recognition as a refugee.

6.1.4 Change of Circumstances

Unlike the forms of cessation discussed thus far which are initiated by the voluntary act of a refugee, cessation due to change of circumstances is the prerogative of an asylum state which is satisfied that protection is once more viable in the refugee's state of origin.[67] The clause was intended to allow

---

1987, at 8, *per* D. Anderson: "[T]he frequent visits to Guatemala of Mr. Morales in 1983. . . [are] not consistent with his claimed fear at that time."

[63] "Visiting an old or sick parent will have a different bearing on the refugee's relation to his former home country than regular visits to that country spent on holidays or for the purpose of establishing business relations": UNHCR, *supra*, note 16, at 29.

[64] To the contrary, Immigration and Refugee Board Decision V89-00618, August 1989, R.L.R.U. Cat. Sig. 10395, at 5, *per* H. Neufeld, held that ". . . to have any chance of success, this claim must be founded upon events occurring after the claimant's most recent departure from Lebanon. . .", thereby penalizing the claimant by estopping him from reliance on the facts of his initial claim.

[65] For example, at a recent meeting of international experts, it was "reaffirmed that voluntary repatriation was, in principle, the best solution to a refugee problem, and that it was desirable and opportune to emphasize the importance of this solution and to develop international cooperation in effecting it. . .": Executive Committee of the High Commissioner's Programme, "Note on Voluntary Repatriation", U.N. Doc. EC/SCP/41 (1985).

[66] "A refugee may return to his home country because he hopes that conditions have improved so that there is no need to fear persecution (for example following the promulgation of an amnesty law), or he may wish to participate in underground activities directed against the regime. Should his optimism prove unfounded, or should he be threatened with prosecution for his illegal work, he may find it advisable to flee the country for the second time": A. Grahl-Madsen, *supra*, note 48, p. 378.

[67] The Canadian legislation rephrases the international obligation in direct terms, providing that "[a] person ceases to be a Convention refugee when. . . the reasons for the person's fear of persecution in the country that the person left, or outside of which the person remained, cease to exist": *Immigration Act*, at s. 2(2)(e) [re-en. 1985, c. 28 (4th Supp.), s. 1]. *Cf. Convention, supra,* note 2, at Art. 1(C)(5) and (6): "This Convention shall cease to apply to any per-

a state to divest itself of the protection "burden" when the government of the home country is judged to have become an appropriate guardian of the rights of its involuntary expatriates:

> To take the case of the aged belonging to the "hard core" of refugees, it could hardly be agreed that the government of a country which had returned to democratic ways should fail to take over the burden of that category of refugees. . . . [France] was quite prepared to continue to assist such refugees so long as such assistance was necessary. But if their country reverted to a democratic regime, the obligation to assist them should not fall perforce upon the French Government. . . . France had merely said that she did not wish to be under an obligation to continue to provide assistance to refugees who could seek the protection of their country of origin.[68]

The drafters' focus on reversion to democracy highlights the magnitude of change which should exist before the consideration of cessation is warranted. First, the change must be of substantial political significance,[69] in the sense that the power structure under which persecution was deemed a real possibility no longer exists. The collapse of the persecutory regime, coupled with the holding of genuinely free and democratic elections,[70] the assumption of power by a government committed to human rights,[71] and a guarantee of fair treatment for enemies of the predecessor regime by way of amnesty or otherwise,[72] is the appropriate indicator of a meaningful change

---

son falling under the terms of Section A if. . . [h]e can no longer, because the circumstances in connexion with which he has been recognized as a refugee have ceased to exist, continue to refuse to avail himself of the protection of the country of his nationality. . . [or] [b]eing a person who has no nationality he is, because the circumstances in connexion with which he has been recognized as a refugee have ceased to exist, able to return to the country of his former habitual residence. . . ."

[68] Statement of Mr. Rochefort of France, U.N. Doc. A/CONF.2/SR.28, at 12-14, July 19, 1951.

[69] *Accord* UNHCR, *supra*, note 16, p. 31; A. Grahl-Madsen, *supra*, note 48, p. 401; G. Goodwin-Gill, *supra*, note 47, p. 51.

[70] *See*, e.g., *Ruben Eduardo Val*, Immigration Appeal Board Decision T83-10592, October 15, 1985, at 5, *per* E. Teitelbaum (". . . Peru today has a democratically elected government. . ."); and *Carlos Anesetti*, Immigration Appeal Board Decision T84-9584, C.L.I.C. Notes 83.12, October 29, 1985, at 2, *per* J. Weisdorf (". . . democratic elections were held in Uruguay in late 1984. . .).

[71] "The Board notes. . . that President Belaunde stated in his inaugural address on 28th July, 1980, that he intends to implement fully the new constitution and to promote the full observance of human rights. . . on 3rd October, 1980 Peru ratified the Optional Protocol to the International Covenant on Civil and Political Rights which provides for individual complaints to be heard by the Human Rights Committee": *Ruiz Angel Jesus Gonzales*, Immigration Appeal Board Decision T81-9746, C.L.I.C. Notes 50.7, November 8, 1982, at 5, *per* U. Benedetti.

[72] *See*, e.g., *Carlos Anesetti*, Immigration Appeal Board Decision T84-9584, C.L.I.C. Notes 83.12, October 29, 1985, at 2, *per* J. Weisdorf (". . . all prohibited persons, including Tupamaros and urban guerillas have been freed and. . . all political parties are presently legal"); and Immigration and Refugee Board Decision M89-01323, R.L.R.U. Cat. Sig. 10200, November 1989, at 10-11, *per* M. Vo (". . . it is significant in this regard that the Polish Parliament, the Sejm, issued on May 30, 1989, a comprehensive pardon regarding all 'political crimes' committed since 1980").

of circumstances. It would, in contrast, be premature to consider cessation simply because relative calm has been restored in a country still governed by an oppressive political structure.[73] Similarly, the mere fact that a democratic and safe local or regional government has been established is insufficient insofar as the national government still poses a risk to the refugee.[74]

Second, there must be reason to believe that the substantial political change is truly effective.[75] Because, as noted in a dissenting opinion in *Ruiz Angel Jesus Gonzales,*[76] ". . . there is often a long distance between the pledging and the doing. . .",[77] it ought not to be assumed that formal change will necessarily be immediately effective:

> . . . there were free elections [in Uruguay] on March 1, 1985 that put an end to 12 years of military government. According to [the U.S. Country Reports], the reestablishment of democracy is complete. I may be permitted to express doubts that in a period of one or two years it would be possible to recover completely from the abuses of a military dictatorship. Good intentions may have existed, of course, but I refuse to believe that there were no chance mishaps.[78]

---

[73] "[A] less profound change should not affect a person's refugee status. . . [T]he present provision should clearly not be construed so as to force a person to accept, more or less at face value, any change of policy of such [an oppressive] regime. In fact, a refugee cannot be expected to submit himself to the very persons who have persecuted or threatened to persecute him": 1 A. Grahl-Madsen, *The Status of Refugees in International Law*, p. 401 (1966). *But see*, e.g., *Venkateswaran Nadarajah,* Immigration Appeal Board Decision T84-9662, March 18, 1986, at 4, *per* U. Benedetti: "The fear of the applicant to return to Colombo is not a well-founded fear as the situation in Colombo since July 1983 has been calm and the applicant's family has not encountered any difficulties."

[74] In *Baldev Saini Singh*, for example, the Board correctly considered the sufficiency of regional protection: "Mr. Saini acknowledged at the hearing that the Akali Dal Party following an election now governs in the Punjab. However, his stated belief is that all power is in the hands of the central Hindu-dominated Congress government and that therefore he is at risk because he is a Sikh and was politically active with the Akali Dal": Immigration Appeal Board Decision T83-9050, March 21, 1985, at 3, *per* G. Tisshaw. In examining the claimant's assertion, however, the Board found that the central government did not in fact pose a risk to the claimant's security. In contrast, the decision in *Nirmal Sagoo Singh* fails to consider the issue of the effectiveness of a change of local or regional government: "Despite the fact that the main Sikh party was elected to power in the Punjab in July, 1985, an event which one would have thought would reasonably have removed any fears which the applicant may have had of returning to the Punjab, he elected to remain in Canada and claim to be a Convention refugee one year after the occurrence": Immigration Appeal Board Decision T87-9841X, January 13, 1988, at 1-2, *per* J. Weisdorf.

[75] This issue was discussed in the decision of the House of Lords in *R. v. Secretary of State for the Home Department, ex parte Sivakumaran,* [1988] 1 All E.R. 193 (H.L.), at 196, *per* Lord Keith of Kinkel: "The question whether such circumstances have ceased to exist can only be one to be determined objectively, in the light of any new circumstances presently prevailing in the country of the person's nationality."

[76] Immigration Appeal Board Decision T81-9746, C.L.I.C. Notes 50.7, November 8, 1982.

[77] *Id.*, at 12, *per* E. Teitelbaum.

[78] *Juan Pedro Diaz*, Immigration Appeal Board Decision M87-1417X, July 27, 1987, at 3, *per* M. Durand.

The formal political shift must be implemented in fact, and result in a genuine ability and willingness to protect the refugee. Cessation is not warranted where, for example, *de facto* executive authority remains in the hands of the former oppressors:

> The fact that there were "above board" elections in Peru in 1980-81, which sent members of various parties and factions to the parliament, does not prove that the applicant does not have a well-founded fear of returning to his country, which is still, as far as executive authority is concerned, a military dictatorship which tolerates no opposition. It is just another case of old wine in new bottles.[79]

Nor can it be said that there has truly been a fundamental change of circumstances where the police or military establishments have yet fully to comply with the dictates of democracy and respect for human rights:

> It was argued that the applicant need no longer be afraid of returning to his homeland as there has been a change in the government since he left. The applicant, however, adduced evidence to show that although the government has changed, members of the Peruvian police and armed forces are still violating human rights and as yet do not appear to be under control by the new government.[80]

In other words, the refugee's right to protection ought not to be compromised simply because progress is being made toward real respect for human rights,[81] even where international scrutiny of that transition is possible.[82] Two mid-1989 judgments of the Immigration and Refugee Board, relating to Poland and Sri Lanka respectively, demonstrate an appropriate concern to see evidence of the real impact of a formal transition of power:

---

[79] *Raul Garcia Zavala*, Immigration Appeal Board Decision 81-1222, C.L.I.C. Notes 45.10, June 29, 1982, at 4, *per* J.-P. Houle.

[80] *Richard Cid Requena Cruz*, Immigration Appeal Board Decision T83-10559, April 8, 1986, at 6, *per* G. Vidal. *Accord Saad Uddin Ahmed*, Immigration Appeal Board Decision T86-10366, August 26, 1987, at 6, *per* E. Teitelbaum: "Having considered the evidence submitted. . . with respect to conditions in Bangladesh, . . . the Board does not find that there was any *significant* change in the behaviour of the military government prior to, during, or after, elections in 1986 which could reasonably be seen to change the claimant's attitude towards it"; and Immigration and Refugee Board Decision T89-00417, R.L.R.U. Cat. Sig. 10051, June 1989, at 8, *per* F. Kapasi: "The panel is of the view that, although the [Polish] accord appears to be a step towards democracy, it cannot be guaranteed that the state security apparatus will honour and accept these recent changes readily. . . ."

[81] *But see Mahibur Rahman Chowdhury*, Immigration Appeal Board Decision T83-10497, C.L.I.C. Notes 90.8, February 6, 1986, at 5, *per* G. Voorhees: "The applicant is a member of a recognized political party; a party that won the 1973 election, had forty members elected in the 1979 election and is still actively working towards an end to martial law. . . ."

[82] *But see* Immigration and Refugee Board Decision T89-01056, R.L.R.U. Cat. Sig. 10349, July 1989, at 10, *per* J. Goldman: "No doubt it will take some time before the State security apparatus accepts and honours the recent changes. As the expert witness stated, some of the abuses which took place prior to the [Polish] accord may continue in smaller, less visible places. However, [the claimant's home of] Gdansk is the birth-place of Solidarity. It is Solidarity's stronghold on which the eyes of the world will rest. We therefore do not believe that there is a valid basis for the claimant's fear of persecution because of his Solidarity activities."

. . . Solidarity calculates that the Communist Party directly or indirectly controls about 900,000 appointments. . . the nomenklatura casts its own shadow. In other words, changing the government does not [necessarily] change much. The panel is of the view that the claimant's fear that the changes in Poland are still too uncertain is supported by the documentary evidence.[83]

Although it is alleged that the scale of military confrontation between the Indian Peacekeeping Force and the Tigers has diminished in recent months, there is still an intense rivalry between the Tamil militant groups for the control of the territory and the population. We agree with the points made by counsel, that the normalization process has not yet achieved political stability and peace for Sri Lanka.[84]

Third, the change of circumstances must be shown to be durable. Cessation is not a decision to be taken lightly on the basis of transitory shifts in the political landscape,[85] but should rather be reserved for situations in which there is reason to believe that the positive conversion of the power structure is likely to last.[86] This condition is in keeping with the forward-looking nature of the refugee definition,[87] and avoids the disruption of protection in circumstances where safety may be only a momentary aberration.

The Convention provides for the exemption from cessation based on change of circumstances for pre-1951 refugees[88] who are able to make a case for not returning home based on "compelling reasons arising out of previous persecution".[89] The intention of the drafters was twofold: first, to recognize the legitimacy of the psychological hardship that would be faced by the victims of persecution were they to be returned to the country responsible

---

[83] Immigration and Refugee Board Decision T89-00903, R.L.R.U. Cat. Sig. 10287, September 1989, at 6, *per* G. Howson.

[84] Immigration and Refugee Board Decision M89-01026, R.L.R.U. Cat. Sig. 10379, June 1989, at 3, *per* S. Wolfe.

[85] UNHCR, *supra,* note 16, at 31. *But see Palwinder Kaur Gill,* Immigration Appeal Board Decision V86-6012, July 11, 1986, at 8, *per* dissenting member D. Anderson; affirmed by Federal Court of Appeal Decision A-476-86, January 22, 1987: "A person could meet the definition of Convention refugee one week, and the next, by reason of political events thousands of kilometres away, no longer meet that definition. Two weeks after that it is perfectly conceivable that the definition would be met once more." *Accord Darshan Lottay Singh,* Immigration Appeal Board Decision V86-6328, February 4, 1987.

[86] *But see Dorothy Robb,* Immigration Appeal Board Decision M84-1364, June 19, 1987, at 4, where the possibility of an adverse electoral result in one year's time was dismissed as irrelevant.

[87] *See* Section 3.1, *supra.*

[88] The exemption applies only to refugees defined by Art. 1(A)(1) of the *Convention, supra,* note 2. The purpose of the clause "was to avert the possibility that [Jewish] refugees of German or Austrian origin living in other countries might be deprived of their refugee status as a result of the restoration of a democratic regime in their country of origin. . . . France would adhere to that view, but was anxious to avoid the possibility that the texts in question might be interpreted in such a way as to give rise to an extension in favour of other groups of refugees. . .": Statements of Mr. Rochefort of France, U.N. Doc. A/CONF.2/SR.28, at 10, July 19, 1951. In contrast, the Canadian legislation in force as of January 1, 1989 extends the exemption to all refugees: *Immigration Act,* at s. 2(3) [en. 1985, c. 28 (4th Supp.), s. 1].

[89] *Convention, supra,* note 2, at Art. 1(C)(5) and (6).

for their maltreatment;[90] and second, to protect the victims of past atrocities from harm at the hands of private citizens, whose attitudes may not have reformed in tandem with the political structure.[91]

The exemption clause in the Convention is not, therefore, structured to provide general humanitarian relief based on factors such as family circumstances or infirmity,[92] but focuses squarely on compelling[93] circumstances which are linked to past persecution. Atle Grahl-Madsen suggests that the existence of a psychological distance between the refugee and her former home, the continued unpopularity in the country of origin of the views or personal characteristics of the refugee, or the severing of familial, social and other linkages between the refugee and her state of origin are the sorts of concerns which warrant exemption from return.[94] In contrast, essentially economic motivations or considerations of personal convenience are not sufficient.[95]

The Canadian legislation adopts these general principles, and extends them to modern day refugees.[96] Insofar as a formal, effective, and enduring change

---

[90] "[T]he framers of the Convention had to take into account the psychological factor connected with the existence of previous persecution: having been persecuted by the government of a certain country, the refugee may have developed a certain distrust of the country itself and a disinclination to be associated with it as its national": N. Robinson, *Convention relating to the Status of Refugees: Its History, Contents and Interpretation*, p. 60 (1953). *Accord* A. Grahl-Madsen, *supra*, note 73, p. 410: "What the drafters of the Convention had in mind was the situation of refugees from Germany and Austria, who were unwilling to return to the scene of the atrocities which they and their kin had experienced, or to avail themselves of the protection of a country which had treated them so badly."

[91] "Even though there may have been a change of regime in his country, this may not always produce a complete change in the attitude of the population, nor, in view of his past experiences, in the mind of the refugee": UNHCR, *supra*, note 16, p. 31. *Accord* N. Robinson, *supra*, note 90, p. 61.

[92] The predecessor IRO exemption clause, in contrast, focused on "compelling family reasons arising out of previous persecution": P. Weis, "The concept of the refugee in international law" (1960), 87 J. de droit international 928, at 980. This formulation was viewed as too liberal by some drafters of the Convention, as a result of which the exemption was reduced to its current form: "Could the family attachments which a refugee might have contracted in his country of residence be regarded as compelling reasons? And was separation from his family to be regarded for that purpose as a compelling family reason?. . . . He was not convinced that compelling family reasons provided sufficient justification": Statement of Mr. Rochefort of France, U.N. Doc. A/CONF.2/SR.28, at 10-11, July 19, 1951.

[93] This adjective was specifically introduced as a qualification to the Israeli proposal in order to constrain the scope of the exemption: Statement of Mr. Petren of Sweden, U.N. Doc. A/CONF.2/SR.28, at 10, July 19, 1951.

[94] A. Grahl-Madsen, *supra*, note 73, pp. 410-11.

[95] This is clear from the fact that the more narrowly defined exclusions in both the IRO Constitution ("purely economic reasons") and the UNHCR Statute ("reasons other than personal convenience") were rejected by the drafters of the Convention in favour of the current standard. *See* A. Grahl-Madsen, *supra*, note 73, pp. 407-10.

[96] "A person does not cease to be a Convention refugee. . . if the person establishes that there are compelling reasons arising out of any previous persecution for refusing to avail himself of the protection of the country that the person left, or outside of which the person remained, by reason of fear of persecution": *Immigration Act*, at s. 2(3) [en. 1985, c. 28 (4th Supp.),

of political structure is found to be in place in the country of origin, there-fore, the Board must go on to consider whether the particular refugee con-tinues to suffer the effects of past persecution,[97] in which case cessation should be withheld.

6.2 Persons Who Benefit from Surrogate National or International Protection

Because the Convention is designed to provide protection only to those who truly require it, persons who have successfully obtained surrogate inter-national or national protection are not within the scope of the definition. Like those who have been restored to the protection of their state of nation-ality or former habitual residence, those with meaningful surrogate protec-tion are deemed to be adequately provided for under international law.

This general category speaks to three distinct situations. First, there are persons who are in receipt of enduring protection or assistance from a special-ized agency of the United Nations itself. Second, some refugees may go on to acquire the citizenship of a new state. Third, formally unprotected per-sons may nonetheless secure the *de facto* protection of a new country on terms substantively similar to those of its nationals. In each of these circum-stances, refugee status may be denied or revoked on the basis of the suffi-ciency of subsisting entitlements.

6.2.1 United Nations Protection or Assistance

This clause of the Convention[98] derives from parallel discussions leading to the adoption of the Statute of the Office of the United Nations High Com-missioner for Refugees.[99] At the time of the Statute's drafting, two special-ized refugee relief agencies were already in existence: the United Nations Relief

---

s. 1]. This extension coincides with a UNHCR recommendation: "The reference [in the Con-vention] to Article 1(A)(1) indicates that the exception applies to 'statutory refugees.' At the time when the 1951 Convention was elaborated, these formed the majority of refugees. The exception, however, reflects a more general humanitarian principle, which could also be applied to refugees other than statutory refugees": UNHCR, *supra*, note 16, p. 31.

[97] "The object of the exception to the effects of a change of circumstances is clearly the con-tinuation of protection for those who have suffered most seriously in their country of origin. . . . [T]he continuing nature of the injuries often suffered by the persecuted is a reason for the excep-tion to be liberally applied": G. Goodwin-Gill, *The Refugee in International Law*, p. 52 (1983).

[98] "This Convention shall not apply to persons who are at present receiving from organs or agencies of the United Nations other than the United Nations High Commissioner for Refu-gees protection or assistance. When such protection has ceased for any reason, without the position of such persons being definitively settled in accordance with the relevant resolutions adopted by the General Assembly of the United Nations, these persons shall *ipso facto* be entitled to the benefits of this Convention": *Convention, supra*, note 2, at Art. 1(D).

[99] *Statute of the Office of the United Nations High Commissioner for Refugees,* Annex to General Assembly Res. 428(V), December 14, 1950 ("*Statute*").

and Works Agency for Palestine Refugees in the Near East (UNRWA),[100] and the United Nations Korean Reconstruction Agency (UNKRA).[101] In part, this exclusion clause was intended to prevent the overlapping of the mandates of UNHCR and these pre-existing agencies.[102] More profoundly, however, it resulted from the strongly held view of Arab states that because the plight of Palestinian refugees was the consequence of the establishment of Israel by the United Nations itself, the UN should bear a more direct and obvious responsibility for their well-being:[103]

> . . . the Palestine refugees. . . differed from all other refugees. In all other cases, persons had become refugees as a result of action taken contrary to the principles of the United Nations, and the obligation of the Organization toward them was a moral one only. The existence of the Palestine refugees, on the other hand, was the direct result of a decision taken by the United Nations itself with full knowledge of the consequences. The Palestine refugees were therefore a direct responsibility on the part of the United Nations and could not be placed in the general category of refugees without betrayal of that responsibility.[104]

The Arab states resisted any move which might decrease the distinct visibility of the Palestinians' predicament, and hence undercut the political will to effect their repatriation:

> If the General Assembly were to include the Palestine refugees in a general definition of refugees, they would become submerged and would be relegated to a position of minor importance. The Arab States desired that those refugees should be aided pending their repatriation, repatriation being the only real solution of their problem. To accept a general definition. . . would be to renounce insistence on repatriation.[105]

In the result, the Statute of the UNHCR provides for an interim suspension of eligibility, so long as the Palestinians' needs in exile are met by the UNRWA.[106]

---

[100] UNRWA was established by General Assembly Resolution 302(IV), December 8, 1949. Its territorial competence extends to Jordan, Syria, Lebanon, and the Gaza Strip.

[101] UNKRA was established by General Assembly Resolution 410(V), December 1, 1950.

[102] "[T]he High Commissioner should not deal with refugee situations under the competence of other agencies of the United Nations": Statement of Mrs. Roosevelt of the U.S.A., 5 UNGAOR at 363, November 29, 1950. *Accord* N. Robinson, *supra*, note 90, p. 64; D. Fowler, "The Developing Jurisdiction of the United Nations High Commissioner for Refugees" (1974), 7 Human Rts. J. 119, at 126; and S. Aga Khan, "Legal Problems Relating to Refugees and Displaced Persons", [1976] Recueil des cours 287, at 299. *But* it is noteworthy that the benefits of protection under the specialized agencies were not truly replicative of the proposed protection function of UNHCR: "The United Nations assistance to Arab refugees was material assistance and could not be compared with the legal protection of the High Commissioner": Statement of Mr. Rochefort of France, 5 UNGAOR at 391, December 4, 1950.

[103] "Political considerations associated with the politics of this area [have] necessitated the United Nations to establish and maintain [UNRWA]": S. Aiboni, *Protection of Refugees in Africa*, p. 31 (1978).

[104] Statement of Mr. Azkoul of Lebanon, 5 UNGAOR at 358, November 27, 1950.

[105] Statement of Mr. Baroody of Saudi Arabia, 5 UNGAOR at 359, November 27, 1950. *Accord* Statement of Mr. Azmi Bey of Egypt, 5 UNGAOR at 358, November 27, 1950.

[106] "[T]he competence of the High Commissioner shall not extend to a person. . . [w]ho con-

The drafters of the Convention were mindful of the Arab preoccupation that formal refugee status would imply mobility for Palestinian refugees, thus potentially undermining the repatriation of the Palestinian community.[107] The concerns of the Arab community[108] ironically coincided with a determination by some Western delegates to avert the prospect of claims to refugee status by Palestinians. The French representative, for example,

> . . . considered that the problems in their case were completely different from those of the refugees in Europe, and could not see how Contracting States could bind themselves to a text under the terms of which their obligations would be extended to include a new, large group of refugees. . . .[109]

Indeed, the American representative warned that the inclusion of Palestinians "would present Contracting States with an undefined problem, and so reduce the number of States in Europe that would find it possible to sign the Convention".[110] Reflecting these concerns, delegates were faced with a draft which provided for the permanent exclusion[111] from the Convention definition of "persons who are at present receiving from other organs or agencies of the United Nations protection or assistance".[112] Realizing that this clause would leave Palestinians completely without aid or protection if UNRWA were to

---

tinues to receive from other organs or agencies of the United Nations protection or assistance. . .": *Statute, supra*, note 99, at Chap. II(7)(c).

[107] The unbending focus on the propriety of repatriation is clear from the comments of Mr. Mostafa Bey, the delegate of Egypt: "[I]t should be noted. . . that the present situation of [Palestinian] refugees was a temporary one, and that the relevant resolutions of the General Assembly provided that they should return to their homes": U.N. Doc. A/CONF.2/SR.19, at 16, November 26, 1951.

[108] "The French representative had rightly recalled that the Arab refugees from Palestine had been excluded from the mandate of the High Commissioner for Refugees as a result of action taken by the delegations of the Arab States at the fifth session of the General Assembly": Statement of Mr. Mostafa Bey of Egypt, U.N. Doc. A/CONF.2/SR.20, at 8, November 26, 1951.

[109] Statement of Mr. Rochefort of France, U.N. Doc. A/CONF.2/SR.19, at 11, November 26, 1951.

[110] Statement of Mr. Warren of the U.S.A., U.N. Doc. A/CONF.2/SR.19, at 23, November 26, 1951. The contrary position of the United Kingdom is noteworthy: "Even if such an influx into Europe did occur, was it conceivable that European countries which had hitherto given refugees certain minimum rights would, even in the absence of a Convention, give the new arrivals less?": Statement of Mr. Hoare of the United Kingdom, U.N. Doc. A/CONF.2/SR.19, at 19, November 26, 1951.

[111] "Turning to the category of refugees who were excluded from the present Convention under paragraph [D], for example, the Palestinian Arabs, in his view the effect of the paragraph as drafted was to make the exclusion permanent. That was, indeed, why the Egyptian representative had submitted his amendment. . . since he wanted to provide for the possible future inclusion of that group within the Convention": Statement of Mr. Hoare of the United Kingdom, U.N. Doc. A/CONF.2/SR.19, at 18, November 26, 1951. *Accord* Mr. Habicht of the International Association of Penal Law, U.N. Doc. A/CONF.2/SR.19, at 27, November 26, 1951: "The phrase 'at present' implied that the Convention should not apply to those persons receiving at a specific time protection or assistance from organs or agencies of the United Nations; it did not imply that when such protection ceased the refugees concerned would come under the protection of the Convention."

[112] U.N. Doc. A/1751, December 19, 1950.

cease operations,[113] the Arab states secured their automatic "deferred inclusion"[114] at such time as specialized relief operations in Palestine might come to an end. It is nonetheless clear from the drafting history that the shared intention of the Arab and Western states was to deny Palestinians access to the Convention-based regime so long as the United Nations continues to assist them in their own region.

More specifically, this exclusion clause applies to all Palestinians eligible to receive UNRWA assistance in their home region.[115] It does not exclude only those who remain in Palestine, but equally those who seek asylum abroad.[116] It affects only Palestinians, since its scope is limited to persons in receipt of UN assistance or protection from a specialized agency (other than UNHCR) in existence in 1951.[117] Under the terms of the Convention, exclusion is automatic once UNRWA eligibility is established.

---

[113] "It was only right and proper that, as soon as the Palestine problem had been settled and the refugees no longer enjoyed United Nations assistance and protection, they should be entitled to the benefits of the Convention. . .": Statement of Mr. Mostafa Bey of Egypt, U.N. Doc. A/CONF.2/SR.20, at 8, November 26, 1951. "It was obvious that, if the Egyptian amendment was rejected, the refugees it was designed to protect might eventually find themselves deprived of any status whatsoever": Statement of Mr. Al Palchachi of Iraq, U.N. Doc. A/CONF.2/SR.29, at 8, July 19, 1951.

[114] Statement of Mr. Rochefort of France, U.N. Doc. A/CONF.2/SR.3, at 10, November 19, 1951. "The object of the Egyptian amendment was to make sure that Arab refugees from Palestine who were still refugees when the organs or agencies of the United Nations at present providing them with protection or assistance ceased to function would *automatically* come within the scope of the Convention" [Emphasis added]: Statement of Mr. Mostafa Bey of Egypt, U.N. Doc. A/CONF.2/SR.29, at 6, July 19, 1951, referring to his amendment, U.N. Doc. A/CONF.2/13. *Accord* 1 A. Grahl-Madsen, *The Status of Refugees in International Law*, p. 263 (1966), p. 263.

[115] "There is reason to believe that Article 1(D) applies not only to those individuals who were actually receiving protection or assistance from UNRWA on 28 July 1951, but also to those individuals who became the concern of UNRWA at any later date, including those born after the signing of the Convention; or, in other words, that Article 1(D) applies to persons within the mandate of UNRWA as a class or category, and not to individual persons": A. Grahl-Madsen, *supra*, note 114, p. 265.

[116] "It would be noted that, whereas in paragraph [D] of article 1 of the draft Convention reference was made to 'persons who are at present receiving. . . protection or assistance', the parallel clause in the Statute of his Office referred to refugees 'who continue to receive. . .'. That difference in wording implied a difference in consequences": Statement of Mr. van Heuven Goedhart, High Commissioner for Refugees, U.N. Doc. A/CONF.2/SR.21, at 12, July 14, 1951. *But see* UNHCR, *supra*, note 16, p. 34: "[A] refugee from Palestine who finds himself outside [the UNRWA operational] area does not enjoy the assistance mentioned and may be considered for determination of his refugee status under the criteria of the 1951 Convention." *Accord* A. Grahl-Madsen, *supra*, note 114, p. 265; G. Goodwin-Gill, *supra*, note 97, p. 57.

[117] "[P]aragraph [D] [is intended] to exclude persons who were defined as those who at the time when the convention came into force were receiving protection or assistance from United Nations organs or agencies. . .": Statement of Mr. Hoare of the United Kingdom, U.N. Doc. A/CONF.2/SR.19, at 20, November 26, 1951. *Accord* Committee of Churches on International Affairs, U.N. Doc. A/CONF.2/NGO/10, at 1, July 6, 1951; A. Grahl-Madsen, *supra*, note 114, p. 264. The clause is not meaningful in relation to those within the mandate of UNKRA (*supra*, note 101): "Since Korean war refugees are regarded in South Korea as citizens and are

While not all Palestinian refugees could meet the criteria of the Convention definition,[118] their wholesale exclusion is inconsistent with a commitment to a truly universal protection system.[119] Happily, Canada has chosen not to apply this part of the Convention definition,[120] as a result of which Palestinian claims in Canada are to be assessed without differentiation of any kind.

6.2.2 Acquisition of a New Nationality

If a refugee cannot resume the protection of her own state, the preferred surrogate is surely the acquisition of citizenship in another country which can effectively ensure her welfare. As was remarked during the drafting of the Convention,

> Both in theory and in practice, naturalization had always been considered as bringing refugee status to an end. . . . [R]efugee status, being abnormal, should not be granted for a day longer than was absolutely necessary, and should come to an end (or, possibly, should never even come into existence) if. . . [the refugee] really had the rights and obligations of a citizen of a given country.[121]

Thus, the Convention provides for the cessation of status when the refugee becomes a citizen of her asylum state or of some other country which is able effectively to protect her.[122]

---

accordingly outside the Convention, paragraph D thus applies in fact only to Palestine refugees in the Near East": C. Pompe, "The Convention of 28 July 1951 and the International Protection of Refugees", published in English as U.N. Doc. HCR/INF/42, May 1958, at 12.

[118] "[T]he obstacle to [the Palestinians'] repatriation was not dissatisfaction with their homeland, but the fact that a Member of the United Nations was preventing their return": Statement of Mr. Azkoul of Lebanon, 5 UNGAOR at 358, November 27, 1950. Under the UNRWA eligibility criteria, a Palestinian need only have lost his home to qualify for assistance; it is not necessary that she show a "well-founded fear of persecution." *See* G. Coles, "Some Reflections on the Protection of Refugees from Armed Conflict Situations" (1984), 7 In Defense of the Alien 78, at 83-84.

[119] *See*, e.g., S. Aiboni, *supra*, note 103, at 32-33; J. Hathaway, "A Reconsideration of the Underlying Premise of Refugee Law" (1990), 31(1) Harvard Intl. L.J. 129. *Accord* Statement of Mr. Warren of the U.S.A., U.N. Doc. A/CONF.2/SR.19, at 21, November 26, 1951: "He had listened with great interest to the United Kingdom representative's lucid explanation of the reasons why he supported the more universal definition of the term 'refugee'. . . unfortunately, the United States delegation could not share it. The United States approach was much more limited." As Gervase Coles has noted, "UNRWA's mandate extends only to assisting [Palestinian refugees], not to protecting them. The Palestinian refugees, therefore, have the unfortunate distinction of being the only group of refugees in the world who are excluded formally from any international protection. . .": *supra*, note 118, at 105.

[120] While the Report to the Minister outlining the new determination system did recommend that Canada apply Art. 1(D) of the Convention (W. Plaut, *Refugee determination in Canada: Proposals for a new system*, p. 60 (1985)), the amended legislation did not incorporate this exclusion clause.

[121] Statement of Mr. van Heuven Goedhart, U.N. High Commissioner for Refugees, U.N. Doc. A/CONF.2/SR.23, at 11, July 16, 1951.

[122] "This Convention shall cease to apply to any person. . . [who] has acquired a new nation-

It is a matter of some dispute whether cessation may result from the involuntary acquisition of a new nationality. On the one hand, this was not the intention of the drafters of the Convention. The representative of the Netherlands moved an amendment expressly to recognize the importance of voluntarism in the choice of a new nationality,[123] but was persuaded that the change was not required[124] since the cessation clause

> . . . was not concerned with the imposition of nationality by an outside authority, but related to the acquisition by a refugee of a new nationality other than that of the country of persecution. Sub-paragraph 3 was designed to meet the case where a refugee in a particular country of refuge paid a brief visit to another country and took advantage of the facilities available there to acquire the nationality of that country. When such a person returned to the country of refuge, the latter would be faced with the situation of his having acquired a new nationality.[125]

It is clear that delegates to the Conference of Plenipotentiaries did not agree that involuntarily acquired citizenship was cause for cessation,[126] and adopted the clause on the understanding that it was restricted to voluntarily secured nationality.

On the other hand, it is true that this clause, unlike the surrounding paragraphs of Article 1(C),[127] does not expressly condition cessation on a voluntary act. Too, substantive symmetry with the dual and multiple nationality provisions of Article 1(A)(2) would argue against considerations of voluntarism. Thus, both scholarly opinion[128] and UNHCR recommendations[129]

---

ality, and enjoys the protection of the country of his new nationality. . .": *Convention, supra,* note 2, at Art. 1(C)(3).

[123] "Substitute for paragraph (3) of Section [C] the following two paragraphs: (3a) Having voluntarily acquired a new nationality; [or] (3b) Having involuntarily acquired a new nationality, he nevertheless avails himself of the protection of the country of his new nationality": U.N. Doc. A/CONF.2/73, July 12, 1951.

[124] Statement of Baron van Boetzelaer of the Netherlands, U.N. Doc. A/CONF.2/SR.23, at 19, July 16, 1951.

[125] Statement of Mr. Hoare of the United Kingdom, U.N. Doc. A/CONF.2/SR.23, at 19, July 16, 1951.

[126] "Automatic acquisition of a new nationality might indeed constitute a form of persecution compelling the person against whom it was directed to seek refuge in another country. . . in his opinion, therefore, an individual could not be compelled to acquire a new nationality": Statement of Mr. Rochefort of France, U.N. Doc. A/CONF.2/SR.23, at 17, July 16, 1951. *Accord* Mr. Herment of Belgium, U.N. Doc. A/CONF.2/SR.23, at 18, July 16, 1951, who ". . . thought it desirable to provide for the case of a refugee in a receiving country who. . . found himself saddled with a nationality he did not wish to possess." *See also* N. Robinson, *Convention relating to the Status of Refugees,* p. 59, (1953).

[127] *See Convention, supra,* note 2, at Art. 1(C)(1), (2) and (4).

[128] "Article 1(C)(3) differs from the previously discussed provisions of Article 1(C) in that its applicability is not subject to the proviso of voluntariness. Consequently, the present provision applies irrespective of the way in which the person concerned acquires a new nationality, whether by naturalization in the strict sense (grant on application), by marriage, or by operation of law in any manner whatsoever": A. Grahl-Madsen, *supra,* note 114, pp. 395-96.

[129] German nationality was conferred on various categories of refugees of German ethnic

urge that the only relevant issue is the effectiveness of the new nationality, however it came to be acquired. Specifically, the refugee must be able to enter her new state of citizenship, reside there with protection against deportation or expulsion,[130] and enjoy a reasonable expectation that her basic human rights will be fully respected. In such circumstances, adequate surrogate protection exists, and refugee status should logically come to an end.

6.2.3 Residence with the Rights and Obligations of a National

This exclusion clause[131] was originally intended simply to bar from international protection all ethnic German refugees from Central and Eastern Europe who had taken up residence in Germany during or following the Second World War.[132] The provision reflected the view that Germany was morally responsible for these migrants,[133] and was in fact meeting their needs by assimilation to its own population,[134] even if they were not always granted formal German nationality. Concern about the diplomatic wisdom of a specific reference to Germany in the Convention[135] led to the formulation

---

origin in Austria by a law of the Federal Republic of Germany on February 22, 1955. Such persons were given one year within which to renounce German citizenship, failing which their citizenship was deemed to be settled in accordance with the law. The UNHCR Executive Committee rendered an advisory opinion that such persons had ceased to be refugees by virtue of the German citizenship thus acquired: U.N. Doc. A/AC.79/37, at para. 129, cited in P. Weis, "The concept of the refugee in international law" (1960), 87 J. du droit international 928, at 978.

[130] G. Goodwin-Gill, *The Refugee in International Law*, p. 50 (1983).

[131] "The Convention shall not apply to a person who is recognized by the competent authorities of the country in which he has taken residence as having the rights and obligations which are attached to the possession of the nationality of that country": *Convention, supra,* note 2, at Art. 1(E).

[132] "This provision was primarily designed to exclude refugees and expellees of German ethnic origin in the Federal Republic of Germany who by virtue of Article 116 of the Basic Law were 'Germans within the meaning of the Basic Law' and, although not possessing German nationality, were treated as if they were German nationals": P. Weis, *supra,* note 129, at 982.

[133] "He did not think that the German Government should be encouraged to shift all responsibility for them to the United Nations": Statement of Mr. Henkin of the U.S.A., U.N. Doc. E/AC.32/SR.3, at 9, January 26, 1950. The Israeli delegate went so far as to characterize the exclusion as a matter of retribution: "It was known that a number of such persons had helped to carry out Hitler's policy even more than the Germans residing in Germany, as they had been able to act under the cover of their new nationality, while preserving their original German nationality. When called upon, they had not hesitated to join the German army, and it was perhaps among them that the most fanatical Nazis had been found. There was no need, therefore, to invoke humanitarian principles in favour of that type of individual who in no way deserved to be granted the status of international refugee": Statement of Mr. Robinson of Israel, U.N. Doc. E/AC.32/SR.15, at 10, January 30, 1950.

[134] "This paragraph is intended to exclude from the benefits of the Convention members of former German minorities outside of Germany who returned to, sought refuge in, or were expelled to Germany, and who are living there. This paragraph reflects the view that these individuals should be and are being assimilated into the German community and are not properly refugees": U.N. Doc. E/AC.32/L.38, at 16, February 15, 1950.

[135] *See,* e.g., Statement of Mr. Rochefort of France, U.N. Doc. E/1703/Add.5, at 5, June

of a generally phrased exclusion of ethnically or culturally affiliated residents of a country who receive the same protection as that provided to nationals.[136]

Ironically, this "politically sensitive" use of general language led to substantial debate in the General Assembly. The Mexican representative opposed the apparent exclusion of Spanish refugees admitted to his country, or of Spanish Basques in France;[137] the delegate of Saudi Arabia argued more generally that "persons forced to flee to a neighbouring State, the inhabitants of which might have similar racial and cultural characteristics, would be denied the protection both of the Convention and of the High Commissioner's Office".[138] French assurances that the clause was aimed only at the German minorities notwithstanding,[139] the original wording was voted down.[140] The revised proposal presented to the Assembly was represented to exclude only "persons involved in mass movements of population due to frontier changes, who possessed the same rights as the inhabitants of the country in which they were currently living",[141] and was further amended to delete any reference to ethnic or cultural kinship, and to focus squarely on the existence of protection genuinely equivalent to that afforded nationals.[142]

Read in this context, exclusion based on *de facto* nationality is truly an exceptional occurrence which implies the effective legal assimilation of the refugee to her host population.[143] Because the clause requires residence in the state willing to confer effective nationality, neither an inchoate right to protection, nor indeed physical presence short of continued residence, is sufficient to warrant exclusion.[144]

Moreover, *de facto* nationality is qualitatively distinct from even long-term

---

26, 1950, who noted that the exclusion clause ". . . would still serve its purpose if. . . [one were to avoid] reference by name to a Government with which, incidentally, a number of states entertain diplomatic relations." *Accord* Statement of Mr. Perez Perozo of Venezuela, U.N. Doc. E/AC.32/SR.43, at 4, September 28, 1950.

[136] The clause considered by the General Assembly provided for the exclusion of ". . . a person who has entered a country with whose nationals he has close ties of ethnic and cultural kinship and, because of such kinship, enjoys the rights and privileges usually attached to the possession of the nationality of such country": U.N. Doc. A/C.3/L.131, at 2, November 30, 1950.

[137] Statement of Mr. Noriega of Mexico, 5 UNGAOR at 376-77, December 1, 1950.

[138] Statement of Mr. Baroody of Saudi Arabia, 5 UNGAOR at 376, December 1, 1950.

[139] Statement of Mr. Rochefort of France, 5 UNGAOR at 376, December 1, 1950.

[140] 5 UNGAOR at 380, December 1, 1950.

[141] Statement of Mrs. Roosevelt of the U.S.A., 5 UNGAOR at 389, December 4, 1950. *Accord* Statement of Mr. Noriega of Mexico, 5 UNGAOR at 390, December 4, 1950; and Statement of Mr. Lequesne of the United Kingdom, 5 UNGAOR at 390, December 4, 1950.

[142] In moving the final language, the representative of New Zealand acknowledged his desire to meet the Saudi Arabian delegate's concern regarding genuine equivalency of rights and obligations: Statement of Mr. Davin of New Zealand, 5 UNGAOR at 394, December 4, 1950, referring to the Statement of Mr. Baroody of Saudi Arabia, 5 UNGAOR at 392, December 4, 1950.

[143] While official naturalization is not required, *de facto* citizens possess the rights and obligations of nationals: N. Robinson, *supra*, note 126, p. 65. *Accord* UNHCR, *supra*, note 16, p. 34.

[144] "The clause refers to a person who has 'taken residence' in the country concerned. This implies continued residence and not a mere visit": UNHCR, *supra*, note 16, p. 34.

residence in a state,[145] since it requires a consequential guarantee of rights to the refugee on terms at least as favourable as those which follow from Convention refugee status.[146] Most critically, the rights of entry and of freedom from removal or expulsion must be clearly conferred and respected,[147] a point emphasized by the Federal Court of Appeal in both *Waclaw Antoni Mihael Hurt v. Minister of Manpower and Immigration*[148] and *Kammy Boun-Leua v. Minister of Employment and Immigration.*[149] As noted in a recent decision to exclude an Iranian with *de facto* refugee status in Denmark, it must also be determined whether "the claimant enjoys the kinds of rights and protection in [the country of effective nationality] which would bring him within the purview of Section E of Article 1".[150] The Board has since

---

[145] This has been confirmed by a series of decisions of the Immigration and Refugee Board. *See*, e.g., Immigration and Refugee Board Decisions M89-01318, in which the Somalian claimant had spent three years in the United States (July 1989, R.L.R.U. Cat. Sig. 10262); M89-00697, involving six years' residence in Nigeria by a Sri Lankan (July 1989, R.L.R.U. Cat. Sig. 10218); M89-00436, dealing with a Ghanaian who spent five years in Israel (April 1989, R.L.R.U. Cat. Sig. 10396); T89-00190, concerning a Somalian who spent eight years in Ethiopia (April 1989, R.L.R.U. Cat. Sig. 10092); and V89-00866, dealing with a refugee from Afghanistan who had lived and worked illegally in Saudi Arabia for six years (March 1990, R.L.R.U. Cat. Sig. 10462). In none of these cases was the long-term residence in another country considered as adverse to the claim.

[146] "The provision contained in Article 1(E) defends its place in the Convention, because persons who enjoy so extensive rights. . . are in no need of the status which the Convention might have given them. . . . In order to be excludable under Article 1(E), a person must be granted a status which in no respect is inferior to that of a Convention 'refugee.' Otherwise the provision may be open to abuse": 1 A. Grahl-Madsen, *The Status of Refugees in International Law*, p. 270 (1966). This test was adopted by Immigration and Refugee Board Decision T89-00374, R.L.R.U. Cat. Sig. 10047, June 1989. However, not even Convention status guarantees full rights to political participation. UNHCR, for example, took the view that ethnic Turks from Bulgaria admitted to Turkey, who were granted all of the civil rights of Turkish citizens but no political participation rights pending nationalization, were excluded under this clause: P. Weis, *supra*, note 129, at 982-84, citing U.N. Docs. A/AC.36/Rev. 1 and A/AC.36/20, at para. 31.

[147] G. Goodwin-Gill, *The Refugee in International Law*, p. 58 (1983); UNHCR, *supra*, note 16, p. 34.

[148] In this case, the Minister argued for denial of refugee status based on Article 1(E), since the Polish claimant had resided in West Germany for five years. The Federal Court noted that ". . . the appellant alleges that he was only able to stay in West Germany by virtue of temporary visas, that he had been unable to obtain status as a permanent resident, that he had been advised the Germans wished to deport him back to Poland and that his temporary visa. . . would not be renewed. In my opinion, this evidence serves to negate, rather than to affirm, the allegation that the appellant had any rights similar to those attached to West German nationality": (1978), 21 N.R. 525 (F.C.A.), at 529, *per* Heald J.; setting aside Immigration Appeal Board Decision T77-9105, March 29, 1977.

[149] "In this case the applicant as a refugee admitted to France can return at least as long as his travel permit, issued by that country to him, is valid. . . . Since he can return to France, which is not the country of his nationality, or where his life or freedom would be threatened, there is no obligation on the Minister to permit him to remain in Canada": Federal Court of Appeal Decision A-578-79, June 17, 1980, at 7, *per* Urie J.

[150] Immigration and Refugee Board Decision T89-00919, August 1989, at 11, *per* E. Rotman.

elaborated this requirement to include respect for the claimant's rights under the Convention and the International Bill of Rights, and even "the *potential* to become a citizen and thus vote in national elections and run for public office".[151] Where these stringent criteria are satisfied, the substance if not the form of a new, surrogate nationality is present, and protection through refugee law is not required.

6.3 Persons Who Do Not Deserve Protection

The drafters of the Convention were preoccupied to avoid the granting of refugee status to both war criminals and individuals who might jeopardize the internal security of asylum countries. The decision to exclude such persons, even if they are genuinely at risk of persecution in their state of origin, is rooted in both a commitment to the promotion of an international morality[152] and a pragmatic recognition that states are unlikely to agree to be bound by a regime which requires them to protect undesirable refugees.[153] Relying on the Universal Declaration of Human Rights'[154] prohibition on the granting of asylum to persons liable to prosecution for "non-political crimes or. . . acts contrary to the purposes and principles of the United Nations",[155] the Convention provides for the mandatory exclusion of three classes of persons: those who have committed crimes against peace and security; serious common law criminals; and individuals who have acted in contravention of the principles and purposes of the United Nations.

While the proscription is not subject to any exceptions,[156] it falls to each

---

[151] Immigration and Refugee Board Decision M90-01972, August 1990, *per* L. Gilad; leave to appeal granted by Federal Court of Appeal Decision 90-A-2406, October 12, 1990. This decision explicitly considers the views of both Grahl-Madsen and Goodwin-Gill, and thoroughly canvasses the range of rights guaranteed to a Sri Lankan *de facto* refugee residing in Denmark.

[152] Statement of Mr. Rochefort of France, 11 UNESCOR (406th mtg.), at 276 (1950). He argued further that ". . . it must be made quite clear that the object was not to specify in the Convention what treatment each country must mete out to individuals who had placed themselves beyond the pale, but only to state whether a country was entitled, in granting refugee status to such individuals, to do so on the responsibility of the High Commissioner and of the United Nations": U.N. Doc. E/AC.7/SR.166, at 4, August 22, 1950.

[153] "The rights of countries of refuge should be safeguarded, as well as the rights of refugees": *Id.*

[154] Indeed, an early formulation of the clause provided that "[n]o person to whom Article 14, paragraph 2 of the aforesaid Declaration is applicable shall be recognized as a refugee": U.N. Doc. E/AC.32/L.3/Corr. 1.

[155] *Universal Declaration of Human Rights*, G.A. Res. 217A (III), December 10, 1948 ("*UDHR*"), at Art. 14(2).

[156] While the United States argued in favour of state discretion to admit or refuse serious criminals (*see* Statement of Mr. Henkin, U.N. Doc. E/AC.32/SR.17, at 9, February 6, 1950), Israel and France (*see* Statement of Mr. Robinson of Israel, U.N. Doc. E/AC.32/SR.17, at 9, February 6, 1950; and Statement of Mr. Rain of France, U.N. Doc. E/AC.32/SR.18, at 3, February 8, 1950) successfully advanced the view that exclusion should be mandatory (*see* Report of the Working Group, U.N. Doc. E/AC.32/L.32, at 3, February 9, 1950). *Accord*

contracting state to decide for itself when a refugee claimant is within the scope of an exclusion clause:

> . . . in the absence of a world government and of a sovereign international court of justice, that power of discretion, which was an essential safeguard both for the real refugee and for the country of refuge, must, perforce, be left to States. The only practical solution was to trust the countries which were willing to grant hospitality.[157]

The asylum state need have only "serious reasons for considering"[158] that the applicant is a criminal described in the exclusion clause; there is no requirement that she have been formally charged or convicted,[159] or even that her criminality be capable of establishment "beyond a reasonable doubt" by a judicial procedure.[160] It is enough that the determination authority have "sufficient proof warranting the assumption of [the claimant's] guilt of such a crime".[161]

6.3.1 Crimes Against Peace and Security

While the drafters of the Convention were unanimously of the view that war criminals should not be entitled to claim refugee status,[162] there was disagreement on two points. First, the United States argued that countries should be allowed to treat war criminals as refugees, although they should not be compelled to do so.[163] Most representatives, however, were strongly of the

---

N. Robinson, *Convention relating to the Status of Refugees*, p. 67 (1953): "Section F is couched in categorical language. . . . It follows that, once a determination is made that there are sufficient reasons to consider a certain person as coming under this section, the country making the determination is barred from according him the status of a refugee."

[157] Statement of Mr. Rochefort of France, U.N. Doc. E/AC.7/SR.166, at 6, August 22, 1950. No response was made to a non-governmental intervention which advocated the determination of exclusion by UNHCR: *see* Statement of the Friends' World Committee, U.N. Doc. A/CONF.2/NGO.7, at 3, July 6, 1951.

[158] The vagueness of this standard was criticized by Mr. Lequesne of the United Kingdom: "The term 'serious reasons' was too vague to justify an important decision. The choice was difficult: it was necessary either to allow governments to take an administrative decision when a judicial decision was called for, or to run the risk of including. . . criminals": 5 UNGAOR (334th mtg.) at 390, December 4, 1950.

[159] A. Grahl-Madsen, *supra*, note 146, p. 277.

[160] As noted by Lord MacDonald of the United Kingdom, this clause "gives to the executive organs of government a power to take what are essentially judicial decisions. . . . [I]t is dangerous to entrust such a power to the executive organs of a government": 5 UNGAOR (325th mtg.) at 670, December 14, 1950. *Accord* Statement of Mr. Bernstein of Chile, U.N. Doc. E/AC.7/SR.165, at 24, August 19, 1950.

[161] N. Robinson, *supra*, note 156, p. 67.

[162] *See*, e.g., Statements of Mr. Rain of France, U.N. Doc. A/AC.32/SR.4, at 8, January 26, 150; of Mr. Makiedo of Yugoslavia, U.N. Doc. A/CONF.2/SR.3, at 7, July 13, 1951; and Mr. von Trutzschler of the Federal Republic of Germany, U.N. Doc A/CONF.2/SR.24, at 8, July 17, 1951.

[163] Indeed, the United States initially argued that "there were no longer any war criminals who had not been punished and there was therefore no need to except them": Statement of

view that discretion of this kind could undermine the integrity of refugee status.[164] Second, Germany opposed incorporation of the definition of war criminals derived from the Charter of the International Military Tribunal (the "Nurnberg Principles"), and advocated reference to the "grave breaches" standard of common Article 147 of the Geneva Conventions instead.[165] This met with opposition based on the importance of safeguarding the jurisprudential clarity already achieved by practice under the Nurnberg Principles.[166]

The compromise which emerged consisted of the mandatory exclusion of an undefined category of persons who had committed "a crime against peace, a war crime, or a crime against humanity, as defined in the international instruments drawn up to make provision in respect of such crimes".[167] This satisfied the majority of delegates who wanted a strong stand against the sheltering of war criminals;[168] the United States was content that the definition was sufficiently vague to allow for the injection of domestic discretion;[169]

Mr. Henkin, U.N. Doc. E/AC.32/SR.5, at 5, January 30, 1950. As a fall-back position, Mr. Henkin suggested that there ought to be "nothing to prevent a State from sheltering war criminals. The basic issue was to determine who would decide that a person was a war criminal. It might be left to the discretion of the receiving country": U.N. Doc. E/AC.32/SR.17, at 9, February 6, 1950.

[164] "A signatory State which extended protection to a war criminal would be going beyond its obligations under the convention. It would, however, be granting special benefits to a category of undesirable persons. . .": Statement of Mr. Robinson of Israel, U.N. Doc. E/AC.32/SR.17, at 9, February 6, 1950. *Accord* Statements of Mr. Cuvelier of Belgium, U.N. Doc. E/AC.32/SR.18, at 2, February 8, 1950; and Mr. Rain of France, U.N. Doc. E/AC.32/SR.18, at 3, February 8, 1950.

[165] "That charter had been approved in 1944 by a limited number of states which had taken part in the last war, and a considerable number of states attending the present conference had not signed it or taken [a] position on it. Reference to that document therefore appeared inappropriate in the draft Convention. . . . By associating the Geneva Conventions with the work of the Conference the humanitarian aims which should govern the convention would be stressed": Statement of Mr. von Trutzschler of the Federal Republic of Germany, U.N. Doc. A/CONF.2/SR.19, at 26, July 13, 1951.

[166] "[N]either the Geneva Conventions nor the Convention on Genocide possessed the solid foundation which the jurisprudence of the International Military Tribunal, and other tribunals which had applied the provisions of article 6 of the Nurnberg Charter, conferred on the 'Nurnberg Principles'": Statement of Mr. Herment of Belgium, U.N. Doc. A/CONF.2/SR.21, at 10, July 14, 1951.

[167] *Convention, supra,* note 2, at Art. 1(F)(a).

[168] "[I]t would be excessively optimistic to state, as did the United States representative, that no more war criminals remained to be dealt with. He was convinced that that was not the case, and it would be intolerable that they should be given the protection of the convention": Statement of Mr. Rain of France, U.N. Doc. E/AC.32/SR.5, at 16, January 30, 1950.

[169] "The object of the provision was to deny the United Nations mantle and international refugee status to war criminals, but as war criminals were difficult to define, and some countries used the term loosely, the determination was left open to the Contracting States in question": Statement of Mr. Henkin of the U.S.A., U.N. Doc. E/AC.7/SR.159, at 13, August 16, 1950.

and Germany was placated by the adoption of a politically neutral formulation.[170]

As customarily interpreted, this exclusion clause therefore bars those who commit three distinct types of crime.[171] First, a "crime against peace" comprises the planning of or participation in an unlawful war. Second, a "war crime" involves the violation of a law of war, including the mistreatment of civilians and prisoners of war, or the infliction of unjustified property damage during wartime. Third, a "crime against humanity" consists of fundamentally inhumane conduct, often grounded in political, racial, religious or other bias. Genocide,[172] slavery, torture, and apartheid[173] are examples of crimes within this category.

An alternative to the plethora of international instruments[174] which now define and describe these crimes against international peace and security has been under construction by the International Law Commission since 1947. Indeed, the drafters of the Convention chose not to elaborate a detailed definition of these crimes partly in deference to the anticipated release of the Commission's *Code of Offences Against the Peace and Security of Mankind*.[175] While still not complete, the draft Code offers a conceptual framework to define crimes within this exclusion clause,[176] and the limited scope of the explanations which may be invoked in relation to them.[177]

The essential nature of a crime against peace and security was elaborated by the Commission in 1987, focusing on the criterion of seriousness:

These are crimes which affect the very foundations of human society. Seriousness can be deduced either from the nature of the act in question (cruelty, monstrousness, barbarity, etc.), or from the extent of its effects (massiveness, the victims being peoples, populations or ethnic groups), or from the motive of the perpetrator (for example, genocide), or from several of these elements.[178]

---

[170] "[T]he London Charter expressly dealt with crimes against humanity committed 'before or during the war', thus excluding such crimes committed at a later date. It would therefore seem logical that the Convention should not include a reference to an instrument of incontestably limited scope": Statement of Mr. von Trutzschler of the Federal Republic of Germany, U.N. Doc. A/CONF.2/SR.24, at 7, July 17, 1951.

[171] *See*, e.g., 1 A. Grahl-Madsen, *The Status of Refugees in International Law*, p. 274 (1966); UNHCR, *supra*, note 16, pp. 35-36.

[172] A. Grahl-Madsen, *supra*, note 171, p. 276.

[173] G. Goodwin-Gill, *The Refugee in International Law*, p. 60 (1983).

[174] UNHCR advocates reference to *inter alia*, the Charter of the International Military Tribunal, the Genocide Convention, and the Geneva Conventions: *supra*, note 16, p. 89. The *Criminal Code*, R.S.C. 1985, c. C-46, also expressly defines "crime against humanity" and "war crime" at s. 7 (3.76) [en. 1985, c. 30 (3rd Supp.), s. 1].

[175] A. Grahl-Madsen, *supra*, note 171, p. 276; N. Robinson, *supra*, note 156, p. 66.

[176] *See* draft Article 1, provisionally adopted by the International Law Commission in 1987: *Report of the International Law Commission to the General Assembly on the Work of its Thirty-Ninth Session* II(2), U.N. Doc. A/CN.4/SER.A/1987/Add.1 (Part 2), at 13 (1987).

[177] Draft Article 9, entitled "Exceptions to the principle of responsibility", had been discussed but not yet adopted by the International Law Commission as of 1987. *See id.* at Part 1, at 7-9.

[178] *Supra,* note 176, at 13.

Intention is a necessary element of such an offence, although some legal experts hold that it may be implied in the case of massive and systematic crimes, such as genocide or apartheid.[179] Because of this *mens rea* requirement, the Commission's draft suggests that three limited exceptions to the general principle of responsibility are available.

First, the leaders of a state may argue self-defence "in respect of acts whose performance was ordered by them or which they carried out in response to an act of aggression directed against their State".[180] This exception should be construed to relate only to offences within the traditional "crimes against peace" category, and recognizes that there is no genuine design to violate the rules against use of force in the context of a strictly defensive engagement in conflict.[181]

Second, it is possible to invoke coercion, state of necessity, or *force majeure*.[182] Essentially, this exception recognizes the absence of intent where an individual is motivated to perpetrate the act in question only in order to avoid grave and imminent peril. The danger must be such that "a reasonable man would apprehend that he was in such imminent physical peril as to deprive him of freedom to choose the right and refrain from the wrong".[183] Moreover, the predicament must not be of the making or consistent with the will of the person seeking to invoke this exception.[184] Most important, the harm inflicted must not be in excess of that which would otherwise have been directed at the person alleging coercion.[185]

These constraints would suggest that the Immigration Appeal Board's exoneration of Chilean torturer *Felix Salatiel Nuñez Veloso*[186] may have been unwarranted. Under pain of execution, the claimant had participated in crimes against humanity which were "totally opposed to his moral, religious and political convictions".[187] Because these actions were committed under duress, it was held that exclusion under Article 1(F) should not follow. Yet the Board failed to inquire whether the human suffering induced by Mr. Nuñez Veloso's actions outweighed the risk to his own well-being, an essential finding for exculpation under the doctrine of coercion.

Third, one may plead an error of law, in the sense of a lack of knowledge of the wrongfulness of the act committed.[188] Clearly, this is not possible in the case of most "crimes against humanity", since actions such as slavery

---

[179] *Id.*

[180] *Supra*, note 177, at 7.

[181] This is consistent with Article 51 of the *Charter of the United Nations*, signed June 25, 1945, entered into force October 24, 1945, 59 Stat. 1031 ("*Charter*").

[182] *Supra*, note 177, at 7.

[183] *Id.*, at 8, citing the *High Command* case, American Military Tribunals, case no. 12, vol. XI, at 509.

[184] *Id.*, at 8, citing the *Krupp* case, American Military Tribunals, case no. 10, vol. IX, at 1439.

[185] *Id.*, at 1445-446.

[186] Immigration Appeal Board Decision 79-1017, C.L.I.C. Notes 11.5, August 24, 1979.

[187] *Id.*, at 3, *per* J.-P. Houle.

[188] *Supra*, note 177, at 8.

or extermination may be classified as obviously wrongful. The specific application of the laws of war, on the other hand, is potentially ambiguous. If, notwithstanding "exertion of the conscience", the individual could not have ascertained the wrongfulness of the actions in question, the requisite intention is absent.[189]

In *Zacarias Osorio Cruz*[190] the Immigration Appeal Board allowed the claim of a deserter from the Mexican army, who admitted active participation in approximately twenty politically motivated executions over a five-year period. He eventually made a daring escape from his unit due to his "awakening political and moral conscience",[191] and claimed refugee status in Canada. In allowing his claim, the Board did not address the question of whether a crime of this sort could admit of a mistake of law, much less whether the claimant had genuinely "exerted his conscience" prior to engagement in actions properly characterized by the Board as "contrary to the most basic international rules of conduct".[192]

However, this case raises quite poignantly the issue of whether an additional form of exculpation rooted in utilitarianism is not warranted. The Board placed emphasis on the fact that Osorio Cruz was the first person to shed light on the crimes against humanity being committed by the Mexican army:

> In deserting from the army and telling the whole world, as it had never been told before, the story of the atrocities committed by officers of the Government of Mexico, Mr. Osorio Cruz betrayed his oath of obedience, became a traitor in the eyes of some Mexican authorities by displaying his strong political disagreement and, without a doubt, the worst punishment reserved for prisoners holding unpopular political opinions awaited him. This is the reason for his fear.[193]

While Osorio Cruz' protracted involvement with crimes against humanity may be too egregious to warrant exculpation on any basis, in the case of a less confirmed criminal one might reasonably consider whether the value of disclosure of previously covert inhumane conduct does not offset the general rule against sheltering an admitted criminal. Since the enforcement of international human rights law is dependent on publicity and moral probation, it may be wise judiciously to exonerate individuals who, though culpable themselves, make it possible to end or curtail crimes against peace and security. This position is not, however, thus far accepted in law.

The commentary which accompanies the International Law Commission draft also fails to suggest a specific "superior order" exception, although

---

[189] *Id.*, at 8, citing *Entscheidungen des Bundesgerichtofes in Strafsachen*, judgment of the German Federal Court, vol. 3 (1953), at 365-66.

[190] Immigration Appeal Board Decision M88-20043X, C.L.I.C. Notes 118.6, March 25, 1988.

[191] *Id.*, at 10, *per* P. Arsenault.

[192] *Id.*, at 11.

[193] *Id.*, at 10.

it notes that soldiers or others following commands may invoke the notions of coercion or error of law, as defined above.[194] In contrast, the Immigration and Refugee Board accepted the claim of a member of a Ghanaian firing squad involved in politically motivated executions under colour of judicial authority, noting that "the claimant is not a person described in Section F [of] Article 1, because he was a private in the Ghanaian Army and killed people in the line of duty".[195] Because criminal responsibility for actions against peace and security is intended to compel subordinates to question the illegitimate exercise of authority, a "superior order" defence would be counterproductive.[196]

In sum, a crime against peace and security is defined by its seriousness, whether based on the nature of the act itself, the extent of its effects, or the motive of the perpetrator. A person who commits such an act is culpable unless a strictly construed exception based on self-defence, coercion, or error of law can be established. Moreover, all of the recognized exceptions to responsibility for crimes against peace and security are inoperative if the facts invoked constitute a breach of a peremptory norm of international law, originate in a fault of the perpetrator, or result in the sacrifice of a greater interest than that protected.[197]

The last question to be addressed is the degree of involvement required to justify criminal liability. While mere presence at the scene of a crime may not be actionable,[198] exclusion is warranted "when the evidence establishes that the individual in question personally ordered, incited, assisted or otherwise participated in the persecution. . . ."[199] In *Fernando Alfonso Naredo Arduengo*,[200] for example, the Immigration Appeal Board disqualified the Chilean applicants who had been employed by that country's secret police:

> Mr. and Mrs. Naredo were members of different four or five mean teams engaged in surveillance, arrests and interrogations, which involved torture and beatings. Both claimed to have been assigned to stand guard and take notes, denying that they personally beat or tortured their victims. Mr. Naredo claims to have participated in eighteen to twenty such operations, ten leading to death. . . . [T]heir actions so clearly an abuse of human rights, set them outside those who can properly seek asylum.[201]

The same holds true for those who make it possible for others to engage in crimes against peace and security:

---

[194] *Supra*, note 177, at 9.

[195] Immigration and Refugee Board Decision T89-00198, July 1989, at 6, *per* J. Gilberger.

[196] A recent Board decision helpfully recognized that ". . . participation — albeit unwilling — in war crimes, could exclude [a claimant]. . . under Article 1(F)(a). . .": Immigration and Refugee Board Decision T89-01690, January 1990, at 11, *per* I. Liebich.

[197] *Supra*, note 177, at 7.

[198] *Fedorenko v. United States*, 449 U.S. 490 (U.S.S.C. 1981).

[199] *Laipenicks v. I.N.S.*, 750 F. 2d 1427, at 1431 (U.S.C.A. 9th Cir. 1985).

[200] Immigration Appeal Board Decision T80-9159, C.L.I.C. Notes 27.13, November 20, 1980.

[201] *Id.*, at 11-14, *per* D. Davey.

That Mr. Giraud did not kill anyone directly is not to his credit. He prepared them for death, which in my view makes him culpable. . . . Mr. Giraud has, in my view, committed a. . . crime against humanity.[202]

6.3.2 Serious Non-Political Crimes

The common law criminality exclusion[203] disallows the claims of persons who are liable to sanctions in another state for having committed a genuine, serious crime, and who seek to escape legitimate criminal liability by claiming refugee status. This exclusion clause is not a means of bypassing ordinary criminal due process for acts committed in a state of refuge,[204] nor a pretext for ignoring the protection needs of those whose transgressions abroad are of a comparatively minor nature.[205] Rather, it is simply a means of bringing refugee law into line with the basic principles of extradition law,[206] by ensuring that important fugitives from justice are not able to avoid the jurisdiction of a state in which they may lawfully face punishment:

Article 14 of the Universal Declaration of Human Rights was concerned with the right of asylum, and its second paragraph constituted a proviso to the general provision of the first paragraph. That second paragraph seemed. . . to be intended to apply to persons who were fugitives from prosecution in another country for non-political crimes, and the effect would seem to be that the provisions of article 14 would not override specific extradition obligations. . . . [T]he Convention mentioned neither the right of asylum nor the principle of extradition. In that connexion, the action of States was governed by treaties

---

[202] *St. Gardien Giraud*, Immigration Appeal Board Decision T81-9669, C.L.I.C. Notes 48.10, October 28, 1982, at 5, *per* E. Teitelbaum; set aside on other grounds by Federal Court of Appeal Decision A-1080-82, September 30, 1983.

[203] "The provisions of this Convention shall not apply to any person with respect to whom there are serious reasons for considering that. . . he has committed a serious non-political crime outside the country of refuge prior to his admission to that country as a refugee": *Convention, supra*, note 2, at Art. 1(F)(b).

[204] "[T]here was no case for denying them the rights envisaged in the Convention, which included all the usual personal rights, such as the right to appear before the courts or to own property. It was wrong that a person whom it might ultimately be necessary to expel should be regarded as a pariah in the meantime": Statement of Mr. Hoare of the United Kingdom, U.N. Doc. A/CONF.2/SR.3, at 15, July 13, 1951.

[205] "He was most anxious that refugees who had committed such crimes as petty thefts in their camp should not thereby be placed once and for all beyond the reach of the Convention. It had been argued that as a matter of civilized treatment that would not occur; if so, he could see no objection to giving the principle legal recognition in the Convention": Statement of Mr. Hoare of the United Kingdom, U.N. Doc. A/CONF.2/SR.24, at 8, July 17, 1951.

[206] "[T]he exception of common law criminals subject to extradition would naturally continue to be applicable": Statement of Mr. Henkin of the U.S.A., U.N. Doc. A/AC.32/SR.5, at 5, January 30, 1950. *Accord* Statement of Mr. Rochefort of France, U.N. Doc. E/AC.7/SR.166, at 4, August 22, 1950. Indeed, the text of the clause adopted by the Economic and Social Council explicitly excluded a person "[i]n respect of whom there are serious reasons for considering that he has committed a crime covered by the provisions of treaties of extradition": 11 UNESCOR (325th mtg.) at 670, December 14, 1950. *See also* A. Grahl-Madsen, *supra*, note 2, at 272-73.

relating specifically to extradition, and it would therefore be for states to take appropriate action in any given case in the light of their obligations under such treaties.[207]

In view of this narrow purpose, the common law criminality clause is subject to several important constraints.

First, it follows from the linkage to extradition that the only allegations of criminality which are relevant to the application of this clause are those which involve acts committed outside a country of refuge,[208] whether in the country of origin[209] or while in transit to an asylum state.[210] As noted by the Canadian representative just prior to the vote on this clause,

> . . . the issue turned on the temporal element, namely, whether a person had committed a crime outside the territory of the receiving country before he had applied for the status of refugee.[211]

Criminal activity in a state of refuge, on the other hand, is appropriately adjudicated through due process of law,[212] with recourse to expulsion or return if the refugee is consequently found to pose a security risk.[213]

Second, the extradition-based rationale for the exclusion clause requires that the criminal offence be justiciable in the country in which it was committed.[214] Insofar as the claimant has served her sentence, been acquitted

---

[207] Statement of Mr. Hoare of the United Kingdom, U.N. Doc. A/CONF.2/SR.29, at 14, July 19, 1951. *Accord* Statement of Mr. Herment of Belgium: "[I]t was possible that, under international law, a refugee convicted of, or charged with, a common-law crime would have necessarily to be handed over to the authorities of his country of origin. Inclusion of the provision in question was therefore imperative": U.N. Doc. A/CONF.2/SR.24, at 9, July 17, 1951.

[208] "His particular preoccupation was that persons who committed crimes in their country of refuge should not be excluded from the application of the Convention": Statement of Mr. Hoare of the United Kingdom, U.N. Doc. A/CONF.2/SR.24, at 13, July 17, 1951. *Accord* Statements of Mr. Petren of Sweden, U.N. Doc. A/CONF.2/SR.29, at 16, July 19, 1951; Mr. Rochefort of France, U.N. Doc. A/CONF.2/SR.29, at 18, July 19, 1951; and Mr. Herment of Belgium, U.N. Doc. A/CONF.2/SR.29, at 24, July 19, 1951. The specific incorporation of this principle was introduced by the representative of Yugoslavia: U.N. Doc. A/CONF.2/SR.29, at 20, July 19, 1951.

[209] Exclusion, of course, does not follow if the criminal law is subverted to attainment of a persecutory end: *see* Section 5.6.1, *supra. Accord* Mr. Herment of Belgium, U.N. Doc. A/CONF.2/SR.29, at 14, July 19, 1951: "[T]he Belgian delegation did not consider that the status of refugee could be denied to a person simply because he had been convicted of a common law offence in his country of origin. In any case, the countries of origin concerned, and their methods of dispensing justice, were well enough known."

[210] In response to a question from the conference president on this issue (U.N. Doc. A/CONF.2/SR.29, at 21, July 19, 1951), the representative of the Netherlands suggested that all crimes committed prior to admission to a country of asylum were relevant: *id.*

[211] Statement of Mr. Chance of Canada, U.N. Doc. A/CONF.2/SR.29, at 26, July 19, 1951. *Accord* Statement of Mr. Bozovic of Yugoslavia, *id.*

[212] "[P]aragraph E would cover any crime committed by a refugee abroad, and its provisions would cease to apply once the refugee had been assimilated into the country of asylum": Statement of Mr. Hoare of the United Kingdom, U.N. Doc. A/CONF.2/SR.29, at 24, July 19, 1951. *See also* UNHCR, *supra*, note 16, at 36.

[213] *See* text at note 233 ff., *infra.*

[214] 1 A. Grahl-Madsen, *The Status of Refugees in International Law*, pp. 291-92 (1966).

of the charges, benefited from an amnesty or otherwise met her obligations under the criminal law, she would be at no risk of extradition, and should not be excluded from refugee status. As Paul Weis has observed,

> It is. . . difficult to see why a person who before becoming a refugee, has been convicted of a serious crime and has served his sentence should forever be debarred from refugee status. Such a rule would seem to run counter to the generally accepted principle of penal law that a person who has been punished for an offence should suffer no further prejudice on account of the offence committed.[215]

Indeed, delegates to the Conference on Territorial Asylum were able to agree that the criminality exclusion should bar only the claims of persons believed to be "still liable to prosecution or punishment".[216]

Third, the drafters recognized the seriousness of refusing to protect a person at risk of persecution, and therefore chose to limit the criminality exception to persons at risk of prosecution or punishment for a serious crime within the realm of extraditable offences.[217] In pressing for a narrowly interpreted exclusion, the British delegate argued against simple incorporation of the non-political crime exclusion from the Universal Declaration of Human Rights:

> But what was meant by considering that a person fell within a category of prosecutions? A person who was prosecuted and convicted would certainly seem to fall within that category. As it stood, therefore, clause (b) would include refugees who had committed a crime, no matter how trivial. . . provided it was not a political crime, and would thus automatically exclude them from the benefits of the Convention. It must be obvious to all that such a proposition was untenable.[218]

This concern that some treaties of extradition envisage removal for insufficiently serious offences convinced the delegates to constrain exclusion to cases of apparently "serious" criminality.[219] The Belgian representative, for example,

> . . . preferred the words "serious crimes". . . to mention of crimes "covered by the provisions of treaties of extradition". . . . Some crimes in respect of

---

[215] P. Weis, "The concept of the refugee in international law" (1960), 87 J. du droit international 928, at 984-86.

[216] U.N. Doc. A/CONF.78/12, February 4, 1977, cited in A. Grahl-Madsen, *Territorial Asylum*, p. 209 (1980).

[217] The French delegate, Mr. Rochefort, ". . . pointed out that a crime was not the same thing as a misdemeanour, and that the term 'crime', in which sense it was used in the Universal Declaration of Human Rights, meant serious crimes": U.N. Doc. A/CONF.2/SR.29, at 18, July 19, 1951. This characterization is particularly important, since the final language of the clause was adopted on the basis of the French formulation, and then translated to English: U.N. Doc. A/CONF.2/L.1/ADD.10, at 3, July 20, 1951.

[218] Statement of Mr. Hoare of the United Kingdom, U.N. Doc. A/CONF.2/SR.29, at 11, July 19, 1951.

[219] This amendment was suggested by the Swiss delegate, Mr. Schurch: U.N. Doc. A/CONF.2/SR.29, at 17, July 19, 1951; and formally moved by Mr. Rochefort of France: U.N. Doc. A/CONF.2/SR.29, at 20, July 19, 1951.

which the offender could be extradited were punishable by only three months' imprisonment, and were obviously not serious.[220]

Atle Grahl-Madsen interprets this clause to mean that only crimes punishable by several years' imprisonment are of sufficient gravity to offset a fear of persecution.[221] UNHCR defines seriousness by reference to crimes which involve significant violence against persons, such as homicide, rape, child molesting, wounding, arson, drugs traffic, and armed robbery.[222] These are crimes which ordinarily warrant severe punishment, thus making clear the Convention's commitment to the withholding of protection only from those who have committed truly abhorrent wrongs.

Fourth, the crime must be an ordinary, common law offence,[223] prosecuted and punished in a non-discriminatory way. As noted in Chapter 5,[224] if the "crime" is an absolute or relative political offence, or if there is evidence of political interference with an otherwise legitimate criminal process by selective prosecution, punitive denial of procedural fairness, or politically inspired sentencing, it cannot accurately be said that the claimant faces a risk of ordinary application of the criminal law.

Finally, and perhaps most important, the risks associated with exclusion from refugee status must not outweigh the harm that would be done by returning the claimant to face prosecution or punishment. Even though a claimant may be a serious criminal, it is possible that the heinous nature of the persecution anticipated in her state of origin counters the extradition-derived logic of her return.[225] The drafters of the Convention were keenly aware of this possibility:

> . . . States which received a request for the extradition of a refugee who had committed a crime of no great consequence from the very government that was likely to persecute him, would be faced with a very difficult decision. On the other hand, States could not be expected to grant asylum to persons committing capital crimes merely because they happened to be exposed at the same time to relatively minor dangers on account of some unimportant political activity. A proper balance must be struck between all the considerations involved.[226]

This requirement to balance harms is echoed in the conference president's summary of the approach to be followed in excluding common law criminals:

---

[220] Statement of Mr. Herment of Belgium, U.N. Doc. A/CONF.2/SR.29, at 20, July 19, 1951.

[221] A. Grahl-Madsen, *supra*, note 214, p. 297.

[222] G. Goodwin-Gill, *The Refugee in International Law*, p. 62 (1983).

[223] *See*, e.g., Statements of Mr. Bozovic of Yugoslavia and Mr. Rochefort of France, U.N. Doc. A/CONF.2/SR.29, at 17, July 19, 1951.

[224] *See* Section 5.6.1, *supra*.

[225] "[I]f, for political reasons, a person is threatened with certain death, imprisonment for life, serious bodily harm or the like upon his eventual return to his country of origin; it would, indeed, seem equitable to recognize him as a refugee, even if he were considered guilty of a truly serious non-political crime. . .": A. Grahl-Madsen, *supra*, note 214, p. 298.

[226] Statement of Mr. Larsen of Denmark, U.N. Doc. A/CONF.2/SR.24, at 13, July 17, 1951.

When a person with a criminal record sought asylum as a refugee, it was for the country of refuge to strike a balance between the offences committed by that person and the extent to which his fear of persecution was well-founded.[227]

To achieve this end, the decision-maker needs to consider the facts of the claim.[228] If the gravity of harm feared by the claimant outweighs the significance of her criminal activity, she is not appropriately excluded under this clause.[229]

There is frequently a confusion between the exclusion of serious, common law criminals under Article 1(F) of the Convention, and the right of a state to expel or return dangerous refugees pursuant to Article 33(2).[230] Article 1(F), inserted at the insistence of countries which perceived themselves to be vulnerable to large flows of refugees,[231] is designed to afford the possibility of pre-admission exclusion on the basis of a relatively low standard of proof[232] ("serious reasons for considering"), and without recourse to a formal trial to assess the criminal charge. The expediency of this recourse is balanced against its very narrow scope: it applies only to persons believed to have committed serious, pre-entry crimes which remain justiciable and the gravity of which outweighs that of the anticipated persecution.

---

[227] Statement of the President, U.N. Doc. A/CONF.2/SR.29, at 23, July 19, 1951.

[228] "In practice, the claim to be a refugee can rarely be ignored, for a balance must also be struck between the nature of the offence presumed to have been committed and the degree of persecution feared": G. Goodwin-Gill, *supra*, note 222, pp. 61-62. While there is authority for this balancing doctrine in the American jurisprudence (*see* M. McAndrew, "The Dictator Dilemma: A Comparison of United States and French Asylum Procedures" (1986), 19 N.Y.U.J. Intl. L. and Policy 1087, at 1089-090), decisions of the Board of Immigration Appeals reject such an approach: *see*, e.g., *Matter of Rodriguez-Coto*, Interim Decision 2985, February 21, 1985, at 3.

[229] UNHCR, *supra*, note 16, at 37; P. Weis, *supra*, note 215, at 986.

[230] "The benefit of the [non-refoulement] provision may not, however, be claimed by a refugee whom there are reasonable grounds for regarding as a danger to the security of the country in which he is, or who, having been convicted by a final judgement of a particularly serious crime, constitutes a danger to the community of that country": *Convention, supra*, note 2, at Art. 33(2). *See*, e.g., Immigration and Refugee Board Decision T89-0245, September 1989, in which the Board inappropriately employed the exclusion clause in Article 1(F)(b) to bar a claimant on the basis of a combination of pre-entry and Canadian criminality for which sentence had been served. This case ought reasonably to have been assessed against the standards of Article 33(2); if met, the claimant would retain refugee status, but lose the benefit of protection against refoulement.

[231] "France's reason for taking such a firm stand on the subject lay in the fact that she had to administer the right of asylum under much more difficult conditions than did countries which were in a position to screen immigrants carefully at their frontiers": Statement of Mr. Rochefort of France, U.N. Doc. A/CONF.2/SR.24, at 13, July 17, 1951. *Accord* Mr. Makiedo of Yugoslavia, U.N. Doc. A/CONF.2/SR.24, at 18, July 17, 1951. These states were concerned not to undermine the possibilities for resettlement of the refugees admitted: "If refugee status was to be granted to criminals, immigration countries could not fail to question its value": Statement of Mr. Rochefort of France, U.N. Doc. A/CONF.2/SR.19, at 7, July 13, 1951.

[232] 1 A. Grahl-Madsen, *The Status of Refugees in International Law*, p. 289 (1966).

Article 33(2), on the other hand, is the original[233] and more broadly applicable criminality provision. It provides the means for states to expel or return refugees who, for example, commit crimes in a state of refuge,[234] or whose past record of criminality in that country or elsewhere is believed to make them undesirable residents, even if they may face extremely serious forms of persecution.[235] Its standard of proof, however, is more exacting: it requires conviction by a final judgment of a particularly serious crime, rather than simply "serious reasons for considering" that a person may be a criminal.[236] Too, it is not enough that the crime committed have been "serious", but it must rather be "particularly serious" and sustain the conclusion that the offender "constitutes a danger to the community".[237]

6.3.3 Acts Contrary to the Principles and Purposes of the United Nations

This last exclusion clause[238] was originally part of the draft provision relating to persons who commit crimes against peace and security.[239] When that exclusion was reformulated in generic terms,[240] the reference to principles and purposes of the United Nations was moved forward to form part of the common law criminality clause modelled on Article 14(2) of the Universal Declaration of Human Rights.[241] The phrase was ultimately detached from this provision as well,[242] resulting in the establishment of failure to abide

---

[233] Indeed, it was argued by the United Kingdom that there was no need for a criminality exclusion in view of Article 33(2): Statement of Mr. Hoare, U.N. Doc. A/CONF.2/SR.24, at 4, July 17, 1951. *Accord* Baron von Boetzelaer of the Netherlands, U.N. Doc. A/CONF.2/SR.29, at 12, July 19, 1951: "Common criminals should not enjoy the right of asylum; but that consideration had already been taken care of in article [33] of the draft Convention. . . ."

[234] *See*, e.g., *I. v. Belgium* (1987), 46 Revue du droit des étrangers 200, in which Belgium relied on Article 33(2) to expel a refugee sentenced to three years' imprisonment in respect of a major theft, cited in (1989), 1(3) I.J.R.L. 392. *Quaere* whether theft is appropriately considered to be a "particularly serious crime", since it would not qualify as even a "serious crime" for purposes of exclusion under Article 1(F)(b): *see* text *supra* at notes 221-222.

[235] "The exclusion clause now refers to crimes committed 'prior to his (the refugee's) admission to that country (i.e. the country of asylum) as a refugee' while persons who have committed a serious crime *in* the country of residence remain refugees, but may in certain conditions be denied asylum and returned to their country of origin (Article 33(2) of the Convention)": P. Weis, *supra*, note 215, at 984.

[236] *Supra*, note 230.

[237] *Id.*

[238] "The provisions of this Convention shall not apply to any person with respect to whom there are serious reasons for considering that. . . he has been guilty of acts contrary to the purposes and principles of the United Nations": *Convention, supra*, note 2, at Art. 1(F)(c).

[239] *See* draft of the Working Group, U.N. Doc. E/AC.32/L.32, at 3, February 9, 1950: "No Contracting State shall apply the benefits of this convention to any person who in its opinion has committed a crime specified in article VI of the London Charter of the International Military Tribunal or any other act contrary to the purposes and principles of the Charter of the United Nations."

[240] *See* text *supra* at note 167.

[241] *Supra*, note 155.

[242] This was proposed by Mr. Bozovic of Yugoslavia: U.N. Doc. A/CONF.2/SR.29, at 20, July 19, 1951.

by the principles and purposes of the United Nations as a free-standing exclusion clause.

The interpretations of this provision mirror its confused drafting history. One position is that the clause was intended to bar enemy collaborators from the Second World War,[243] and is therefore of little contemporary relevance. Some argue that violation of the principles and purposes of the United Nations is essentially coterminous with crimes against peace and security,[244] such as genocide[245] or a war crime.[246] Others take the view that the clause implies a duty to refrain from the subversion of an asylum state,[247] or even of the refugee's state of origin.[248] A fourth theory is that the barring of persons who fail to respect the principles and purposes of the United Nations is intended to exclude any person who acts in a manner inconsistent with basic human rights,[249] for example by engaging in acts of discrimination[250] or opposing the right to self-determination.[251] Finally, it is argued that the clause

---

[243] Statement of Mr. Henkin of the U.S.A., U.N. Doc. E/AC.7/SR.160, at 16, August 18, 1950. *Accord* P. Weis, *supra*, note 215, at 986.

[244] "His delegation held that the phrase in question applied to — and hence excluded — war criminals, ordinary criminals and certain individuals who, though not guilty of war crimes, might have committed acts of similar gravity against the principles of the United Nations, in other words, crimes against humanity": Statement of Mr. Rochefort of France, U.N. Doc. E/AC.7/SR.166, at 4, August 22, 1950.

[245] Statement of Mr. Rochefort of France, U.N. Doc. E/AC.7/SR.160, at 15, August 18, 1950.

[246] Statement of Mr. Schurch of Switzerland, U.N. Doc. A/CONF.2/SR.29, at 17, July 19, 1951. *Accord* C. Pompe, "The Convention of 28 July 1951 and the International Protection of Refugees", published in English as U.N. Doc. HCR/INF/42, May 1958, at 13: "What is to be understood by this last expression — over and above war crimes which are separately mentioned — is not made clear by the authors of the Convention."

[247] Statements of Mr. Hoare of the United Kingdom, U.N. Doc. A/CONF.2/SR.24, at 4, July 17, 1951; and of Mr. Chance of Canada, U.N. Doc. A/CONF.2/SR.24, at 16, July 17, 1951.

[248] "[E]ach state is obligated under international laws to prevent any act which may endanger the security of other nations from being committed in its jurisdictional territory. [It] naturally flows that each state is obligated to prevent refugees in its territory from engaging in political activities against the government of their country": K. Kawahara, "Analysis of Results of the First Session of the International Conference on Territorial Asylum" in International Institute of Humanitarian Law, ed., *Round Table on Some Current Problems of Refugee Law*, p. 26 (1978).

[249] "The general principle of respect for human rights has been developed specifically through the Universal Declaration and the 1966 Covenants, so that an individual who has denied or restricted the human rights of others may thus be argued to fall within the exception": G. Goodwin-Gill, *The Refugee in International Law*, pp. 63-64 (1983).

[250] The Indian delegate, Mr. Desai, noted that he knew of ". . . one case where a refugee running a licensed hotel had refused to admit coloured people. In such cases, the individual refugee would be acting contrary to the purposes and principles of the Charter and should not enjoy the protection of the Convention": U.N. Doc. E/AC.7/SR.160, at 17, August 18, 1950. *Accord* Statement of Mr. Rochefort of France, U.N. Doc. E/AC.7/SR.160, at 20, August 18, 1950: "A refugee who, as in the case cited by the Indian representative, practised racial discrimination, would be thereby abusing the hospitality of the country of refuge."

[251] This possibility was raised by the Chilean representative, Mr. Bernstein: U.N. Doc. E/AC.7/SR.160, at 18, August 18, 1950. *See also* G. Goodwin-Gill, *supra*, note 249, p. 65.

disfranchises those who fail to respect any major initiative of the United Nations, including not only respect for human rights, but also such causes as the fights against hijacking and hostage-taking.[252]

The multiplicity of possible interpretations bears witness to the concern of several delegates that the vagueness of the clause left it open to misconstruction or abuse.[253] Moreover, all of these interpretations are substantively problematic. The exclusion of collaborators, war criminals and persons guilty of crimes against humanity can be achieved under Article 1(F)(a),[254] thus rendering the "principles and purposes" exclusion redundant. Concern with persons intending to subvert the asylum state can be addressed under Article 33(2),[255] while exclusion on the basis of efforts to topple the regime of a refugee-producing state seems misplaced in view of the United Nations' commitment to human rights and self-determination.[256] The exclusion of those who breach human rights standards or who fail to support other goals of the world community is more compelling,[257] but the range, detail, and relative obscurity of such standards would work a real hardship in the case of the average citizen, who generally looks only to domestic law to understand her duties.

The Charter of the United Nations lists four purposes of the organization: to maintain international peace and security; to develop friendly and mutually respectful relations among nations; to achieve international cooperation in solving socio-economic and cultural problems, and in promoting respect for human rights; and to serve as a centre for harmonizing actions directed to these ends.[258] These basic purposes bind member states through a series of principles set out in Article 2, including respect for sovereign equality; good faith fulfilment of obligations; peaceful settlement of disputes;

---

[252] *Id.*

[253] "[W]hile not questioning the good faith of the representative of France, [he] recalled that there had been instances in which tyrants had imprisoned their political enemies on the pretext that they were enemies of the United Nations and of democracy. . . . [T]he Committee should avoid restrictive language, which would be open to abuse": Statement of Mr. de Alba of Mexico, U.N. Doc. E/AC.7/SR.160, at 19, August 18, 1950. *Accord* Statements of Mr. Brohi of Pakistan, U.N. Doc. E/AC.7/SR.160, at 16, August 18, 1950; of Miss Meagher of Canada, U.N. Doc. E/AC.7/SR.165, at 23, August 19, 1950; and of Mr. Bernstein of Chile, *id.*

[254] *See* Section 6.3.1, *supra.*

[255] *Supra*, note 230.

[256] Citing the various United Nations resolutions in support of freedom fighters, Sam Aiboni concludes, "It can therefore hardly be held that the activities of these Movements are contrary to the purposes and principles of the United Nations. Rather the opposite is true": S. Aiboni, *Protection of Refugees in Africa*, p. 141 (1978).

[257] "The principles referred to were defined in the United Nations Charter and the Universal Declaration of Human Rights. An individual who, without having committed a crime against humanity, had violated human rights, for instance, by the exercise of discrimination, could be considered to have committed 'acts contrary to the purpose and principles of the United Nations'": Statement of Mr. Giraud of the Secretariat, U.N. Doc. E/AC.7/SR.166, at 9, August 22, 1950.

[258] *Charter, supra,* note 181, at Article 1.

refraining from use of force against the territorial integrity or political independence of another state; and promotion of the work of the United Nations.[259] It is clear that these principles speak essentially to governments,[260] and that most individuals can violate even the spirit of the purposes and principles only through the commission of a crime against peace and security, or of a serious criminal offence. The independent utility of this exclusion clause is thus somewhat elusive.

During the drafting of the Convention, however, it was suggested that this exclusion clause is a response to those who have "abused positions of authority"[261] by failing to exercise political power in a manner which is respectful of the requirements of the Charter:

> The provision was not aimed at the man-in-the-street, but at persons occupying government posts, such as heads of States, ministers and high officials. . . .
> By a turn of events, the persecutor might himself become a refugee. . . [in which case] there could be no compulsion on a State to provide asylum and in no case could it be provided in the name of the Charter or of the Universal Declaration of Human Rights. . . .[262]

More specifically, the concern was that

> [i]t was possible that a petty tyrant, after committing a crime against humanity, might not be prosecuted by his country of origin, where his crime against the United Nations might be considered as a normal act. . . . [I]n the absence of a world government and of a sovereign international court of justice, that power. . . must, perforce, be left to States.[263]

A sensible and purposeful interpretation of this exclusion clause, advocated by the United Nations,[264] is therefore that it is intended to enable states effectively to act as agents of the international community in bringing to bear basic norms of acceptable international conduct against government officials who ought reasonably to understand and respect them, and to avoid tarnishing refugee status by the admission to protection of those who have exploited their political authority to jeopardize the well-being of individuals, their nation, or the world community.[265]

---

[259] *Id.*, at Article 2.

[260] "It was difficult to see how an individual could commit acts contrary to the purposes and principles of the Charter of the United Nations, membership of which was confined to sovereign States": Statement of Mr. Bernstein of Chile, U.N. Doc. E/AC.7/SR.160, at 15, August 18, 1950. *But see* Statement of Mr. Rochefort of France, U.N. Doc. E/AC.7/SR.166, at 5, August 22, 1950: "So far as acts contrary to the purposes and principles of the United Nations were concerned, the first question which arose was whether such acts could be committed by individuals. An affirmative reply to that question was given by articles 14 and 30 of the Universal Declaration of Human Rights." *Accord* Statement of Mr. Giraud of the Secretariat, who relied on individual liability under international criminal law: U.N. Doc. E/AC.7/SR.166, at 8, August 22, 1950.

[261] Statement of Miss Meagher of Canada, U.N. Doc. E/AC.7/SR.166, at 10, August 22, 1950.

[262] Statement of Mr. Rochefort of France, U.N. Doc. E/AC.7/SR.166, at 6, August 22, 1950.

[263] *Id.*

[264] UNHCR, *supra*, note 16, p. 38.

[265] *See* 1 A. Grahl-Madsen, *The Status of Refugees in International Law*, p. 286 (1966).

7

The Challenge of Humane Protection in a Self-Interested World

There is no right to freedom of movement between states. General principles of international law recognize the right to leave one's country, and to return to it, but impose no duty on other states to permit entry. The International Bill of Rights recognizes only a right of individuals to seek asylum, with no concomitant duty on states to in fact accede to such requests.

Refugee law constitutes a narrow exception to this norm of autodetermination of immigration policy. Refugee law is a politically pragmatic means of reconciling the generalized commitment of states to self-interested control over immigration to the reality of coerced migration. Since the early part of this century, governments have recognized that if they are to maintain control over immigration in general terms, they must accommodate demands for entry based on particular urgency. To fail to do so is to risk the destruction to those broader policies of control, since laws and institutional arrangements are no match for the desperate creativity of persons in flight from serious harm. By catering for a subset of those who seek freedom of international movement, refugee law legitimates and sustains the viability of the protectionist norm.

The challenge for states has always been the definition of refugee status — the exception to the rule — in terms which are sufficiently broad to encompass those whose need to move is unassailable, yet simultaneously to tailor and constrain the scope of the refugee class to meet the self-interested preoccupations of asylum states. Perhaps because the Convention was the first refugee accord to attempt this task in a universal political forum, it exhibits acute concern for the protection of the self-defined interests of states, as attested to by the comments of one non-governmental observer to the Conference which adopted it:

> The Conference was about to adopt a legal definition of the term "refugee". But in the course of the work it had so far completed it had by inference so defined that term that truth and justice demanded that the general impression thus created should be rectified. . . . Its decisions had at times given the impression that it was a conference for the protection of helpless sovereign states against the wicked refugee. The draft Convention had at times been in danger of appearing to the refugee like the menu at an expensive restaurant, with every course

231

crossed out except, perhaps, the soup, and a footnote to the effect that even the soup might not be served in certain circumstances.[1]

The result is in many ways lamentable from a protection perspective, as is clear from the Convention's exclusive focus on those who have successfully escaped the jurisdiction of their home state; the provision of asylum only to those who meet objective criteria of risk; the preoccupation with avoiding serious harm, rather than with fully liberating the human person; the deference to effective national protection; the insistence on some form of discrimination or differentiation in assessing risk; and, of course, the denial of status to those who, from the vantage point of the asylum state, do not need or deserve recognition as refugees. The Convention's structure clearly derives from a minimalist commitment of states to the effectuation of guarantees of human dignity. Since there is little to suggest that governments would be inclined to act more generously today, the first purpose of this book has been to suggest ways in which a philosophy of humane protection can reasonably be accommodated within the framework of the definition as adopted.

The second challenge to the Convention's continued viability comes from the dissipation of the cold war, Eurocentric political landscape to which it was initially addressed. As contemporary protection concerns become increasingly distinct from those of post-war Europe, the risk of the Convention definition becoming a mere legal anachronism is real. To some extent, of course, regional refugee arrangements, institutional programs, discretionary national initiatives, and the evolution of customary legal standards have mitigated the significance of the Convention definition's conceptual flaws. Yet because the Convention has been adhered to by two-thirds of the countries of the world, and because so many states have modelled their own protection regimes around it, the Convention definition is of more than mere historical interest. In at least the medium term, the fair-minded and contextually sensitive application of the Convention definition represents the best hope for a universal legal commitment to the security of the forcibly displaced. This book's second goal has therefore been to illustrate the adaptability of the Convention's core precepts to new modes of state disfranchisement which force people to migrate. By linking the substantive concern of refugee law to general international legal standards of fundamental human dignity, an effective parallel can be drawn between the protection needs of contemporary refugees and those of the refugees whose predicament was known to the drafters of the Convention.

There is, of course, no guarantee that even a humane interpretation of those of the Convention's core precepts which remain relevant today can sustain indefinitely the fragile political consensus upon which refugee law is premised. The current system faces potentially irreconcilable challenges from

---

[1] Statement of Mr. Rees of the International Council of Voluntary Agencies, U.N. Doc. A/CONF.2/SR.19, at 4, November 26, 1951.

governments with an ever-narrowing sphere of concern, and from increasing numbers of persons coerced to flight by the failure of states to meet even their most essential duties of protection. This collision of interests seems destined to result in the reconsideration of the mechanisms of protection, and may require the equation of refugee status with something less than even the current limited notion of asylum if the needs of a more broadly defined class of involuntary migrants are to be met. Because refugee law is, after all, the creation of largely self-interested nation states, it may ultimately prove impossible to define access to asylum more generously than as we know it today.

Bibliography

Adelman, Howard, "Refuge or Asylum: A Philosophical Perspective" (1988), 1 J. Refugee Studies 7.

Aga Khan, Sadruddin. "Legal Problems Relating to Refugees and Displaced Persons", [1976] Recueil des cours 287.

Aiboni, Sam. *Protection of Refugees in Africa* (1978). Uppsala: Svenska inst. for internationell ratt, Uppsala University.

Alston, Phillip. "The Universal Declaration at 35: Western and Passé or Alive and Universal?" (1983), 31 I.C.J. Rev. 60.

Anker, Deborah. "Defining a 'Social Group'" (1983), 6 Imm. J. 15.

————. "American Immigration Policy and Asylum" (1987), 38(4) Harvard L. Bull. 4.

————. "Discretionary Asylum: A Protection Remedy for Refugees Under the Refugee Act of 1980" (1987), 28 (1) Virginia J. Intl. L. 1.

Anker, Deborah and Carolyn Blum. "New Trends in Asylum Jurisprudence" (1989), 1 Intl. J. Refugee L. 67.

Anker, Deborah and Michael Posner. "The Forty Year Crisis: A Legislative History of the Refugee Act of 1980" (1981), 82 San Diego L.Rev. 1.

Beyer, Gunther. "The Political Refugee: 35 Years Later" (1981), 15 Intl. Migration Rev. 26.

Blum, Carolyn. "Who is a Refugee? Canadian Interpretation of the Refugee Definition" (1986), 1 Imm. J. 8.

————. "Legal Perspectives on U.S. Jurisprudence Regarding Central American Refugee Claims" (1987), 7 (1) Refuge 12.

Botelho, Angela. "Membership in a Social Group: Salvadoran Refugees and the 1980 Refugee Act" (1985), 8 Hastings Intl. Comp. L.Rev. 305.

Brill, Kenneth D. "The Endless Debate: Refugee Law and Policy and the 1980 Refugee Act" (1983), 32 Cleveland State L.Rev. 117.

Burke, Scott W. "Compassion Versus Self-Interest: Who Should Be Given Asylum in the United States?" (1984), 8 Fletcher Forum 311.

Chamberlain, Margaret D. "The Mass Migration of Refugees and International Law" (1983), 7 Fletcher Forum 93.

Chemille-Gendreau, Monique. "Le concept de réfugié en droit international et ses limites" (1981), 28 Pluriel 3.

Coles, G.J.L. "Some Reflections on the Protection of Refugees from Armed Conflict Situations" (1984), 7 In Defense of the Alien 78.

————. "The Human Rights Approach to the Solution of the Refugee Problem: A Theoretical and Practical Enquiry", in A. Nash, ed., *Human Rights and the Protection of Refugees under International Law*, p. 195 (1988). Montreal: Canadian Human Rights Foundation.

_____. "Approaching the Refugee Problem Today", in G. Loescher and L. Monahan, eds., *Refugees and International Relations*, p. 373 (1989). Oxford: Oxford University Press.

Cox, Theodore N. "Well-Founded Fear of Being Persecuted: The Sources and Application of a Criterion of Refugee Status" (1984), 10 Brooklyn J. Intl. L. 333.

DeVecchi, Robert P. "Determining Refugee Status: Towards a Coherent Policy", [1983] World Refugee Survey 10.

Dirks, Gerald E. "The Green Paper and Canadian Refugee Policy" (1975), 7 (1) Cdn. Ethnic Studies 61.

_____. *Canada's Refugee Policy: Indifferences or Opportunism?* (1977). Montreal: McGill-Queen's University Press.

_____. "A Policy Within a Policy: The Identification and Admission of Refugees to Canada" (1984), 17 Cdn. J. Pol. Sci. 279.

Evans, Alona E. "Political Refugees and the United States Immigration Laws: Further Developments" (1972), 66 A.J.I.L. 571.

Fish, Hamilton, Jr. "A Congressional Perspective on Refugee Policy", [1983] World Refugee Survey 48.

Foighel, I. "Legal Status of the Boat People" (1979), 48 Nordisk Tidsskrift for Intl. Ret. 217.

Fong, Chooi. "Some Legal Aspects of the Search for Admission into Other States of Persons Leaving the Indo-Chinese Peninsula in Small Boats" (1981), 52 British Y.B. Intl. L. 53.

Fowler, Dulcey. "The Developing Jurisdiction of the United Nations High Commissioner for Refugees" (1974), 7 Human Rts. J. 119.

Fragomen, A.T., Jr. "The Refugee: A Problem of Definition" (1970), 3 Case Western Reserve J. Intl. L. 45.

Frelick, Bill. "Conscientious Objectors as Refugees", in V. Hamilton, ed., *World Refugee Survey: 1986 in Review* (1987). U.S. Committee for Refugees.

Gagliardi, Donald P. "The Inadequacy of Cognizable Grounds of Persecution as a Criterion for According Refugee Status" (1987-88), 24 Stanford J. Intl. L. 259.

Garvey, J. "Toward a Reformulation of International Refugee Law" (1985), 26 Harvard Intl. L.J. 483.

Ghoshal, A. and T. Crowley. "Refugees and Immigrants: A Human Rights Dilemma" (1983), 5 Human Rts. Q. 327.

Gibney, Mark. "A 'Well-Founded Fear' of Persecution" (1988), 10(1) Human Rts. Q. 109.

Gibney, Mark and M. Stohl, "Human Rights and U.S. Refugee Policy', in Mark Gibney, ed., *Open Borders? Closed Societies? The Ethical and Political Issues* (1988). New York: Greenwood Press.

Gilbert, Geoffrey S. "Right of Asylum: A Change of Direction" (1983), 32 I.C.L.Q. 633.

Goodwin-Gill, Guy. *International Law and the Movement of Persons Between States* (1978). Oxford: Clarendon Press.

_____. "Entry and Exclusion of Refugees: The Obligations of States and the Protection Function of the Office of the UNHCR" (1980), Michigan Y.B. Intl. L. Studies 291.

_____. *The Refugee in International Law* (1983). Oxford: Clarendon Press.

_____. "Non-Refoulement and the New Asylum Seekers" (1986), 26(4) Virginia J. Intl. L. 897.

_____. "Refugees: The Functions and Limits of the Existing Protection System", in A. Nash, ed., *Human Rights and the Protection of Refugees under International Law*, p. 149 (1988). Montreal: Canadian Human Rights Foundation.

Grahl-Madsen, Atle. "Further Development of International Refugee Law" (1964), 34 Nordisk Tidsskrift for Intl. Ret. 159.

_____. *The Status of Refugees in International Law* (1966, 1972). Leyden: A.W. Sijthoff.

_____. *Territorial Asylum* (1980). Stockholm: Almqvist & Wiksell International.

_____. "International Refugee Law Today and Tomorrow" (1982), 20 Archiv des Völkerrechts 411.

_____. "The League of Nations and the Refugees" (1982), 20 A.W.R. Bull. 86.

_____. "Identifying the World's Refugees" (1983), 467 Annals A.A.P.S.S. 11.

_____. "Protection of Refugees by Their Country of Origin" (1986), 11(2) Yale J. Intl. L. 362.

Greatbatch, Jacqueline. "The Gender Difference: Feminist Critiques of Refugee Discourse" (1989), 1(4) Intl. J. Refugee L. 518.

Greig, D.W. "The Protection of Refugees and Customary International Law" (1983), 8 Australian Y.B. Intl. L. 108.

Grey, Julius H. *Immigration Law in Canada* (1984). Scarborough, Ontario: Butterworths.

Gross, Douglas. "The Right of Asylum Under United States Law" (1980), 80 Columbia L.Rev. 1125.

Hailbronner, Kay. "Non-Refoulement and 'Humanitarian' Refugees: Customary International Law or Wishful Legal Thinking?" (1986), 26(4) Virginia J. Intl. L. 857.

Hathaway, James C. "The Evolution of Refugee Status in International Law: 1920-1950" (1984), 334 I.C.L.Q. 348.

_____. "'Irregular' Asylum Seekers: What's All the Fuss?" (1988), 8(2) Refuge 1.

_____. "Selective Concern: An Overview of Refugee Law in Canada" (1988), 33(4) McGill L.J. 676.

_____. "A Reconsideration of the Underlying Premise of Refugee Law" (1990), 31(1) Harvard Intl. L.J. 129.

Hathaway, James C. and Michael Schelew. "Persecution by Economic Proscription: A New Refugee Dilemma" (1980), 28 Chitty's L.J. 190.

Helton, Arthur C. "Persecution on Account of Membership in a Social Group as a Basis for Refugee Status" (1983), 15 Columbia Human Rts. L.Rev. 39.

Henkin, L. "International Human Rights and Rights in the United States", in Theodor Meron, ed., *Human Rights in International Law: Legal and Policy Issues* (1984). Oxford: Clarendon Press.

Heyman, M. "Redefining Refugee: A Proposal for Relief for the Victims of Civil Strife" (1987), 24 San Diego L.Rev. 449.

Hofman, Rainer. "Refugee-Generating Policies and the Law of State Responsibility" (1985), 45 Zeitschrift Auslandisches Offentliches 694.

Holborn, Louise W. *The International Refugee Organization: A Specialized Agency of the United Nations: Its History and Work, 1946-1952* (1956). Oxford: Oxford University Press.

Howard, Rhoda. "Contemporary Canadian Refugee Policy: A Critical Assessment" (1980), 6(2) Cdn. Public Policy 361.

Hull, David. "Displaced Persons: 'The New Refugees'" (1983), 13 Georgia J. Intl. Comp. L. 755.

Huyck, Earl E. and Leon F. Bouvier. "The Demography of Refugees" (1983), 467 The Annals Am. Academy 39.

Hyndman, Patricia. "Refugees Under International Law with a Reference to the Concept of Asylum" (1986), 60 Australian L.J. 148.

———. "The 1951 Convention Definition of Refugee: An Appraisal with Particular Reference to the Sri Lankan Tamil Applicants" (1987), 9 Human Rts. Q. 49.

Independent Commission on International Humanitarian Issues. *Refugees: The Dynamics of Displacement* (1986). London: Zed Books.

———. *Winning the Human Race?* (1988). London: Zed Books.

Indra, Doreen. "Gender: A Key Dimension of the Refugee Experience" (1987), 6(3) Refuge 3.

Iognat-Prat, Michel. "L'évolution du concept de réfugié: Pratiques contemporaines en France" (1981), 28 Pluriel 13.

Jackson, J. "Measuring Human Rights and Development by One Yardstick" (1985), 15 California W. Intl. L.J. 453.

Jaeger, Gilbert. "Status and International Protection of Refugees", in International Institute of Human Rights, ed., *Lectures Delivered at the Ninth Study Session of the International Institute of Human Rights* (1978). Strasbourg: International Institute of Human Rights.

———. "The Definition of 'Refugee': Restrictive versus Expanding Trends", [1983] World Refugee Survey 5.

Jennings, R.Y. "Some International Law Aspects of the Refugee Question" (1939), 20 British Y. Intl. L. 98.

Johnson, Anders. "The International Protection of Women Refugees: A Summary of Principal Problems and Issues" (1989), 1(2) Intl. J. Refugee L. 221.

Joyce, James Avery. *The New Politics of Human Rights* (1978). New York: St. Martin's Press.

Julien-Laferrière, François. "Réflexions sur la notion de réfugié en 1978" (1978), 17 A.W.R. Bull. 30.

_____. "Bulletin de jurisprudence française" (1984), 3 Clunet 119.

Kawahara, Kenichi. "Analysis of Results of the First Session of the International Conference on Territorial Asylum", in International Institute of Humanitarian Law, ed., *Round Table on Some Current Problems of Refugee Law* (1978). San Remo: International Institute of Humanitarian Law.

Keely, Charles B. and Patricia J. Elwell. *Global Refugee Policy: The Case for a Development-Oriented Strategy* (1981). New York: Population Council.

Krenz, Frank E. "The Refugee as a Subject of International Law" (1966), 15 I.C.L.Q. 90.

LaForest, Gerald. *Extradition to and from Canada* (1977). Toronto: Canada Law Book Co.

Lamar, Sandra J. "Those Who Stand at the Door: Assessing Immigration Claims Based on Fear of Persecution" (1983), 18 New England L.Rev. 395.

Lapenna, Enrico. "Territorial Asylum — Developments from 1961 to 1977 — Comments on the Conference of Plenipotentiaries" (1978), 16 A.W.R. Bull. 1.

Le, Tang and Michael Esser. "The Vietnamese Refugee and U.S. Law" (1981), 56 Notre Dame Lawyer 656.

Leduc, François. "L'Asile territorial et Conférence des Nations Unies de Genève, Janvier 1977" (1977), 23 Ann. française de droit intl. 221.

Lentini, Elizabeth J. "The Definition of Refugee in International Law: Proposals for the Future" (1985), 5 Boston College Third World L.J. 183.

Loescher, Gilburt D. and J. Scanlan, "Human Rights, U.S. Foreign Policy, and Haitian Refugees" (1984), 26(3) J. Interamerican Studies 313.

Marino-Menendez, Fernando. "El concepto de refugiado en un contexto de derecho internacional general" (1983), 35(2) Revista española de derecho internacional 337.

Marrus, Michael. *The Unwanted: European Refugees in the Twentieth Century* (1985). New York: Oxford University Press.

Martin, David A. "Large-Scale Migrations of Asylum Seekers" (1982), 76 A.J.I.L. 598.

Martin, David A., in C. Sumpter. "Mass Migration of Refugees — Law and Policy" (1982), 76 A.S.I.L.P. 13.

Maynard, P. "The Legal Competence of the United Nations High Commissioner for Refugees" (1982), 31 I.C.L.Q. 415.

Mbaya, Etienne-Richard. *La communauté internationale et les mouvements des populations en Afrique* (1985). Abidjan: Editions Yaba.

McAndrew, Melissa. "The Dictator Dilemma: A Comparison of United States and French Asylum Procedures" (1986), 19 N.Y.U.J. Intl. L. and Policy 1087.

Melander, Goran. "The Protection of Refugees" (1974), 18 Scandinavian Studies in Law 153.

————. "Refugees in Orbit" (1978), 16 A.W.R. Bull. 59.

Mushkat, R. "Hong Kong as a Country of Temporary Refuge: An Interim Analysis" (1982), 12 Hong Kong L.J. 157.

Nash, Alan. *International Refugee Pressures and the Canadian Public Policy Response* (1989). Institute for Research on Public Policy.

Nathan-Chapotot, R. *La qualification internationale des réfugiés et personnes déplacées dans le cadre des Nations Unies* (1949).

Nicolaus, Peter. "La notion de réfugié dans le droit de la R.F.A." (1985), 4 A.W.R. Bull. 158.

Patrnogic, J. "Refugees — A Continuing Challenge" (1982), 30 Annuaire de droit international médical 73.

Petrini, Kenneth R. "Basing Asylum Claims on a Fear of Persecution Arising from a Prior Asylum Claim" (1981), 56 Notre Dame Lawyer 719.

Pick, Grant. "People Who Live on Hope — and Little Else" (1983), 11 Student Lawyer 12.

Plaut, W. Gunther. *Refugee determination in Canada: Proposals for a new system* (1985). Ottawa: Minister of Supply and Services Canada.

Plender, Richard. "Admission of Refugees: Draft Convention on Territorial Asylum" (1977), 15 San Diego L.Rev. 45.

————. *International Migration Law* (1988). Dordrecht, Netherlands: Martinus Nijhoff.

Pompe, C.A. "The Convention of 28 July 1951 and the International Protection of Refugees", [1956] Rechtsgeleerd Magazyn Themis 425, published in English as U.N. Doc. HCR/INF/42, May 1958.

Posner, Michael. "Who Should We Let In?" (1981), 9 Human Rts. 16.

Rickard, Delia. "The Rhetoric and the Reality" (1986), Legal Services Bull. 214.

Rizvi, Zia. "Causes of the Refugee Problem and the International Response", in A. Nash, ed., *Human Rights and the Protection of Refugees under International Law*, p. 107 (1988). Montreal: Canadian Human Rights Foundation.

Roberts, Brian. "Can the Boat People Assert a Right to Remain in Asylum?" (1980), 4 U. Puget Sound L.Rev. 176.

Robinson, N. *Convention relating to the Status of Refugees: Its History, Contents and Interpretation* (1953). New York: Institute of Jewish Affairs.

Roth, David. "The Right of Asylum Under United States Immigration Law" (1981), 33 U. Florida L.Rev. 539.

Ryan, Michael C.P. "Political Asylum for the Haitians?" (1982), 14 Case Western Reserve J. Intl. L. 155.

Saari, V. and R. Higgins Cass. "The United Nations and the International Protection of Human Rights: A Legal Analysis and Interpretation" (1977), California W. Intl. L.J. 591.

Scott, C. "The Interdependence and Permeability of Human Rights Norms: Towards a Partial Fusion of the International Covenants on Human Rights" (1989), 27(4) Osgoode Hall L.J. 769.

Sexton, Robert C. "Political Refugees, Nonrefoulement and State Practice: A Comparative Study" (1985), 18 Vanderbilt J. Transntl. L. 731.

Shacknove, Andrew E. "Who is a Refugee?" (1985), 95 Ethics 274.

Shimada, Yukio. "The Concept of the Political Refugee in International Law" (1975), 19 Japanese Ann. Intl. L. 24.

Sieghart, Paul. *The International Law of Human Rights* (1983). Oxford: Clarendon Press.

Simmance, A.J.F. "Refugees and the Law", [1981] New Zealand L.J. 550.

Simpson, J. *Refugees: Preliminary Report on a Survey* (1938).

————. *The Refugee Problem* (1939). Oxford: Oxford University Press.

Sinha, S.P. "Human Rights: A Non-Western Viewpoint" (1981), 67 Archiv für Rechts und Sozial Philosophie 76.

Smith, Rogers M. "Refugees, immigrants and the claims of the nation-state", [1987] Times Literary Supplement 1422 (December 25-31, 1987).

Starke, J.G. "Major Trans-Frontier 'Flows' of Refugee-Type Civilians" (1983), 57 Australian L.J. 366.

Thomas, J., in A. Woods, ed., "Refugees: A New Dimension in International Human Rights" (1976), 70 A.S.I.L.P. 58.

Tompkin, Cheryl. "A Criminal at the Gate: A Case for the Haitian Refugee" (1982), 7 Black L.J. 387.

Trubek, D. "Economic, Social, and Cultural Rights in the Third World: Human Rights Law and Human Needs Programs", in Theodor Meron, ed., *Human Rights in International Law*, p. 205 (1984). Oxford: Clarendon Press.

Tsamenyi, B.M. "The 'Boat People': Are They Refugees?" (1983), 5 Human Rts. Q. 348.

Turack, Daniel. *The Passport in International Law* (1972). Lexington, Mass.: Lexington Books.

United Nations High Commissioner for Refugees. *Handbook on Procedures and Criteria for Determining Refugee Status* (1979). Geneva: Office of the United Nations High Commissioner for Refugees.

van der Veen, Job. "Does Persecution by Fellow-Citizens in Certain Regions of a State Fall Within the Definition of 'Persecution' in the Convention Relating to the Status of Refugees of 1951?" (1980), 11 Netherlands Y.B. Intl. L. 167.

Vernant, Jacques. *The Refugee in the Post-War World* (1953). London: Allen & Unwin.

Vierdag, E. "The Country of 'First Asylum': Some European Aspects", in D. Martin, ed., *The New Asylum Seekers: Refugee Law in the 1980s* (1988). Dordrecht, Netherlands: Kluwen Academic Publishers.

Watson, J. "Legal Theory, Efficacy and Validity in the Development of Human Rights Norms in International Law" (1979), 3 U. Illinois L. Forum 609.

Weis, Paul. "Legal Aspects of the Convention of 25 July 1951 relating to the Status of Refugees" (1953), 30 British Y. Intl. L. 478.

_____. *Nationality and Statelessness in International Law* London: Stevens & Sons Ltd.; repr. of 1956 ed. (1979). Westport, Conn.: Hyperion Pr., Inc.

_____. "The concept of the refugee in international law" (1960), 87 J. du droit international 928.

_____. "Convention Refugees and *De Facto* Refugees", in G. Melander and P. Nobel, eds., *African Refugees and the Law* (1978). Uppsala: Scandinavian Institute of African Studies.

_____. "The Draft United Nations Convention on Territorial Asylum" (1979), 50 British Y.B. Intl. L. 151.

Wildes, Leon. "The Dilemma of the Refugee: His Standard for Relief" (1983), 4 Cardoza L.Rev. 353.

Woods, Patricia A. "The Term 'Refugee' in International and Municipal Law: An Inadequate Definition in Light of the Cuban Boatlift" (1981), ASILS Intl. L.J. 39.

Woodward, Peter. "Political Factors Contributing to the Generation of Refugees in the Horn of Africa" (1987), 9(2) Intl. Relations 111.

World Peace Through Law Centre. *Toward the Second Quarter Century of Refugee Law* (1976). Washington, D.C.

Wydrzynski, Christopher J. "Refugees and the *Immigration Act*" (1979), 25 McGill L.J. 154.

_____. *Canadian Immigration Law and Procedure* (1983). Aurora, Ontario: Canada Law Book.

Young, Stephen. "Who is a Refugee? A Theory of Persecution" (1982), 5 In Defense of the Alien 38.

Zimmer, Jana. "Political Refugees: A Study in Selective Compassion" (1978), 1 Loyola L.A. Intl. Comp. L. Ann. 121.

Zolberg, Aristide R. "The Formation of New States as a Refugee-Generating Process" (1983), 467 The Annals Am. Academy Pol. Soc. Science 24.

Index

243

Health care, right to: 111, 117, 123-124
Hijacking: 228
Homosexuality: *see* Sexual orientation
Hostage-taking: 228
Housing, right to: 111, 120-121
Human rights: 8, 31, 70, 104-105, 114-116, 125, 136, 189-191, 219, 227-228
— Derogation from: 109-110, 172
— Evidence of respect for: 80-83, 200
— Violation of, as basis for claim: 92-97; 20-27, 91-97, 138, 158-159, 172-173
Humanitarian refugees: *see* De facto refugees; Generalized harm or oppression

Illegal departure: *see* Departure
Illegal entry of refugees: *see* Entry into asylum state
Immigration control: 1-2, 231-233
Immigration offences: *see* Entry into asylum state
Inability to protect: *see* Agents of persecution
Indiscriminate harm: *see* Generalized harm or oppression
Innate or immutable characteristics, fear on account of: 160-161
Integrity, attack on: 113 fn.119, 115
Inter-American Court of Human Rights: 132
Intermediate states: *see* 'Direct flight' rule
Internal conflicts: *see* War
Internal refugees: 29-32, 133-134
International law Commission: 217-220
International law, customary: *see* Customary international law
International Refugee Organization: 5-6, 61, 66-69, 99, 204 fns.92, 95
'Irregular' asylum seekers: 47, 51

Kinship: *see* Family

Language, fear on account of: 144
Latin America: *see* Organization of American States
Law of return, Israeli: 47
League of Nations: 2-4, 99, 117 fn.151, 135-136
Leave and return, right to: 40, 109, 173
Life, right to: 103, 107-109, 112, 114-115, 132
Livelihood, right to earn: *see* Work

Marital status, fear on account of: 162
Marriage: 197, 210 fn.128
Medical care, right to: *see* Health care
Membership of a particular social group: *see* Social group
Membership principle: *see* Civil or political discrimination
Military: 125-126, 201-202